Production and
Exchange in Eurasia

YALE UNIVERSITY PUBLICATIONS IN ANTHROPOLOGY

EDITORIAL COMMITTEE

Richard L. Burger
Curatorial Editor-in-Chief
Charles J. MacCurdy Professor of Anthropology, Yale University
Chair, Yale Council on Archaeological Studies
Curator of Anthropology, Yale Peabody Museum

Oswaldo Chinchilla Mazariegos
Associate Professor of Anthropology
Department of Anthropology, Yale University
Curator-in-charge of Anthropology, Yale Peabody Museum

Anne P. Underhill
Professor of Anthropology
Department of Anthropology, Yale University
Curator of Anthropology, Yale Peabody Museum

The Yale University Publications in Anthropology series, published by the
Yale University Department of Anthropology and the Yale Peabody Museum,
is supported by the Theodore and Ruth Wilmanns Lidz Endowment Fund for Excellence
in Scholarly Publications, dedicated to the dissemination of scholarly research and
study of the world and its cultures.

The Yale University Publications in Anthropology series embodies the results
of researches in the general field of anthropology directly conducted or sponsored by
the Yale University Department of Anthropology and the Yale Peabody Museum
Division of Anthropology. Occasionally other manuscripts of outstanding quality
that deal with subjects of special interest to the faculty of the Department of
Anthropology may also be included.

Distributed by Yale University Press
NEW HAVEN AND LONDON

For quantity purchases and exam copies for coursework,
and a complete list of available titles in this series visit
www.yalebooks.com or yalebooks.co.uk.

Production and Exchange in Eurasia

In Commemoration of Zeng Lingyi

Edited by Anne P. Underhill

NUMBER 99

Published by
the Yale University Department of Anthropology
and the Yale Peabody Museum

Distributed by
Yale University Press
NEW HAVEN AND LONDON

Yale

YALE UNIVERSITY PUBLICATIONS IN ANTHROPOLOGY
NUMBER 99

Rosemary Volpe
Publications Manager

Sally H. Pallatto
Cover Design, Title Page Illustration

Claire Purnell
Book Production

Index by Cynthia Col, PhD

Front cover: Fourteenth century CE Yuan dynasty of China (Mongol period) blue-and-white porcelain plate in the Yale Peabody Museum collections (YPM ANT 207740). Photograph by Richard House/Yale University Art Gallery.

Back cover: Zeng Lingyi analyzing porcelain sherds using a scanning electron microscope at the Yale Institute for the Preservation of Cultural Heritage in 2017. Photograph by Ellery Frahm.

Dedication page: Zeng Lingyi excavating a burial at the fourteenth-century CE (Mongol Empire period) site of Ikh Khungui. Photograph by Batdalai Byambatseren.

The article "Fuliang Ceramics Bureau Officer and Governor (浮梁磁局大使和督陶官)" by Zeng Lingyi (曾令怡), *Journal of the National Museum of China* 4:63–71, 2012, is reprinted courtesy of the National Museum of China Editorial Department. © 1994–2022 China Academic Journal Electronic Publishing House. All rights reserved. http://www.cnki.net.

© 2024 Yale University. All rights reserved.
This book may not be reproduced, in whole or in part, including illustrations, in any form (beyond that copying permitted by Sections 107 and 108 of the U.S. Copyright Law and except by reviewers for the public press), without the written permission of the publisher.

Yale Peabody Museum
Yale University
P. O. Box 208118
New Haven CT 06520-8118 USA
peabody.yale.edu

Distributed by Yale University Press
new haven and london
www.yalebooks.com | yalebooks.co.uk

ISBN 978-0-913516-35-5
ISSN 1535-7082
Printed in the United States of America

Library of Congress Control Number: 2024944764

This paper meets the requirements of ANSI/NISO Z39.48-1992 (Permanence of Paper).
10 9 8 7 6 5 4 3 2 1

Dedicated to the memory of
Zeng Lingyi (曾令怡)
PhD candidate in the Department of Anthropology, Yale University

Contents

ix List of Figures
xiii List of Tables
xv Preface

1   One   **The Contributions of Zeng Lingyi to Eurasian Archaeology**
Daniela WOLIN, *Skidmore College*
Yu LUO, *University of Puget Sound*

7   Two   **Fire at Zhoukoudian: Is There Evidence for Its Production and Cultural Transmission?**
Ellery FRAHM, *Yale University*

29   Three   **Ceramic Petrography in China: Past Approaches and Future Directions**
Andrew WOMACK, *Furman University*
LU Qingyu, *Shandong University*

47   Four   **Late Neolithic Painted Pottery Traditions at Huangguashan and Fengbitou along the Taiwan Strait: A Case Study**
HE Yahui, *Stanford University*

67   Five   **The Introduction of Horses into Yinxu during the Late Shang Dynasty: A Brief Review**
FAN Rong, *Yale University*

87   Six   **Iron Age Sheep Management at Delgerkhaan Uul: A Tale of Two Graves**
Sarah PLEUGER-DREIBRODT, *University of Edinburgh*
Mandakh DAVAASUREN *Mongolian Academy of Science*
Sarah PEDERZANI, *University of La Laguna*

117   Seven   **Production and Distribution of Early Period Yue Wares in China in the Second through Sixth Centuries CE**
WU Shuang, *Guangxi Normal University*
CHEN Hongbo, *Guangxi Normal University*
WANG Lei, *Guangxi Normal University*
ZHENG Jianming, *Fudan University*

141	Eight	**Carnelian Beads During the Mongol Period of Mongolia**
		Asa CAMERON, *Yale University*
		Bukhchuluun DASHZEVEG, *Yale University*
163	Nine	**Household Scale Metallurgical Production in Mongolia: Implications for Local Community Independence**
		William R. GARDNER, *ASM Affiliates, Hilo, Hawaii*
		Jang-Sik PARK, *Hongik University*
		Jargalan BURENTOGTOKH, *National University of Mongolia*
177	Ten	**A Translation of "Debating the Legitimate Succession of the Liao, Song, and Jin (辯遼宋金正統)" by Xiu Duan (修端), 1234 CE**
		KOH Choon Hwee, *University of California, Los Angeles*
207	Eleven	**浮梁磁局大使和督陶官**
		"Commissioner of the Fuliang Porcelain Bureau" and "Officials that Oversee Porcelain Production" [during the Yuan Dynasty of China]
		ZENG Lingyi, *Yale University*
		Translated and annotated by SHEN Dewei, *City University of Hong Kong*
219	Twelve	**Porcelain in the Yuan Period of the Mongolian Empire: Moving from Portable X-ray Fluorescence Analysis toward Political Economy Insights**
		ZENG Lingyi, *Yale University*
		WANG Qingzhu, *Shandong University*
		Mandakh DAVAASUREN, *Mongolian Academy of Sciences*
		Chunag AMARTUVSHIN, *National University of Mongolia*
		Ellery FRAHM, *Yale University*
241	Index	

Figures

Chapter Two

- 10   Figure 2.1.   One of the crania of "*Sinanthropus pekinensis*" by Franz Weidenreich.
- 12   Figure 2.2.   Basic stratigraphic section of Zhoukoudian Locality 1.
- 17   Figure 2.3.   The Zhoukoudian Locality 1 diorama at the National Museum of China.
- 21   Figure 2.4.   Sites with evidence of fire production and approximate dates.

Chapter Four

- 50   Figure 4.1.   The location of the sites of Huangguashan and Fengbitou.
- 53   Figure 4.2.   Analysis of Huangguashan painted pottery paste.
- 54   Figure 4.3.   Evidence of coiling in the paste in Huangguashan painted pottery.
- 55   Figure 4.4.   Interior rim painted sherds from the Huangguashan site.
- 55   Figure 4.5.   Width of painted lines on sherds sampled in the 2012 survey.
- 56   Figure 4.6.   Evidence of firing in Huangguashan painted pottery.
- 57   Figure 4.7.   Pottery vessel types at the Huangguashan site.
- 60   Figure 4.8.   Coiling feature in Fengbitou painted pottery paste.
- 61   Figure 4.9.   Painted pottery vessel types at the Fengbitou site.

Chapter Five

- 72   Figure 5.1.   Changes in the types of horse mouthpieces at Yinxu.
- 75   Figure 5.2.   Sex and age composition of horses from sacrificial pits at Wuguancun North Locality.
- 77   Figure 5.3.   Integration of knowledge about horses into the Shang system.

Chapter Six

- 88   Figure 6.1.   Map of Mongolia showing sites mentioned in the text.
- 93   Figure 6.2.   Slab burial DMS 1396A in Delgerkhaan Uul.
- 93   Figure 6.3.   Xiongnu ring burial DMS 777A in Delgerkhaan Uul.
- 96   Figure 6.4.   Sheep skull deposition in situ in slab burial DMS 1396A.
- 96   Figure 6.5.   Age group distribution of sheep individuals from DMS 1396A.
- 97   Figure 6.6.   Faunal deposition in Xiongnu burial DMS 777A.
- 97   Figure 6.7.   Distribution of taxa deposited in Xiongnu burial DMS 777A.
- 99   Figure 6.8.   Age group distribution of sheep individuals from DMS 777A.
- 102   Figure 6.9   Time series plots of $\delta^{13}C$ and $\delta^{18}O$ of *Ovis* sp.

Chapter Seven

124	Figure 7.1.	The location of tombs in southern China yielding early Yue wares.
124	Figure 7.2.	The location of tombs in northern China yielding early Yue wares.
126	Figure 7.3.	Early celadon wares from southern China.
127	Figure 7.4.	Number of early celadon wares from Zhejiang and Jiangsu tombs.
130	Figure 7.5.	Number of kiln sites with celadon wares in the Shangyu area.
131	Figure 7.6.	The number and distribution of kiln sites in different areas of Zhejiang.
132	Figure 7.7.	An exposed dragon kiln in Zhejiang Province.
135	Figure 7.8.	Three kinds of kiln furniture.

Chapter Eight

144	Figure 8.1.	Mongol period carnelian long bead (MG22) from Gorzgoriin uvur.
144	Figure 8.2.	Mongol period carnelian short bead (MG25) from Ereen.
145	Figure 8.3.	Carnelian bead surface find from Khalzan Shireg.
146	Figure 8.4.	Necklace and artifacts from the elite cave burial at Tsagaan Khanan.
146	Figure 8.5.	Reconstruction of the Tsagaan Khanan beads.
150	Figure 8.6.	Jayaatu Khan (Төвтөмөр), emperor of the Yuan dynasty.
150	Figure 8.7.	Chabi (Чаби), empress and consort of Kublai Khan.
152	Figure 8.8.	Rinchinbal Khan (Ринчинбал), emperor of the Yuan dynasty.
152	Figure 8.9.	Temür Khan (Төмөр), emperor of the Yuan dynasty.
153	Figure 8.10.	Külüg Khan (Хайсан), emperor of the Yuan dynasty.
153	Figure 8.11.	Buyantu Khan (Аюурбарбад), emperor of the Yuan dynasty.

Chapter Nine

165	Figure 9.1.	The archaeological site of Tsagaan Ereg (TVP-180).
167	Figure 9.2.	Two furnace structures in the southeast sector of the living area.
168	Figure 9.3.	The general appearance of the iron objects under consideration.

Chapter Eleven

| 209 | Figure 11.1. | The jurisdiction of Jiangzhe Province, Raozhou Circuit, and Fuliang. |

CHAPTER TWELVE

227	FIGURE 12.1.	Backscattered electron image of a white-glazed porcelain sherd from Avraga, Khentii Province.
228	FIGURE 12.2.	SEM-EDS measurements of SiO_2 versus Al_2O_3 in porcelain pastes.
228	FIGURE 12.3.	SEM-EDS measurements of Na_2O versus CaO in porcelain pastes.
229	FIGURE 12.4.	SEM-EDS measurements of K_2O versus FeO + MgO in porcelain pastes.
229	FIGURE 12.5.	SEM-EDS measurements of FeO versus MgO in porcelain pastes.
231	FIGURE 12.6.	pXRF measurements of Mn versus As for cobalt blue pigments.
231	FIGURE 12.7.	pXRF measurements of Fe/Mn versus Mn/Co ratios for cobalt blue pigments.
232	FIGURE 12.8.	pXRF measurements of K versus Ca for glaze on porcelain sherds.
232	FIGURE 12.9.	pXRF measurements of Rb versus Y for glaze on the porcelain sherds.
233	FIGURE 12.10.	pXRF measurements of Zr versus Nb for glaze on the porcelain sherds.
233	FIGURE 12.11.	pXRF measurements of Sr versus Ca for glaze on the porcelain sherds.

Tables

Chapter Four
- 51 Table 4.1. Huangguashan painted pottery sherds examined in Fujian Province.
- 59 Table 4.2. Fengbitou painted pottery sherds examined at the Yale Peabody Museum.

Chapter Five
- 71 Table 5.1. The early horse-related objects at the Yinxu site.

Chapter Six
- 98 Table 6.1. Distribution of skeletal elements in the Xiongnu ring burial (DMS 777A).
- 101 Table 6.2. Sampled sheep M/2s from mortuary contexts in Delgerkhaan Uul.
- 106 Appendix 6.1. Oxygen and carbon isotope data from sheep teeth at Delgerkhaan Uul.

Chapter Seven
- 120 Table 7.1. Porosity, absorbency, and firing range of ceramic samples.
- 121 Table 7.2. Major historical eras of Zhejiang Province and southern China.
- 123 Table 7.3. Tomb sites with early Yue wares from different eras.
- 129 Table 7.4. Kiln sites in second- to sixth-century CE Zhejiang Province.
- 134 Table 7.5. Data for dragon kiln sites in Shangyu District.

Chapter Nine
- 169 Table 9.1. Mass and chemical composition of metal fragments from Tarvagatai.

Chapter Ten
- 180 Table 10.1. Historical timeline of China's dynasties.

Chapter Eleven
- 213 Table 11.1. Offices of Fuliang Prefecture (or County) and their ranks.
- 213 Table 11.2. Offices of the Fuliang Porcelain Bureau and their ranks.

Preface

The goal of this volume is to encourage international collaborative research about lifeways in early Asia. The creation of this work was motivated by the desire to honor the remarkable research of Zeng Lingyi (曾令怡). Before she lost her hard-fought battle with illness in 2020, Lingyi had inspired many by her multiple achievements, courageous archaeological fieldwork, insightful analyses of relevant historical data, promising initial results from her analyses of porcelains, concern with the welfare of others, and her joy of life.

Lingyi's pioneering research was centered on craft production and exchange in the Mongol Empire, from the thirteenth to fourteenth centuries CE. She insisted from the beginning that such research required a de-emphasis on modern political borders and holistic consideration of both archaeological and historical data. This book takes this perspective as its model by presenting new archaeological and historical research focusing on China and Mongolia over a broad time range, from the Paleolithic period to the Mongol Empire. More publications concerning the rich archaeological heritage of this region are needed. We hope that this volume will inspire more young scholars to develop collaborative research projects on production and exchange in different areas of Asia and beyond.

Acknowledgments

I am very grateful to each author and to the two anonymous reviewers for their thoughtful comments about a wide range of issues. We owe special thanks to the Yale Peabody Museum's publications manager Rosemary Volpe for her expertise and guidance in improving our manuscript, and to Yale University Publication in Anthropology faculty director Richard Burger for his continual encouragement. Many thanks to Carmen Cusmano for completing our book after the retirement of Rosemary Volpe. Fan Rong, Daniela Wolin, Wang Qingzhu, Bukhchuluun Dashzeveg, and Shen Dewei provided invaluable assistance. Each contributor to this volume feels fortunate to have had the opportunity to share part of Zeng Lingyi's life journey.

Editor's Note

In this book, Chinese names are presented with surnames before given names (in full or by initials).

Anne P. Underhill, *Yale University*

CHAPTER ONE

THE CONTRIBUTIONS OF ZENG LINGYI TO EURASIAN ARCHAEOLOGY

Daniela WOLIN and Yu LUO

This volume commemorates the life and scholarship of Zeng Lingyi, a PhD candidate in the Department of Anthropology at Yale University until illness overtook her in 2020. Lingyi was a remarkable archaeologist whose pioneering dissertation explored the production, exchange, and consumption of ceramic vessels across Eurasia during the Mongol Empire from about the thirteenth through fourteenth centuries CE. She joined the graduate program at Yale in 2013 after earning a master of arts in history that year at the Jingdezhen Ceramic University, with a focus on archaeology and museology. In 2008 she earned her bachelor's degree from Peking University in both law and economics. Adhering to her ideals and passions, she dropped her original plan for a prestigious law career and changed her academic focus to archaeology—a decision only a person with firm beliefs and extraordinary courage would make. Throughout her time at these different institutions Lingyi earned a reputation of being a diligent student, a brilliant scholar, and a kind-hearted person. She leaves behind a legacy that will inspire current and future generations of archaeologists to come.

Lingyi's work as a graduate student at Yale (US National Science Foundation grant BCS-1746779; see Chapter 12) used the systematic study of porcelain to examine how growth in historical trade networks and the increased connectivity of societies spanning multiple geographical areas under Mongol rule transformed ceramic production and exchange. Porcelain vessels are a unique medium, whose form and decoration can easily be altered to meet the functional and aesthetic needs of different groups (Gerritsen and McDowall 2012:4). The dynamic nature of porcelain makes it ideal for studying global connections in the past (Finlay 2010; Gerritsen 2020), particularly during periods of heightened interaction. To this end, Lingyi traced diachronic and synchronic patterns in the production, circulation, and consumption of porcelain, shedding light on how this material linked together people from a range of social identities across Eurasia (e.g., Zeng 2013).

Mindful of the limitations and biases of the written and material records, Lingyi skillfully navigated and interwove different lines of textual, archaeological, and visual evidence. This ranged from macroscopic observations of the elaborate motifs adorning porcelain vessels to the use of scientific techniques such as scanning electron microscopy with energy-dispersive X-ray spectroscopy, energy-dispersive X-ray fluorescence, and portable X-ray fluorescence to study the composition of the pigments used in the decorations. The interdisciplinary methodological approach that Lingyi brought to her work serves as a valuable model for historians and anthropologists who seek to examine the exchange of materials, technology, and aesthetics (e.g., Brook 2008; Gerritsen and McDowall 2012).

Building on Lingyi's research, this volume contributes to recent endeavors within the humanities and social sciences to reimagine conventional understandings of the vast region stretching from East Asia to the Middle East (Perdue, Siu, and Tagliacozzo 2015). By focusing on the holistic investigation of the entirety of ceramic networks—from how porcelain was made and distributed over space to the varied cultural meanings and values of vessels consumed in different locales—Lingyi successfully struck a balance between elucidating macroscale connections across Eurasia, while simultaneously illuminating the unique conditions of specific local contexts. Lingyi brought anthropological theory to the forefront of her work by moving beyond material culture to emphasize the flows of information, technology, and people that wove such vibrant networks over time and space.

The chapters within this book are aligned with Lingyi's research interests and the methodologies that she used. Here we publish Lingyi's preliminary results (Chapter 12) and we take inspiration from her research by expanding on two broad themes that formed the basis of her work: production and exchange. To highlight the historical trajectory that created the interconnected world that Lingyi studied, the chapters are organized roughly chronologically. We include in our temporal scope research on sites, artifacts, and texts leading up to and through the Mongol period. While some of the studies consider large-scale interactions, others focus more closely on site-level analyses or analytical methods. Together they provide a *longue durée* perspective on the interconnectedness of this region, as reflected in the exchange of goods, technology, plants and animals, and beliefs.

The earliest exchange of technology can be found in our hominin past with the shared knowledge of stone tool production. Less clear was the process whereby the controlled use of fire was added to this toolkit. Drawing on the latest information from continuing excavations at the site of Zhoukoudian in northern China, Frahm (Chapter 2) evaluates whether the use of fire, like other technological innovations, was culturally transmitted or independently arose across hominin populations. Harnessing fire not only provided warmth, protection, and the ability to cook food, but it also made possible the production of the earliest pottery in Asia, which began in the Paleolithic (e.g., Wu et al. 2012).

A key theme in this volume is production, with an emphasis on pottery. As in the present, ceramic vessels had myriad functions in the past. Some were used in everyday life for cooking, storage, or consumption; others were reserved for specific occasions, such as ritual feasting; and some were created solely to be buried in elaborate mortuary rituals. Archaeologists seek to understand these varied uses through a suite of macroscopic and microscopic analyses, both noninvasive and destructive, which when situated in the larger archaeological context, can tell us about a range of topics, including the organization of labor, dietary traditions, and religious practices (Rice 2015).

The second, and related, theme of this volume is exchange. Interregional interaction creates new venues for the exchange of different goods and raw materials, religious practices, and technologies. Increased mobility facilitated by animals for transport and wheeled vehicles contributed to the exchange of goods, information, and technology over vast areas of Eurasia. Translocal objects were incorporated into local traditions, value systems, and beliefs, while simultaneously serving as markers of sociopolitical status or group identity (Womack 2024). The archaeological study of exchange thus draws on a number of sources and techniques, including textual evidence, compositional analyses, and tracing the form, function, and stylistic motifs of objects.

Ceramic production is an elaborate, multi-step process that includes raw material acquisition, preparing the clay, forming an object, applying a surface treatment, and firing. Variation in the materials and methods of production can be observed through the careful analysis of a vessel's clay, temper, and slip or glaze. Womack and Lu (Chapter 3) outline the history and use of petrography in China, a technique that uses thin sections of pottery to assess the composition of clay and mineral inclusions. This method can help archaeologists uncover where objects were produced, who produced them, and how they were used across time and space.

Similarities in ceramics across space can result from the movement of people, sharing of technology, and the exchange of objects. Using macro- and microscopic observations about the paste, decoration, firing technique, and form of painted pottery, He (Chapter 4) examines the exchange of ceramic technology and finished vessels in southern China and Taiwan during the Late Neolithic. Suggesting that a diversity of interactions may have been simultaneously occurring, this chapter serves as an important reminder that archaeologists must consider how different interactions in the past could produce similar archaeological signatures.

In Eurasia, a crucial factor that facilitated the exchange of people, goods, and ideas was the widespread adoption of horses, which afforded past groups the ability to traverse long distances and allowed for the formation of nomadic states in the Eurasian steppe (Honeychurch 2015). Fan (Chapter 5) examines the archaeological and paleographic evidence for the introduction of horses during China's Bronze Age. Remains from the Late Shang period at Yinxu (Anyang) indicate that, while horses were integrated into a well-established belief system, new cultural activities and ritual practices were formed around them.

Diachronic variation in human–animal interactions in regions such as the Eurasian steppe, on the other hand, can reflect changes in subsistence practices brought on by sociopolitical shifts. Pleuger and colleagues (Chapter 6) use zooarchaeological information, including isotope analysis, to examine faunal remains from two burials—one from the Late Bronze Age/Early Iron Age and another from the Xiongnu period. The authors note that despite standardization in mortuary practices across large regions, subsistence practices likely varied locally.

Shifting the focus to craft production across Eurasia, the subsequent chapters consider specific tools, materials, and technologies that were used and adapted. Careful documentation of the workshops where objects were manufactured can provide important insights into craft production. Wu and colleagues (Chapter 7) examine the emergence of a type of celadon produced in China during the second through sixth centuries CE called Yue ware. Analysis of the distribution of sites with kilns and the contents of burials reveals that the production and use of Yue wares were initially relatively limited, before becoming more widespread. Understanding the specific trajectory of celadon provides more information about the adoption of new technologies.

Besides the application of technologies, the introduction of nonlocal materials through exchange networks can alter the production and consumption of locally produced objects. This is particularly true for small objects such as beads, which are easy to transport over long distances. Cameron and Dashzeveg (Chapter 8) trace changes in the manufacture of beads in Mongolia during the Mongol period. They find that carnelian, a material used for bead production in earlier periods, was no longer widely exploited. The authors suggest that this change may be due to a new preference for beads that were made from nonlocal materials.

One particular type of material that deserves attention in understanding the Mongol period was metal, because of the high demand for horse gear, armor, weapons, and tools during that time. While evidence for this industry was uncovered at the capital of Karakorum (e.g., Park and Reichert 2015), many questions remain about the production and exchange of metal across the empire. Gardner and colleagues (Chapter 9) present evidence for small-scale metallurgical production uncovered at the Mongol period site of Tsagaan Ereg in Mongolia. The authors' research counters previous arguments that the mobile lifestyle of pastoralists was not conducive to activities such as metallurgy.

Apart from archaeological emphasis on material objects, historical texts–ranging from personal letters to legal manuscripts–also record many aspects of daily life. Large political shifts, such as the numerous dynastic changes in China, are well documented in the textual record. Koh (Chapter 10) presents a translation of one such passage dating to the Jin dynasty (1115-1234 CE) and debated during the Yuan dynasty in China. The text illuminates what a select group of people thought about the upheaval entailed in the process of succession. Koh's chapter is an important reminder that sociopolitical change was not a monolithic experience for people living in expansive polities.

Finally, the volume seeks to highlight the work that Lingyi carried out in graduate school. From the very beginning of her archaeological career Lingyi was drawn to porcelain, the significance of which in world history merits special attention. During her time as a master's student at Jingdezhen Ceramic University, Lingyi analyzed the production, use, and exchange of porcelain during the Yuan dynasty of China (1271–1368 CE). Her research not only highlighted different firing techniques used in porcelain manufacture (Zeng 2012a), but also sought to examine the lives of those who would have interacted with these vessels, from the officers in charge of ceramic production to craftspeople working at the kiln sites, to literati painters that influenced the aesthetics at the time (Zeng 2012b, 2013). The results of this study have been translated into English by Shen (Chapter 11) in an effort to bring her important research to a wider audience.

As part of her dissertation research as a doctoral candidate at Yale University, Lingyi analyzed ceramic vessels from across Eurasia. With the help of her colleagues, a portion of her results are published here (Chapter 12). Using portable X-ray fluorescence and scanning electron microscopy with energy-dispersive X-ray spectroscopy, Lingyi examined the composition of the glazes, pigments, and pastes of blue-and-white glazed pottery from Mongolia, to better understand political economy during the Yuan dynasty. While her work will never see its completion, Lingyi's study-in-process of the pigments used to create blue-and-white porcelain would have made an immeasurable contribution to the field.

Collectively, this volume shows the need for more subtle and comparative narratives that consider the complexities of the contexts in which materials were produced, exchanged, and consumed. Being attentive to the various social strata, religious environments, and politico-economic settings involved in these processes, we piece together a picture of an "interlinked but highly differentiated" worlding system that is not simply a "Eurasian ecumene" (Gerritsen and McDowall 2012:7). Using a regional perspective, rather than an empire- or state-focused perspective, we consider production and exchange within the larger context of Eurasian societies, tracing the varied ways that complex societies grew and the processes that articulated adjacent societies in networks of mutual transformation.

The scholars who have contributed to this volume represent Lingyi's colleagues, former Yale classmates, mentors, and friends. We spent time with her in the classroom and the field, at conferences, and in our homes. We hope to honor Lingyi by highlighting her contributions to the field of archaeology, both in terms of her grounded research and her enduring impact on the scholarship and lives of everyone who was fortunate enough to have known her.

Acknowledgments

We are grateful to Rosemary Volpe at the Yale Peabody Museum and Richard Burger, Yale Department of Anthropology, faculty director of the Yale University Publications in Anthropology series, and a committee member for Lingyi, for making this book possible. The thoughtful comments of two anonymous reviewers were very helpful. Revisions by the first author were carried out at The Hebrew University of Jerusalem as part of the "The Wall" project (ERC grant 882894).

References

BROOK, TIMONTHY. 2008. *Vermeer's Hat: The Seventeenth Century and the Dawn of the Global World.* New York: Bloomsbury Press. 272 pp.

FINLAY, ROBERT. 2010. *The Pilgrim Art: Cultures of Porcelain in World History.* Berkeley: University of California Press. 440 pp.

GERRITSEN, ANNE. 2020. *The City of Blue and White: Chinese Porcelain and the Early Modern World.* Cambridge: Cambridge University Press. 332 pp. https://doi.org/10.1017/9781108753104

GERRITSEN, ANNE, AND STEPHEN MCDOWALL. 2012. Global China: Material culture and connections in world history. *Journal of World History* 23(1):3–8. https://doi.org/10.1353/jwh.2012.0008

HONEYCHURCH, WILLIAM. 2015. *Inner Asia and the Spatial Politics of Empire: Archaeology, Mobility, and Culture Contact.* New York: Springer. 332 pp. https://doi.org/10.1007/978-1-4939-1815-7

PARK, JANG-SIK, AND SUSANNE REICHERT. 2015. Technological tradition of the Mongol Empire as inferred from bloomery and cast iron objects excavated in Karakorum. *Journal of Archaeological Science* 53:49–60. https://doi.org/10.1016/j.jas.2014.10.005

PERDUE, PETER C., HELEN F. SIU, AND ERIC TAGLIACOZZO. 2015. Introduction: Structuring moments in Asian connections. In: Eric Tagliacozzo, Helen F. Siu, and Peter C. Perdue, eds. *Asia Inside Out: Changing Times.* Cambridge, MA: Harvard University Press. pp. 1–22. https://doi.org/10.4159/harvard.9780674736207

RICE, PRUDENCE. 2015. *Pottery Analysis.* 2nd ed. Chicago: University of Chicago Press. 592 pp.

WOMACK, ANDREW. 2024. Translocal identity construction among Neolithic and Bronze Age communities in northwestern China. *Journal of Anthropological Archaeology* 74:101585. https://doi.org/10.1016/j.jaa.2024.101585

WU, XIAOHONG, CHI ZHANG, PAUL GOLDBERG, DAVID COHEN, YAN PAN, TRINA ARPIN, AND OFER BAR-YOSEF. 2012. Early pottery at 20,000 years ago in Xianrendong Cave, China. *Science* 336(6089):1696–1700. https://doi.org/10.1126/science.1218643

ZENG, LINGYI. 2012a. Investigation report on kiln sites at the west side of Jingdezhen Ceramic Institute in Xianghu Town. *Zhongguo Taoci Gongye* 19(3):62–68. [in Chinese.]

—2012b. Fuliang ceramics bureau officer and governor. *Zhongguo Guojia Bowuguan Guankan* 4:63–71. [in Chinese.]

—2013. "A Study of the Craftsmen in Official Kilns of the Yuan Dynasty and on the Type and Time of Yuan Blue-and-white Porcelains" [master's thesis]. Jiangxi, China: Jingdezhen Ceramic University, School of Ceramic Art. 68 pp. [in Chinese.]

CHAPTER TWO

FIRE AT ZHOUKOUDIAN:
Is There Evidence for Its Production and Cultural Transmission?

Ellery FRAHM

The means by which innovations—whether social, behavioral, or technological—spread is often a topic of importance among archaeologists, no matter where or when their research interests lie. For example, Zeng Lingyi, whom this volume memorializes, explored mechanisms behind the emergence and maintenance of the Mongol Empire, which spanned large distances and encompassed ethnically diverse peoples. To do so, she investigated the spread of porcelain technologies throughout what is now China, Mongolia, and Iran, as well as the production, use, and distribution of the products. Her hypothesis was that porcelain technologies were initially controlled and restricted by high-level elites as a way to create prestige goods that served to symbolize their power and, in turn, the political hierarchy. Eventually the knowledge to produce porcelain spread sufficiently for it to become more commonplace and accessible to local, intermediate-level elites who sought to raise their social status. At the same time, she expected to identify among porcelain decorations increasing stylistic infusions through time from various cultural traditions (e.g., Islamic motifs). Her research focus, in this sense, involved the social roles of a particular innovation and its transmission—or lack thereof—within a metapopulation, part of the vast and ongoing conversation in our field involving the means by which innovations spread (e.g., Burmeister and Bernbeck 2017; Stockhammer and Maran 2017; Spataro and Furholt 2019; Erb-Satullo 2020).

The transmission of innovations is no less interesting to Paleolithic archaeologists. We speak of transitions, revolutions, milestones, and frontiers during the Pleistocene while noting the shortcomings of these terms (e.g., Goren-Inbar et al. 2000; McBrearty and Brooks 2000; D'Errico 2003; Monnier 2006; Camps and Chauhan 2009). A central question is to what extent the transmission of innovations versus their autochthonous emergence can be identified in the deep past. Addressing this question depends, in my view, on three major factors: (1) agreement about what constitutes archaeological evidence for the innovation of interest, (2) preservation and visibility of that evidence in the record, and (3) chronological resolution sufficient to recognize any patterns in its spatiotemporal distribution.

Consider, for example, the rise of Levallois lithic technology (that is, removal of distinctive flakes by striking a prepared, tortoise-shaped lithic core), which is considered the hallmark of the Lower to Middle Paleolithic transition, and it is alternatively characterized as the replacement of so-called Mode 2 lithic technology by Mode 3 (Clark 1969). It is appealing to consider the spread of Levallois lithic technology from the perspective of cultural or demic diffusion, or both, because archaeologists have often regarded this technology as counterintuitive and, in turn, widely contend that it must be taught to a novice under the guidance of an expert (e.g., Eren, Bradley, and Sampson 2011). Visibility within the archaeological record is good because lithic artifacts preserve well. Additionally, there is a general consensus about what constitutes Levallois technology (Boëda 1995), although debate on certain details remains, such as which factors control the shape of the resulting artifacts (e.g., Brantingham and Kuhn 2001; Lycett and von Cramon-Taubadel 2013). Until recently, however, chronological resolution has been low, making it a challenge to recognize clear spatiotemporal trends on the emergence and spread of Levallois technology. For decades, the prevailing idea was that this innovation was carried out of Africa by a population of archaic humans as they spread into and across Eurasia (e.g., Akhilesh et al. 2018). This notion, though, was undermined by precise dates for the Armenian site of Nor Geghi 1 (Նոր Գեղի 1), which records a local development of Levallois (Mode 3) lithic technology alongside the presence of Acheulean (Mode 2) lithic technology (Adler et al. 2014). The site's dating (a *terminus post quem* of 308 ± 3 ka and a *terminus ante quem* of 441 ± 6 ka from $^{40}Ar/^{39}Ar$ dating) is a result of its volcanic setting, and its timing is incompatible with a simple out-of-Africa origin for Levallois technology (Adler et al. 2014). Instead, the evidence from Nor Geghi 1 as well as other sites suggests that the emergence of Levallois technology was not a singular one. Instead, this shift independently occurred within dispersed populations of archaic humans who, due to a shared technological heritage, came across the same innovation via experimentation.

MacDonald et al. (2021) argue that archaeological indicators of fire use become visible around the world at about 400,000 years ago and onward, and they cast this as the first recognizable instance of cultural transmission in the archaeological record. One central assumption to their argument is that the change from Mode 1 (Oldowan choppers) to Mode 2 (Acheulean bifacial handaxes) lithic technology was not cultural in nature. Instead, they see this shift in lithic technology as a demographic change—that is, the technological change reflects, in their view, hominin dispersals. Specifically, MacDonald et al. (2021) point to the spatiotemporal distribution of the earliest handaxes in the archaeological record: 1.7 Ma in Africa, 1.4 to 1.2 Ma in the Levant, and 0.6 to 0.7 Ma in Europe. Their argument is essentially that "it took hundreds of thousands of years from the first appearance…before handaxe technology first showed up in the technological repertoire of the early occupants of Europe…[so] the Acheulean record seems more consistent with a demic scenario [and] even suggests a genetic transmission scenario" (MacDonald et al. 2021:8). The logic of their argument does not seem especially strong, although such ideas are far from uncommon in the literature (Corbey et al. 2016). Of course, if "it took hundreds of thousands of years" (MacDonald et al. 2021:8) for a different technology to spread, once considered a case of cultural transmission, it would undercut their claim.

The control of fire, MacDonald et al. (2021) hold, differs. Specifically, they suggest that it fits the spatiotemporal pattern of cultural transmission. Their hypothesis relies heavily on prior research on the European record, especially a study by Roebroeks and Villa (2011). In that research, Roebroeks and Villa (2011) propose that "good evidence" of fire use emerges at European archaeological sites during marine isotope stages (MIS) 11 to 9 (around 424 to 300 ka), remains at a low level from MIS 8 to 6 (around 300 to 130 ka), and rises dramatically from MIS 5 onward (around 130 ka and later). There are no European sites, they maintain, with "good evidence" of fire from MIS 12 or earlier (around 478 ka and before). MacDonald et al. (2021) view this as evidence that "fire use was very rare to nonexistent" before MIS 11. For the Levant, they follow the assessment of Shimelmitz et al. (2014) that "habitual" use of fire emerged around 350 ka. Northern Africa is represented in their hypothesis by one site, Jebel Irhoud (جبل إيغود) in Morocco, with evidence of fire at around 300 ka (Richter et al. 2017). For sub-Saharan Africa, MacDonald et al. (2021) cite a review by Bentsen (2014) of fire use in the Middle Stone Age (around 350 to 35 ka). They contrast a few contentious cases of purported fire before 400 ka (e.g., Wonderwerk Cave in South Africa at around 1 Ma [Berna et al. 2012]; Koobi Fora in Kenya at around 1.5 Ma [Hlubik et al. 2017, 2019]) with the more frequent instances of fire after 400 ka, claiming that this apparent trend indeed reflects the reality of the deep past more than it does taphonomic forces or small sample sizes, or both.

All of these chronological details are important for understanding and critiquing the hypothesis of MacDonald et al. (2021). Specifically, they propose that the apparent pattern of fire use from around 400 ka onward reflects the rapid transmission of a technological innovation, due to cultural interactions, within a broad metapopulation that perhaps included multiple species of hominins:

> A striking characteristic of the fire signal that emerges from the archaeological record is the strong increase in evidence for fire use across a wide geographic area and in (geologically speaking) the same period and in different hominin subpopulations…. We also point to archaeological data that, independent of the fire record and somewhat younger, strongly supports the interpretation of the existence of cultural diffusion in the later part of the Middle Pleistocene, particularly the archaeological record of a specific stone-working technology (namely, the Levallois technique). (MacDonald et al. 2021:3)

In suggesting that the transmission of fire technology is analogous to the spread of Levallois lithic technology, MacDonald et al. (2021) seem to ignore its independent emergence in geographically dispersed hominin populations, from which the technology subsequently diffused in somewhat sporadic ways, as attested by its spread between MIS 9 and 6 (about 337–191 ka; Adler et al. 2014). Outside of the Near East, Asia is represented in the hypothesis of MacDonald et al. (2021) by just one site: Zhoukoudian (周口店). As a result, this site is somewhat key to supporting their hypothesis. In this chapter, I consider not only the most recent evidence for—and against—the use and production of fire by *Homo erectus* at Zhoukoudian Locality 1, but also its newest chronometric dates, which directly contradict the age listed MacDonald et al. (2021) for the site, thereby potentially jeopardizing important aspects of their argument.

Background on Zhoukoudian Locality 1

The story of Zhoukoudian (formerly transliterated as Choukoutien) and the discovery and loss of its *Homo erectus* ("Peking Man") fossils are worthy of a feature film. It should be emphasized that Peking Man is not singular, but analogous to the obsolete phrase Neanderthal Man. Not only were six crania (Figure 2.1) discovered, but also various other bones represent, at minimum, forty individuals. It is also often unrecognized, especially in the Western literature, that "Zhoukoudian" describes a highly complex locale with more than twenty-seven Pleistocene hominin and faunal sites. Specifically, it is Zhoukoudian Locality 1 that is known as the Peking Man site. It is a 40 m sequence comprised of seventeen

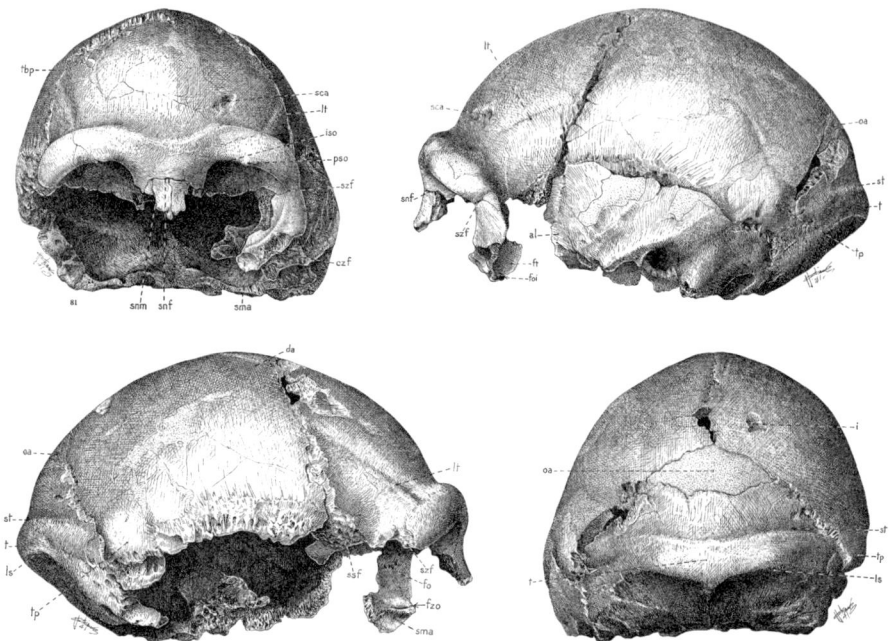

FIGURE 2.1. One of the crania of "*Sinanthropus pekinensis*" (the original species designation) as illustrated by German anatomist and physical anthropologist Franz Weidenreich (1873–1948). From Weidenreich (1943:359, 361, 363, pls. XXX, XXXI, XXXII).

geological layers, thirteen layers with mammalian fossils, and ten layers with lithic artifacts. In addition, the site has been investigated for more than a century now and much has changed in archaeology over that time. Zhoukoudian is locally known as Longgushan (龙骨山, Dragon Bone Hill), offering a clue about its discovery.

The 1890s discovery of "Java Man" fossils (originally *Anthropopithecus erectus*, now recognized as *Homo erectus*) in Indonesia led European paleontologists to explore elsewhere in Asia for additional human ancestors. Jia and Huang (1984) perhaps best detail the discovery of Zhoukoudian Locality 1. Most versions of the story report that a German physician purchased fossils from a Beijing apothecary around the start of the twentieth century. The fossils, regarded as dragon bones, had been collected locally and had high medicinal value for the treatment of various ailments. Fossil hunters saw the potential of these apothecaries' suppliers as a paleontological resource. Boxes and boxes of purchased fossils were shipped to Germany, where paleontologist Max Schlosser recognized the molar of an unknown hominin species among them. Swedish geologist Johan Gunnar Andersson was aware of Schlosser's discovery when he was hired as a mining advisor by the Chinese government in 1914. In 1918, Andersson visited the area of Zhoukoudian and he was brought to Jigushan (鸡骨山, Chicken Bone Hill), where abundant rodent fossils had been misidentified by the locals. This location is now known as Zhoukoudian Locality 6. Andersson also recognized that the locale was once a cave and that its compacted sediments had been exposed by the quarrying of the once-surrounding limestone. In 1921, Andersson returned with Austrian paleontologist Otto Zdansky and American paleontologist Walter Granger. At what is now

Locality 1 they identified the mandible of an extinct deer species and lithic artifacts made from quartzite. Later, working with Canadian paleontologist Davidson Black, they found two hominin teeth. The paleontologists were able to convince the world of their discovery when, in 1929, the first cranium was found. By the 1940s, it was argued that the Peking Man (first ascribed to *Sinanthropus pekinensis*) and Java Man fossils should be integrated into a single species: *Homo erectus* (Weidenreich 1940; Mayr 1950).

The tale of the six Locality 1 hominin crania (all but one of which has since been lost) is no less interesting and remains one of the best mysteries in the history of paleoanthropology (e.g., Jia and Huang 1990). In 1937, before the onset of World War II, Japan invaded China, including Beijing and its outskirts. Fieldwork at Zhoukoudian was suspended (except for surreptitious visits by Pei Wen-Chung [Pei Wenzhong]). In 1941, as war intensified, it was decided that the hominin fossils should be sent overseas for safekeeping, so five crania and other bones were crated for transport to the United States. The two crates, though, disappeared, and the fossils were never seen again. What happened to them has been discussed and debated at length, even in the popular press (e.g., Melvin 2005; Wayman 2011; Wong 2012; Yong 2012). Did the crates make it onto a vessel that was sunk? Were the fossils stolen? Did they make it onto a train to the port or were they hidden along the way? The latest twist in the story is from the son of a US Marine who, stationed at the port city in 1947, encountered a crate full of bones while digging a foxhole during a firefight. Local paleontologists and historians believe that they have identified this location, but the area is now a large parking lot in the middle of an industrial zone. For now the fate of the fossils is a mystery and only one of the original six skulls is available for study.

Since the end of World War II excavations at Zhoukoudian Locality 1 have been punctuated due, in part, to larger trends in paleoanthropological and archaeological research. Some trends (e.g., regional surveys) led to pauses, whereas others (e.g., paleoenvironmental reconstruction and geomorphological investigations) led to a reinvigoration of research at the site. A recurring topic has been the processes of site formation, especially with respect to the cave's formation and subsequent evolution. Already in the 1920s, the chief geologist, Li Chi (Li Ji) had recognized that Locality 1 deposits were trapped between limestone walls and that the lowest deposits were fluvial (i.e., these sediments were laid down by running water; Li C. 1927). Indeed, the karstic landscape of Zhoukoudian is much more complex than was originally appreciated. Joints and fissures occur in the Ordovician limestone throughout the hillside. Some of these joints are vertical and others are horizontal (Ren and Liu 1985). Locality 1 reflects a vertical expansion of a fissure along a joint in the dissolved and eroded limestone. The entrances to this site changed through time, including, for at least some of the cave's existence, openings in the ceiling.

Today the site can be described geologically as a 40-m-thick infill of sediments within a vertical karstic fissure. Seventeen layers have been recognized in this stratigraphic sequence (Figure 2.2). The lowest levels (layers 11 to 17) principally reflect fluvial deposition. Layers 6 to 10 are breccia, a result of weathering limestone cave walls and ceiling, interbedded with silt- and sand-sized sediment. Layer 5 is composed of travertine (i.e., calcite flowstone deposited by the dissolved limestone). The topmost strata (layers 1 to 4) are silt, travertine, and limestone breccia from the collapse of the cave ceiling. Mammalian fossils occur throughout the sequence between layers 1 and 13. Hominin fossils and lithic artifacts were found between layers 1 and 10, but most were concentrated in two proposed cultural horizons: a lower one in layers 8/9 and 10 and an upper one in layers 3 and 4 (e.g., Chiu et al. 1973; Shen G. et al. 2009).

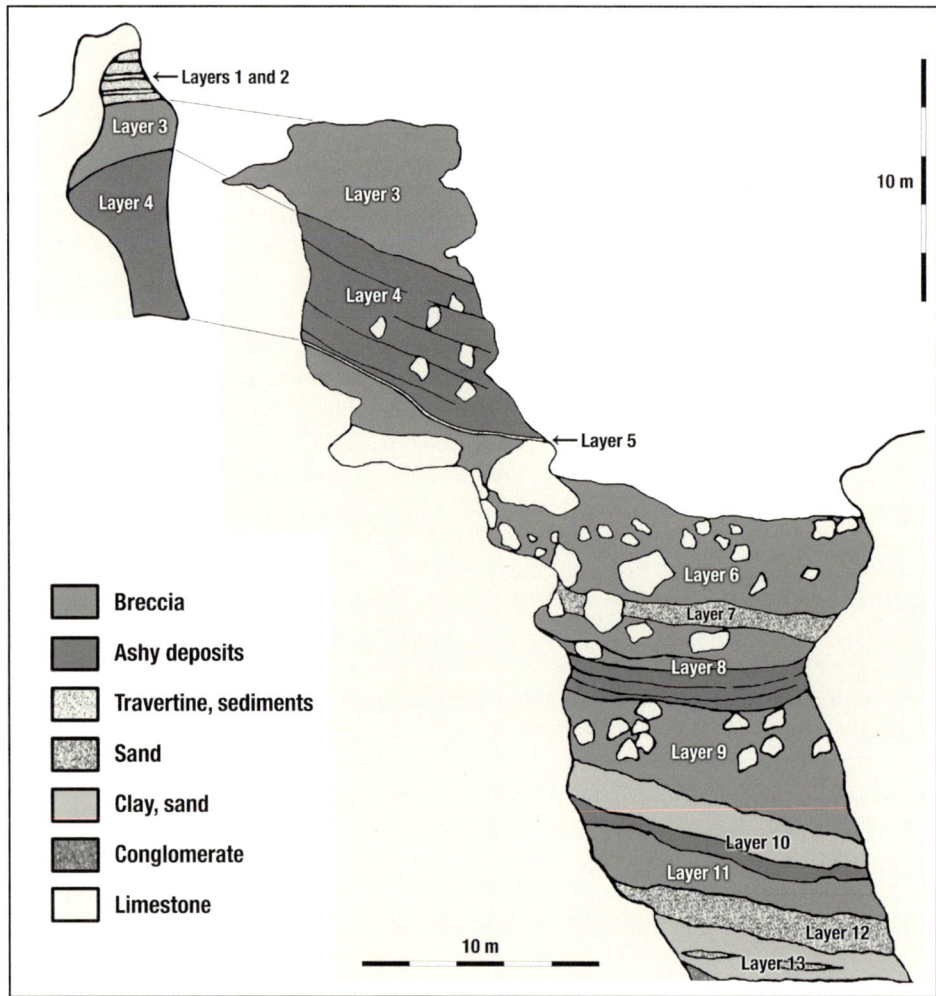

Figure 2.2. Basic stratigraphic section of Zhoukoudian Locality 1. After Binford and Ho (1985); Zhou et al. (2000); Gao et al. (2017).

The quartzite lithic artifacts first recognized by Andersson and colleagues have been reexamined in recent years, leading to the revision of earlier conclusions (Li F. 2016; Shen, Zhang, and Gao 2016). Most of the artifacts are quartzite flakes. According to some descriptions (Teilhard de Chardin and Pei 1932), many pieces might even be unworked fragments. It is worth stressing that quartzite is notoriously challenging to interpret given its irregular fracture compared with cherts and other high-quality lithic raw materials. Extremely few cores, from which flakes were removed, were reported, but this might require an amendment. For example, at least one of the purported "chopper tools" is instead more likely a core from which flakes were struck (Shen, Zhang, and Gao 2016). No bifacially shaped artifacts are known, and even the presence of retouched or resharpened edges is unclear (e.g., Teilhard de Chardin and Pei [1932] imply the occurrence of retouch along purported scrapers, but Black et al. [1933]

note that there was no intentional retouch, merely edge damage due to use). Li Feng (2016) concluded that past assertions (e.g., Pei 1932; Zhang S.S. 1983; Pei and Zhang 1985) of prevalent bipolar reduction (i.e., knapping in which the core is placed on a stone anvil and hit with a hammerstone) were vastly overestimated. Furthermore, the quartzite is not as exotic a raw material as once believed. Li Feng et al. (2011) conducted a survey of the surrounding hills and identified several quartz and quartzite outcrops from which the artifacts could have derived. Hence, the material is very local. In addition, lithic analysis conducted by Li Feng (2016) of the layer 4 and 5 artifacts led to the conclusion that the assemblage is a highly expedient one, consistent with procurement from nearby outcrops rather than curation of tools made from a more distant source of lithic material. A purported sandstone "tool" (Jia 1959) in layer 13, well below any hominin remains (i.e., layer 10 and above), likely reflects the natural accumulation of material in the cave (Binford and Ho 1985).

Much of the site's revision has focused on how the hominin, faunal, and other remains entered the cave. Was the cave actually occupied by hominins, or did natural forces, such as carnivores or water, introduce the remains? These forces were likely not at the forefront of archaeologists' minds during the first few decades of excavation. Today, though, it is better appreciated that bones can be introduced to sites and modified by varied means: not only hominins but also carnivores, rodents, raptors, and flowing water, among other possibilities. Although Black et al. (1933) noted the potential for carnivore influence at Locality 1, these discussions came to prominence in the 1980s (e.g., Binford and Ho 1985; Binford and Stone 1986; Jia 1989) and have also resurfaced in recent decades (e.g., Boaz et al. 2000, 2004; Boaz and Ciochon 2001, 2004; Yang, Wallace, and de Vries 2014). Binford and colleagues (Binford and Ho 1985; Binford and Stone 1986), based on a fraction of the excavated materials, argued that the ungulate (i.e., hoofed mammals) remains were accumulated by predation (i.e., hyenas or wolves), hominin scavenging, or both, when carcasses were brought inside the cave for protection from other scavengers.

A challenge to this interpretation from Binford and colleagues is that Locality 1 was occupied for two to three hundred millennia (as discussed in the following section). It is plausible that the mechanisms by which remains accumulated in the cave varied during that considerable length of time. Further work, however, has largely substantiated that natural forces, not hominins, were primarily responsible for the assemblage found in the cave. For example, Boaz et al. (2004) concluded that two-thirds of the hominin remains have bite marks or other modifications that can be attributed to carnivores such as hyenas or wolves, also the probable reason for marked skeletal fragmentation. Zhang Shuangquan et al. (2016) examined the layer 3 cervid (i.e., sika deer) remains recovered during the 2009–2010 excavations. They ruled out the role of hominins in the formation of this faunal assemblage, and carnivores, rodents, raptors, and water currents were largely irrelevant as well. Instead, Locality 1 probably functioned as a natural trap, at least during the deposition of layer 3, while the high frequency of sika deer remains is merely an indication of the species' propensity for accidents. Such scenarios have important implications regarding evidence for—and against—fire at Zhoukoudian Locality 1, as discussed later in this chapter.

Dating of Zhoukoudian Locality 1

Given the claims of MacDonald et al. (2021) regarding the diffusion of fire use around 400 ka, testing their hypothesis (or at least the possible role of Zhoukoudian Locality 1 within it) necessitates accurate and precise dates for the site. It has been common to chronologically place the stratigraphic layers with hominins and lithic artifacts between 300 ka (for layer 4, part of the upper cultural horizon) and 500 ka (for layer 10, part of the lower cultural horizon) (see Zhou C. et al. 2000). As elaborated below, the most reliable dates for Zhoukoudian Locality 1 are considerably closer to 780 to 400 ka, from the ages from independent techniques applied to the best materials for dating (Shen G. et al. 2009).

Crucially, MacDonald et al. (2021:2) state that the evidence for fire at Zhoukoudian Locality 1 falls within the same timeframe that they propose for the cultural diffusion of fire use:

> The putative fire evidence from Zhoukoudian (China) has been much debated, with recent work identifying traces of anthropogenic fires in a layer for which the age estimates obtained vary per dating technique but all point to the 500- to 250-ka range (i.e., to the same period in which we see fire use emerge in western Eurasia).

The reality, though, is much more complex. In short, it is certainly not the case that "all [dates] point to" the 500 to 250 ka age range. Either the dates noted by MacDonald et al. (2021) have been cherry-picked to yield a result favorable to their interpretation, or these authors simply have not critically evaluated the chronological research that has been conducted at this site. For example, it is true that Wu, Ren, and Zhu (1985) put the hominin presence at the site between 460 and 230 ka; however, such dates in older studies are problematic and have since been superseded by more reliable dates from the twenty-first century. In addition, some of the dating confusion, especially in the secondary literature, likely results from the great complexity of the Zhoukoudian area. It is frequently overlooked, particularly in the Western literature, that the district consists of numerous Pleistocene hominin and fauna sites, so it is not hard to mistakenly attribute the dates from another locality to Locality 1 (the Peking Man site) specifically.

It is not an exaggeration to state that virtually every possible dating technique has been applied to the Zhoukoudian deposits (e.g., uranium–palladium dating [Yuan et al. 1991]; fission-track dating [Liu S. et al. 1985]; amino acid racemization [Zhou Y. 1989]), although most of these techniques were tried in the 1980s or 1990s. Not all of them, though, are equally reliable, at least not for a complex and deeply stratified site such as Zhoukoudian Locality 1. For example, applying electron spin resonance (ESR) dating to fossil deer teeth, Huang et al. (1991) dated layers 3 and 4 to 282 ± 45 ka. The accuracy of this dating technique, which measures the accumulation of unpaired electrons in a substance such as tooth enamel from its exposure to natural radiation, depends on several key factors. For example, the rate of radiation exposure must be precisely known and the measurement of that dose rate in the present is assumed to be representative of the site's entire depositional history, in this case spanning hundreds of millennia (not necessarily a valid assumption). Additionally, ESR dating can be affected by mineralization changes in teeth enamel, potentially even resetting the signal. Consequently, without corroboration by an independent dating technique, ESR dates should be regarded with caution in many settings. Unfortunately, the lack of recent volcanic activity within this region means that highly accurate dating techniques, such as potassium–argon (K–Ar) and argon–argon (Ar–Ar) dating, cannot be applied to the site.

It is not uncommon to see dates reported between 200 and 300 ka for the upper (i.e., youngest) layers of Zhoukoudian Locality 1. An age of 230 ka for the topmost strata (layers 1 to 3) derives from early uranium–thorium (U–Th) dating of nonhominin faunal remains (Zhao et al. 1985). Bones, though, can be susceptible to alteration of the uranium contents during burial, meaning that the amount of uranium in the bones (a crucial variable in calculating ages using this technique) can change, invalidating the result. There have also been advances during the intervening decades in the mass spectrometry protocols involved in such age determinations. U-series dating is more reliable using speleothems (i.e., flowstones, very dense and pure calcites) rather than fossil materials, because the uranium content does not change over time (Ludwig and Renne 2000; Richards and Dorale 2003). Fortunately, the topmost stratigraphic layers of the site contain several interbedded calcite flowstone layers that can be reliably U–Th dated, and newer measurements using thermal ionization mass spectrometry yield better age determinations. Using this approach, Shen Guanjun et al. (1996, 2001) suggested dates of 400 ± 8 ka for layers 1 and 2, around 500 ka for the upper portion of layer 5, and at least 600 ka or earlier for the lower part of layer 5, which is essentially the limit of U-series dating. Given this limit, the site's lowest layers have been dated by other techniques. Furthermore, Zhou Chunlin et al. (2000) link the site's sediment stratigraphy and global $\delta^{18}O$ climate variations and, as a result, propose an age of at least 400 ka for layer 3, consistent with the U–Th dates.

The lower layers of Zhoukoudian Locality 1 are also considerably older than Wu, Ren, and Zhu (1985) and others had first proposed. At the bottom of layer 13, the lowest stratum with (nonhominin) fossils, lies the Brunhes/Matuyama (B/M) paleomagnetic boundary, indicating a reversal in the direction of Earth's magnetic field (Qian, Zhang, and Yin 1985). This reversal has been dated to around 780 ka (Spell and McDougall 1992). More recently, Shen Guanjun et al. (2009) used the production and subsequent radioactive decay of cosmogenic isotopes ($^{26}Al/^{10}Be$) in quartz as a means to date the lower stratigraphic layers. When sediments become deeply buried, such as the lower strata of the site, cosmogenic isotope production ends and decay begins. This dating technique can be applied not only to quartz-bearing sediments, but also to quartzite lithic artifacts. For example, Shen Guanjun et al. (2009) tested the isotope ratios in three quartzite artifacts from layers 8 and 9 that yielded a mean age of 720 ± 130 ka. Taken together, the sediments and artifacts yield an age of 770 ± 80 ka for layers 7 through 10, consistent with the B/M reversal boundary.

Similar to Zhou Chunlin et al. (2000), Shen Guanjun et al. (2009) also correlated the site's stratigraphy with global climatic variations. Given the geochronological framework, the upper layers (around 400 ka for layers 1 to 3) should reflect MIS 11 (around 424–374 ka), which, as indicated by its odd number, was an interglacial (i.e., warm) phase. The B/M boundary at the bottom of layer 13 should correlate with MIS 19 (around 790–761 ka), another interglacial period. The mammalian fossil remains also provide clues about climate and chronology. For example, layer 5 contains fauna that unambiguously reflect a warm climate (Liu Z.-C. 1985; Zhou Chunlin et al. 2000), corresponding to the MIS 13 interglacial phase (around 524–478 ka). This is consistent with the U–Th dates for layer 5 (Shen et al. 1996, 2001). The strata above (layer 4) and below (layer 6) principally contain fauna indicative of a colder climate (Liu Z.-C. 1985; Zhou C. et al. 2000), consequently corresponding to the glacial MIS 12 (around 478–424 ka) and MIS 14 (around 563–524 ka) periods, respectively. Furthermore, layers with largely cold-adapted fauna were composed of breccia, loess, and blocks of limestone from ceiling collapse, reflecting cooler and drier times (Liu Z.-C. 1985; Zhou C. et al. 2000; Goldberg et al. 2001; Shen G. et al. 2009). Conversely, warm-adapted faunas were found in layers composed of water-deposited (fluvial) sediments and flowstones, reflecting warmer and wetter times. Accordingly, the clays, sands, and other sediments found in the lower layers reflect warmer phases. Limited oxygen isotope data for the fauna likewise support the shifts in climate. The $\delta^{18}O$ values from *Equus* teeth are consistent with layers 4 and 8/9 as glacial phases and layers 10 and 11 as interglacial ones (Gaboardi, Deng, and Wang 2005). Such climate data are important not only for site chronology, but also for considering the prevalence of fire on the landscape. As is clear to us today, as the climate changes, wildfires are becoming more common and more severe as fuel dryness increases with less moisture and more severe droughts. Thus, we must keep in mind that fire likely would naturally occur more often during the dry periods and those layers that are associated with cultural horizons (i.e., layers 4 and 8/9) reflect drier glacial times.

Fire and Zhoukoudian Locality 1

Particularly in the secondary literature, it is almost taken as an unquestionable fact that fire was used, and even skillfully controlled, by hominins inside the Zhoukoudian Locality 1 cave; however, there is no such consensus to be found in nearly a century's worth of excavations, observations, and literature from the site. Given the cultural significance ascribed to early control of fire at Zhoukoudian (Cheng 2019), it is no surprise that this has been hotly debated. Here I endeavor to follow the main threads of this issue through the literature, both quite recent and several decades old, to present the current status of the debate. The principal challenge is distinguishing, after more than half a million years have passed, between the presence of fire either in or around the cave versus the use and control of fire by hominins inside the cave. It is common in books and museum displays (Figure 2.3) to see a reconstruction of life inside the cave with hominins tending to, even gathered around, fire inside a hearth, often stone-lined and fed by gathered firewood. In assembling the relevant information for a review and analysis, though, the null hypothesis must be that there was natural fire on the landscape surrounding Zhoukoudian, not anthropogenic fire inside it. Natural fires exist and their frequency changes with climate. Therefore, we should start from the position of first assuming any fire was natural in origin and consider what evidence would allow us to clearly accept the hypothesis of an anthropogenic origin.

It is frequently mentioned that the original excavators noted the presence of ash and a potential for fire inside the cave. Even this simple statement is actually complex. The development of this idea has been traced by Binford and Ho (1985) and Goldberg et al. (2001). These authors point out that the "ash" deposits of, for example, layers 4 and 10 were not initially regarded as such by Teilhard de Chardin and Young (1929), who reported them to be laminated clay and sand. As discussed shortly, later researchers concurred with this identification (Weiner et al. 1998; Goldberg et al. 2001). It seems that the notion of burning and ashy deposits came from Henri Breuil, usually known as Abbé Breuil, the French priest and prehistorian (Binford and Ho 1985; Goldberg et al. 2001). Teilhard de Chardin in 1930 sent a calcined deer bone to Breuil in Paris, and he thought that it had been burned (Breuil 1932a, 1932b). At about the same time, Black (1932) sent sediment samples to Paris for analysis. The results indicated the presence of elemental carbon (i.e., carbon not present in chemical compounds such as carbonates) in the sediment potentially as soot or fine charcoal debris. In December 1931, Breuil visited the site and Pei pointed out a dark layer of sediment, from which apparent soot-covered rocks and burnt bone were removed (Breuil 1932b). The Geological Survey of China also identified a thin black layer as fine charcoal particles, perhaps the same sediment sampled for testing by Black (1932). Thereafter, the deposits of layers 4 and 10, sometimes 4 to 6 m thick, were interpreted as deep ash accumulations. The observed laminations of red, yellow, and dark sediment came to be interpreted as deeply stratified in situ hearths (Black et al. 1933). Thus, there was an

FIGURE 2.3. The diorama of Zhoukoudian Locality 1 at the entrance of the *Ancient China* exhibition hall in the National Museum of China in Beijing. Among various activities being carried out by hominins inside the cave, one individual (lower right) is blowing on the flames of a hearth to keep it burning. Photo credit: E. Frahm.

extrapolation, due at least in part to the suggestion of Breuil, from burnt bone and a carbon-bearing layer to overlapping hearth features in deep ashy deposits.

Black (1932) did consider that the presence of charcoal particles, which later analyses confirmed (Stringer 1985; Shen C. et al. 2004), could reflect burnt material that originated from outside the cave and was washed inside. This would have been consistent with the cave's formation processes as they were understood at the time by Teilhard de Chardin and Young (1929:184): "Locality 1 has to be understood, not as an underground, water-drained, fissure, but as an ancient, gradually filled, open-air cave." There were hackberry seeds also recovered from the deposits, but Binford and Ho (1985) pointed out that the seeds could reflect droppings from owls, raptors, or other animals who had consumed the fruit, not hominins. Furthermore, Binford and colleagues proposed that the burnt bones and purported ashy deposits likely represented the natural combustion and subsequent mineralization of animal droppings, rather than anthropogenic hearths (Binford and Ho 1985; Binford and Stone 1986). Such interpretations were received with a mix of support and disbelief, and certainly some elements of their arguments were stronger than others. Perhaps their best contribution to the debate is that, with taphonomy squarely in mind, Binford and colleagues started from a position that natural forces were more responsible for the site than hominins were, bringing it into better alignment with other Pleistocene cave sites. This was the explicit null hypothesis, which is essentially the approach followed in this chapter.

The initial identification of layers 4 and 10 as sand and silt, rather than ash (Teilhard de Chardin and Young 1929), was supported by later microscopic and microchemical techniques (e.g., Weiner et al. 1998; Goldberg et al. 2001), and other scholars have agreed that such examinations are crucial to clarify misleading macroscopic observations and to better understand depositional forces (e.g., Hu et al. 2019). Because of the large-scale excavations at Zhoukoudian Locality 1 over many decades, Weiner et al. (1998) collected sediments from a preserved stratigraphic profile near a wall of the site. During cleaning of the profile, layer 10 yielded forty-two macrofauna bones. Of these, six bones were uniformly gray, black, or turquoise in hue, and their surface residues were shown by Fourier-transform infrared spectroscopy (FTIR) to be consistent with burnt bone organic matrix. The remaining bones were yellow with black speckles. Chemical analyses revealed the surfaces to instead be oxide-stained by the depositional environment. Of the 278 microfauna bones also recovered, seven had been burned. Therefore, a portion, but far from a majority, of the bones showed chemical evidence of burning, not staining from manganese or other oxides. Weiner et al. (1998) considered these burnt bones the best evidence for fire, at least near the site. Since the ceiling was open at times, however, they were not necessarily burned in situ.

Micromorphological analysis of layers 4 and 10 indicated low-energy deposition of sediments by water (Weiner et al. 1998; Goldberg et al. 2001). For example, the purported "hearths" in layer 10, on microscopic examination, were revealed to be finely laminated silt and clay sediments interbedded with fragments of organic matter, and there was no charcoal noted. The laminations of such fine sediments, which were visible in petrographic thin sections, are characteristic of their accumulation in a low-energy alluvial environment, such as slow-flowing or standing water in a small pool. Pieces of limestone were derived from the cave walls or were brought into the cave by runoff or mudflows, a mechanism that could also have transported faunal remains and other material from the outside. In fact, the Zhoukou River flowed through this crevasse in the deep past. In addition, microscopic fragments of animal bone were observed to be well rounded from alluvial transport or carnivore digestion, or both.

Layer 4 yielded similar results. In particular, reddish areas in this layer were a result of fine, silt-sized hematite (iron oxide, Fe_2O_3) particles that chemically precipitated during diagenesis (Weiner et al. 1998). The occurrence of abundant hematite hints that, during its deposition, the sediments in this layer were rich in organic material, which depleted the local oxygen content and mobilized the iron oxide. As the iron oxide encountered more oxygen, it precipitated as fine grains of hematite. Such conditions can also lead to silica (SiO_2) mobility and clay formation. Both of these processes were also observed in layer 4 (e.g., veins of newly formed and deposited quartz, silicified clays), providing support for the diagenetic origin of the bright-red hematite (Weiner et al. 1998; Karkanas et al. 2000). As further evidence that the hematite was not produced by localized heating, FTIR and elemental tests established that fragments of limestone within the sediment had not been thermally altered (Weiner et al. 1998).

There were limited indicators of ash in layers 4 and 10, but not enough to support labeling them as ashy deposits from abundant hearth features. Naturally, much of the challenge is due to the passage of about half a million years. Fresh wood ash primarily consists of fine-grained calcite (the same mineral that makes up limestone) and a fairly small amount of "siliceous aggregates," which are minerals from the soil embedded within an amorphous, siliceous (i.e., silica-rich) matrix that is biological in origin (Weiner et al. 1998). Layer 10 consists, as determined by Weiner et al. (1998), of quartz (about 45%), clay minerals (about

15%), and carbonated apatite (about 40%), which could potentially reflect a reaction between calcite and phosphate from groundwater. There was a small quantity of mineral clusters, which, in a scanning electron microscope, broadly resembled siliceous aggregates but showed no traits that indicated a biological origin (e.g., the presence of plant phytoliths). FTIR and elemental analyses showed that, because of diagenesis, the clay minerals had been secondarily silicified and, hence, Weiner et al. (1998) argued that the mineral aggregates were a product of the same geochemical process. Their inference, in turn, was that the carbonated apatite did not reflect altered wood ash. Later observations revealed the remnants of rhombic- or lozenge-shaped calcite crystals, which could indicate wood ash (Goldberg et al. 2001); however, the origins of this potential ash might still lie outside of the cave.

During more recent excavations at Zhoukoudian Locality 1, the reddened sediments and mineral aggregates of layer 4 have been revisited. These studies have reached different conclusions about both phenomena but, frustratingly, without critically engaging with the previous interpretations. Zhong et al. (2014), for instance, argue that the mineral clusters are indeed biologically derived siliceous aggregates from wood ash. Unfortunately, the one scanning electron microscopy image in their article shows severe electrical charging that obscures most of the details, and it does not show any of the characteristics necessary to demonstrate a biological origin (e.g., phytoliths). Furthermore, their X-ray diffraction spectra established that the mineral clusters included hydrated, potassium-bearing micas (e.g., muscovite), which are common in silt and lose their water molecules when heated to high temperatures (i.e., in a hearth). Ultimately, it seems as though Zhong et al. (2014) perhaps better supported the interpretations of Weiner et al. (1998) and Goldberg et al. (2001) than their own argument in favor of in situ fire production. Similarly, Zhang Yan et al. (2014) mapped the reddened sediments using magnetic susceptibility. They argue that localized areas of high magnetic susceptibility and, in turn, concentrated hematite reflect the locations of hearths, and the mapped susceptibility measurements indeed look compelling. The challenge, though, is that the data do not confront the issue of diagenetic hematite, as argued by Weiner et al. (1998). The circular "hearths" may simply reflect small pools of water in which fine hematite particles precipitated. The key problem is essentially equifinality, whereby multiple causes can lead to quite similar outcomes.

Ideally, potential hearth features and heat-altered lithic artifacts would be in direct association, but such evidence is presently lacking. Pei and Zhang (1985) report one lithic artifact, a simple chopping tool, that had been exposed to enough heat to crack. It might be one of the two fire-cracked rocks that is pictured by Gao et al. (2017), the other of which looks to be an unmodified pebble. It is difficult to see whether the purported chopper has simply fractured into the shape evocative of a tool or if it might instead be a flake core, as Shen, Zhang, and Gao (2016) note about "chopping tools" at the site. Beyond these brief reports, it is unclear how common or scarce fire-altered rocks are and what proportion of them are unambiguously artifacts rather than simple pebbles or limestone blocks. Guo et al. (1980, 1991) attempted to date lithic artifacts from layer 10 using the fission-track technique; however, this tends to be more of a relative, not absolute, technique because of the variables involved (i.e., like ESR, dates depend on very precisely knowing the ambient radiation levels over hundreds of millennia). Guo et al. (1980, 1991) argued that the fission-track results revealed the lithics had been heated around 462 ± 45 ka, roughly the suspected age of the layer at the time of their study. We know now, though, that layer 10 is much older—around 770 ± 80 ka. Thus, their date is so far off as to be indicative of nothing except, perhaps, confirmation bias.

Where does this leave the issue of fire at Zhoukoudian Locality 1? There was, at the very least, fire nearby. There are some burnt bones, a few fire-cracked rocks, probable charcoal particles reflected by the presence of elemental carbon, and perhaps limited (but not unambiguous) remnants of ash. The problem is that each of these materials could have existed on the landscape and been transported into the cave by water or wind, thereby increasing the chances for natural, rather than anthropogenic, fires being the causes. It must also be kept in mind that the site is large, the stratigraphy (see Figure 2.2) is much more complex than implied, the layers were deposited over immense periods of time, and the excavations have completely removed large portions of the site, all contributing to the challenge of locating possible hearth features. Ideally, addressing this issue in the future will not depend on a chance discovery of, for example, fire-cracked lithics, heated sediments, and burnt bones in direct association with charcoal and related evidence.

There are, though, other scientific means to investigate fire use during the Pleistocene (Goldberg, Miller, and Mentzer 2017). A potential line of investigation involves combustion-produced compounds that, unlike elemental carbon, remain near a burning location. As demonstrated by Brittingham et al. (2019), polycyclic aromatic hydrocarbons (PAHs) are created during combustion, and they can differ in structure (i.e., the number of rings of molecules) and mobility. The abundance of light PAHs (three to four rings) can reveal wildfires across the wider landscape, while heavy PAHs (five to six rings) reflect localized particulate emissions from burning wood. A high ratio of heavy-to-light PAHs would hint at hearths as the cause, whereas the reverse would suggest wildfires were the culprit. For now, though, the degree to which the Zhoukoudian hominins used fire to cook food, stay warm, and provide light remains unclear.

Conclusions

Zhoukoudian Locality 1 offers, according to some (Attwell, Kovarovic, and Kendal 2015), the best evidence for the independent innovation of fire use, creation, and maintenance; however, as laid out above, there is still, after nearly a century of study, no "smoking gun" for anthropogenic fire inside the cave. There was fire, at least, near the site, but taphonomy and equifinality have confounded the unambiguous identification of hearth features. If one is convinced that evidence for fire use by the Zhoukoudian hominins is already sufficient, the site can debunk the hypothesis of MacDonald et al. (2021), whereby the ability to create and maintain fire was the first culturally transmitted innovation. If, though, one finds that the evidence does not yet rise to the level of rejecting the null hypothesis that the fire was naturally occurring, there remains more research to do. This outcome does not diminish the importance of Zhoukoudian Locality 1. In fact, it highlights a crucial need for continued investigation as the site remains central to answering questions about the innovation of fire use and its effects on human evolution. Testing the hypothesis of MacDonald et al. (2021) still largely relies on the future findings from Locality 1.

For now, considering the hypothesis from MacDonald et al. (2021) is predicated on Pleistocene archaeological sites with more conclusive scientific evidence of fire use (Figure 2.4). Several of the earliest purported instances of fire use in eastern Africa—Koobi Fora (patches of reddened sediment at 1.5 Ma; Bellomo 1994; Hlubik et al. 2017, 2019) and Chesowanja (burnt clay at 1.4 Ma; Gowlett et al. 1981) in Kenya as well as Gadeb in Ethiopia (fire-cracked rocks at 1.5 Ma; Barbetti et al. 1980)—remain quite debatable. Wonderwerk

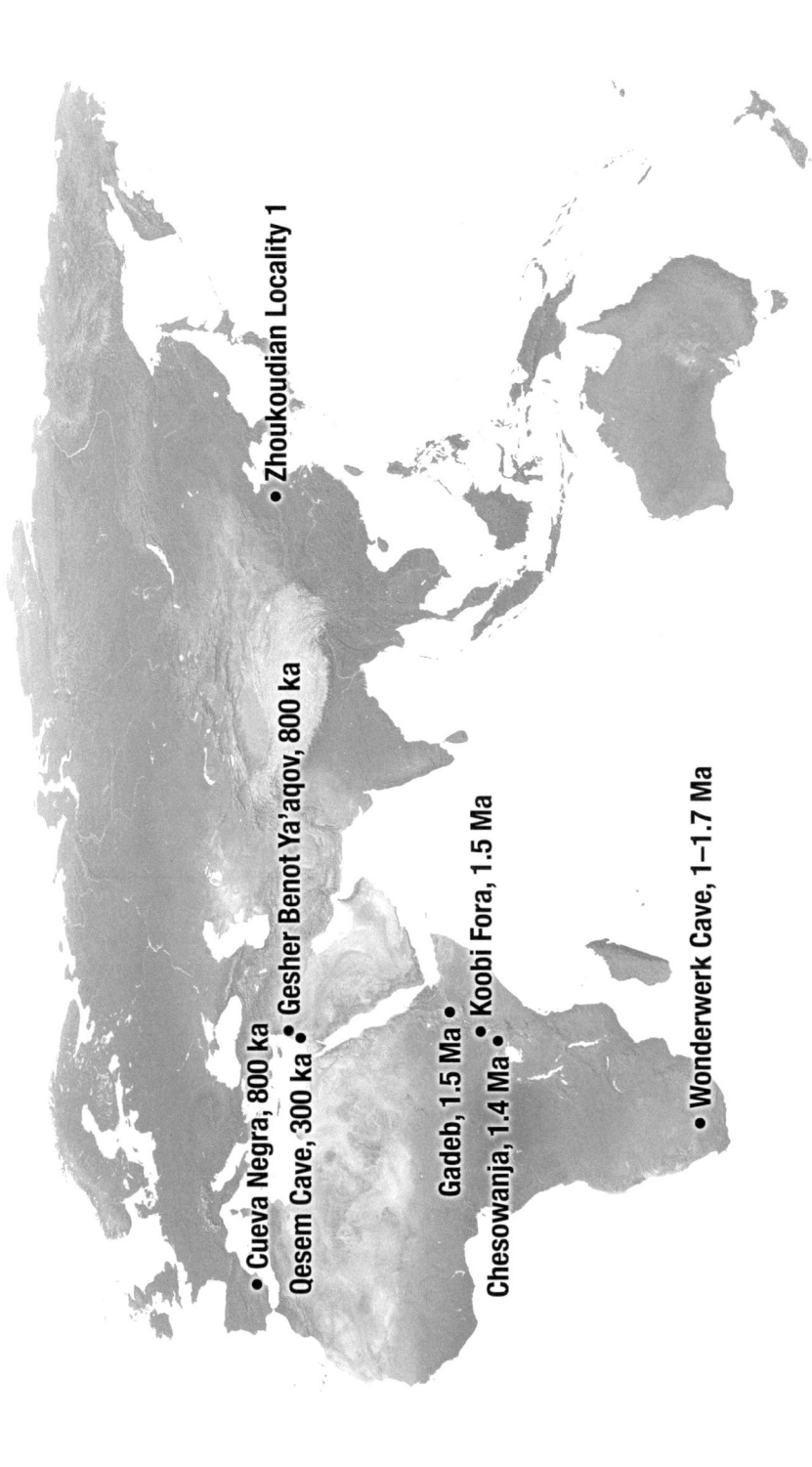

Figure 2.4. Sites with evidence of fire production and approximate dates. Digital elevation data from SRTM3 (NASA Shuttle Radar Topography Mission, SRTM Plus, dataset Version 3.0, 2013).

Cave in South Africa; however, has much clearer evidence for intentional fire use by 1 Ma and perhaps as early as 1.7 Ma (Beaumont 2011; Berna et al. 2012). At around 800 ka there is support for fire at Cueva Negra in southeastern Spain (Rhodes et al. 2016) and at Gesher Benot Ya'aqov (בקעי תונב רשג) in Israel (Alperson-Afil and Goren-Inbar 2010). Not far from the latter site, however, fire use appears much later, around 300 ka, at Qesem Cave (תרעמ קסם; Karkanas et al. 2007). These dates and geographic distributions are much patchier than implied by MacDonald et al. (2021) and are similar to those for the appearance of Levallois technology, which, as argued by Adler et al. (2014), best fits a model in which this technological shift independently occurred within dispersed hominin populations rather than as a result of cultural or population diffusion across the landscape. MacDonald et al. (2021) highlight that, in the Near East, evidence for fire use rises after about 350 ka (e.g., Qesem Cave); however, this region is a key corridor between Africa and Eurasia. Thus, it is challenging to explain highly dispersed control of fire at around 800 ka, spanning from southern Africa to western Europe to eastern Asia, and yet a lack of such control in the vast areas between them. Zhoukoudian Locality 1 remains one of the best locales in the world to potentially show that the use and maintenance of fire could have independently arisen in Asia.

Acknowledgments

My sincere thank you to Anne Underhill, Richard Burger, and Rosemary Volpe for their roles in making this publication in honor of Lingyi happen. Anonymous reviewers are thanked for improving the clarity of this chapter. I considered Lingyi to be one of "my" students and I still feel her loss deeply. This book will never capture her light and warmth, but I hope that it shows to all readers how much Lingyi was loved by her friends and colleagues.

References

ADLER, DANIEL S., KEITH N. WILKINSON, SIMON BLOCKLEY, DARREN F. MARK, RON PINHASI, BEVERLY A. SCHMIDT-MAGEE, SAMVEL NAHAPETYAN, CAROLINE MALLOL, FRANCESCO BERNA, PHIL J. GLAUBERMAN, ET AL. 2014. Early Levallois technology and the Lower to Middle Paleolithic transition in the Southern Caucasus. *Science* 345(6204):1609–1613. https://doi.org/10.1126/science.1256484

AKHILESH, KUMAR, SHANTI PAPPU, HARESH M. RAJAPARA, YANNI GUNNELL, ANIL D. SHUKLA, AND ASHOK K. SINGHVI. 2018. Early Middle Palaeolithic culture in India around 385–172 ka reframes Out of Africa models. *Nature* 554: 97–101. https://doi.org/10.1038/nature25444

ALPERSON-AFIL, NIRA, AND NAAMA GOREN-INBAR. 2010. *The Acheulian Site of Gesher Benot Ya'aqov. Volume 2, Ancient Flames and Controlled Use of Fire.* New York: Springer Dordrecht. 120 pp. (Vertebrate Paleobiology and Paleoanthropology.) https://doi.org/10.1007/978-90-481-3765-7

ATTWELL, LAURA, KRIS KOVAROVIC, AND JEREMY KENDAL. 2015. Fire in the Plio-Pleistocene: The functions of hominin fire use, and the mechanistic, developmental and evolutionary consequences. *Journal of Anthropological Sciences* 93:1–20. https://doi.org/10.4436/JASS.93006

BARBETTI, MIKE, J. D. CLARK, F. M. WILLIAMS, AND M. A. J. WILLIAMS. 1980. Palaeomagnetism and the search for very ancient fireplaces in Africa: Results from a million-year-old Acheulian site in Ethiopia. *Anthropologie* 18:299–304. https://www.jstor.org/stable/44602417

BEAUMONT, PETER B. 2011. The edge: More on fire-making by about 1.7 million years ago at Wonderwerk Cave in South Africa. *Current Anthropology* 52(4):585–595. https://doi.org/10.1086/660919

BELLOMO, RANDY V. 1994. Methods of determining early hominid behavioral activities associated with the controlled use of fire at FxJj 20 Main, Koobi Fora, Kenya. *Journal of Human Evolution* 27(1–3):173–195. https://doi.org/10.1006/jhev.1994.1041

BENTSEN, SILJE EVJENTH. 2014. Using pyrotechnology: Fire-related features and activities with a focus on the African Middle Stone Age. *Journal of Archaeological Research* 22:141–175. https://doi.org/10.1007/s10814-013-9069-x

BERNA, FRANCESCO, PAUL GOLDBERG, LIORA KOLSKA HORWITZ, JAMES BRINK, SHARON HOLT, MARION BAMFORD, AND MICHAEL CHAZAN. 2012. Microstratigraphic evidence of in situ fire in the Acheulean strata of Wonderwerk Cave, Northern Cape province, South Africa. *Proceedings of the National Academy of Sciences* 109(20):E1215–E1220. https://doi.org/10.1073/pnas.1117620109

BINFORD, LEWIS R., AND CHUAN KUN HO. 1985. Taphonomy at a distance: Zhoukoudian, "The cave home of Beijing Man?" *Current Anthropology* 26(4):413–442. https://doi.org/10.1086/203303

BINFORD, LEWIS R., AND NANCY M. STONE. 1986. Zhoukoudian: A closer look. *Current Anthropology* 27(5):453–475. https://doi.org/10.1086/203469

BLACK, DAVIDSON. 1932. Evidences of the use of fire by *Sinanthropus*. *Bulletin of the Geological Society of China* 11(2):107–108. https://doi.org/10.1111/j.1755-6724.1932.mp11002002.x

BLACK, DAVIDSON, PIERRE TEILHARD DE CHARDIN, CHUNG-CHIEN YOUNG, AND WEN-CHUNG PEI. 1933. *Fossil Man in China: The Choukoutien Cave Deposits with a Synopsis of Our Present Knowledge of the Late Cenozoic in China*. Peiping: Geological Survey of China and Section of Geology of the National Academy of Peiping. 174 pp. (Geological Memoirs, Series A, 11.)

BOAZ, NOEL T., AND RUSSELL L. CIOCHON. 2001 March. The scavenging of "Peking Man": New evidence shows that a venerable cave was neither hearth nor home. *Natural History* 110(2):46–51. http://hdl.handle.net/2246/6507

—2004. *Dragon Bone Hill: An Ice-Age Saga of* Homo erectus. Oxford: Oxford University Press. 232 pp. https://doi.org/10.1093/acprof:oso/9780195152913.001.0001

BOAZ, NOEL T., RUSSELL L. CIOCHON, QINQI XU, AND JINYI LIU. 2000. Large mammalian carnivores as a taphonomic factor in the bone accumulation at Zhoukoudian. *Acta Anthropologica Sinica* 19(Suppl.):224–234.

—2004. Mapping and taphonomic analysis of the *Homo erectus* loci at Locality 1 Zhoukoudian, China. *Journal of Human Evolution* 46(5):519–549. https://doi.org/10.1016/j.jhevol.2004.01.007

BOËDA, ERIC. 1995. Levallois: A volumetric construction, methods, a technique. In: Harold L. Dibble and Ofer Bar-Yosef, eds. *The Definition and Interpretation of Levallois Technology*. Madison, WI: Prehistory Press. pp. 41–68. (Monographs in World Archaeology 23.)

BRANTINGHAM, P. JEFFREY, AND STEVEN L. KUHN. 2001. Constraints on Levallois core technology: A mathematical model. *Journal of Archaeological Science* 28(7):747–761. https://doi.org/10.1006/jasc.2000.0594

BREUIL, HENRI. 1932a. Le feu et l'industrie lithioue et osseuse à Choukoutien [Fire and the lithic and osseous industry at Choukoutien]. *Bulletin of the Geological Society of China* 11:17–154. https://doi.org/10.1111/j.1755-6724.1932.mp11002004.x

—1932b. Le feu et l'industrie de pierre et d'os dans le gisement du "Sinanthropus" à Choukoutien [Fire and the stone and bone industry in the "Sinanthropus" deposit at Chou Kou Tien]. *L'Anthropologie* 42:1–17.

BRITTINGHAM, ALEX, MICHAEL T. HREN, GIDEON HARTMAN, KEITH N. WILKINSON, CAROLINA MALLOL, BORIS GASPARYAN, AND DANIEL S. ADLER. 2019. Geochemical evidence for the control of fire by Middle Palaeolithic hominins. *Scientific Reports* 9:15368. https://doi.org/10.1038/s41598-019-51433-0

BURMEISTER, STEFAN, AND REINHARD BERNBECK, EDS. 2017. *The Interplay of People and Technologies: Archaeological Case Studies on Innovation*. Berlin: Edition Topoi. 294 pp. (Berlin Studies of the Ancient World 43.) https://doi.org/10.17171/3-43

CAMPS, MARTA, AND PARTH CHAUHAN. 2009. *Sourcebook of Paleolithic Transitions: Methods, Theories, and Interpretations*. New York: Springer Press. 574 pp. https://doi.org/10.1007/978-0-387-76487-0

Cheng, Yinghong. 2019. *Discourses of Race and Rising China.* New York: Palgrave Macmillan. 335 pp. https://doi.org/10.1007/978-3-030-05357-4

Chiu, Chung-Lang, Yü-min Gu, Yin-Yun Zhang, and Shen-Shui Chang. 1973. Newly discovered *Sinanthropus* remains and stone artifacts at Choukoutien. *Vertebrata Palasiatica* 11:109–131. [in Chinese.]

Clark, Grahame. 1969. *World Prehistory: A New Outline.* 2nd ed. Cambridge: Cambridge University Press. 331 pp.

Corbey, Raymond, Adam Jagich, Krist Vaesen, and Mark Collard. 2016. The Acheulean handaxe: More like a bird's song than a Beatles' tune? *Evolutionary Anthropology* 25(1):6–19. https://doi.org/10.1002/evan.21467

D'Errico, Francesco. 2003. The invisible frontier: A multiple species model for the origin of behavioral modernity. *Evolutionary Anthropology* 12(4):188–202. https://doi.org/10.1002/evan.10113

Erb-Satullo, Nathaniel L. 2020. Archaeomaterials, innovation, and technological change. *Advances in Archaeomaterials* 1(1):36–50. https://doi.org/10.1016/j.aia.2020.11.003

Eren, Metin I., Bruce A. Bradley, and C. Garth Sampson. 2011. Middle Paleolithic skill level and the individual knapper: An experiment. *American Antiquity* 76(2):229–251. https://doi.org/10.7183/0002-7316.76.2.229

Gaboardi, Mabry, Tao Deng, and Yang Wang. 2005. Middle Pleistocene climate and habitat change at Zhoukoudian, China, from the carbon and oxygen isotopic record from herbivore tooth enamel. *Quaternary Research* 63(3):329–338. https://doi.org/10.1016/j.yqres.2005.02.006

Gao, Xing, Shuangquan Zhang, Yue Zhang, and Fuyou Chen. 2017. Evidence of hominin use and maintenance of fire at Zhoukoudian. *Current Anthropology* 58(516):S267–S277. https://doi.org/10.1086/692501

Goldberg, Paul, Christopher E. Miller, and Susan M. Mentzer. 2017. Recognizing fire in the Paleolithic archaeological record. *Current Anthropology* 58(S16):S175–S190. https://doi.org/10.1086/692729

Goldberg, Paul, Steven Weiner, Ofer Bar-Yosef, Q. Xu, and J. Liu. 2001. Site formation processes at Zhoukoudian, China. *Journal of Human Evolution* 41(5):483–530. https://doi.org/10.1006/jhev.2001.0498

Goren-Inbar, Naama, Craig S. Feibel, Kenneth L. Verosub, Yoel Melamed, Mordechai E. Kislev, Eitan Tchernov, and Idit Saragusti. 2000. Pleistocene milestones on the Out-of-Africa corridor at Gesher Benot Ya'aqov, Israel. *Science* 289(5481):944–947. https://doi.org/10.1126/science.289.5481.944

Gowlett, J. A. J., J. W. K. Harris, D. Walton, and B. A. Wood. 1981. Early archaeological sites, hominid remains and traces of fire from Chesowanja, Kenya. *Nature* 294:125–129. https://doi.org/10.1038/294125a0

Guo, Shilun, Shunsheng Liu, Shengfen Sun, Feng Zhang, Shuhua Zhou, Xiuhong Liao, Ruiying Hu, Wu Meng, Pengfa Zhang, and Jingfa Lin. 1980. Age determination of Peking Man by fission track dating. *Chinese Science Bulletin* 25:535–536.

—1991. Fission track dating of the 4th layer of the Peking Man Site. *Acta Anthropologica Sinica* 10(1):73–77. [in Chinese.] https://doi.org/10.16359/j.cnki.cn11-1963/q.1991.01.011

Hlubik, Sarah, Francesco Berna, Craig Feibel, David Braun, and John W. K. Harris. 2017. Researching the nature of fire at 1.5 Mya on the site of FxJj20 AB, Koobi Fora, Kenya, using high-resolution spatial analysis and FTIR spectrometry. *Current Anthropology* 58(S16):S243–S257. https://doi.org/10.1086/692530

Hlubik, Sarah, Russell Cutts, David R. Braun, Francesco Berna, Craig S. Feibel, and John W. K. Harris. 2019. Hominin fire use in the Okote Member at Koobi Fora, Kenya: New evidence for the old debate. *Journal of Human Evolution* 133:214–229. https://doi.org/10.1016/j.jhevol.2019.01.010

Hu, Yuanfeng, Bin Zhou, Yang Pang, and Xiangchun Xu. 2019. A review of study methods and progress on hominid use of fire. *Quaternary Sciences* 39(1):240–257. [in Chinese.] https://doi.org/10.11928/j.issn.1001-7410.2019.01.22

Huang, Peihua, Sizhao Jin, Renyi Liang, Zhongjia Lu, Lizhen Zheng, Zhenxin Yuan, Zhaomeng Fang, and Bingxi Cai. 1991. Study of ESR dating for burying age of the first skull of Peking Man and chronological scale of the cave deposit in Zhoukoudian Site Loc. 1. *Acta Anthropologica Sinica* 10(2):107–115. [in Chinese.]

Jia [Chia], Lanpo. 1959. Report on excavations at the *Sinanthropus* site in 1958. *Palaeovertebrata et Paleoanthropoligica* 3(1):41-45. [in Chinese.]1(1):21–26.

—1989. On problems of the Beijing-man site: A critique of new interpretations. *Current Anthropology* 30(2):200–205. [in Chinese.] https://doi.org/10.1086/203727

Jia, Lanpo, and Weiwen Huang. 1984. *Excavation of Zhoukoudian Peking Man Site.* Beijing: Science and Technology Press. 54 pp. [in Chinese.]

—1990. *The Story of Peking Man: From Archaeology to Mystery.* Translated by Zhiqi Yin. Beijing: Foreign Languages Press. 280 pp.

Karkanas, Panagiotis, Ofer Bar-Yosef, Paul Goldberg, and Steve Weiner. 2000. Diagenesis in prehistoric caves: The use of minerals that form in situ to assess the completeness of the archaeological record. *Journal of Archaeological Science* 27(10):915–929. https://doi.org/10.1006/jasc.1999.0506

Karkanas, Panagiotis, Ruth Shahack-Gross, Avner Ayalon, Mira Bar-Matthews, Ran Barkai, Amos Frumkin, Avi Gopher, and Mary C. Stiner. 2007. Evidence for habitual use of fire at the end of the Lower Paleolithic: Site-formation processes at Qesem Cave, Israel. *Journal of Human Evolution* 53:197–212. https://doi.org/10.1016/j.jhevol.2007.04.002

Li, C. 1927. The Chow K'ou Tien fossil deposits. *Bulletin of the Geological Society of China* 6(3–4):337–344. https://doi.org/10.1111/j.1755-6724.1927.mp63-4007.x

Li, Feng. 2016. An experimental study of bipolar reduction at Zhoukoudian locality 1, north China. *Quaternary International* 400:23–29. https://doi.org/10.1016/j.quaint.2015.08.064

Li, Feng, Chunxue Wang, Decheng Liu, Xiaoling Zhang, Shuangquan Zhang, and Xing Gao. 2011. Vein quartz procurement at layers 4–5 of the Zhoukoudian locality 1. *Quaternary Sciences* 31(5):900–908. [in Chinese with English abstract.] http://www.dsjyj.com.cn/en/article/id/dsjyj_10540

Liu, S., F. Zhang, R. Hu, J. Liu, S. Guo, and S. Zhou. 1985. Dating Peking Man site by fission-track method. In: Rukang Wu, Mei'e Ren, and Xianmo Zhu, eds. *Multi-disciplinary Study of the Peking Man Site at Zhoukoudian.* Beijing: Science Press. pp. 241–245. [in Chinese.]

Liu, Ze-Chun. 1985. Sequence of sediments at Locality 1 in Zhoukoudian and correlation with loess stratigraphy in northern China and with the chronology of deep-sea cores. *Quaternary Research* 23(2):139–153. https://doi.org/10.1016/0033-5894(85)90025-0

Ludwig, Kenneth R., and Paul R. Renne. 2000. Geochronology on the paleoanthropological time scale. *Evolutionary Anthropology* 9(2):101–110. https://doi.org/10.1002/(SICI)1520-6505(2000)9:2<101::AID-EVAN4>3.0.CO;2-W

Lycett, Stephen J., and Noreen von Cramon-Taubadel. 2013. A 3D morphometric analysis of surface geometry in Levallois cores: Patterns of stability and variability across regions and their implications. *Journal of Archaeological Science* 40(3):1508–1517. https://doi.org/10.1016/j.jas.2012.11.005

MacDonald, Katharine, Fulco Scherjon, Eva van Veen, Krist Vaesen, and Wil Roebroeks. 2021. Middle Pleistocene fire use: The first signal of widespread cultural diffusion in human evolution. *Proceedings of the National Academy of Sciences* 118 (31):e2101108118. https://doi.org/10.1073/pnas.2101108118

Mayr, Ernst. 1950. Taxonomic categories in fossil hominids. *Cold Spring Harbor Symposia on Quantitative Biology* 15:109–118. https://doi.org/10.1101/SQB.1950.015.01.013

McBrearty, Sally, and Alison S. Brooks. 2000. The revolution that wasn't: A new interpretation of the origin of modern human behavior. *Journal of Human Evolution* 39(5):453–563. https://doi.org/10.1006/jhev.2000.0435

Melvin, Sheila. 2005. "Archaeology: Peking Man, still missing and missed." *New York Times*, October 11, 2005. https://www.nytimes.com/2005/10/11/health/archaeology-peking-man-still-missing-and-missed.html

Monnier, Gilliane F. 2006. The Lower/Middle Paleolithic periodization in western Europe: An evaluation. *Current Anthropology* 47(5):709–744. https://doi.org/10.1086/506280

Pei, Wen-Chung. 1932. Notice of the discovery of quartz and other stone artifacts in the Lower Pleistocene hominid-bearing sediments of the Choukoutien cave deposit. *Bulletin of the Geological Society of China* 11(5):109–146. https://doi.org/10.1111/j.1755-6724.1932.mp11002003.x

Pei, Wenzhong, and Senshui Zhang. 1985. *A Study on the Lithic Artifacts of* Sinanthropus. Beijing: Science Press. 277 pp. (Palaeontologia Sinica 12.) [in Chinese.]

Qian, F., J. Zhang, and W. Yin. 1985. Magnetic stratigraphy from the sediment of west wall and test pit of Locality 1, at Zhoukoudian. In: Rukang Wu, Mei'e Ren, and Xianmo Zhu, eds. *Multi-disciplinary Study of the Peking Man Site at Zhoukuodian*. Beijing: Science Press. pp. 251–254. [in Chinese.]

Ren, Mei'e, and Z. C. Liu. 1985. Development of Peking Man's cave in relation to early man at Zhoukoudian, Beijing. In: Tung-sheng Liu, ed. *Quaternary Geology and Environment of China*. Beijing: China Ocean Press. pp. 186–193. [in Chinese.]

Rhodes, S. E., M. J. Walker, A. López-Jiménez, M. López-Martínez, M. Haber-Uriarte, Y. Fernández-Jalvo, and M. Chazan. 2016. Fire in the Early Palaeolithic: Evidence from burnt small mammal bones at Cueva Negra del Estrecho del Río Quípar, Murcia, Spain. *Journal of Archaeological Science: Reports* 9:427–436. https://doi.org/10.1016/j.jasrep.2016.08.006

Richards, David A., and Jeffrey A. Dorale. 2003. Uranium-series chronology and environmental applications of speleothems. *Reviews in Mineralogy and Geochemistry* 52(1):407–460. https://doi.org/10.2113/0520407

Richter, Daniel, Rainer Grün, Renaud Joannes-Boyau, Teresa E. Steele, Fethi Amani, Mathieu Rué, Paul Fernandes, Jean-Paul Raynal, Denis Geraads, Abdelouahed Ben-Ncer, et al. 2017. The age of the hominin fossils from Jebel Irhoud, Morocco, and the origins of the Middle Stone Age. *Nature* 546:293–296. https://doi.org/10.1038/nature22335

Roebroeks, Wil, and Paola Villa. 2011. On the earliest evidence for habitual use of fire in Europe. *Proceedings of the National Academy of Sciences* 108(13):5209–5214. https://doi.org/10.1073/pnas.1018116108

Shen, Chen, Xiaoling Zhang, and Xing Gao. 2016. Zhoukoudian in transition: Research history, lithic technologies, and transformation of Chinese Palaeolithic archaeology. *Quaternary International* 400:4–13. https://doi.org/10.1016/j.quaint.2015.10.001

Shen, Chengde, Weixi Yi, Ying Yang, Yanmin Sun, Changzhu Jin, Tungsheng Liu, and Bingxi Cai. 2004. Concentrations of "elemental carbon" in samples from the Peking Man Site at Zhoukoudian and the possibility of their application in the development of evidence for the use of fire by humans. *Chinese Science Bulletin* 49(6):612–616. https://doi.org/10.1360/03wd0209

Shen, Guanjun, Xing Gao, Bin Gao, and Darryl E. Granger. 2009. Age of Zhoukoudian *Homo erectus* determined with $^{26}Al/^{10}Be$ burial dating. *Nature* 458:198–200. https://doi.org/10.1038/nature07741

Shen, G., D. Gu, B. Gahleb, Z. Yuan, and B. Cai. 1996. Preliminary results on U-series dating of Peking Man Site with high precision TIMS. *Acta Anthropologica Sinica* 15:210–217. [in Chinese.]

Shen, Guanjun, Teh-Lung Ku, Hai Cheng, R. Lawrence Edwards, Zhenxin Yuan, and Qian Wang. 2001. High-precision U-series dating of Locality 1 at Zhoukoudian, China. *Journal of Human Evolution* 41(6):679–688. https://doi.org/10.1006/jhev.2001.0516

Shimelmitz, Ron, Steven L. Kuhn, Arthur J. Jelinek, Avraham Ronen, Amy E. Clark, and Mina Weinstein-Evron. 2014. "Fire at will": The emergence of habitual fire use 350,000 years ago. *Journal of Human Evolution* 77:196–203. https://doi.org/10.1016/j.jhevol.2014.07.005

Spataro, Michela, and Martin Furholt, eds. 2019. *Detecting and Explaining Technological Innovation in Prehistory*. Leiden: Sidestone Press Academics. 250 pp. (Scales of Transformation 8.) https://doi.org/10.59641/i1801lu

Spell, Terry L., and Ian McDougall. 1992. Revision to the age of the Brunhes–Matuyama boundary and the Pleistocene geomagnetic polarity time scale. *Geophysical Research Letters* 19(12):1181–1184. https://doi.org/10.1029/92GL01125

Stockhammer, Philipp W., and Joseph Maran, eds. 2017. *Appropriating Innovations: Entangled Knowledge in Eurasia, 5000–1500 BCE*. Oxford: Oxbow Books. 296 pp. https://doi.org/10.2307/j.ctt1vgw6v1

Stringer, Chris B. 1985. Discussion and criticism: On Zhoukoudian. *Current Anthropology* 26(5):655. https://doi.org/10.1086/203356

Teilhard de Chardin, Pierre, and Wen-Chung Pei. 1932. The lithic industry of the *Sinanthropus* deposits in Choukoutien. *Bulletin of the Geological Society of China* 11(4):315–364. https://doi.org/10.1111/j.1755-6724.1932.mp11004001.x

Teilhard de Chardin, Pierre, and C. C. Young [Z. Yang]. 1929. Preliminary report on the Chou Kou Tien fossiliferous deposit. *Bulletin of the Geological Society of China* 8(3):173– 202. https://doi.org/10.1111/j.1755-6724.1929.mp8003002.x

Wayman, Erin. 2011. "The mystery of the missing hominid fossils." *Smithsonian Magazine,* December 7, 2011. https://www.smithsonianmag.com/science-nature/the-mystery-of-the-missing-hominid-fossils-1985559/

Weidenreich, Franz. 1940. Some problems dealing with ancient man. *American Anthropologist* 42:375–383. https://www.jstor.org/stable/663229

—1943. *The Skull of* Sinanthropus pekinensis: *A Comparative Study on a Primitive Hominid Skull*. Pehpei, Chungking: Geological Survey of China. 484 pp. (Paleontologia Sinica, New Series D 10, Whole Series 110.)

Weiner, Steve, Qinqi Xu, Paul Goldberg, Jinyi Liu, and Ofer Bar-Yosef. 1998. Evidence for the use of fire at Zhoukoudian, China. *Science* 281(5374):251–253. https://doi.org/10.1126/science.281.5374.251

Wong, Kate. 2012. "Report from former U.S. Marine hints at whereabouts of long-lost Peking Man fossils." *Scientific American,* March 22, 2012. https://blogs.scientificamerican.com/observations/report-from-former-u-s-marine-hints-at-whereabouts-of-long-lost-peking-man-fossils/

Wu, Rukang, Mei'e Ren, and Xianmo Zhu. 1985. *Multi-disciplinary Study of the Peking Man Site at Zhoukoudian*. Beijing: Science Press. [in Chinese.]

Yang, Deming, Ian J. Wallace, and Dorien de Vries. 2014. Peking man: New research. *Evolutionary Anthropology* 23(5):162–163. https://doi.org/10.1002/evan.21420

Yong, Ed. 2012. "Lost treasures: Peking Man's bones." *New Scientist,* February 1, 2012. https://www.newscientist.com/article/mg21328502-500-lost-treasures-peking-mans-bones/

Yuan, Sixun, Tiemei Chen, Shijun Gao, and Yanqiu Hu. 1991. Study on uranium series dating of fossil bones and teeth from Zhoukuodian site. *Acta Anthropologica Sinica* 10:189–193. [in Chinese.]

Zhang, S. S. 1983. Bipolar flakes as a bond of ancient culture in China. *Fossils* 4:6–8. [in Chinese.]

Zhang, Shuangquan, Fuyou Chen, Yue Zhang, Jingshu Li, Xiaoling Zhang, and Xing Gao. 2016. A taphonomic study on the skeletal remains of *Cervus* (*Sika*) *grayi* from layer 3 of the Peking man site at Zhoukoudian during the 2009–2010 field seasons. *Quaternary International* 400:36–46. https://doi.org/10.1016/j.quaint.2015.09.081

Zhang, Yan, Zhengtang Guo, Chenglong Deng, Shuangquan Zhang, Haibin Wu, Chunxia Zhang, Junyi Ge, Deai Zhao, Qin Li, Yang Song, and Rixiang Zhu. 2014. The use of fire at Zhoukoudian: Evidence from magnetic susceptibility and color measurements. *Chinese Science Bulletin* 59(10):1013–1020. https://doi.org/10.1007/s11434-013-0111-7

Zhao, S., M. Xia, C. Zhang, M. Liu, S. Wang, Q. Wu, and Z. Ma. 1985. Uranium-series dating of Peking man site. In: Rukang Wu, Mei'e Ren, and Xianmo Zhu, eds. *Multi-disciplinary Study of the Peking Man Site at Zhoukoudian*. Beijing: Science Press. pp. 246–250. [in Chinese.]

Zhong, Maohua, Congling Shi, Xing Gao, Xinzhi Wu, Fuyou Chen, Shuangquan Zhang, Xingkai Zhang, and John W. Olsen. 2014. On the possible use of fire by *Homo erectus* at Zhoukoudian, China. *Chinese Science Bulletin* 59(3):335–343. https://doi.org/10.1007/s11434-013-0061-0

Zhou, Chunlin, Zechun Liu, Yongjin Wang, and Qiaohua Huang. 2000. Climatic cycles investigated by sediment analysis in Peking Man's Cave, Zhoukoudian, China. *Journal of Archaeological Science* 27(2):101–109. https://doi.org/10.1006/jasc.1999.0428

Zhou, Yihua. 1989. Amino acid dating of Peking Man and Dingcun Man. *Acta Anthropologica Sinica* 8:177–181. [in Chinese.] https://doi.org/10.16359/j.cnki.cn11-1963/q.1989.02.01

CHAPTER THREE

CERAMIC PETROGRAPHY IN CHINA:
Past Approaches and Future Directions

Andrew WOMACK and LU Qingyu

Thin section petrography, also sometimes referred to as petrology, involves the systematic identification, and in some cases quantification, of inclusions in ceramic fabrics as well as other aspects of the paste, as viewed through a transmitted light microscope in polarized and cross polarized light (Rea 1989). Over the last century thin section petrography has been used alongside other techniques, such as bulk chemical analysis to identify raw materials, forming techniques, firing methods, and postdepositional processes, allowing archaeologists to explore topics including raw material sourcing, organization of production, circulation and exchange, and producer identity (Quinn 2013). Despite the usefulness and relatively low cost of this technique, its application in many areas of the world, including China, has until recently been quite limited. Here we review the development of this method before diving into recent applications and future trajectories for its use in China.

Background on Ceramic Thin Section Petrography

Thin section petrography was first developed in the mid-1800s by Henry Clifton Sorby, who adopted techniques from zoology for creating transparent thin sections of material mounted on glass and analyzing them under a microscope (Worley 2009). Sorby published the first known work using thin section petrography for analysis of geological samples (Sorby 1851). While Sorby initially only worked with geological thin sections, later in life he also applied this technique to archaeological materials, including Roman and Medieval ceramics, as well as bricks and tiles from England. His results, however, were only presented in lectures and were not formally published (Worley 2009). Additional small-scale studies were undertaken on archaeological ceramics in Europe and North America in the late 1800s and early 1900s; however, it was not until the 1930s that more systematic studies using thin section petrography for classification and provenance studies were done (Quinn 2013).

Shepard's (1936, 1939) work on Native American ceramics from New Mexico, USA, was the first large-scale petrographic study that connected ceramic paste recipes to specific geological formations to identify production locales. Significant growth in petrographic research coincided with the general rise in archaeometric analysis in the 1960s though 1980s, particularly with applications in North America and the Mediterranean (Quinn

2013). Beginning in the 1980s formalized descriptions of inclusions in ceramic fabrics were adopted, with Whitbread's (1995) seminal work adding formal descriptions of the clay matrix using terminology adopted from soil micromorphology. Around the same time Stoltman pioneered the application of a quantitative point-counting approach, adopted from sedimentary geology to his studies of ceramics from the Mississippi Valley (Stoltman 1989, 1991, 2001), providing a complimentary analytical method to more traditional qualitative, descriptive approaches.

In recent years advances in archaeological applications of thin section petrography have been used in other areas, including China, along with advances in automated point counting, image analysis, and online open-access data sharing. Traditionally, barriers to the application of ceramic petrography have included the extensive training that is typically needed to be able to competently analyze a sample as well as the time needed for the actual analysis, which can take several hours per sample. In addition, time is needed to select the sample, create the thin section, and analyze the resulting data. While comprehensive training is still necessary, automated point-counting stages and recording software such as the PETROG digital petrography system (Conwy Valley Systems Limited, United Kingdom; www.petrog.com) have significantly reduced the time needed for point counting, while also speeding up data entry and analysis. At the same time, image analysis software, such as ImageJ (W.S. Rasband, 1997–2018, ImageJ, US National Institutes of Health, Bethesda, Maryland, USA; https://imagej.net/ij/,), has been used to assist with counting of mineral inclusions and voids, and assess attributes such as roundedness (Aprile, Castellano, and Eramo 2019). Perhaps the most significant breakthrough, however, has been the development of open-access online databases, such as Petrodatabase (Quinn et al. 2011), that allow for petrographers to view hundreds or thousands of comparative ceramic and geological samples from various areas of the world to better understand and contextualize their own results.

While thin section petrography is now a well-established technique, it has only relatively recently been applied systematically in China. In this chapter we will provide a history of early efforts, summarize more recent advances and uses, and then chart future directions for applications of petrography to Chinese archaeological ceramics.

Early Applications of Ceramic Petrography to Materials from China

The earliest known application of thin section petrography for analyzing archaeological materials from China actually dates back to some of the earliest archaeological work in the country. In the 1920s Swedish geologist Johan Gunnar Andersson and his Chinese colleagues surveyed and excavated at dozens of Neolithic and Bronze Age (about 8000–1000 BCE) sites in eastern and northwestern China as part of their work for the Geological Survey of China. Much of the material gathered during excavations and purchased in local markets was eventually shipped to Sweden, where it was housed in the newly established Museum of Far Eastern Antiquities in Stockholm (Andersson 1943; Myrdal 2021). While much of the material was returned to China per Andersson's agreement with the Chinese government, a significant portion, including hundreds of whole vessels and thousands of ceramic sherds, remained in Sweden (Fiskesjö and Chen 2004). There Andersson, his colleagues, and students, including Nils Palmgren, Margit Bylin-Althin, and Bo Sommarström, analyzed the ceramic materials (Hein et al. 2021).

Bylin-Althin in the 1930s used macroanalysis and thin section petrography to understand the makeup of pottery from different cultural periods. Bylin-Althin focused on Qijia-style pottery (齐家; 2300–1500 BCE) and, with the help of geologist Gunnar Beskow, examined some samples in thin section. While the details of the analysis are unknown, the results did support Bylin-Althin's division of Qijia pottery into different classes by paste type (Bylin-Althin 1946).

In the 1960s some of Andersson's Majiayao-style (马家窑; 3200–2000 BCE) materials were also examined by the Swedish geologist Nils Sundius, who used thin section petrography, chemical analysis, and refiring to examine technological aspects of these ceramics. While only a small number of samples were examined, the results largely hold up. Sundius's descriptions of pastes match modern analyses of Majiayao material, while his refiring experiments demonstrated that Majiayao wares had typically been fired to 800 to 950 °C (Sundius 1961).

In China, the first application of petrography also dates to the 1960s, with the work of Zhou, Zhang, and Zheng (1964). Zhou and colleagues investigated the physical and chemical properties of Neolithic and Bronze Age pottery, including from the Shang (商代; 1600–1046 BCE) and Western Zhou dynasties (西周; 1046–771 BCE), in the Yellow River Basin. The petrographic portion of their analysis focused on describing the inclusions and fabric of ceramic sherds, but much like Bylin-Althin's work, they only used the results to classify the pottery into various categories. This is not surprising given the focus at that time on typological classification. However, this did mark the first time that this type of analysis was applied within China. Unfortunately, despite these relatively early studies, the technique was not more widely applied and to our knowledge was not used again in China, or on Chinese material abroad, until the 1990s.

Early Applications of Ceramic Petrography in China: 1990s to 2000s

New studies of ceramics using thin section petrography began in the mid-1990s in China. Despite sporadic efforts to apply petrography to Chinese materials, these did not coalesce into a more coherent specialization until the publication of works specifically focused on petrographic methods for archaeology in Chinese, beginning in 2010. In general, scholars using thin section petrography in this period were seeking answers to a wide variety of questions, ranging from the technology used to create various types of porcelain to sourcing of Neolithic pottery in eastern and central China. Most studies used multiple methods, such as petrography and X-ray diffraction (XRD) or inductively coupled plasma mass spectrometry (ICP-MS) analysis; however, most researchers only worked with very small sample sizes, making the results of these early efforts difficult to fully assess. Generally thin section petrography during this period was still in the experimental phase, where it was seen as a useful tool for analysis but was often only used to address a small range of questions and only applied to very small samples of pottery.

Porcelain and Proto-porcelain
The first of these earlier works, by Peng et al. (1993), focused on Song dynasty (宋代; 960–1279 CE) porcelain. While it may seem unusual to apply petrography to such fine, high-fired wares, in this case the researchers were focused on the structural relationship

between pottery body and glaze as well as the size and type of any inclusions in the paste. The results of the study allowed for a technological comparison of paste preparation and glaze application in various types of porcelain from Qingshan, Hubei Province. A similar study on proto-porcelain from sites in both northern and southern China was also undertaken in the late 2000s (Xia, Zhu, and Wang 2009) and once again used petrography to explore inclusion size, this time with the aid of digital image analysis. The results generally pointed to differences in particle sizes in pottery from different regions. To our knowledge, this latter study marks the first time automated image analysis was applied to studies of pottery thin sections in China.

Neolithic Pottery

Chi et al. (1995) used a now common combination of XRD and petrography to analyze Neolithic Dawenkou-style ceramics from the Huating (花厅) site in Xinyi County, Jiangsu Province. The study analyzed twenty-five samples in an attempt to determine which were made locally and which, if any, were imported to the site from elsewhere. Using their results the researchers divided the pottery into three groups: (1) locally produced, (2) produced in other areas of the Dawenkou culture (大汶口; 3900-2400 BCE), and (3) those of unknown origin. However, the researchers only examined large geological areas in narrowing down potential pottery origins, did not examine any geological samples, did not examine trace elements in the XRD analysis, and also mostly sampled fineware sherds, limiting the usefulness of petrography. However, despite potential issues with this study, this did mark one of the first instances in China where petrography was used alongside chemical analysis techniques to attempt to determine the provenance of ancient pottery.

The use of thin section petrography for analysis of Dawenkou-style ceramics continued into the new millennium, with Xu Anwu et al.'s (2000) study of a particular type of ceramic vessel, *daokouzun* (大口尊), from two sites: Yuchisi (尉迟寺) in Anhui Province and Dazhujiacun (大朱家村) in Shandong Province. The goal of this study was to examine whether production at either site was largely local or whether many ceramics were imported from elsewhere. The results pointed to most sherds at Dazhujiacun being produced locally, while the sherds from Yuchisi seemed to have multiple origins. However, between the two sites only eleven samples were analyzed with thin section petrography. Therefore, significantly larger samples sizes are needed from each site to clarify the accuracy of these results.

A third study of Neolithic period pottery in China comes from the early Neolithic site of Shuangdun (双墩; around 5000 BCE), located in Anhui Province. There, Zhu et al. (2005) used a combination of XRD, Raman spectroscopy, petrography, and scanning electron microscopy with energy-dispersive X-ray spectroscopy (SEM-EDS) to analyze black pottery found at the site. Specifically, they wanted to investigate how the black color of the pottery was created. Their analysis revealed that the black was from carbon, which was seen at high levels in the inner and outer layers of the pottery paste. Since this study was focused only on the color of the pottery, however, the application of a wide range of techniques was unfortunately not used to address any other questions of pottery production or origins.

Historic Period Pottery

A second set of studies from the early 2000s focused on perhaps the most well-known archaeological find in China, the terracotta warriors of the first emperor of the Qin dynasty (秦代; 221-206 BCE), Qin Shi Huangdi. In this case Shan et al. (2003) used inductively coupled plasma atomic emission spectroscopy (ICP-AES) and petrography to examine nine samples from four warrior statues. The results showed that the warriors were all constructed using coarseware paste with inclusions that likely came from the vicinity of nearby Lishan Mountain. They also concluded that the firing temperature was relatively low, likely pointing to an open firing environment. A second study, by Rong and Lan (2005), used thin section petrography to examine seven samples from the warriors. Rong and Lan concluded that local sand was used as a temper and that the statues were made with molds. They were then fired in a reducing atmosphere, possibly contradicting the findings of the previous study, which pointed to the potential use of open firings. This second study was partially undertaken to assist with the preservation and reconstruction of the warrior statues. The petrographic results from these studies largely match those seen in later, more thorough studies of the warrior statues (discussed below).

Additional research on pottery from the historical period focused on Han dynasty (汉代; 206 BCE–220 CE) tomb wares; however, in this case, instead of focusing on production methods and location, the focus was on the pigment used to paint these items. Using a combination of petrography, Raman spectroscopy, and SEM-EDS, Xia et al. (2008) analyzed painted pottery from Han tombs in Shanxi and Shandong Provinces. Petrography in particular was used to analyze the distribution and thickness of the paint layers, while the other methods were used to identify the chemical composition of the pigments. The researchers found that a variety of pigments were used to decorate the pottery, including cinnabar, red lead, Chinese purple ($BaCuSiO_6$), hematite, magnetite, and kaolin clay. The discovery of Chinese purple in Shandong was the first time the use of this type of unusual, synthetic pigment was seen in this area.

Other work on pottery from the historical period comes from outside China, where Lois Bray (2001) completed a master's thesis on thirty-three sherds of gray, wheel-made pottery from the late Shang dynasty capital site of Anyang (occupied around 1300–1046 BCE). Bray used a combination of thin section petrography, XRD, and bulk chemical analysis. Bray also analyzed some soil samples from Anyang to understand the chemical composition of potential local raw materials. The results revealed that the samples were all made of the same raw materials that were most likely sourced locally near Anyang. While this study was one of the first by an international researcher to compare pottery and local soil samples, it unfortunately did not lead to a larger trend of international petrographic work at that time.

A second, more comprehensive international study of Shang pottery by Stoltman et al. (2009) used sixty-one thin sections of ceramics, as well as raw materials from two locales at the site of Yinxu (殷墟). This study was relatively unusual in that a wide variety of ceramics were analyzed, including vessels, pipes, bronze casting materials, and raw materials. This study had clear goals relating to the provenance and production of ceramics, focusing on identifying local raw materials, distinguishing locally made versus nonlocal items, and then exploring what implications the presence of nonlocal items might have on our understanding of production and exchange in Shang society. This study was also the first we know of to use quantitative analysis (that is, point counting) on Chinese materials. Their results pointed to the complexity of the Shang ceramic industry, with potters at Anyang using a variety of raw materials, including at least one that is likely nonlocal, and processing techniques to manufacture a wide variety of items. Overall the study answered several questions relating to sourcing, production techniques, and organization of production, and provided an excellent example of the multitude of questions that thin section petrography can be used to answer. In many ways, this work heralded a new era of petrographic studies in China, when an increasing number of researchers began to use this method to its full potential.

Recent Advances in Petrographic Analyses of Chinese Ceramics: 2010 to the Present

The landscape of ceramic thin section petrography began to change rapidly in China in the early 2010s, with the publication in Chinese of several works on the methods of ceramic petrographic analysis. These methodological publications spurred a wave of ceramic petrographic research by Chinese scholars, while at the same time small but increasing numbers of international researchers also began publishing results of petrographic studies on Chinese ceramic materials. Although the overall landscape of research remained fragmented, with concentrations of studies in some geographic regions and a complete lack of petrographic analysis in others, there was still significant growth in the sheer number of studies that used petrography, as well as the sophistication of the application of this method to Chinese materials.

Methodological Publications

The first systematic introduction in Chinese to the application of thin section petrography for Chinese archaeological materials was published by Duan (2010). This was followed soon thereafter by Wang Meng's (2011) short work on the role of petrographic analysis for identifying pottery provenance and exchange. Wu and Chen (2018) expanded on these earlier works with a more comprehensive discussion of both the uses and limitations of ceramic petrography as an analytical method. Of particular note, this work pointed to the importance of using petrography as a means of investigating the entire *chaîne opératoire* of ceramic production, while also discussing how results from petrography can be better interpreted when used alongside other approaches, including experimental archaeology and ethnoarchaeological comparison (Wu S. and Chen 2018). A series of articles on ceramic petrography, alongside other methods used to investigate ceramic technology, have been published in recent years (Bao and Zheng 2020, 2021a, 2021b). These works have provided detailed discussions of the methods used in thin section petrography and have continued to focus attention on applications of this method.

International collaborative research and methodological training has also played a key role in the expansion of petrographic methods in China. A long-standing collaboration between scholars at Shandong University, Yale University, and the University of Wisconsin–Madison has resulted in several publications that include petrographic analysis of ceramics from Shandong as a key component. On the methodological front, Lu, Wang, and Luan (2020) published on the advantages and challenges of combining ceramic petrography and bulk chemical analysis to analyze ancient ceramics, while also providing step-by-step information on how to best undertake this type of research. Lu, Wang, and Wang (2021) followed up on this work with the first comprehensive overview of petrographic analysis in China, which is the first systematic review of its kind in a Chinese publication. Together, these works throughout the last decade have made thin section petrography more accessible to scholars throughout China, resulting in the large number of works reviewed in the following section.

Recent Advances in Petrographic Analysis of Neolithic and Bronze Age Ceramics

The application of ceramic petrography has been particularly robust in the study of Neolithic and Bronze Age (about 8000–1000 BCE) societies of ancient China, where the main focus has been on understanding pottery production technology as well as circulation and exchange of pottery vessels and their contents. While chemical compositional analysis remains the preferred method for answering questions relating to production and exchange, perhaps due to relative ease of use and data interpretation, petrography is gaining steam for its ability to distinguish between inclusions and other aspects of pottery paste that may be chemically homogeneous, but distinct in visual analysis. This is particularly useful since in some areas of China, particularly the northern loess plateau, vast areas contain clay and soil that are not easy to separate by chemistry alone (see Hung [2021] as an example). A significant amount of research has taken place in several regions, including the east coast and northwest, with more sporadic research in other areas such as northern, central, and southern China.

East Coast

On the east coast, the aforementioned international collaboration has produced a number of works focused on Dawenkou (3900-2400 BCE) and Longshan (龙山; 2400-1800 BCE) ceramics, investigating topics including the production and circulation of Longshan period white pottery (Lu et al. 2019; Druc et al. 2021) as well as the organization of pottery production at the sites of Liangchengzhen (两城镇) and Dantu (丹土) (Druc et al. 2018; Lu et al. 2023). The results of these studies showed that Longshan white pottery production does not seem to be centered on a single production locale, but likely occurred at several sites, with white pottery circulated throughout local regions in Shandong Province. Other wares were produced at each site using local raw materials—with little evidence of extensive circulation of pottery or raw materials, or major changes in production practices—between the Dawenkou and Longshan periods. One other study of unusual Neolithic pottery from eastern China comes from Cui (2013), who analyzed egg-shell black pottery using a variety of methods, including petrography. Their results point to Longshan egg-shell pottery being produced independently at each site where it was used during the Longshan period, with clear variation in clay chemistry as well as clay preparation and forming methods.

Lu et al. (2024) have also recently combined petrography and chemical composition analysis to explore different types of pottery excavated from the Jinzhai site (金寨; 5200–4300 BCE) in Anhui Province. The results reveal that Dawenkou-style pottery, Liangzhu-style pottery, and Yangshao-style pottery unearthed at the site were all locally produced, while Qujialing-style pottery was likely procured via exchange. From the dating of the finds they suggested that there was extensive exchange and interaction among different regional cultures at the Jinzhai site.

Northwest

In the northwest, pottery from the Majiayao (3200–2000 BCE) and Qijia (2300–1500 BCE) periods has seen some of the more intensive petrographic research. Womack and colleagues focused on a comparative analysis of pottery from several sites in the Tao River valley of Gansu Province (Womack 2017; Womack et al. 2019, 2023), concluding that while pottery production took place at several sites, there was also significant circulation of pottery between sites in both mortuary and daily use settings. They also found that pottery production traditions, including paste recipes, did not change significantly between the Majiayao and Qijia periods, despite significant shifts in pottery forms and decoration. Dammer (2021) and Dammer et al. (2023) followed up on this work with a petrographic analysis of clay samples as well as Majiayao pottery from Qinghai and Gansu Provinces held in the Museum of Far Eastern Antiquities in Stockholm, Sweden. The results indicate that production knowledge was likely shared among potters at sites scattered across this region. Hein and Stilborg (2019) used the same collections to analyze a wide variety of Neolithic and Bronze Age pottery from this region, showing that while pottery technology remains relatively consistent in the Neolithic and early Bronze Age, there is a radical shift in paste recipes in the middle Bronze Age (beginning about 1500 BCE). They also analyzed unusual Majiayao period double-ware sherds and discussed the technological and social implications of these impressive pieces (Stilborg and Hein 2021).

Other work in the northwest has focused on pottery from specific sites, such as the early bronze working site of Xichengyi (西城驿; 2100–1600 BCE) in the Hexi Corridor. There, Yu et al. (2017) used X-ray fluorescence (XRF) and petrographic analysis to understand the origins of pottery recovered from the site. Their results suggest that at least some of the pottery was circulated into the site from other areas from the late Majiayao to the Siba (1700–1300 BCE) periods. A separate study on Majiayao pottery from two cemetery sites in Qinghai Province focused on identifying the composition of paint using a combination of chemical and petrographic analyses (Yang et al. 2013). The results showed that the black pigment was magnetite and manganese, red was made using hematite, and white was made from quartz—all of which could be locally sourced.

Other Regions
Petrographic research in other areas of China has been more scattered, with work in northern central China including studies of pottery from the Xinglongwa (兴隆洼; 6000–5000 BCE; Y. Li 2020) site as well as the Haminmangha site (哈民忙哈; 3500–3000 BCE; Duan et al. 2018), both in Inner Mongolia. For the former, the scholars examined pottery from several phases of the site, finding that production and processing technology remained largely the same over time. The Haminmangha research focused on understanding potential influence from Hongshan-style pottery; however, the researchers found that even Hongshan-influenced pottery was still being made with local raw materials. Other recent studies in this region looked at the Shimao (石峁) site (2300–1800 BCE) and analyzed a wide variety of pottery to understand production practices. Womack, Liu, and Di (2021) and Liu et al. (2022) both concluded that multiple local production groups were engaged in producing a variety of pottery vessels; however, only a small amount of pottery was likely circulating in from outside the immediate region. Guo Meng, Sun, and Shao (2023) used petrography along with X-ray and macroanalysis to determine that the potter's wheel was used to produce some types of vessels at Shimao.

In western central China, Jiang (2018) analyzed pottery from the sites of Baodun (宝墩; 2700–1700 BCE), Sanxingdui (三星堆; 1700–1150 BCE), and Shierqiao (十二桥; Shang and Zhou periods) in the Chengdu Plain to investigate pottery production and circulation. Jiang found that typical inclusions in pottery from all sites and periods most likely come from local sediments. Notably, this is one of the only studies to use quantitative point counting in its approach. Lin (2013) used petrography as well chemical analysis and standardization analysis in a study of Bronze Age pottery production in the Chengdu Plain. The results revealed that pottery production was most likely organized at the household or community level, while knowledge and finished products were transferred throughout the wider region. Moving farther east, Bonomo (2018) used a combination of petrography and portable X-ray fluorescence (pXRF) to analyze late Neolithic and early Bronze Age pottery from the Yiluo River valley in Henan Province. He found that at each of three sites analyzed pottery production was overwhelming local, from the Yangshao (仰韶; 5000–3000

BCE) down to the Erlitou period (二里头; 1900–1500 BCE), suggesting that changes in other aspects of social organization did not significantly impact pottery production and distribution. A second study in Henan, by Zhang Xianrui (2018), focused on pottery from the Yangshao, Qujialing (屈家岭), and Longshan period site of Guowan (沟湾), which is located between the northern Central Plain and the Jianghan Plain. While this region was typically thought to have been a key corridor for exchange between groups in the northern and southern plains regions, Zhang found that virtually all pottery from this site was in fact made locally and not imported from other areas.

Slightly farther south in Hubei Province, Guo Yi et al. (2018) examined pottery from the Neolithic Diaolongbei (雕龙碑) site using petrography and instrumental neutron activation analysis. They found that from 4300 to 3200 BCE all pottery was produced locally, while from 3200 to 2800 BCE there was increasing evidence of some pottery being circulated into the site from outside the local region, providing evidence for changes in pottery sourcing over time. Moving east, there have been several studies on pottery from Anhui Province. Zhang Youyin, Zhu, and Wu (2020) examined pottery production at the Lingjiatan site (凌家滩; 3600–3300 BCE), finding that, while different raw materials were used to produce different types of pottery vessels, all these materials come from the local area. Other studies in Anhui have focused on specific pottery production methods, such as the use of plant temper. Wu Weihong and Qiu (2020) used petrography to analyze pottery from Sunjiacheng (孙家城; 3800–2300 BCE), finding that plant temper was used in the production of specific types of pottery, perhaps to alter the water absorption levels in raw clay and thus the drying times of pottery items. Finally, Xu Wenting (2017) examined pottery from the Neolithic through Western Zhou periods at the site of Mopanshan (磨盘山) in Anhui, once again looking at rates of water absorption. They found that absorption was highest in the earliest pottery, lowest in Liangzhu (良渚) period pottery, and raised again in the Western Zhou (1046–771 BCE), perhaps speaking to changes in pottery production technology and firing temperatures over time.

Recent Applications of Petrography to Historical Ceramics: 2010 to the Present

Along with significant research on Neolithic and Bronze Age pottery, there have also been several studies that used thin section petrography solely on pottery from the dynastic periods. These studies have focused on topics ranging from bronze production to painted tomb wares to origins and production of the Qin dynasty terracotta warriors. Beginning with the late Shang dynasty, Stoltman et al. (2018) built on their earlier work at Anyang with a study on ceramic artifacts associated with bronze production, including molds, models, and cores. They found that, unlike what was previously thought, these items were not made of unaltered loess soils, but instead were carefully prepared using levigation and the addition of sand and lime. Similar results were gained by Chastain (2019) in his dissertation research on the same topic, but on material from Western Zhou sites. He concluded that casting molds were specially made from highly processed loess that was reduced to quartz silt, with only enough clay to hold them together.

Petrographic investigations of production processes have also focused on objects from the tomb of Qin Shi Huangdi, founder of the Qin dynasty. Zhang Shangxin et al. (2019) analyzed fragments of the acrobatic figures and found that different amounts of temper were used in different parts of the bodies of these complex statues. Quinn et al. (2017) have looked at multiple aspects of production of the terracotta warriors, using petrographic analysis to examine fragments of the warriors as well as other objects from the tomb area. Like previous studies, they found that the warriors were made near the tomb site with local raw materials, including sand and clay, which were processed centrally before being used by various local workshops.

Moving on to the Han dynasty, Wei (2012) used a combination of petrography, XRD, XRF, SEM, and other techniques to examine painted pottery from tombs in the Yulin area of Shanxi Province. Examining the pigments used to decorate these vessels, Wei found that black was made of carbon, white of bone and kaolin, red of cinnabar and hematite, and other colors used ultramarine and Chinese purple. The pottery itself was produced using locally available materials. Another study looking at coatings of ceramics as well as ceramic bodies focused on ceramic exchange between Myanmar and southern China. Kivi (2019) examined sherds from seven types of vessels from Myanmar, as well as several from southern China, and found that, while the glaze on some sherds from Myanmar seems to have been influenced by southern Chinese glazing practices, other glazing practices were most likely influenced from local southeast Asian glassmaking traditions. Other dissertation research has focused on petrographic and pXRF analysis of Kitan Liao (916–1125 CE) earthenware pottery from northern China; however, this analysis (Ross-Sheppard 2016) focused mostly on establishing baseline groupings of pottery and connecting pXRF results with petrographic groupings and did not answer specific research questions.

Other research on historical ceramics has largely examined porcelain production, beginning with proto-porcelains of the Shang dynasty. Li Wenjing et al. (2021) used petrography and chemical compositional analysis to explore production steps for proto-porcelain at the late Shang capital of Yinxu, Anyang, Henan Province. They found that these glazed wares had high calcium and low iron contents, which is typical of later porcelain, and were fired to 1167 °C. Other research on porcelain using thin section petrography includes a study on Yue celadons from Zhejiang Province, where Wu Shuang (2019) examined porcelain and other ceramic wares, finding that different raw materials and production processes were used to make these different types of vessels. Another study on porcelains of the Tang (618–907 CE) and Song dynasties used petrography to examine the microstructure of clay and glaze layers seen in porcelain of these time periods (Wang E. et al. 2020). Overall, research on historical ceramics in China has been even more sporadic than predynastic research. In general, there have only been significant amounts of research in a few concentrated regions, a trend we hope to see spread to other regions in the future.

Future Directions of Petrographic Analysis in China

As can be seen from our literature review, while there has been a significant increase in the application of thin section petrography to ceramic archaeological materials in the past decade, overall the field is still highly fragmented in regard to examination of materials from various time periods and geographic regions, as well as the questions researchers are seeking to answer. We suggest that this fragmentation has multiple causes. In the first place, formal training in petrographic analysis has only become available in China in recent years and a lack of publications prior to the 2010s meant that many scholars were unfamiliar with this method. Therefore, the concentrations of ceramic research, particularly on Neolithic and Bronze Age materials from the east coast and northwest, has been in part due to the significant participation of international researchers working in these two areas. In the case of Shandong, long-term collaborations between Chinese and American scholars have allowed for the training of a new generation of archaeologists in petrographic methods, who are now applying these more widely throughout the province (see Lu et al. [2019] as an example). In the northwest, researchers affiliated with the Tao River Archaeological Project established initial petrographic groupings as well as a database hosting results (Womack and Hein 2018), which other scholars are now building on both locally and expanding to adjacent regions such as Shaanxi Province.

A second potential factor in the piecemeal application of ceramic petrography may be that the questions this technique is best at answering have not been particularly apparent, based on the earliest petrographic work published in Chinese. The few petrographic studies before the 1990s of Chinese ceramics mostly focused on classification of pastes, which was not particularly novel compared to the main focus of that period on typological classification. Even in the 1990s to early 2000s the few studies that existed simply attempted to answer whether certain types of pottery could have been produced locally or not. These did not engage with the many other aspects of ceramic production and use where petrography can potentially provide insight, such as raw material sourcing and processing, organization of labor and production steps, potter identity and communities of practice, paste recipe standardization, and post-depositional processes, among others. Therefore, thin section petrography has remained a technique for which it is difficult to receive training and mentorship, and which is not seen as more useful than other, more accessible methods, such as bulk chemical analysis. Since petrographic analysis has also remained largely qualitative in application in China, perhaps it has also lacked the clear "scientific" appearance and relatively straightforward interpretability of results that approaches such as XRD or ICP-MS provide.

However, it is clear from the extensive use of thin section petrography in other parts of the world, such as the Mediterranean and southwestern United States, that there is a wealth of information this technique can provide about ceramic production, interaction, identity, and social organization, and that the more work is done in a region, the more useful the results can be. Therefore, for ceramic petrography to truly become a useful method for understanding the past in China, two main developments need to occur: (1) questions asked of petrography need to be broadened, and (2) methods and data need to be standardized and shared among researchers. As seen in many recent articles, archaeologists have tended to use a wide variety of research techniques, including SEM, XRD, pXRF, and LA-ICP-MS, among others, to analyze ceramics from ancient China. However, in many cases, the questions they are seeking to answer are very limited (for example, simply asking what pigments are made of or whether pottery could have been produced locally). While these questions are relatively easy to answer using these methods, they do little to shed light on more complicated, but more interesting, questions that can actually tell us about how people lived, interacted, and organized themselves in the past. For petrography to actually be worth the time, money, and expertise needed to use the technique, petrographers need to first rethink the questions they are asking of their samples. Luckily, some scholars in China have started pushing petrography in this direction, including Wu Shuang and Chen's (2018) discussion of the *chaîne opératoire* and ethnographic and experimental comparison, and Lu, Wang, and Wang's (2021) discussion of limitations currently restricting the usefulness of petrography in China.

Additionally, ceramic thin section petrography is most helpful when there is a significant collection of data to compare one's results to. In areas such as the US southwest,

Europe, and the Mediterranean, many publications, use of replicable well-defined methods, and the availability of open-source online databases have all contributed to the success of petrographic methods in answering a wide variety of questions about past societies. While some specific regions of China now have seen a significant amount of research and a fledgling bilingual database with standardized methods has been created (Womack and Hein 2018), it will take many more years of concentrated research for a comprehensive understanding of regional paste recipes to be formed. However, in regions where significant work has taken place, the payoffs are already becoming clear. For example, in northwestern and eastern China we now have a good understanding of both ceramic raw materials, production practices, and organization spanning from the Neolithic to the Bronze Age. In the northwest we now also have clear evidence of ceramic circulation between sites (Womack et al. 2023), while in Shandong it seems that local production and consumption were the norm for hundreds of years, despite significant changes in vessel forms and use (Lu et al. 2023). So while there is a long way to go in advancing petrographic studies in China, there are also many important insights that can be gained from this type of systematic work.

Conclusions

Thin section petrography was first applied to materials from China beginning in the 1930s, yet over the next eighty years use of this technique in China was very rare. This was likely due to several factors, including a lack of training opportunities and publications on the topic in Chinese, as well as an overall focus in ceramic studies on typological analysis. It is only in the past decade with the publication of multiple papers on petrographic methods in Chinese as well as increased international training opportunities that there has been a more concentrated application of this method to archaeological ceramics. In general, a few regions, such as the northwest and Shandong Province, have seen a significant number of research papers that use petrography, due at least in part to the presence of long-term international collaborations in these areas, while other regions have seen more sporadic efforts by Chinese or foreign researchers. Many of these research projects have focused on application of a variety of methods to relatively narrow questions such as paste, paint, or glaze recipes, while larger archaeological questions relating to topics such as *chaîne opératoire*, labor organization, and social interaction are only recently being addressed. We suggest that increasing engagement with these topics will be critical for both demonstrating the usefulness of petrography and creating a better understanding of the past in China.

Personal Note

We had the privilege of studying with Lingyi during her graduate work at Yale, where we all focused our research on Chinese ceramics. While Lingyi used other methods in her research, we think she would appreciate this addition to the history of ceramics research in China. In class, the office, the lab, and in the field Lingyi was dedicated to her research, while also always making time for friends. She would never turn down a dinner or party invitation and was invariably kind and elegant, but she would also make jokes that were absolutely hilarious. She is deeply missed.

References

Andersson, Johan G. 1943. *Researches into the Prehistory of the Chinese*. Stockholm: Museum of Far Eastern Antiquities. 516 pp.

Aprile, Anna, Giovanna Castellano, and Giacomo Eramo. 2019. Classification of mineral inclusions in ancient ceramics: comparing different modal analysis strategies. *Archaeological and Anthropological Sciences* 11:2557–2567. https://doi.org/10.1007/s12520-018-0690-y

Bao, Yi, and Jianming Zheng. 2020. New advances in archaeological research on ancient ceramic science and technology since the 21st century (introduction). *Wenwu Tiandi* 2020(12):89–95. [in Chinese.]

—2021a. New advances in archaeological research on ancient ceramic technology since the 21st century (part I). *Wenwu Tiandi* 2021(1):104–110. [in Chinese.]

—2021b. New advances in archaeological research on ancient ceramic technology since the 21st century (part 2). *Wenwu Tiandi* 2021(2):96–99. [in Chinese.]

Bonomo, Michael F. 2018. Ceramic production and provenance in the Yiluo basin (Henan, China): Geoarchaeological interpretations of utilitarian craft production in the Erlitou state. *Archaeological Research in Asia* 14:80–96. https://doi.org/10.1016/j.ara.2017.02.005

Bray, Lois M. 2001. "Petrographic, X-ray Diffraction, and Chemical Analysis of Pottery from Anyang, China" [master's thesis]. University of Minnesota, Duluth. Retrieved from the University Digital Conservancy, https://hdl.handle.net/11299/212461

Bylin-Althin, Margit. 1946. The Sites of Ch'i Chia P'ing and Lo Han T'ang in Kansu. *Bulletin of the Museum of Far Eastern Antiquities* 18:383–498.

Chastain, Matthew L. 2019. "The Ceramic Technology of Bronze-casting Molds in Ancient China: Production Practices at Three Western Zhou Foundry Sites in the Zhouyuan Area" [dissertation]. Massachusetts Institute of Technology. ProQuest Dissertations & Theses Global (27715886). https://www.proquest.com/dissertations-theses/ceramic-technology-bronze-casting-molds-ancient/docview/2314593465/se-2

Chi, Jinqi, He Xixue, Gongyi Zhiyuan, Houben Zou, Zunguo Wang, Feng Qian, Tiemei Chen, and Wenming Yan. 1995. Analysis of the origin of Neolithic ancient pottery in Xinyi County, China. *Zhongguo Kejidaxue Xuebao* 25(3):302–308. [in Chinese.]

Cui, Wei. 2013. "Analysis on the Technological Origins and Related Problems of Egg-shell Black Pottery Unearthed from Yuhui Site" [dissertation]. University of Science and Technology of China. [in Chinese.]

Dammer, Evgenia. 2021. "Technological Transfer in Production of Majiayao-style Pottery between Neolithic Communities in Northwest China" [dissertation]. University of Oxford, United Kingdom. ProQuest Dissertations & Theses Global (28979140). https://www.proquest.com/dissertations-theses/technological-transfer-production-majiayao-style/docview/2607477040/se-2

Dammer, Evgenia, Anke Hein, and Michela Spataro. 2023. An exploration of potential raw materials for prehistoric pottery production in the Tao River Valley, Gansu Province, China. *Geoarchaeology* 39(2):122–142. https://doi.org/10.1002/gea.21984

Druc, Isabelle, Anne Underhill, Fen Wang, Fengshi Luan, and Qingyu Lu. 2018. A preliminary assessment of the organization of ceramic production at Liangchengzhen, Rizhao, Shandong: Perspectives from petrography. *Journal of Archaeological Science: Reports* 18:222–238. https://doi.org/10.1016/j.jasrep.2017.12.050

Druc, Isabelle, Anne Underhill, Fen Wang, Fengshi Luan, Qingyu Lu, Qitao Hu, Mingjian Guo, and Yanchang Liu. 2021. Late Neolithic white wares from southeastern Shandong, China: The tricks to produce a white looking pot with not much kaolin. Results from petrography, XRD and SEM-EDS analyses. *Journal of Archaeological Science: Reports* 35:102673. https://doi.org/10.1016/j.jasrep.2020.102673

Duan, Tianjing. 2010. Applications of ceramic petrography analysis in the study of prehistoric pottery origins and interactions. *Bianjiang Kaogu Yanjiu* 2010(00):305–315. [in Chinese.]

Duan, Tianjing, Shiqi Ma, Shanshan Li, and Yuhan Chen. 2018. Petrographic analysis of pottery from the Haminmangha site (2010–2011), Inner Mongolia. *Asian Archaeology* 2:43–50. https://doi.org/10.1007/s41826-018-0014-3

Fiskesjö, Magnus, and Xingcan Chen. 2004. *China before China: Johan Gunnar Andersson, Ding Wenjiang, and the Discovery of China's Prehistory*. Stockholm: Museum of Far Eastern Antiquities. 159 pp. (Monograph series 15.)

Guo, Meng, Zhouyong Sun, and Jing Shao. 2023. Use of the potter's wheel at Shimao, Shaanxi, China. *Archaeological Research in Asia* 36: 100468. https://doi.org/10.1016/j.ara.2023.100468

Guo, Yi, Quyi Jiang, Yan Liu, Weidong Huang, Yaoli Wu, and Yimin Yang. 2018. Provenance analysis of pottery from the Neolithic Diaolongbei site, Hubei Province, China by using NAA and petrography analysis. *Journal of Archaeological Science: Reports* 21:200–2007. https://doi.org/10.1016/j.jasrep.2018.07.009

Hein, Anke, and Ole Stilborg. 2019. Ceramic production in prehistoric northwest China: Preliminary findings of new analyses of old material from the Museum of Far Eastern Antiquities, Stockholm. *Journal of Archaeological Science: Reports* 23:104–115. https://doi.org/10.1016/j.jasrep.2018.10.022

Hein, Anke, Andrew Womack, Ole Stilborg, and Evgenia Dammer. 2021. Investigating prehistoric pottery from the Gansu-Qinghai region (northwest China): From Andersson's first excavations to contemporary research. *Bulletin of the Museum of Far Eastern Antiquities* 82:231–272.

Hung, Ling-yu. 2021. Painted Pottery Production and Social Complexity in Neolithic Northwest China. Anke Hein and Andrew Womack, eds. Oxford: BAR Publishing. 214 pp. (BAR International Series 3045, Archaeology of East Asia 5.)

Jiang, Baiyi. 2018. Preliminary petrographic analysis of prehistoric pottery unearthed in Chengdu Plain. *Sichuan Wenwu* 2018(2):80–89. [in Chinese.]

Kivi, Nicholas. 2019. "Reverse Engineering of Ancient Ceramic Technologies from Southeast Asia and South China" [master's thesis]. University of Arizona. 192 pp. ProQuest Dissertations & Theses Global (13426471). https://www.proquest.com/dissertations-theses/reverse-engineering-ancient-ceramic-technologies/docview/2187686796/se-2

Li, Wenjing, Jian Zhu, Yuling He, Jigen Tang, Jianming Zheng, Guangming Zhou, Quanzheng Yao, Guoding Song, and Changsui Wang. 2021. Origin and technology of primitive porcelain unearthed from Anyang Yin ruins. *Huaxia Kaogu* 2021(3):94–105. [in Chinese.]

Li, Yuanqiu. 2020. Preliminary petrographic and compositional analysis of pottery unearthed from the Xinglonggou site, Aohan Banner, Inner Mongolia. *Sichuan Wenwu* 2020(-4):110–118. [in Chinese.]

Lin, Kuei-chen. 2013. "Pottery Production and Social Complexity of the Bronze Age Cultures on the Chengdu Plain, Sichuan, China" [dissertation]. University of California, Los Angeles. 567 pp. ProQuest Dissertations & Theses Global (3564444). https://www.proquest.com/dissertations-theses/pottery-production-social-complexity-bronze-age/docview/1400829785/se-2

Liu, Nani, Siran Liu, Kunlong Chen, Zhouyong Sun, Jing Shao, Nan Di, and Anding Shao. 2022. Chemical and petrographic analyses of pottery unearthed from the east parapet stone-faced wall of the Huangchengtai platform at the Shimao site. *Kaogu Yu Wenwu* 2:155–160. [in Chinese.]

Lu, Qingyu, Zhi Liu, Andrew Womack, Jiayan Tian, and Fen Wang. 2023. A preliminary analysis of pottery from the Dantu site, Shandong, China: Perspectives from petrography and WD-XRF. *Journal of Archaeological Science: Reports* 47:103710. https://doi.org/10.1016/j.jasrep.2022.103710

Lu, Qingyu, Fen Wang, and Fengshi Luan. 2020. Comprehensive analysis of pottery origin: Methods and Practices. *Southeast Culture* 2020(5):27–35. [in Chinese.]

Lu, Qingyu, Fen Wang, Fengshi Luan, De'an Wen (Anne Underhill), Isabelle Druc, and Sun Bo. 2019. Petrography and chemical composition analysis of Longshan culture white pottery in Dinggong and its surrounding sites. *Kaogu* 2019(10):106–120. [in Chinese.]

Lu, Qingyu, Qi Wang, and Fen Wang. 2021. Pottery petrography and its application in archaeology. *Jianghan Kaogu* 2021(2):109–115. [in Chinese.]

Lu, Qingyu, Fen Wang, Xiaolei Zhang, Hao Wu, Chengcheng Jiang, Fengshi Luan, and Anne Underhill. 2024. Analysis of the pottery provenance of Jinzhai site, Xiaoxian County, Anhui Province, China. *Kaogu* 2024(1):102–113. [in Chinese.]

Myrdal, Eva. 2021. Editor's preface: 100th anniversary of the discovery of the Yangshao culture by Johan Gunnar Andersson (1874–1960). *Bulletin of the Museum of Far Eastern Antiquities* 82:5–22.

Peng, Changqi, Xinjian Jiao, Chen Wenxue, and Haifeng Tian. 1993. Petrographic study on northern Song dynasty porcelain and kiln ware in Qingshan, Wuchang. *Jianghan Kaogu* 1993(3):72–76. [in Chinese.]

Quinn, Patrick S. 2013. *Ceramic Petrography: The Interpretation of Archaeological Pottery and Related Artefacts in Thin Section.* Oxford: Archaeopress. 260 pp. https://doi.org/10.2307/j.ctv1jk0jf4

Quinn, Patrick, Dominic Rout, Luke Stringer, Timothy Alexander, Alasdair Armstrong, and Sam Olmstead. 2011. Petrodatabase: An on-line database for thin section ceramic petrography. *Journal of Archaeological Science* 38(9):2491–2496. https://doi.org/10.1016/j.jas.2011.04.024

Quinn, Patrick S., Shangxin Zhang, Yin Xia, and Xiuzhen Li. 2017. Building the terracotta army: Ceramic craft technology and organisation of production at Qin Shihuang's mausoleum complex. *Antiquity* 91(358):966–979. https://doi.org/10.15184/aqy.2017.126

Rea, William J. 1989. Petrology—history. In: Donald R. Bowes, ed. *Petrology.* Boston: Springer. pp. 452–456. (Encyclopedia of Earth Sciences Series.) https://doi.org/10.1007/0-387-30845-8_183

Rong, Bo, and Desheng Lan. 2005. Polarizing microanalysis of terracotta pottery. *Science of Conservation and Archaeology* 2005(3):35–39.

Ross-Sheppard, Callan. 2016. "The Archaeology of Kitan/Liao Subaltern Unglazed Earthenware Ceramics: Optical, Petrographic and Geochemical Approaches" [master's thesis]. McGill University, Montreal, Canada. 175 pp. ProQuest Dissertations & Theses Global (28250832). https://www.proquest.com/dissertations-theses/archaeology-kitan-liao-subaltern-unglazed/docview/2509280146/se-2

Shan, Jie, Juanzuo Zhou, Changsui Wang, Ping Qiu, Zhongli Zhang, Junxiao Zhu, and Yinglan Zhang. 2003. Preliminary study on mineral source and sintering method of terra-cotta warriors in Qinling. *Hejishu* 2003(4):299–305. [in Chinese.]

Shepard, Anna O. 1936. The technology of Pecos pottery. In: Alfred V. Kidder, ed. *The Pottery of Pecos,* Volume 2. New Haven, CT: Published for Phillips Academy by Yale University Press. pp. 389–588. (Papers of the Southwestern Expedition 5, 7.)

—1939. Appendix A: Technology of La Plata pottery. In: Earl H. Morris, ed. *Archaeological Studies in the La Plata District, Southwestern Colorado and Northwestern New Mexico.* Washington, DC: Carnegie Institution of Washington. pp. 249–287. https://hdl.handle.net/2027/mdp.39015008501440

Sorby, Henry C. 1851. On the microscopical structure of the Calcareous Grit of the Yorkshire coast. *Quarterly Journal of the Geological Society of London* 7:1–6. https://doi.org/10.1144/GSL.JGS.1851.007.01-02.05

Stilborg, Ole, and Anke Hein. 2021. A tale of two wares: An unusual type of Late Neolithic vessels from Gansu Province, China. *Bulletin of the Museum of Far Eastern Antiquities* 82:273–321.

Stoltman, James B. 1989. A quantitative approach to the petrographic analysis of ceramic thin sections. *American Antiquity* 54(1):147–160. https://doi.org/10.2307/281336

—1991. Ceramic petrography as a technique for documenting cultural interaction: an example from the upper Mississippi Valley. *American Antiquity* 56(1):103–120. https://doi.org/10.2307/280976

—2001. The role of petrography in the study of archaeological ceramics. In: Paul Goldberg, Vance T. Holliday, and C. Reid Ferring, eds. *Earth Sciences and Archaeology.* Reprint. New York: Springer Science and Business Media. pp. 297–326.

Stoltman, James B., Zhichun Jing, Jigen Tang, and George Rapp. 2009. Ceramic production in Shang societies of Anyang. *Asian Perspectives* 48(1):182–203. https://www.jstor.org/stable/42928758

Stoltman, James B., Zhanwei Yue, Zhichun Jing, Jigen Tang, James H. Burton, and Mati Raudsepp. 2018. New insights into the composition and microstructure of ceramic artifacts associated with the production of Chinese bronzes at Yinxu, the last capital of the Shang dynasty. *Archaeological Research in Asia* 15:88–100. https://doi.org/10.1016/j.ara.2017.11.002

Sundius, Nils. 1961. *Some Aspects of the Technical Development in the Manufacture of the Chinese Pottery Wares of Pre-Ming Age*. Stockholm: Museum of Far Eastern Antiquities. 33 pp.

Wang, Enyuan, Yingfei Xiong, Yibing Zhu, and Jingwei Wu. 2020. Regional microstructural characteristics between the body and glaze of ancient Chinese ceramics. *Ceramics International* 46(14):22253-22261. https://doi.org/10.1016/j.ceramint.2020.05.303

Wang, Meng. 2011. Experimental design and reflection on the composition and dissemination of a pottery. *Zhongguo Wenwu Bao* 2011(23):6. [in Chinese.]

Wei, Lu. 2012. "Research on Protection of Han Dynasty Painted Pottery Collected in Yulin Area" [dissertation]. Northwest University, Xi'an, Shaanxi, China. [in Chinese.]

Whitbread, Ian K. 1995. *Greek Transport Amphorae: A Petrological and Archaeological Study*. Athens: British School at Athens. 453 pp.

Womack, Andrew. 2017. "Crafting Community: Exploring Identity and Interaction through Ceramics in Late Neolithic and Early Bronze Age Northwestern China" [dissertation]. Yale University. 491 pp. ProQuest Dissertations & Theses Global (10783474). https://www.proquest.com/dissertations-theses/crafting-community-exploring-identity-interaction/docview/2023467751/se-2

Womack, Andrew, and Anke Hein. 2018. China Ceramic Petrography Database. In: Andrew Womack and Anke Hein, eds. Open Context. Released: 2018-10-30. http://opencontext.org/projects/2c5addea-41d5-4941-b2bd-672bc1e60448. https://doi.org/10.6078/M79Z930G

Womack, Andrew, Xinwei Li, Zhiwei Guo, Hui Wang, Jing Zhou, and Rowan Flad. 2023. From local to long-distance: Neolithic and Bronze Age ceramic networks in north-western China. *Antiquity* 97(395):1119–1137. https://doi.org/10.15184/aqy.2023.119

Womack, Andrew, Li Liu, and Nan Di. 2021. Initial insights into ceramic production and exchange at the early Bronze Age citadel at Shimao, Shaanxi, China. *Archaeological Research in Asia* 28:100319. https://doi.org/10.1016/j.ara.2021.100319

Womack, Andrew, Hui Wang, Jing Zhou, and Rowan Flad. 2019. A petrographic analysis of clay recipes in Late Neolithic north-western China: Continuity and change. *Antiquity* 93(371):1161–1177. https://doi.org/10.15184/aqy.2019.132

Worley, Noel. 2009. Henry Clifton Sorby (1826–1908) and the development of thin section petrography in Sheffield. In: Patrick S. Quinn, ed. *Interpreting Ssilent Artefacts: Petrographic Aapproaches to Archaeological Ceramics*. Oxford: Archaeopress. pp.1–9.

Wu, Shuang. 2019. "Technology Selection: Research on Early Yue Kiln Production in the Shangyu Area" [dissertation]. Fudan University, Shanghai, China. [in Chinese.]

Wu, Shuang, and Chun Chen. 2018. Ceramic lithofacies analysis and archaeological information refining. In: Xianzhu Wu, ed. *Scientific and Technological Archaeology and Cultural Relics Protection Technology*. Beijing: Science Press. pp. 77–87. [in Chinese.]

Wu, Weihong, and Zhenwei Qiu. 2020. A preliminary study on plant-tempered pottery from the Sunjiacheng site in Huining, Anhui Province. *Jianghan Kaogu* 2020(4):92–101. [in Chinese.]

Xia, Ji, Jian Zhu, and Changsui Wang. 2009. Particle size analysis and origin exploration of proto-porcelain paste. *Nanfang Wenwu* 2009(1):47–52. [in Chinese.]

Xia, Yan, Shuangcheng Wu, Shengkuan Cui, Yufu Lan, Zhiguo Zhang, Weifeng Wang, and Qianli Fu. 2008. Study on the pigments of pottery painted from Han tomb unearthed in Wei'an, Shanxi Province, Shandong Province. *Wenwu Baohu Yu Kaogu Kexue* 2008(2):13–19. [in Chinese.]

Xu, Anwu, Xiaoyong Yang, Zaijing Sun, Changsui Wang, Jihuai Wang, Zhonghe Liang, and Xingcan Chen. 2000. Preliminary study on the origin of Dakouzun in Dawenkou culture. *Kaogu* 2000(8):87–92. [in Chinese.]

Xu, Wenting. 2017. "Study on Production Technology and Origins of Pottery Unearthed from the Mopanshan Site in Langxi, Anhui Province" [dissertation]. Nanjing University, Jiangsu, China. [in Chinese.]

Yang, Zhenzhen, Yin Xia, Liqin Wang, Zhiwei Gao, and Desheng Lan. 2013. Scientific analysis and research on colored pottery of Majiayao culture in Minhe County, Qinghai Province. *Wenwu Baohu Yu Kaogu Kexue* 3(3):81–92. [in Chinese.]

Yu, Yongbin, Xiaohong Wu, Jianfeng Cui, Guoke Chen, and Hui Wang. 2017. Science and technology analysis and research on pottery of the Xichengyi site in Zhangye, Gansu Province. *Kaogu* 2017(07):108–120. [in Chinese.]

Zhang, Shangxin, Qianli Fu, Yu Ma, Weixing Zhang, Weifeng Wang, Yin Xia, and Xiaoyang Fang. 2019. Petrographic thin section analysis of pottery pieces of the acrobatic terracotta figures unearthed from the Qin mausoleum. *Wenwu* 02:72–78. [in Chinese.]

Zhang, Xianrui. 2018. "Study on the Making Technology and Origin of Prehistoric Pottery Unearthed from Gouwan Site" [master's thesis]. Zhengzhou University. [in Chinese.]

Zhang, Youyin, Jian Zhu, and Weihong Wu. 2020. Petrographic analysis of pottery unearthed from Lingjiatan site in Anhui Province. *Nanfang Wenwu* 2020(3):159–164. [in Chinese.]

Zhou, Ren, Fukang Zhang, and Yongpu Zheng. 1964. A scientific summary of pottery craft in The Neolithic and Shang and Zhou dynasties of China. *Kaogu Xuebao* 1964(1):1–27. [in Chinese.]

Zhu, Tiequan, Changsui Wang, Dali Xu, and Jun Wu. 2005. Preliminary study on carbonizing technology of black pottery from the Shuangdun site. *Wenwu Baohu Yu Kaogu Kexue* 2:1–8. [in Chinese.]

CHAPTER FOUR

LATE NEOLITHIC PAINTED POTTERY TRADITIONS AT HUANGGUASHAN AND FENGBITOU ALONG THE TAIWAN STRAIT:
A Case Study

HE Yahui

Interregional migration stands out as a pivotal characteristic among early maritime inhabitants. It is widely accepted that the roots of seafaring coincide with the initiation of interactions across the Taiwan Strait during the Neolithic period, marked by the emergence and advancement of canoe-making techniques (Jiao, Lin, and Rolett 2002:308–310, 317). Numerous scholars posit that these interactions began as early as 4000 BCE, manifesting in the form of migration by proto-Austronesians (Chang 1969, 1995; Sung 1980; Tsang 1992, 2001; Chang and Goodenough 1996; Jiao 2005, 2021; Rolett, Guo, and Jiao 2007; Hung and Carson 2014; Hung 2019).

To investigate early Austronesian seafaring and migration, scholars have analyzed archaeological remains using diverse approaches. For instance, the geological sourcing of stone adzes with X-ray fluorescence (XRF), inductively coupled plasma mass spectrometry (ICP-MS) techniques, and petrographic thin-section techniques suggests that people in southeast mainland China obtained raw materials either from the Penghu Archipelago in the Taiwan Strait or from the Fujian coast as early as 5,000 years ago. These studies indicate the possible development of exchange networks across the Taiwan Strait during the middle Neolithic period (Guo et al. 2005; Rolett, Guo, and Jiao 2007; Jiao et al. 2011). Furthermore, recent genetic and archaeobotanical studies have provided multiple lines of evidence for communication across the Taiwan Strait. For example, Wang et al.'s (2021) genetic study implies that people from Taiwan predominantly originated from farming groups in the Yangtze River valley, with a small portion related to the northern lineage associated with the Yellow River basin. Archaeobotanical evidence reveals that both millet and rice agriculture spread from mainland China to Taiwan around 3000 BCE (Deng, Hung, Carson, et al. 2018; Deng, Hung, Fan, et al. 2018; Ge et al. 2019).

Multiple lines of evidence have unveiled early interactions between mainland China and Taiwan across today's Taiwan Strait. Scholars have long observed similarities in Neolithic pottery between southeast mainland China and western Taiwan. However, a comprehensive comparative study on the ceramic traditions in these two regions remains limited. A more thorough examination of pottery from both areas would be beneficial for understanding the nature of ceramic traditions in southeast mainland China and Taiwan, as well as their implications. In this chapter, I specifically focus on painted pottery from the Huangguashan (黄瓜山) culture and the Fengbitou (凤鼻头) culture dated to the Late

Neolithic period. The aim is to gain a deeper understanding of how pottery technology traditions developed in southeast mainland China and the western coast of Taiwan, shedding light on sociocultural relationships in prehistory across the Taiwan Strait. One challenge is the need for more precise dating of sites.

The consensus among specialists is that Neolithic ways of life continued in southern China and Taiwan longer than on the northern Chinese mainland. There is agreement that the Erlitou site and associated culture should be classified as Bronze Age, given the evidence for production of bronze vessels after about 1900 BCE (see Liu and Chen 2012). The Late Neolithic period of the southern Chinese mainland and Taiwan extended roughly from around 2000 to 100 BCE although there is variation by region (see Jiao 2013; Pearson 2023). My discussion below refers to the efforts of scholars to compare pottery vessels from the northern Longshan/Lungshan culture (about 2600–1900 BCE; Liu and Chen 2012) found in southern sites.

Archaeological Background and Pottery Assemblages from the Southern Neolithic Period

Scholars have noted that there are several similarities in the pottery of Neolithic mainland China and Taiwan, based on their study. It is suggested that the earliest interaction can be traced to the early Neolithic period, during which the Dabenkeng/Tapenkeng (大坌坑) culture originated from the mainland of China, since the typical cord marks appear on pottery sherds in both southeast mainland China and the Dabenkeng culture (Sung 1980; Chang 1995; Bellwood 2000; Tsang 2001; Jiao 2005; Liu and Chen 2012; Li 2013). Dabenkeng corded wares are quite large and thick. The paste is very coarse, with large amounts of coarse-grained inclusions of quartz and other minerals. The primary forms of the vessels are bowls and jars. The surface decorations are mainly cord marks and line incisions. The Corded Ware culture spans from the early to the middle Neolithic, characterized by cord-mark patterns. Usually, corded wares have coarse paste containing a large amount of sand or grit inclusions of quartz and mica. Two basic shapes of vessels are present: bowl and jar. In the late Neolithic period, in addition to the painted pottery mentioned above, the pottery of the Yuanshan (圓山) culture is relatively coarse.

During the late Neolithic there are two primary cultures in western Taiwan, Yuanshan in the northwest and Fengbitou in the south. The pottery sherds of the Yuanshan culture present reddish-brown pigment with a line or dot decoration pattern on the pottery, which is similar to the pigment decoration on the pottery of mainland China. Scholars propose that according to archaeological findings there is more than one origin of the Yuanshan culture. The painted pottery of Yuanshan may have been influenced by the mainland cultures in China (see the summary in Jiao [2007]). At the Fengbitou site in southwestern Taiwan, the pottery assemblage also takes on some similar features with those in the mainland of China. At Fengbitou there is more than one pottery horizon, including painted wares, fine red wares, sandy red and gray wares, and black wares. K. C. Chang 张光直 (1969) argued that the fine red ceramic wares from the "Lungshanoid culture" share many features with archaeological cultures in Jiangsu, that sandy red ware and the painted pottery group are closely related to the culture in Fujian, and that the black pottery horizon must have originated from the Liangzhu (良渚) culture in the lower Yangtze River area. There are multiple identifiable derivations of Neolithic Fengbitou wares and these have a close relationship with mainland China pottery (Chang 1969:233). Jiao (2007) suggests that the Huangguashan culture in southeast mainland China, characterized by the painted patterns on the pottery sherds, may have been the source for the appearance of the painted pottery in western Taiwan. However, a systematic comparison between the pottery remains from Fujian and Taiwan is still limited. This paper aims to contribute to this research agenda.

Ceramics Included in the Study and Methodology

In preparation for researching the pottery of this region, I collected basic data on sherds from the Huangguashan culture of southeast mainland China in Xiapu, Fujian Province. I also examined sherds from the Fengbitou site collected by Chang (1969) and housed in the Yale Peabody Museum at Yale University. This paper focuses on discussing the painted pottery from the Huangguashan and Fengbitou cultures, both belonging to the late Neolithic period (He 2015).

Methodologically, the first step involved gathering basic information on the sherds, including the color of the paste or paint, the diameter of the rim or base, and the type of decoration, with a particular emphasis on rim sherds. To introduce the primary characteristics of the sherds, I used Microsoft Excel and JMP statistical software, version 12 (JMP Statistical Discovery, LLC; https://www.jmp.com), for the analysis of these basic data and to compare technologies for forming and decorating pots, as well as the preparation of pastes. For this I used a portable Dino-Lite digital microscope with DinoXcope software, version 2.4.1 (Dunwell Tech, Inc.; https://www.dinolite.us) to analyze the paste. The images of paste were then sorted to examine various paste groups. Following Druc's (2015) criterion for digital microscope analysis, sherds were sorted according to paste appearance, with two to three samples chosen from each sorted group.

A ceramic paste may contain minerals and rock fragments of different geological origins, resembling a sediment of heterogeneous composition. Druc (2015) categorizes common minerals found in pottery paste, including felsic minerals (quartz, feldspars) and mafic minerals (micas, amphiboles, pyroxenes). Scales and visual comparison charts adapted from sedimentology, such as those for measuring or estimating grain angularity, abundance, and degrees of sorting, have been used to aid ceramic analysis in classifying and describing inclusions in archaeological pastes (Rice 2015). My study follows Druc's methodology to record granulometric scale (see Druc 2015:16). Additionally, a simple angularity scale, degrees of grain sorting, and mineral types, using Druc's book, are compared. Finally, the paste colors were recorded to provide information on the firing atmosphere of the pottery vessels.

Painted Pottery at Huangguashan in Southeast Mainland China

The Huangguashan site is situated in the hills of Xiapu County, Fujian Province, facing the Dongwu Gulf (Figure 4.1). Discovered in 1987, the site underwent two excavations (Fujian Provincial Museum 1994, 2004). A typical shell mound site, Huangguashan features ten cultural layers. The Neolithic layers, located in the fourth and fifth strata, contain many artifacts, such as lithic tools, bone tools, and pottery. Notably, the Huangguashan pottery is characterized by a substantial quantity of painted pottery, along with unpainted sandy sherds. The data presented here is derived from the archaeological study conducted in 2014 (Table 4.1).

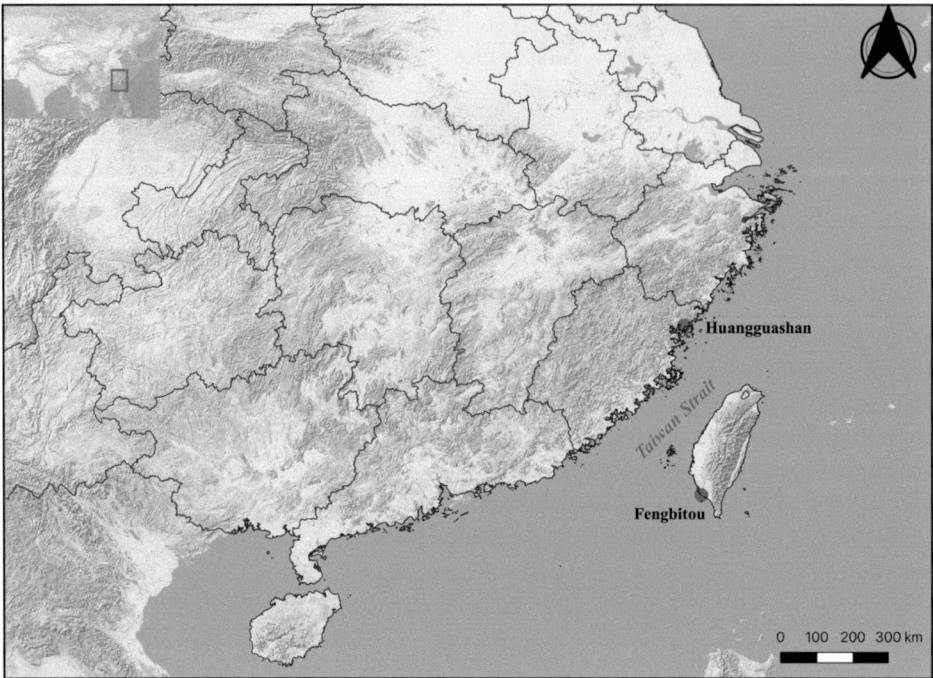

FIGURE 4.1. The location of the Huangguashan and Fengbitou archaeological sites.

Paste

Concerning raw materials, most of the painted pottery pastes are tempered, with subangular and medium-sized minerals. Fine pottery sherds with minimal grains (inclusions) indicate strict selection of raw materials for painted pottery (Figure 4.2). Microscope analysis provides evidence of coiling during the production of painted pottery (Figure 4.3). The finishing process involved the use of a slow-wheel technique, leaving spiral lines on the rims or necks of pottery vessels. Burnishing on the rim of painted pottery is also evident.

Decoration

The decoration of Huangguashan pottery is characterized by diversity, encompassing inclusion, impression, and painting. Most vessels have a combination of designs, with painted pottery often featuring a blend of decorations, such as incisions and ridges. There are two distinct types of painted decoration. One involves geometric pattern painting, while the other entails a more random and simple application of slips on the vessels. Instances of painted pottery with simple slipping are typically impressed or incised before painting, featuring techniques like cord-marking, net impression, ridges, dentate incision, and others. However, a significant number are undecorated, although specific incision patterns have been identified on some sherds. For example, there is an incised Y on the interior rim of the sherd (Figure 4.4).

Typically, after preparing pastes and decorations like impression or incision, potters proceed to paint the vessels. Two kinds of painted pottery are distinguished by the slips on the sherds. This section delves into various types of slip decoration and painting tools, with a discussion on slip colors reserved for the firing section. In analyzing the pottery

TABLE 4.1. Huangguashan site painted pottery sherds examined in Fujian Province, China, listed by paste, pattern, and color.

Decoration pattern	Paste surface and color							Total number of sherds
	Sand-tempered				Fine clay			
	Orange red	Gray and red	Orange yellow	Gray	Orange red	Orange yellow	Gray	Gray and orange red	
Red slip									
Net and cord mark		1							1
Cord mark			1			1	1	1	4
Net	1					1		1	3
Plain				1		3	1		6
Ridge						1			1
Black slip									
Basket						1			1
Net						1			1
Cord mark	1					1			2
Black paint									
Triangle			1		1				2

Continued

TABLE 4.1 CONTINUED

Decoration pattern	Paste surface and color								
	Sand-tempered				Fine clay				Total number of sherds
	Orange red	Gray and red	Orange yellow	Gray	Orange red	Orange yellow	Gray	Gray and orange red	
Red paint									
Irregular lines	1					6	3		10
Parallel lines						1	2		3
Leaf			1						1
Triangle					1	3	1		5
Spiral					1				1
Total	3	1	3	1	3	19	8	3	41

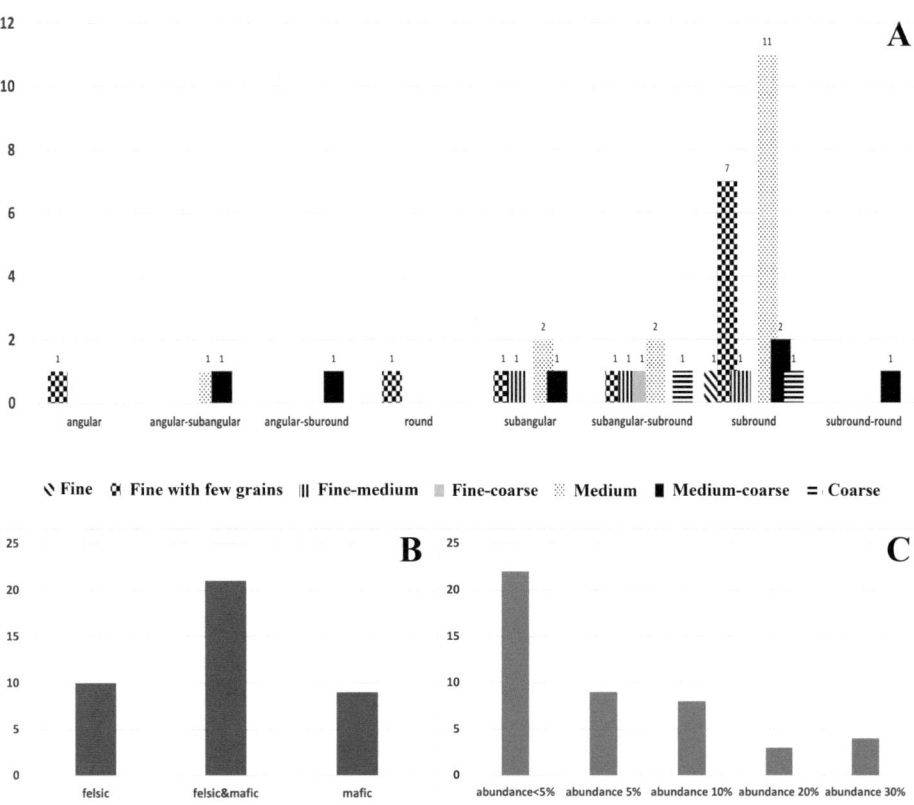

FIGURE 4.2. Analysis of Huangguashan painted pottery paste. **A.** Shape and fineness of minerals. **B.** Different types of temper. **C.** Grain abundance.

decorations, aspects such as style, element, combination, and configuration are considered. The styles of pottery vessels are classified as abstract, iconic, or geometric (Rice 2015:389). Obviously, the painted decoration of Huangguashan pottery primarily adopts a geometric style, featuring elements like long and wide, or short and narrow, lines, including triangles. The selection of these elements is closely linked to the potters' tools. Diverse elements contribute to a range of decorations, including parallel-line, cross-line, curve-line, leaf, and triangle patterns. The combination of painting involves several predetermined combinations of decoration for different parts of the vessels. The position of painted decorations may have significance in relation to specific uses or aesthetic considerations.

Data from a 2012 survey (He 2019) indicates that cross-line, parallel-line, curve-line, and leaf decorations are predominantly on the exterior of the sherds. Cross-line decoration is mainly distributed on the exterior body with some on the exterior rims, while parallel-line decoration is seen relatively widely on the exterior rims and bodies of pottery vessels. Curve-line decoration is primarily painted on the exterior of pottery bodies. Significantly, the combination of triangle and curve-line decorations are exclusively found on the interior of rims (Figure 4.4). This may suggest a standard practice of potters or, it may identify specific communities adopting the fixed pattern.

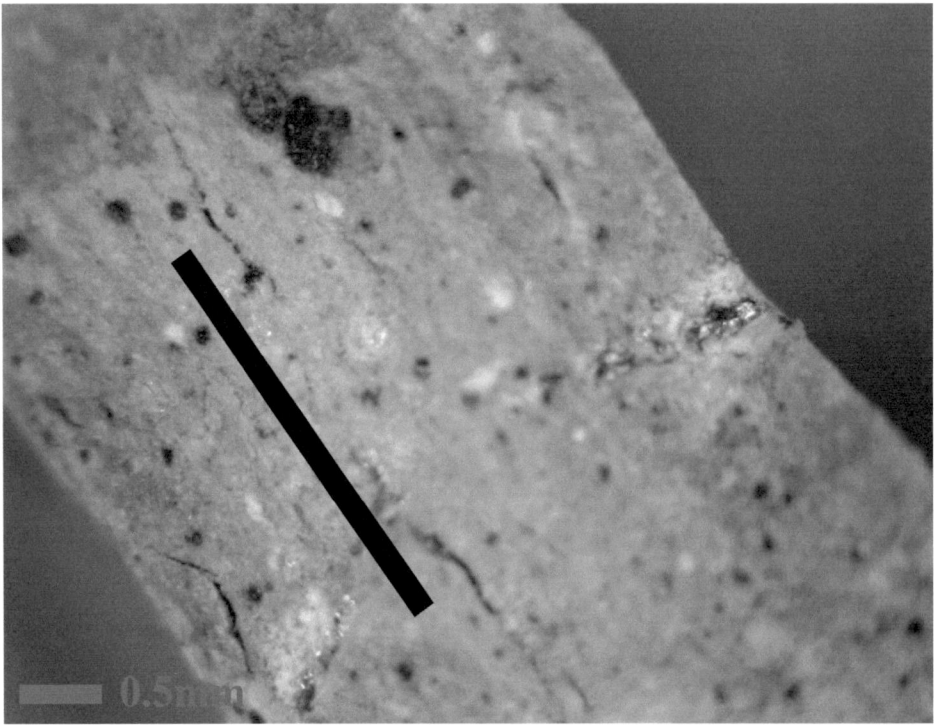

Figure 4.3. Evidence of coiling in the paste of a Huangguashan painted sherd. Photo credit: He Yahui.

The sources of painting tools are diverse, dependent on the shape and width of lines on the sherds (Figure 4.5; He 2019). It is evident that cross-line painting was more random with a relatively large width range. In contrast, the change in width for curve-line and parallel-line painting is relatively less noticeable. This irregular pattern suggests potters used more random tools, while for more regular patterns tools were narrower and more standardized.

Firing

The analysis reveals that the pastes of the majority of the painted pottery have shades of orange-red or yellow, while the color of interior pastes tends toward gray (Figure 4.6). Most painted pottery underwent firing in an oxidization atmosphere, with temperatures not exceeding 600 to 700 °C, attributed to the relatively limited presence of quartz. However, there is a possibility that the temperature could have reached up to 800 °C, considering the notable hardness of Huangguashan painted pottery and the fine quality of the clay. The study of raw materials for Huangguashan painted pottery indicates a meticulous selection process, emphasizing the fineness of the paste. Slip colors predominantly lean toward black, occasionally featuring dark red hues. Electron microscope analysis highlights the main chemical compositions as iron oxide (Fe_2O_3) and manganese(II) oxide (MnO), which, during firing, manifest as black to dark red (He 2019).

FIGURE 4.4. Interior rim painted sherds from the Huangguashan site. Photo credit: He Yahui.

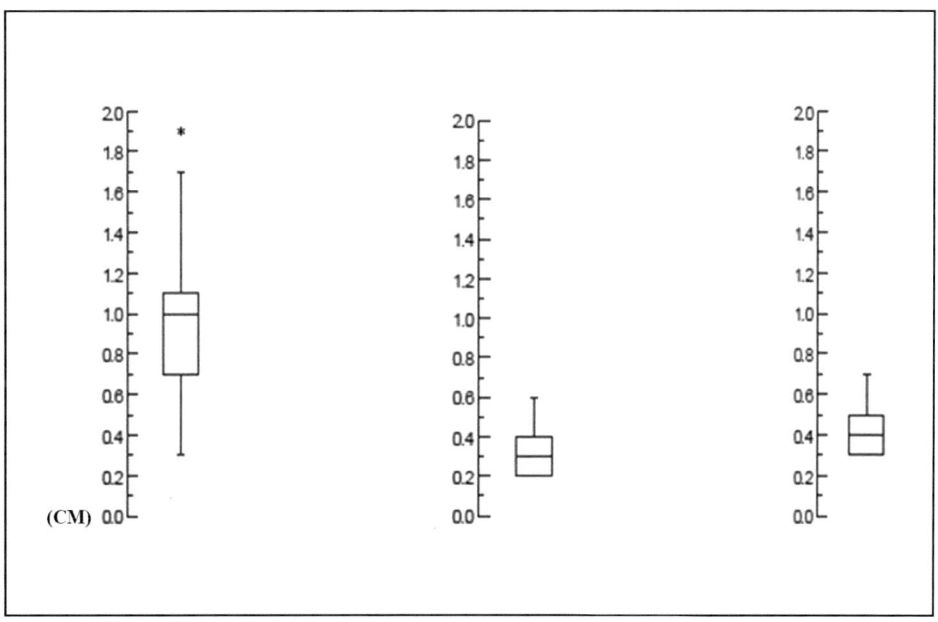

FIGURE 4.5. Width of painted lines on sherds sampled in the 2012 survey. **A.** Cross-line decoration. **B.** Curve-line decoration. **C.** Parallel-line decoration. After He (2019, fig. 9).

Typology

The majority of pottery sherds from the second excavation consists of bowls, jars, pedestal bowls, and cups (Figure 4.7). Jars (*guan*, 罐) play a significant role in the Huangguashan pottery assemblage, encompassing both painted and unpainted varieties. Using my observations and Jiao's (2007) classification, painted jars can be broadly categorized into four types.

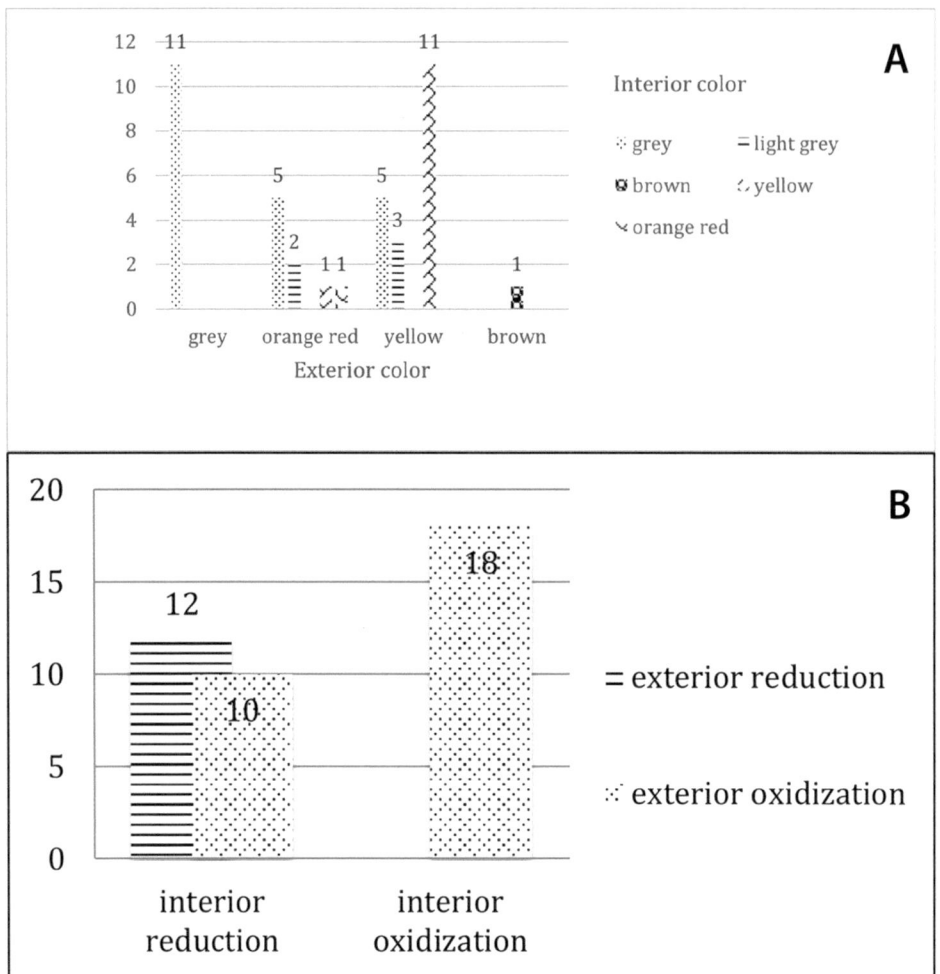

FIGURE 4.6. Evidence of firing in Huangguashan painted pottery paste. **A.** Paste colors. **B.** Number of oxidization and reduction pastes.

Type I features a flared rim and lip, while Type II has a relatively vertical rim and lip, with ridges on the neck and paint usually applied on the shoulder. Type III presents an inward restrained lip, a ridge on the belly, and a fully painted body. Lastly, Type IV is characterized by vertical rims.

Other types of pottery vessels include bowls (*wan*, 碗), bowls with pedestals, and cups (*bei*, 杯). However, because of limited materials, the classification of bowls, pedestal bowls, and cups does not distinguish between unpainted and painted pottery vessels. Drawing from the first excavation report and my observations, there are four types of bowls.

Type I boasts a vertical rim, round wall, and round base. Type II features an inward rim, round wall, and round base, while Type III has a flared rim and wall, a flat base, and ridges around the walls. Lastly, Type IV showcases an inward rim, flared wall, flat base, and ridges around the walls of pottery. For pedestal bowls, three types are identified: Type

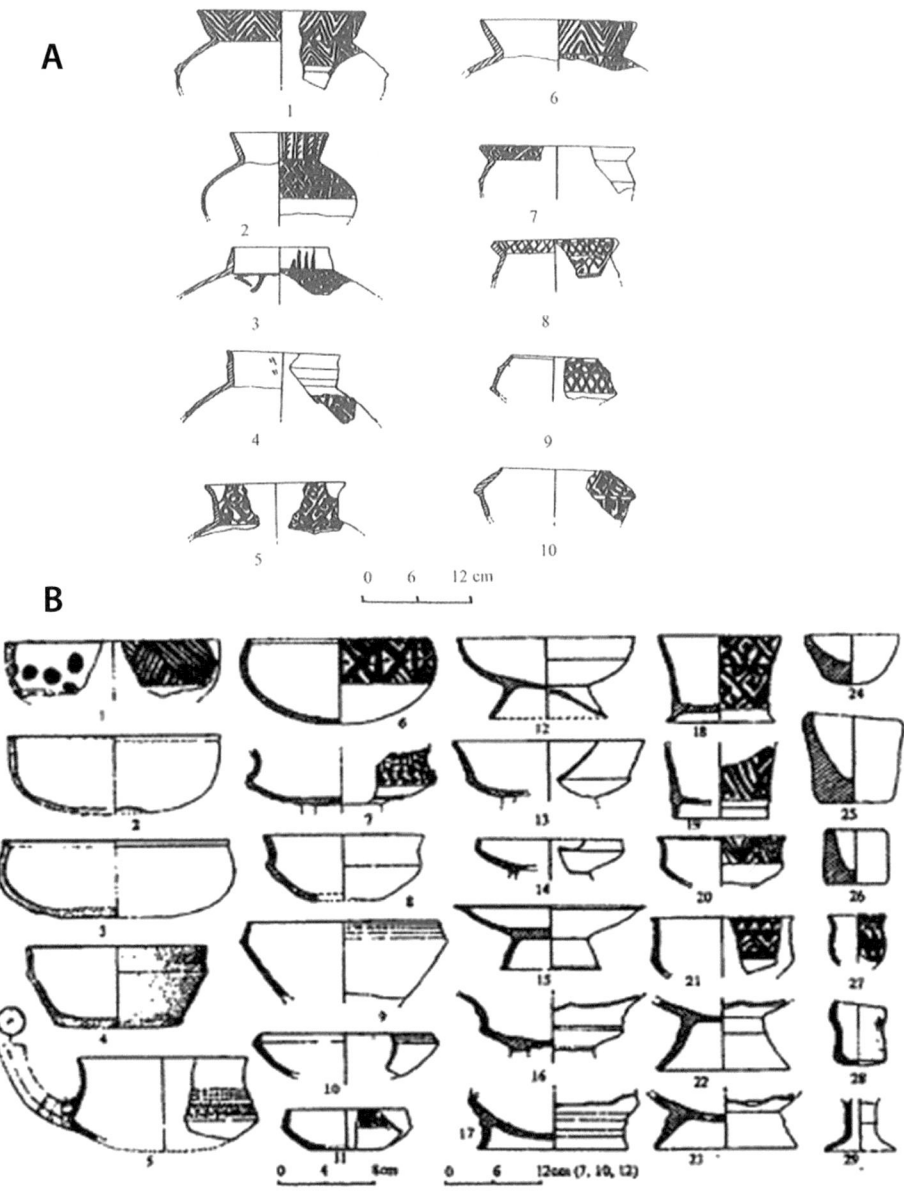

FIGURE 4.7. Pottery vessel types at the Huangguashan site. **A.** Painted jars. Type I: 1, 2, 6, 7; Type II: 5; Type III: 9, 10; Type IV: 3, 4. After Jiao (2007: 232). **B.** Bowls, pedestal bowls, and cups. *Bowl.* Type I: 1, 2, 11; Type II: 3, 6; Type III: 7, 8, 10; Type IV: 4, 9. *Pedestal bowl.* Type I: 13, 15, 16; Type II, 14; Type III: 12, 22, 23. *Cup.* Type I: 24; Type II: 25, 26, 28; Type III: 27. After Jiao (2007:229).

I with both a flared rim and a lip, Type II with a flared rim and a flat lip, and Type III with a roundish rim and a flat lip. In the case of cups, three distinct types are identified: Type I with a round rim and a round base, Type II with a flared rim and a flat base, and Type III with a flared rim, a restricted neck, and a round base.

Painted Pottery at Fengbitou in Western Taiwan

The Fengbitou site is situated in Linyaun District, Gaoxiong County, in southwestern Taiwan, at coordinates 22° N, 120° E (see Figure 4.1). Positioned on a small terrace above the 25 m contour line, approximately 400 m north of the Kaoxiong–Linyuan main road, the prehistoric remnants span the entire hill in an area extending around 500 m from east to west and 300 m from north to south. The Yale–National Taiwan University Project excavation of Fengbitou took place in 1965 at a total of thirteen loci. It uncovered various types of Fengbitou pottery, including painted pottery, fine red pottery, black pottery, and sandy pottery. This section specifically focuses on painted pottery (Table 4.2).

Paste
Staff at the Yale Peabody Museum gave me permission to sample a small quantity of sherds for analysis with DinoXcope. The micro-photographs provide insight into the basic mineral shapes, predominantly ranging from subround to subangular, with a prevailing medium fineness. The primary temper consists of a blend of mafic and felsic materials. From my observations of the sampled sherds, it is evident that coiling was the principal manufacturing technique (Figure 4.8). Vessel rims were meticulously finished using a slow wheel and, on occasion, the bodies of the pottery vessels underwent burnishing after coiling.

Decoration
The slip applied to the painted pottery of the Fengbitou culture predominantly has red or dark red hues. The fundamental elements of the painting patterns encompass lines, dots, and other similar features. Common patterns include parallel lines, wavy lines, net zones, dot painting, and triangles forming zones or bands meticulously applied to the exterior or interior, or both, of the rims and bodies. The overall composition adheres to the principles of symmetry and repetition. The painting tools were brushes used either singly or bundled together to create these intricate patterns (Chang 1969:83–88).

Firing
The exterior color of Fengbitou pottery ranges from red to orange red, while the interior is predominantly gray, as determined through microscope study. The estimated firing temperature for these pottery items is in the range of 550 to 600 °C (Chang 1969).

Typology
The primary vessel types of Fengbitou painted pottery comprise jars, bowls, and cups (Figure 4.9), as for Huangguashan pottery. However, Chang (1969) also includes a form described as a "beaker." In common classificatory schemes used by archaeologists, vessel forms are typically categorized as plates, dishes, bowls, jars, and vases (Rice 2015). While

TABLE 4.2. Fengbitou site painted pottery sherds examined at the Yale Peabody Museum listed by paste, pattern, and color.

Decoration pattern	Paste surface and color					Total
	Sand-tempered				Fine clay	
	Orange red	Brown	Dark red	Gray and orange red	Orange red	
Black slip					1	1
Red slip	5					5
Parallel line	19	4	1	2	11	37
Net	4	1			1	6
Triangle	2					2
Wave line	1					1
Parallel line and dot	1					1
Line painting	4		1			5
Line and dot	4				1	5
Triangle and parallel line	1				1	2
Spiral	1					1
Total	42	5	2	2	15	66

beaker is often recognized as a distinct type, defined as "a vessel whose height is greater than its rim diameter…and which is of suitable size and shape for drinking forms," for the purpose of this chapter I classify beakers as part of the group "cups," a practice commonly seen in mainland China excavation reports. Another reason is the lack of whole vessels clearly indicating the form of these vessels.

Jars are the most prevalent form, characterized by a collar distinct from the body, with the wall of the collar being vertical or slightly flaring. The diameter typically ranges from 10 to 20 cm. According to observations, jars can be categorized into three types based on the shape of the lips. Type I features a flared rim and a flat lip. Type II consists of jars with a flared rim and a roundish lip. Type III includes jars with a roundish rim and a flat lip. For these types, a ridge is occasionally applied around the body. The base for jars is usually roundish, flat, or concave.

Painted bowls are generally shallow and wide, with thick lips. Observations identify two basic types of bowls. Type I features a roundish rim and an inward lip, while Type II has a flared rim and an inward lip. The shapes of Fengbitou painted cups are relatively simple. From observations and Chang's research, it is suggested that cups primarily have a slightly flared mouth. The first type includes cups with a cylindrical wall and the second type encompasses those with a roundish wall.

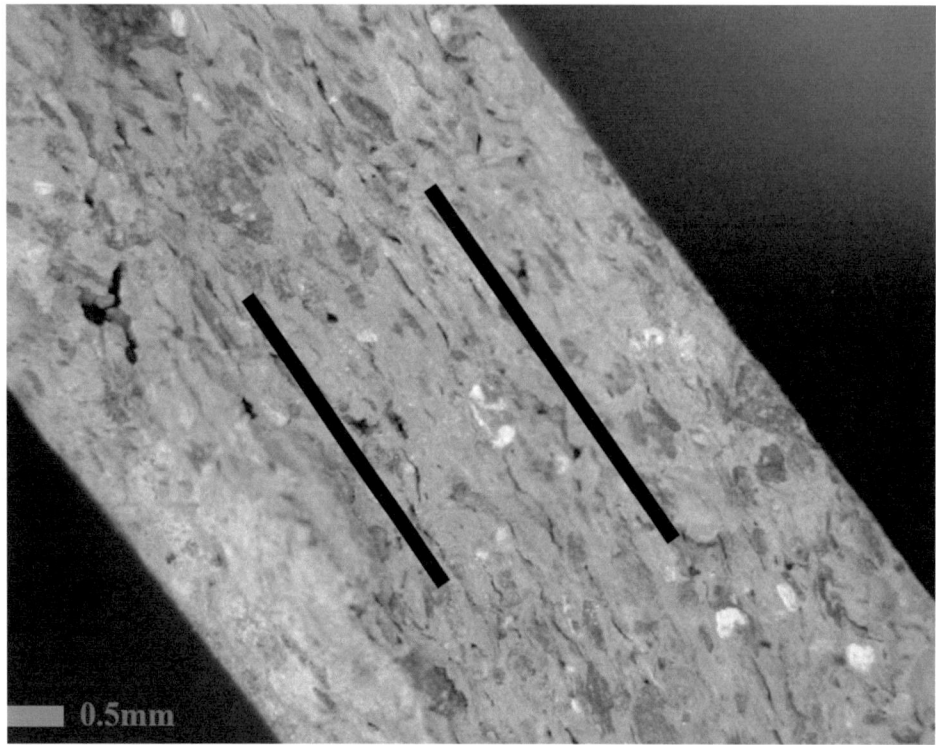

Figure 4.8. Coiling feature (lines) in Fengbitou painted pottery paste. (YPM. ANT. 221961). Photo credit: He Yahui.

Discussion

Pottery Traditions along the Taiwan Strait

Pottery in western Taiwan was categorized into horizons by Chang's early studies (Chang 1969:191–220). The Fengbitou culture, from the late Neolithic period, comprises a painted pottery horizon, fine red pottery horizon, fine black pottery horizon, and sandy pottery horizon contemporaneous with the Huangguashan culture. In the late Neolithic, the pottery pastes for both cultures were tempered and the mineral particle size was predominantly medium. For Huangguashan and Fengbitou painted pottery, the particles were relatively small, possibly intentionally filtered by potters. These high-quality pottery types might have had specific uses. The primary technique for making paste was hand-coiling, supplemented by burnishing for the pottery bodies; the slow-wheel technique was commonly used for the rims.

During the late Neolithic period the Huangguashan culture was distinctive for its painted pottery, which features geometric decorations such as parallel lines, cross lines, curve lines, leaves, and triangles. Incisions, like the typical Y incision on the interior rims, were also applied. Fengbitou pottery had similar geometric painting patterns, including parallel lines, cross lines, curve lines, and triangles. These were fired in an atmosphere that had sufficient oxygen, indicated by the paste colors. However, the firing time might not have been long enough, or the temperature not high enough, resulting in the gray or black color of the paste interior.

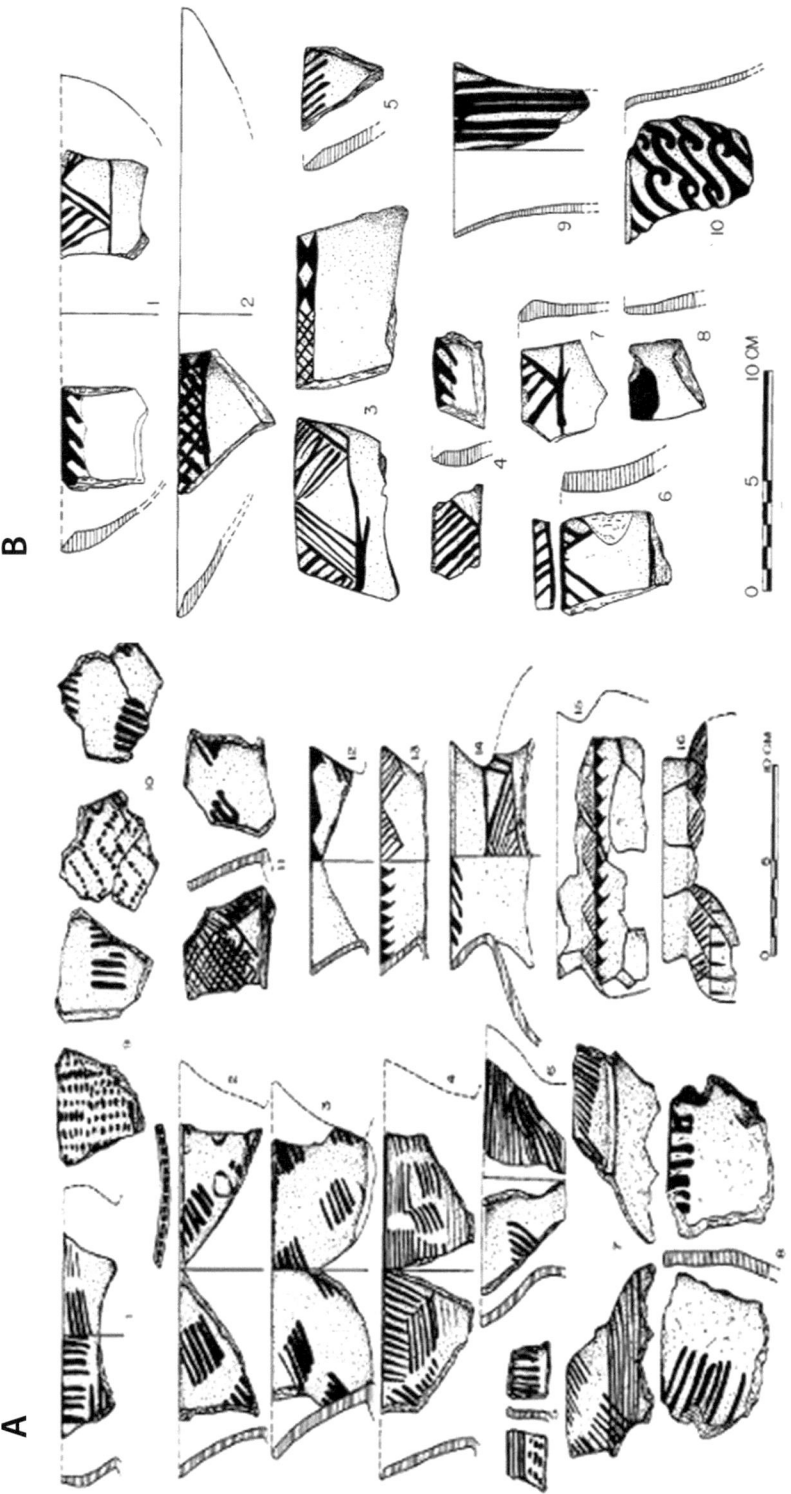

FIGURE 4.9. Painted pottery vessel types at the Fengbitou site. **A.** Bowls, cups, and jars. Type I: 2, 6, 12, 13; Type II: 3, 4; Type III: 1. After Chang (1969:85). **B.** Bowls and cups. Bowl. Type I: 1; Type II: 2. Cup. Type I: 9; Type II: 10. After Chang (1969:84).

During this period, jars, bowls, and cups were the primary vessel types in both southeast mainland China and western Taiwan. Although pedestal bowls were not very common in western Taiwan during the Neolithic, cups were densely present in both cultures during the late Neolithic period. The basic shapes were cylindrical and with straight walls. Both late Neolithic Huangguashan painted cups and Fengbitou painted cups had geometric decorations on the exterior of the whole body.

Proto-Austronesian Migration and Cross-strait Interactions during the Late Neolithic

There has been extensive debate regarding the nature of interactions among the people of southeast mainland China and Taiwan. Several prevailing theories attempt to explain the early interactions in this area. Bellwood (2007) contends that demographic pressure, spurred by the introduction of rice agriculture, was a key driver for early expansion. Chang and Goodenough (1996) argue that trade served as the motivation for people to navigate from southeast China to Taiwan. Kirch (1997) posits that family division and the ideology of founder lineages compelled ancient Austronesians and their Polynesian descendants to expand into the Pacific. Tsang (2001) maintains that specialized adaptations to the maritime environment were the ultimate driving force. Jiao (2007) suggests that, during different periods, there were multiple causes for Proto-Austronesian dispersals across the Taiwan Strait. The primary mechanism, according to Jiao, should be maritime adaptation, enabling them to explore beyond their immediate environment. The search for new land and resources likely played a significant role in early population migrations across the Taiwan Strait. Nevertheless, the well-developed rice agriculture and increased contact with inland populations during the late Neolithic period could be considered a new mechanism. Demographic pressure and the potential threat of new immigrants from inland areas may have further prompted population expansions from mainland China to Taiwan.

Exchange networks serve not only as conduits for the exchange of goods, but also play a crucial role in facilitating the flow of information and fostering social relationships, encompassing political affiliations, kinship alliances, and even adversarial connections (e.g., Brumfiel and Earle 1987; Rice 2015). In the context of pottery-driven interactions, various motivations underpin the exchange processes. First, migration becomes a pivotal factor, where individuals traverse from one locale to another, potentially transporting pottery or sharing pottery-making techniques as part of their migratory practices. Second, the desire to retain a distinctive identity in new surroundings prompts individuals to actively produce specific types of pottery, marked by unique forms or decorations, each laden with personal or cultural significance. Commonalities may manifest in aspects such as paste composition, decorative elements, or vessel types. Pastes could show similarities, sharing common tempers like shells or specific minerals. Decorative patterns, especially painted motifs found on sherds from both mainland China and Taiwan, may bear striking resemblances. Distinctive types of pottery vessels, requiring specialized skills, could also be replicated, as exemplified by the black pottery of the Fengbitou site. A third possibility involves potters acquiring specialized techniques in response to consumer demands. The fourth scenario suggests the transportation of pottery vessels across regions as part of a trade mechanism. In typical trade scenarios, vessels earmarked for exchange usually conform to uniform forms, decorations, and paste. Trade items might consist of specific vessel types or those with decorations deemed valuable or purposeful (see the summary in Rice [2015]).

The possibility emerges that mainland migrants initiated pottery production in western Taiwan during the early Neolithic period. Over time, the scope of interaction expanded beyond mere migration to encompass the exchange of pottery-making techniques. This evolution could be attributed to the demands of specific groups or the assertion of identity for cohesive community bonds. Shared characteristics among pottery vessels from different cultures become evident, such as the similarity in geometric painting decorations observed in Huangguashan and Fengbitou pottery.

Revisiting Chang's Opinions about "Lungshanoid" Pottery in Western Taiwan

In his 1969 book, K. C. Chang raised the culture conception of Lungshanoid, which has been discussed extensively in later archaeological studies of the region.

> Except for the corded ware layers, and despite internal variations, the artifacts excavated from the entire Fengbitou site can be said to belong to the same culture—the Lungshanoid. The name is derived from the Lungshanoid horizon that has been characterized for the Neolithic cultures on the eastern and southeastern coasts of mainland China. (Chang 1969:60)

> Before the advent of historical civilizations in the southeast coastal areas of China—Shang and Western Zhou in the northern regions and Eastern Zhou in the south, but Qin and Han throughout and intensively—the prehistoric cultures were broadly grouped into two major cultural horizons, Lungshanoid and Geometric. Except for Yuanshan, the cultures on the western coast of Taiwan fall within the Lungshanoid category without any serious questions. The Lungshanoid horizon of southeast China, however, is a very broad integrative concept, and it includes a number of more restricted local and temporal manifestations. (Chang 1969:226)

In this context, the overarching term Lungshanoid culture is broadly used to encapsulate the Lungshanoid horizon. It is essential to exercise caution, recognizing that not all archaeological materials from Taiwan during this period neatly align with the characteristics of the Lungshanoid culture. For instance, the pottery of the Fengbitou culture can be subdivided into distinct groups, some of which do not conform to the traits of the Lungshanoid culture. Scholars advocate for the use of different or more localized names to account for this diversity, emphasizing the need for nuanced terminology instead of a sweeping cultural label that may oversimplify the varied cultures present in Taiwan and mainland China.

Since the late 1970s, alternative terms have been proposed by scholars in Taiwan to replace Lungshanoid. Sung Wenxun (1980) suggested that each phase of the Lungshanoid culture should be regarded as distinct cultures in southwestern Taiwan, albeit maintaining the acknowledgment of firm connections between Taiwan and China during the Neolithic period.

In the 1980s Chang introduced the concept of the Chinese interactive sphere, drawing from a growing body of archaeological evidence for shared ceramic styles across regions. The aim of this concept was to reevaluate and clarify regional variation in archaeological remains and to discern a trajectory toward homogenization during the Longshan cultural period, roughly 4,000 to 5,000 years ago. The interactive sphere encompasses diverse regions, stretching from the Liao River region in the north to Taiwan and the Pearl River delta in the south, and extending westward to present-day Gansu, Qinghai, and

Sichuan. Scholars distinguish between these regions using different horizons or horizon styles. They infer that through interactions among people from various regional cultures traces of interconnected relationships gradually emerged, while distinct indigenous social norms also were maintained (Chang 1987:234–294). Chang (1995) later identified Fengbitou culture as representative of the fine cord-marked ware culture. While Chang posits regional differences, he contends that central and southern Taiwan collectively belong to the Fengbitou culture.

Scholars like Tsang and Jiao, while differing in certain terminologies, generally align with Chang's perspective that different phases should be grouped into a more inclusive entity. Jiao specifically advocates for the term Fengbitou culture to encompass this archaeological entity (Jiao 2007:100–101). On observation and comparison, I agree that considering them as a cohesive entity under the term Fengbitou culture provides a more comprehensive framework. This facilitates a nuanced understanding of the region during this temporal phase and allows for an exploration of the interactions between this region and southeastern mainland China. The term Lungshanoid culture may still be aptly applied to the Fengbitou fine black pottery, which shares certain similarities with the earlier Longshan culture of mainland China (discussed above).

Conclusions

In summary, this research offers a preliminary exploration of late Neolithic painted pottery in southeast mainland China and western Taiwan using a comparative analysis of paste, decoration, firing, and typology. Current findings reveal dynamic and intensive interactions across the Taiwan Strait, encompassing the exchange of cultural materials, production technologies, and agricultural practices. Future investigations should use additional methodologies, including petrographic and chemical analyses, on a broader range of pottery samples from diverse sites in both mainland China and western Taiwan. Furthermore, residue analysis presents an avenue for delving into how people engaged in varied culinary and consumption practices with these pottery vessels.

Acknowledgments

This paper is a revised version of my master's thesis for the Archaeological Studies program at Yale University. The research was made possible through the Michael Coe Fieldwork Fund and the Council on East Asian Studies Summer Travel and Research Grant at Yale University. I extend my gratitude to Dr. Anne Underhill, Dr. William Honeychurch, and Dr. Jiao Tianlong for their valuable suggestions and comments on my research project and thesis writing. Special thanks are due to Wu Chunming, curator of the Xiapu County Museum in Fujian Province, and Dr. Li Kuang-ti at the Institute of History and Philosophy, Academic Sinica, as well as to the researchers at the Yale Peabody Museum (Roger Colten, Rebekah DeAngelo, Maureen White, and Erin Gredell), for their assistance with the pottery sherd sampling process. Two reviewers and Dr. Underhill provided valuable comments on the manuscript. Any errors are solely my responsibility.

Reflecting on my academic journey with Lingyi, I am overwhelmed with gratitude for her presence as both a friend and a colleague. Lingyi served as a wellspring of inspiration, a pillar of strength, and a treasured companion. In her professional pursuits she consistently demonstrated diligence and unwavering dedication to her research. As a friend Lingyi's kindness and nurturing demeanor enriched our personal bonds. Looking back to our old days filled with tons of laughter, Lingyi's passing is a tremendous loss for each of us. I consider myself fortunate to have Lingyi and other friends who have fostered a sense of community within our archaeology circle at Yale. Together we have created a supportive and familial environment that enhances our collective academic experience.

References

BELLWOOD, PETER. 2000. Formosan prehistory and Austronesian dispersal. In: David Blundell, ed. *Austronesian Taiwan: Linguistics, History, Ethnology, and Prehistory*. Berkeley, CA: Phoebe A. Hearst Museum with Shung Ye Museum of Formosan Aborigines. pp. 337–365.

—2007. *Prehistory of the Indo-Malaysian Archipelago*. Rev. ed. Canberra: ANU E Press. 386 pp. https://doi.org/10.22459/PIMA.03.2007

BRUMFIEL, ELIZABETH M., AND TIMOTHY K. EARLE, EDS. 1987. *Specialization, Exchange, and Complex Societies*. Cambridge: Cambridge University Press.

CHANG, KWANG-CHIH.1969. *Fengpitou, Tapenkeng, and the Prehistory of Taiwan*. New Haven: Yale University, Department of Anthropology. 279 pp. (Yale University Publications in Anthropology 73.)

—1987. *The Archaeology of Ancient China*. 4th ed. New Haven: Yale University Press. 450 pp. https://aaeportal.com/?id=-20247

—1995. Taiwan Strait archaeology and proto-Austronesian. In: Rengui Li, ed. *Austronesian Studies Relating to Taiwan*. Taipei: Academia Sinica. pp. 161–183.

CHANG, KWANG-CHIH, AND WARD GOODENOUGH. 1996. Archaeology of southeastern coastal China and its bearing on the Austronesian homeland. *Transactions of the American Philosophical Society*, New Series 86(5):36–56. https://doi.org/10.2307/1006620

DENG, ZHENHUA, HSIAO-CHUN HUNG, MIKE T. CARSON, PETER BELLWOOD, SHU-LING YANG, AND HOUYUAN LU. 2018. The first discovery of Neolithic rice remains in eastern Taiwan: Phytolith evidence from the Chaolaiqiao site. *Archaeological and Anthropological Sciences* 10:1477–1484. https://doi.org/10.1007/s12520-017-0471-z

DENG, ZHENHUA, HSIAO-CHUN HUNG, XUECHUN FAN, YUNMING HUANG, AND HOUYUAN LU. 2018. The ancient dispersal of millets in southern China: New archaeological evidence. *The Holocene* 28(1):34–43. https://doi.org/10.1177/0959683617714603

DRUC, ISABELLE C. 2015. *Atlas of Ceramic Pastes: Components, Texture and Technology*. Blue Mounds, WI: Deep University Press. 132 pp.

FUJIAN PROVINCIAL MUSEUM. 1994. Report on archaeological excavations at the Huangguashan site. *Fujian Wenbo* 1:3–37. [in Chinese.]

—2004. Report on the second archaeological excavations at the Huangguashan site in Xiapu, Fujian. *Fujian Wenbo* 3:1–18. [in Chinese.]

GE, WEI, SHU YANG, YUTONG CHEN, SHIHUA DONG, TIANLONG JIAO, MIAO WANG, MENGYANG WU, YUNMING HUANG, XUECHUN FAN, XIJIE YIN, ET AL. 2019. Investigating the late Neolithic millet agriculture in Southeast China: New multidisciplinary evidence. *Quaternary International* 529:18–24. https://doi.org/10.1016/j.quaint.2019.01.007

GUO, ZHENGFU, TIANLONG JIAO, BARRY V. ROLETT, JIAQI LIU, XUECHUN FAN, AND GONGWU LIN. 2005. Tracking Neolithic interactions in Southeast China: Evidence from stone adze geochemistry. *Geoarchaeology: An International Journal* 20(8):765–776. https://doi.org/10.1002/gea.20082

HE, YAHUI. 2015. "Analysis of Ceramic Traditions in Neolithic Southeast Mainland China and Western Taiwan" [master's thesis]. Yale University.

—2019. A study on the painted pottery from the Huangguashan culture. *Nanfang Wenwu* 6:89–100. [in Chinese.]

Hung, Hsiao-Chun. 2019. Prosperity and complexity without farming: The South China Coast, c. 5000–3000 BC. *Antiquity* 93(368):325–341. https://doi.org/10.15184/aqy.2018.188

Hung, Hsiao-Chun, and Mike T. Carson. 2014. Foragers, fishers and farmers: Origins of the Taiwanese Neolithic. *Antiquity* 88(342):1115–1131. https://doi.org/10.1017/s0003598x00115352

Jiao, Tianlong. 2005. Prehistoric population migrations and regional interactions across the Taiwan Strait. *Dongfang Kaogu* 2:15–38. [in Chinese.]

—2007. *The Neolithic of Southeast China: Cultural Transformation and Regional Interaction on the Coast.* Youngstown, NY: Cambria Press. 286 pp.

—2013. The Neolithic archaeology of Southeast China. In: Anne P. Underhill, ed. *A Companion to Chinese Archaeology.* Malden, MA: Wiley-Blackwell. pp. 599–611.

—2021. Archaeology of Southeast China and the search for an Austronesian homeland. *Social Sciences in China* 42(1):161–170. https://doi.org/10.1080/02529203.2021.1895522

Jiao, Tianlong, Zhengfu Guo, Guoping Sun, Maoliang Zhang, and Xiaohui Li. 2011. Sourcing the interaction networks in Neolithic coastal China: A geochemical study of the Tianluoshan stone adzes. *Journal of Archaeological Science* 38(6):1360–1370. https://doi.org/10.1016/j.jas.2010.10.029

Jiao, Tianlong, Gongwu Lin, and Barry Rolett. 2002. Early seafaring in the Taiwan Strait and the search for Austronesian origins. *Journal of East Asian Archaeology* 4(1):307–319. https://doi.org/10.1163/156852302322454576

Kirch, Patrick V. 1997. *The Lapita Peoples: Ancestors of the Oceanic World.* Oxford: Blackwell Publishers. 376 pp. (The Peoples of South-East Asia and the Pacific.)

Li, Kuang-ti. 2013. First farmers and their coastal adaptation in prehistoric Taiwan. In: Anne P. Underhill, ed. *A Companion to Chinese Archaeology.* Malden, MA: Wiley-Blackwell. pp. 612–633. https://doi.org/10.1002/9781118325698.ch30

Liu, Li, and Xingcan Chen. 2012. *The Archaeology of China: From the Late Paleolithic to the Early Bronze Age.* Cambridge: Cambridge University Press. 498 pp.

Pearson, Richard J.. 2023. *Taiwan Archaeology: Local Development and Cultural Boundaries in the China Seas.* Honolulu: University of Hawai'i Press. 272 pp.

Rice, Prudence M. 2015. *Pottery Analysis: A Sourcebook.* Chicago: University of Chicago Press. 561 pp.

Rolett, Barry V., Zhengfu Guo, and Tianlong Jiao. 2007. Geological sourcing of volcanic stone adzes from Neolithic sites in Southeast China. *Asian Perspectives* 46(2):275–297. https://doi.org/10.1353/asi.2007.0018

Sung, Wenxun. 1980. Archaeological perspectives on Taiwan. In: Chi-lu Chen, ed. *Taiwan in China.* Taipei: Central Cultural Relics Supply Society. pp. 93–220. [in Chinese.]

Tsang, Cheng-Hwa. 1992. *Archaeology of the P'eng-hu Islands.* Taipei: Institute of History and Philology, Academia Sinica. 492 pp.

—2001. Maritime adaptations in prehistoric Southeast Chine: Implications for the problem of Austronesian expansion. *Journal of East Asian Archaeology* 3(1):15–46. https://doi.org/10.1163/156852301100402750

Wang, Chuan-Chao, Hui-Yuan Yeh, Alexander N. Popov, Hu-Qin Zhang, Hirofumi Matsumura, Kendra Sirak, Olivia Cheronet, Alexey Kovalev, Nadin Rohland, Alexander M. Kim, et al. 2021. Genomic insights into the formation of human populations in East Asia. *Nature* 591(7850):413–419. https://doi.org/10.1038/s41586-021-03336-2

CHAPTER FIVE

THE INTRODUCTION OF HORSES INTO YINXU DURING THE LATE SHANG DYNASTY:
A Brief Review

FAN Rong

Horses are an inseparable part of life in many cultures in the world and are particularly useful on the Eurasia steppes. They aid in transportation of goods, human mobility and warfare. Horse manure can be used as fuel, horse skin and horsehair can be made into ropes and boots, and horse meat and milk provide food and drink (Li Y. and Sun 2013). In North America, horses enabled Native Americans on the Great Plains to hunt bison and travel across vast distances with loads of goods (Curry 2023). In contemporary China, horses are important in the daily life of pastoralists who mainly live in Inner Mongolia, Xinjiang, Ningxia, Gansu, and a few other Chinese provinces. Throughout the history of China, horses played significant roles, especially in warfare. Before King Wuling of the Zhao state (赵武灵王) adopted the nomadic pastoralists' mounted archery to form an independent cavalry regiment in 307 BCE, horse-drawn chariots had been an important part of military forces during periods of warfare (Guo 2004). The mobility and military potency provided by horses, chariots, and accompanying soldiers are believed to have been among the main factors that sustained the victory of the Western Zhou over the Shang, and later the Qin over neighboring states during the Warring States period (481–221 BCE; Yang H. 2008).

Tracing back the history of horses in China, there is no clear evidence that domesticated horses lived in the Central Plain, where the political centers of early China were located, until the Late Shang dynasty (around 1300–1046 BCE; Xia-Shang-Zhou Chronology Project Team 2000:60–61). The earliest clear evidence of domesticated horses was found at the Yinxu site in Anyang, Henan Province. These horses appeared relatively suddenly, as if out of nowhere, as animals of the highest prestige and seemingly associated with warfare (Yuan 2003). In addition, the Shang elite integrated horses into their rituals and value system in a very short time. From the Late Shang dynasty, the importance of horses in warfare began to be highly valued in China and thereafter persisted in Chinese history as an enduring cultural and political factor.

The importance of the horse in the Shang dynasty raises several interesting questions: Where were these horses from? When did they arrive and how did they get there? What roles did these horses play in the Shang people's life when they first appeared? What did it take to acquire this large number of horses in a relatively short time? And how were they integrated into the Shang system so quickly? Here I briefly review both the Chinese and English literature on the issues raised by these questions. By piecing together pertinent archaeological discoveries such as oracle bone inscriptions and historical records, as well as the very latest archaeological evidence, I aim to sort out some of the mysteries related to the introduction of horses to the Shang state and how the Shang people managed their horse resources.

This chapter is dedicated to my beloved friend Zeng Lingyi, who devoted herself to bridging the archaeology of the East and the West. I hope this review might take her unfinished wishes a microstep farther and serve as an initial reference for scholars in English-speaking countries who are interested in the introduction of horses to early China, particularly at Yinxu during the Late Shang dynasty.

Horses before Shang

Wild horses have been in China since the Paleolithic period (Wang G. and Dong 2020). Fragmentary horse remains have been unearthed in early contexts in China's northeast, north, northwest and southwest regions (Tie 2015:241). These horses are all identified as *Equus przewalskii* Poliakov (Yuan 2003). As the climate changed during the Neolithic period, around 4000 to 2300 BCE, horses gradually became restricted to the north and northwest of China. Horse remains were found mainly in the north, especially in the northwest, in modern Gansu, Qinghai, and Ningxia provinces (Tie 2015). During the terminal Neolithic period around 2000 BCE a few remains of horses were discovered in the middle and lower reaches of the Yellow River valley as well. For instance, horse bone fragments were identified at the Chengziya site in Zhangqiu, Shandong Province (Fu 1934), and at the Baiying site in Tangyin, Henan Province (Fang, Sun, and Zhao 1980). However, except for a few exceptions in Xinjiang (see below for more details), almost all of the other horse remains pre-dating the Late Shang period are loose teeth or bone fragments, and the majority of these remains are from mundane contexts such as garbage pits or stratigraphic layers (Tie 2015; Kikuchi 2019; Wang G. and Dong 2020). Besides difficulties in differentiating wild from domesticated horses caused by the fragmentary condition of the bones and teeth, the scattered distribution and small number of horses in each site also indicate that these horses were not intensively involved in the daily lives of people, but were deposited at these sites because of other activities, such as hunting and meat consumption.

The turning point when horses suddenly appeared in large numbers and were handled in an orderly manner was at Yinxu during the early phase of the Late Shang (Kikuchi 2019). The time was equivalent to the Yinxu Phase II, which is dated between the late reign of King Wu Ding (武丁, 1250–1192 BCE) and possibly the reigns of King Zu Geng (祖庚) and King Zu Jia (祖甲), approximately around 1200 BCE (Xia-Shang-Zhou Chronology Project Team 2022:518). At this time a large number of horses appear in Shang burials and sacrificial pits. For example, a total of 117 horses were unearthed from thirty out of forty pits from the group of sacrificial features in the north locality of Wuguancun (武官村; CASS Anyang Team 1987). Horses recovered from burials were mostly interred with chariots. Likewise, horse-pulled chariots were recovered in the Central Plain (Kikuchi 2019). This new phenomenon at Yinxu suggests that the horses and chariots were most likely imported from elsewhere (Chen Xingcan 2002; Linduff 2003; Yuan 2003; Yuan and Flad 2005b).

The Introduction of Horses to Yinxu

The origin of the Yinxu horses is complicated. According to written records, Shang elites had many ways to acquire horses. In addition to Shang horse specialists raising them locally, they were captured during warfare and presented to the Shang as tribute or received through gift exchanges from neighboring polities (Wang Y. 1999). The multiple origins of the Yinxu horses are supported by the results of strontium isotope analyses. Five out of ten sampled horses from locations at Yinxu, including Xiaomintun (孝民屯), Tiyuchang (体育场), Baijiazhuang Eastern Locality (白家庄东地), and Tiesanlu (铁三路), were born and raised locally, and another five were born in other locations (Zhao, Li, and Yuan 2015). Unfortunately, the chronological phases of these horses are not noted and therefore verifying that these horses were all from the same Late Shang period is not possible. After their initial appearance, horses were rapidly adopted into the Shang system. Having locally bred horses would not be surprising as part of integrating horses into Shang elite culture. What is most intriguing is the decision to adopt horses into a Central Plain system that had long been centered on agricultural subsistence strategies where the mobile skills of pastoralism were quite underdeveloped. Before Yinxu Phase II domesticated horses were very few, or even nonexistent, in the Central Plain. Although rare, domesticated horses and related horse objects could have appeared in the Shang territory at a slightly earlier time, but so far evidence is lacking. Rather than simply taking horses as war trophies, the Shang people adopted and quickly modified the use of horses for their own needs and forms of practice. Sorting out when, where, and how the Shang people received the earliest horses and horse-related objects may shed light on Shang strategies in building their military, their horse-related belief system, and the horse's importance to Shang central power.

The Earliest Horses and Horse-related Objects at Yinxu

One of the earliest Shang archaeological features with horses are eleven groups of sacrificial pits out of fifteen unearthed at the Wuguancun north locality, dated to the early phase of Yinxu culture. In thirty-six of these pit features, a total of 125 sacrificial victims were unearthed, including three humans, 117 horses, one elephant, one pig, and one fox (CASS Anyang Team 1987). These horses did not have ornaments nor were any other objects buried with them. However, in twenty-seven of the pits the horse counts are even numbers, such as two, four, six, and eight horses buried in a single pit. Excavators proposed that the even number of buried horses indicates that these horses might have been chariot horses sacrificed as war captives since, at that time, chariots were drawn by teams of two horses (CASS Anyang Team 1987:1068). Another noteworthy phenomenon is the elephant found in the sacrificial pits at this locality. Only two elephants have been discovered after almost two thousand pits were uncovered at Yinxu at the time of the Wuguancun north locality excavation, suggestive of the rarity and importance of the more numerous horses in associated features. As many as forty-four presumably rare horses were sacrificed during a single ritual event at Wuguancun, signaling that rituals held at this site were extraordinarily important (CASS Anyang Team 1987:1070).

Bridle and harness parts are direct evidence for horses having been used in chariot teams. According to Chang Huaiyin's (2019) review, the earliest horse bridle parts and chariot parts at Yinxu are from around Yinxu Phase II (Table 5.1). The earliest yoke cover, from unit 1136–1137 at Houjiazhuang, was potentially dated between Yinxu Phase I and Phase II, which is possibly a group of ritual pits associated with burial M1443. Because it is possible that the earliest chariots may have been pulled by animals other than horses, here I only discuss horse bridles that are directly indicative of horse use, but not other early chariot parts.

At the Xiaotun palace locality both horses and the combination of horses with chariots were discovered (see Table 5.1). These objects have distinctive patterns, which were gradually modified overtime. For instance, horse bits changed from one form having a bronze bar mouthpiece connected to bronze cheek pieces with pegs or spikes to guide horse movement to one having connecting rings separate from the mouthpiece, similar to a modern bar bit (see Anthony 2007:194; Chang 2019; Figure 5.1).

To answer how the Shang people derived these styles and forms of the earliest horse-related objects and whether, before adoption of the horse, such devices were used on other animals, archaeologists still need to do more research.

Origins of the Yinxu Horses

The earliest horses at Yinxu were used in rituals along with other prestigious animals, such as the elephant, and the earliest horse-related objects and chariots were discovered within the royal palace region in association with bronze weapons (Yang B. 1984; CASS Anyang Team 1987). Considering the large number of horses sacrificed, the patterns of how they were buried, and their elaborate ornaments, these horses were certainly imported from elsewhere. What accompanied these early horses was also extremely important, including chariot technology, harnessing methods, equestrian knowledge and skills, and symbolic systems of value and meaning. The arrival of these "packages" of technology, animals, and skillsets raises a key question: Where were these horses possibly from? As mentioned above, there is barely any evidence for horses on the Central Plain before the Late Shang. As Linduff (2003:147–148) once pointed out, the communities in the Yellow River basin were usually settled close to rivers with arable land and the agriculturalist of the Central Plain did not need horses for transport or labor. In contrast, the dry climate and rocky mountainous terrain to the north and west of the Central Plain is an environment better suited to the use of horses in daily life for transportation, herding, and other daily tasks.

Scholars have proposed two potential routes for the introduction of horses to Yinxu. One is a western route through the Xinjiang–Gansu corridor, and another is a northwestern route via Inner Mongolia. Honeychurch (2015:193) points out that these two routes are, of course, not exclusive and at this time there is not enough evidence to state that either one was primary. To trace the possible origins of the early Yinxu horses it is essential to sort out horse remains and horse-related objects that predate the Late Shang period when the horses are already known from Yinxu. Several horse skeletons uncovered in Xinjiang predate the Late Shang critical period of 1200 BCE. One horse rib from the Tangbalisay cemetery in Nilka County is dated to 1605 to 1585 BCE (Wang Y., Yuan, and Ruan 2019), and horse remains from the stone residential structure at the Husta site in Bortala Mongol Autonomous Prefecture in Xinjiang are dated to around 1400 to 1121 BCE (CASS ^{14}C Laboratory 2020:117–118). In addition, some of these remains may have served purposes that are different from the horse bone fragments found at the sites in the upper and lower Yellow River basin. For instance, two complete horse skulls uncovered from the floors of the Har-Oro walled fortress site, which is about 3 km north of the central Husta site, were dated to around 1608 to 1501 BCE. In preparation for an enemy on foot or on horseback, these two horse skulls may be associated with defense of the fortress site (Jia X. et al. 2016; Jia P. et al. 2018).

TABLE 5.1. The early horse-related objects at the Yinxu site. Modified from Chang (2019, Tables 1, 2, 3, and 4).

Locality	Unit	Context	Associated human remains	Type of object	Phase
Houjiazhuang	1136–1137	—	—	Yoke cover	Possibly between I and II
Xiaotun	M164	1 horse	1	Horse bit, browband pendant	II
Xiaotun	M202	2 horses	3	Browband pendant	II
Xiaotun	M20	4 horses and 2 chariots	3	Yoke cover, horizontal drawbar decoration	II
Xiaotun	M40	2 horses and 1 chariot	3	Yoke cover, horizontal drawbar decoration	II

Though horse discoveries are still sporadic, the relative abundance of horse remains and variety in horse use may indicate that this far western region may be a possible origin of the horses at Yinxu. However, horses predating the Late Shang period in China are still extremely few and the area of northwestern Xinjiang where these dated horse remains were recovered is far from the Central Plain. From the perspective of artifact styles associated with horses at Yinxu, contacts between the Shang and northern steppe groups who are known to have kept horses may be a more plausible region for initial horse introductions to Yinxu. The earliest objects with actual horse depictions are dated to Yinxu Phase II, but interactions between the Shang state and the northern steppe may have started earlier. A few northern style objects have been found in burials that are dated to late Yinxu Phase I, which is believed to be the early reign of King Wu Ding. For instance, northern style shaft-hole bronze axes were found in sacrificial pit M10 of the late Yinxu Phase I in the palace area in the northern village of Xiaotun (Zhu 2013:25).

Early interaction between the Shang state and the northern steppe can be traced to the Zhukaigou (朱开沟) cultural period (around 2100–1300/1200 BCE; Wei and Feng 2020). Remains from the Zhukaigou culture are distributed mainly in the east of the Ordos plateau. During the Erligang and the early Yinxu period, about 1500 to 1300 BCE, Zhukaigou cultural communities dominated the entire Hetao region and extended as far east as northern Shaanxi (Lv 2002). Bronze daggers, knives, and personal accessories found in the Zhukaigou burials and the late phase of the settlement are of Karasuk style originating in south Siberia (Linduff 1997:21; Liu L. and Chen 2012:321–322; Honeychurch 2015:189). In addition, pottery vessel assemblages and chronological changes, especially of *li* tripods, at

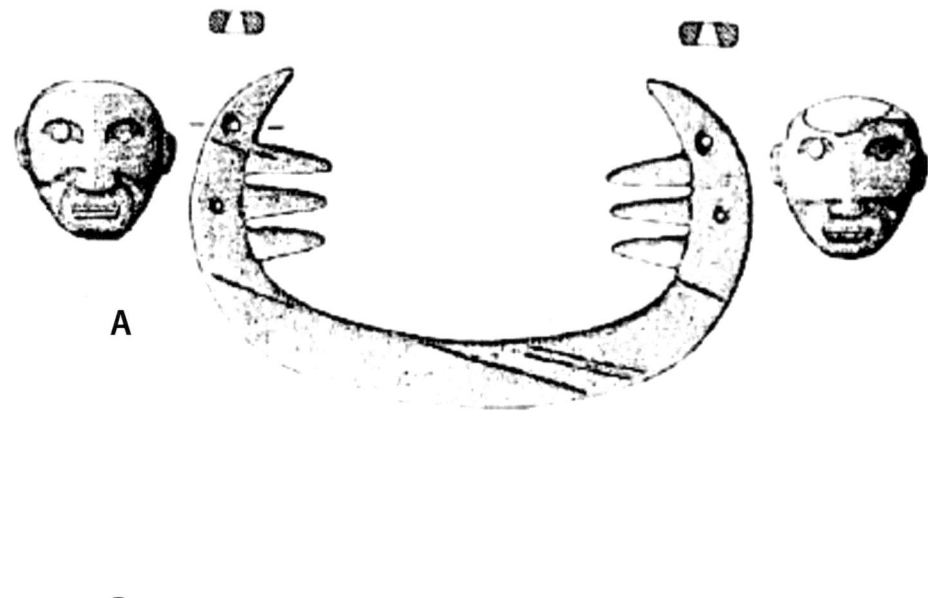

FIGURE 5.1. Changes in the types of horse mouthpieces at Yinxu. **A.** Horse bit from Xiaotun (grave M164, R009121), Yinxu Phase II. **B.** Horse bit from 04Dasikong (M231, 53), Yinxu Phase IV. **C.** Horse bit with connecting rings from 04Dasikong (M226, 61), Yinxu Phase IV. Adapted from Chang (2019:60, fig. 1).

the Tazhao (塔照) site near Beijing reveal frequent interactions between the local Shang culture and external cultures, possibly from the upper Zhangjiayuan (张家园) cultural period of the Tazhao site in northern Shanxi, dated to around 1408 to 930 BCE (Beijing Municipal Institute of Cultural Relics 1999:420–421; Ma 2009:43). Still another possibility is Shelach's (2009:133) argument that the Northern Bronzes Complex may be traced along a transmission route through southeastern Inner Mongolia via groups of the Upper Xiajiadian culture. Such northern style bronze objects are found in many contexts in Yinxu, including sacrificial pits with bronze knives and axes in which the majority of sacrificed humans were decapitated; knives with animal heads also are found in tombs and horse-chariot pits (Zhu 2013). Zhu (2013) further argues that these northern style objects indicate frequent interactions between the Shang state and the northern steppe groups that lived in present western Shanxi, northeastern Shaanxi, and northern Hebei provinces.

The origins of these northern styles can be traced to the Eurasian steppe regions farther west. Nevertheless, Wang Peng (2021) points out that knives with mushroom-shaped handles, with animal head-shaped handles, and with three protruding buttons are seen from northern China, Mongolia, and southern Siberia, but not the western steppe. He (2020) instead proposes an alternative northern route for bronzes and steppe contacts ranging from Liaoning Province to the east and the Jinshan plateau to the west. A particular kind of dagger with animal head pommels was unearthed from burials in Yinxu, including M1713 at the West locality of Yinxu, in grave M20 at Xiaotun, and in grave Huayuanzhuang Donglu M54. The pommels of these daggers take the shape of horses, cattle, sheep, deer, and tigers. He (2020:35) thinks that these various animal-shaped pommels at Yinxu are mimicking the original form of the typical horse-head-shaped daggers. Wang Peng (2018) points out that some ornamentations and motifs on pottery and bronze objects at Yinxu resemble ones from the late Bronze Age in southern Siberia and Kazakhstan at about 1300 BCE. Wang Peng (2018) further argues that the styles of artifacts indicate direct contacts and mutual exchange of material culture, including the possibility that some people from communities with horses and horse knowledge may have resided at Yinxu for a time. Some objects related to the horse harnesses found at Yinxu and Laoniupo (老牛坡) in Shaanxi resembles the Western Asiatic style, such as rod-shaped bits with loops and rectangular cheek pieces. Takahama (2020) argues that this type of harness was introduced to China from the west, while chain-type horse bits were invented by the Shang. This horse equipment and horse-related objects were first discovered in the north and scholars have concluded that these items were brought to Yinxu.

Wang Wei (1998) and Barbieri-Low (2000) propose that chariots were transmitted through the northern steppe, from southeast of the Ural Mountains through an area south of the Altai Mountains to Mongolia, Shanxi, and then finally to Yinxu. According to Wu (2011), the earliest parts of chariot packages were from the horse-chariot sacrificial pits M20 and M40 from the Xiaotun Yi Qi (乙七基址) architectural foundation site in Anyang (Shi 1972), and the tomb passageways of M1 and M18 at the Qiaobei (桥北) site in Fushan (浮山), Shanxi Province (Qiaobei Archaeological Team 2006). Among these burials, M1 from the Qiaobei site is dated to about Yinxu Phase II on the basis of the typology of grave goods (Zhao 2012:15–24).

Interactions with the aforementioned cultures might be the sources from which Shang high elites acquired knowledge, skills, and inspiration to begin keeping horses locally. The initial introduction of horses and chariots from the north, from Mongolia, Inner Mongolia, and the west (such as from Xinjiang), could have been through a number of interactive processes, including exchange, warfare, or political alliances (Linduff 2002; Zhu 2013).

Logistics of Transporting the First Horses
Some scholars argue that the Shang dynasty ruled over a vast land during the Late Shang period. At its peak, the Shang territory reached to northern Hebei Province in the north, southern Henan Province in the south, the central Shaanxi plain to the west, and eastern Shandong to the east (Li B. 2006). Another argument is that the Shang territory shrank

during the Late Shang period. The Shang king controlled only a region north of the Yellow River valley, north to Xingtai in Hebei Province, Puyang to the east, and the eastern foothills of the Taihang Mountains to the west (CASS IA 2003). Neither of the proposed regions covered lands deemed to have herding cultures or that would have been suitable for horses as natural habitats. The distance between Yinxu and Inner Mongolia is over 800 km and horses may have been coming from even farther afield. Transporting herds of horses over such distances would have taken an incredible amount of effort as well as technical prowess. Factors one must consider to accomplish such a journey would have included weather, water, and grazing resources, as well as keeping the horses under control while moving. Horse experts almost certainly would have been involved in transporting any number of horses over distances and possibly some of these people eventually arrived at Yinxu together with the horses.

Given the hardship of transporting horses over such a long distance, three scenarios are imaginable given the scale of early horse sacrificial events at Yinxu. First, horses might have been introduced and integrated into the Shang system in small numbers gradually before they were sacrificed during these events in large numbers. Second, there may have been multiple "way stations" that could supply and support longer distance movements of larger herds. For example, the Yinxu Phase II chariot-packages found at the Qiaobei site in Shanxi could have represented a transit point along the route between the Shang royal state and the polities to the west (e.g., Tian 2021). Finally, the horses sacrificed in these events could have come from multiple regions—some closer and some farther—and could have been specifically acquired over time for the event. Besides possible long-distance movements, tribute to the Shang elites might have been one way of acquiring horses (Liu Y. and Cao 2004). According to the oracle bone inscriptions unearthed from the locality of Huayuanzhuang East, horses were provided to Yinxu as tribute sent from a place or a person called Zhu (貯) or Ning (宁) from the reign of the King Wu Ding until the middle phase of Yinxu (Liu Y. and Cao 2004).

Even though a systematic analysis of the sex and age of horses used in rituals throughout Yinxu is still needed, the age composition of the horses from the sacrificial pits at the Wuguancun North locality indicates that the animals selected for rituals were mostly young male horses (Figure 5.2A) and the majority of these horses were between the ages of 7 and 11 years old (Figure 5.2B).

According to Meng (2005), castrated riding horses between the ages of 3 and 15 are in their physical prime and therefore of highest use-value. The lack of young horses may suggest three possibilities. First, as proposed by the excavators, these were chariot horses used in battle contexts and captured during conflicts (CASS Anyang Team 1987). If so, the presence of female horses may support this assumption. Next, the Shang high elite may have kept female and young horses for breeding. Last of all, the horses transported may have initially been quite young, but the process of movement took time and therefore on reaching Yinxu they were older, or possibly the youngest and weakest horses may have perished, leaving only mature horses. These three possibilities are not exclusive and some combination may have contributed to the age profile of contexts such as those at Wuguancun. In any case, the age composition of the early horses indicates that the purpose of the initial arrival of a large number of horses to Yinxu may have not been merely battle-captured animals or those intended for a sacrifice, but rather part of a more encompassing strategy that included preparation for horse and chariot use in Shang warfare.

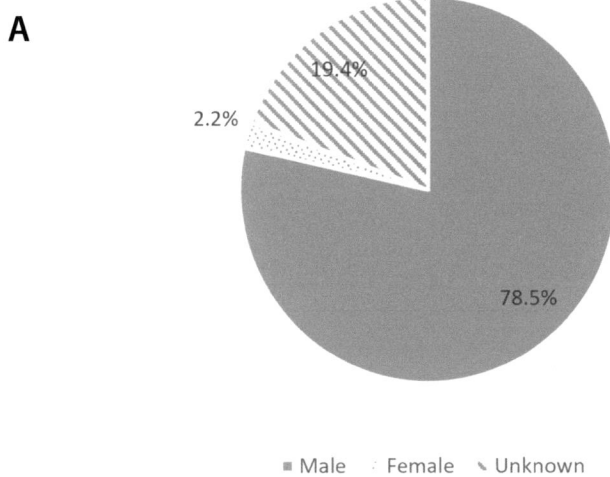

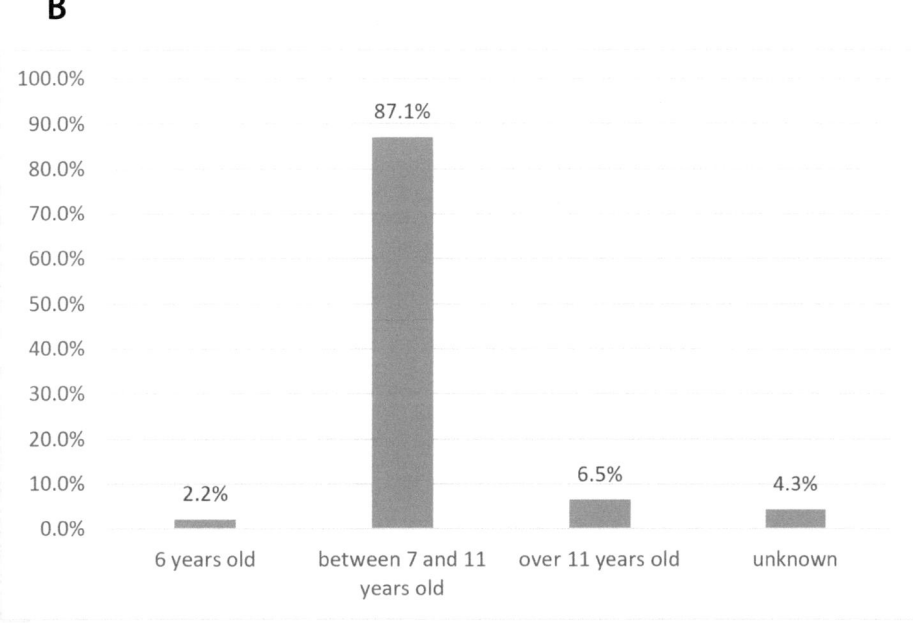

FIGURE 5.2. Sex (A) and age (B) composition of the horse remains from the sacrificial pits at the Wuguancun North locality. Modified from CASS Anyang Team (1987:1068).

The integration of horses into the Shang system after the initial rituals seems rapid, as if the elite of the Shang had strategies in mind for keeping, supporting, and using horses in various ways. However, we must remember that the timing we observe from archaeological finds probably does not represent the very first experience with horses. When horses initially appear archaeologically at Yinxu, in sacrificial pit contexts they are associated with the highest status and greatest prestige, indicating their direct association with state royalty. Such status could not have been instantaneous and instead suggests that their value and meaning must have taken time to develop locally. Therefore, considering the long history of interactions between the Shang state and horse-keeping groups located to the west and north, I hypothesize that the introduction of horses into Yinxu was gradual, accumulative, and possibly represents a process over a long span of time and not suddenly or out of nowhere, as much research argues. Probably there were events that occurred between 1300 and 1200 BCE that stimulated and accelerated the integration of horses into the Shang system.

Integration of Horses into the Shang System

The elaborate display of horses and chariots found in various archaeological contexts at Yinxu reflect an intricate system of understanding about horses. These systems involved knowledge of horses, horse husbandry, horse-related skills, and relevant beliefs. Knowledge about horses was the foundation of the entire system. It enabled horse husbandry, which supported the development of horse-related skills, and it eventually facilitated the elaborate display of horses and chariots in large tombs. Reciprocally, the intention and desire of using horses and chariots as symbols of social status in turn supported the horse husbandry system (Figure 5.3).

As mentioned earlier, horses were not common on the Central Plain before the Late Shang. Once horses and chariots appeared at Yinxu—and, as explained above, I expect that they did so earlier than the archaeological record so far suggests—the integration and infusion of horses into the Shang system was seemingly rapid. Through horse management and usage, the Shang high elites established their unique system that served their ritual and political purposes.

Horse Management during the Shang Dynasty

Facilities for horse management were most likely directly supervised by the kings and high elites. Oracle bone inscriptions state that "the king raised horses in stables" ("王畜马于兹牢"; CASS IHS 1981:3603; Yuan 2003). Although kings may not have directly raised horses by themselves, such records show that horses during the Late Shang were held in the highest regard. The Shang elite had a complete system to manage horses. According to Chen Enzhi (1987), the corpus of oracle bone inscriptions by the Chinese Academy of Social Sciences Institute of Archaeology (CASS IA 1965) recorded forty-nine characters of horses. For example, the Wu Ding period oracle inscriptions include such horse-related characters as *Ma* (马), *Duo Ma* (多马), and *Ma Xiaochen* (马小臣). These records reveal the horse system in the Shang dynasty, which maintained quality criteria used to assure the horses used in the palace were the best of those given in tribute by other states (Chen E. 1987). Horse physiognomy might have also been established as a system of symbolic value early on. The Shang people identified individual horses by their colors and personalities rather than by groups (Wang G. and Dong 2020, 2021). Types of horses were named based on their coat color. For instance, pure brown horses were called *dong* (駧) and variegated horses were called *bo* (驳) (Chen E. 1987:339). Color and size were evaluated in the selection process of

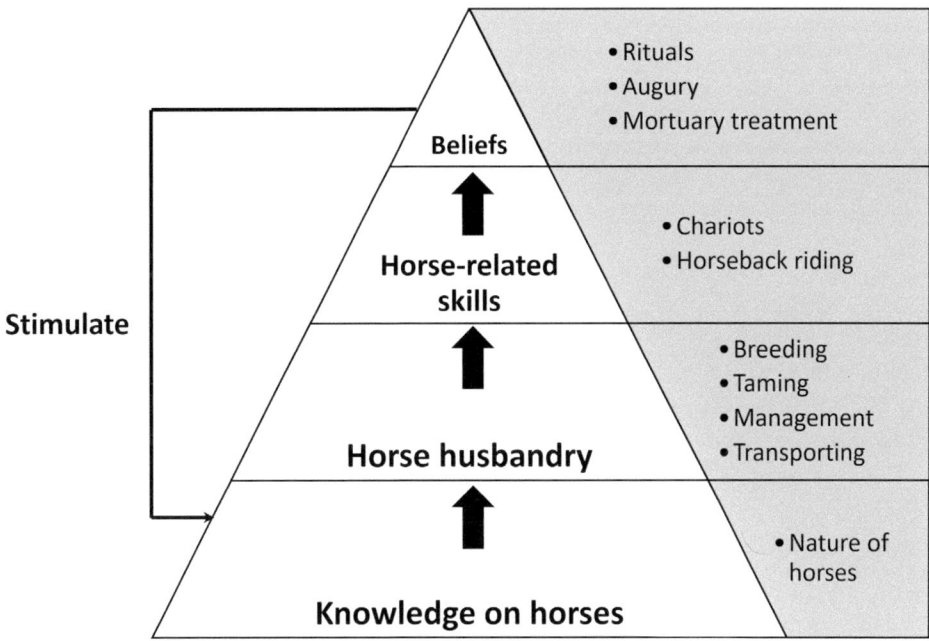

FIGURE 5.3. Illustration showing the integration of knowledge about horses into the Shang system.

ritual sacrifices (Xie 1959:48). It is also possible that the Shang people may also have begun castration of horses, although we still lack this evidence (Xie 1959:37). In all contexts, the knowledge and symbolic systems that the Shang used to place value on certain kinds of horses was likely derived from the places and cultures from where horses originated and then added to and developed through Shang concepts of value.

The Shang had official positions to manage horses, such as *Ma Xiaochen*, a status position which may have served multiple roles in the Shang dynasty. These officials generally served to manage horses and they also joined military actions (Wang G. 1986; Cao 2018:77). *Ma* and *Duo Ma* are also found in inscriptions about military attacks (Wang G. 1986:114). Horses had a significant role in the military. The number of chariots and horses in both oracle bone inscriptions and archaeological sites indicate that the Shang people managed to collect, raise, and train horses to prepare them for warfare within the Shang territory. The horse-raising system shows that the Shang people were knowledgeable about horses (Wang G. and Dong 2020, 2021). This kind of knowledge would take generations of experimentation, experience, and practice and could have been a major contribution of steppe peoples who likely began and facilitated horse husbandry at Yinxu. Given the large number of sacrificed horses, the horse-raising industry must have reached an unprecedented level that could support frequent and large-scale sacrificial rituals, as were seen during the late reign of King Wu Ding.

Horse Use during the Shang Dynasty
Horses and related remains are mostly found in the royal cemetery, bronze workshop in Xiaomintun, and occasionally in the bone workshop site at Dasikong (大司空). Horses and

chariots are mainly found close to the entrances of a tomb, or on tomb entry ramps (Chen Xiang 2021:37). In addition to being mere sacrificial animals, horses played additional roles in the lives of Shang elites (Chen Z. 1994:416). Horses were often mentioned in oracle bone inscriptions in auguries. For instance, more than thirty pieces of inscribed oracle bones out of 689 unearthed from the East locality of Huayuanzhuang record horse-related content (Liu Y. and Cao 2004). In the pit H3 oracle bone inscriptions (Liu Y. and Cao 2004), auguries regarding horses covered a range of activities in daily life, including whether the horse herd was safe, inquiring as to the health of horses, whether certain horses were suitable for sacrificial rituals or hunting, and which were best as chariot horses (Wang Y. 1999; Liu Y. and Cao 2004:8). No other animal in the Shang court received such intense attention as did the horse.

In addition to use in warfare, horses and chariots were an important element in the Shang royal hunt (Fiskesjö 2001:114–115). The Shang kings often sent out scouts to check on the weather and report road conditions before a hunt. During hunting, the Shang kings dispatched horses to startle prey. In oracle bone inscriptions "horses go first" (马其先) appears many times and usually followed by "the king then followed" (王兑从) (translated from Wang Y. [1999:64]). In both cases, horses were sent out before the king's departure, possibly to prepare charioteering before the king came. Using horses in these activities suggests that the Shang elites profoundly understood the nature of horses, or at least trusted horses. They knew how to maximize the advantages of horses to make sure the king was safe and for the hunting events to go smoothly.

Horses in Rituals

In contrast to previous eras in China, horses at Yinxu were found in elite contexts (see above). Horses were put in separate areas and concentrated in an area distinct from other domesticated animals like dogs, sheep, and pigs (Yuan and Flad 2005a). The unique mortuary practices involving horses at Yinxu as well as oracle bone inscriptions reveal that rituals associated with horses were likely conducted by kings for ancestor memorials and veneration rituals (Yuan and Flad 2005a). Additionally, horses were offered to male ancestors in veneration rituals. In oracle bone inscriptions male ancestors such as Da Yi (大乙), Da Ding (大丁), Lin Xin (廪辛), Zu Jia (祖甲), Zu Yi (祖乙), and Zi Gui (子癸) were venerated by way of horse sacrifices. While seven female ancestors were venerated in the H3 auguries, none of them were offered horses (Liu Y. and Cao 2004). The H3 oracle inscriptions were unearthed from the pit H3 excavated at the east locality of Huayuanzhuang (花园庄东地), which are dated to the early reign of King Wu Ding (cited from Liu Y. and Cao [2004]).

Besides being used as sacrificial offerings for important occasions such as ancestor veneration, horses occasionally were at the center of ritual acts. In the sacrificial pit H33 at the south locality of Xiaotun (小屯南地), the horse was in the center and surrounded by three adult humans and two children. One of the adult humans was decapitated and one had a bronze arrow next to his or her left leg. The two children were likewise dismembered (CASS Anyang Team 1975:30). This arrangement led to an assumption that the ritual was centered on the horse. And the bones of this horse seemed to command respect. Despite the large number of horses unearthed, horse bones are rarely found as raw materials in bone tool workshops in Yinxu. The majority of raw materials for bone tools are from cattle (Campbell et al. 2011; CASS Anyang Team 2015; Li Z. 2018:97). Horses at Yinxu were highly valued in rituals presumably because they were conceived of as powerful and independent animals. However, exceptions to this pattern also seem to be present. One of the recent discoveries worth noting is a large sacrificial trench at the Huanbei Shang city (洹北商城) dating to the Middle and Late Shang periods. The excavation revealed a large number of bones from dismembered animals, including horses (Li Y. and Wang 2023). These horse remains were buried along with dismembered cattle, pigs, and birds. Even though the exact age of the horse remains is unclear, the excavators date the 19.36 m sacrificial trench to the Yinxu, Late Shang period (cited by (Li Y. and Wang [2023:1]). The Yinxu period at Huanbei Shang city dates to Yinxu Phase I (reviewed by He and Yue [2011:16]). If the date of this layer with horse remains is consistent with the Yinxu Phase I and the horses prove to be domesticated (ideally using a DNA analysis), they will be the earliest found in Shang territory. However, the most recent study suggests that the trench is dated to Yinxu Phase III (Du and He 2024), about 1205 to 1080 BCE (Xia-Shang-Zhou Chronology Project Team 2022:196), when the first group of horses appeared in Yinxu. A few issues remain intriguing. First, the horses found in this trench were buried with livestock that were commonly seen, which is in stark contrast to other early Yinxu horses mentioned previously in this review. Were the horses consumed as food or for ritual feasting? Are there similar patterns of consumption seen for other animals? Did the presence of these horses signal a further integration of horses into the ritual and belief system of the Shang? Or, was there a slight "downgrade" of the prestige of horses that had become more common by this time period? Investigations including a larger sample of Yinxu horses for ^{14}C dating may provide answers about the dynamic roles that horses played in Late Shang societies.

Horse-related Objects

According to Meng, Li, and Li (2017:411), horse and chariot ornaments and horse tacks had been unearthed from over fifty tombs at Yinxu by the time their paper was published. Horses, horse-related objects, and chariots were usually buried close to entrances and ramps of large tombs. In some tombs, only horses were found. For example, twenty-eight horses were found at the WKGM tomb: sixteen horses buried in three pits on the north ramp and twelve horses in three pits on the south ramp. Even though no chariots accompanied the horses, the headstalls found on the horse skulls suggest that these horses may have served as chariot-pulling horses (Meng, Li, and Li 2017). In some cases, large tombs do not have actual horse remains or chariots, but instead are provisioned with horse ornaments and horse tack, such as burial M1311 at the Xibeigang (西北岗) locality (Zhu 2013:18–19). Horse tack at Yinxu mainly included horse whips and bow-shaped objects. The exact functions of the bow-shaped objects are still debated (e.g., Lin 1998; Sun 2001; Teng 2011). The interpretation represented by Lin (1998) proposes that these objects were attached to a belt that wrapped around the horse chariot driver's waist as rein holders. Wang Peng (2021) argues that these bow-shaped objects may have been used as restraints to keep the riders and passengers balanced on a moving chariot. In either case, scholars have reached a consensus that the bow-shaped objects were definitely associated with horses and chariots. Even though horse equipment might have been initially imported, the Shang people improved these objects to adjust to their needs. For example, horse bits were one piece when introduced to Yinxu and Shang artisans eventually reformed them into multiple pieces with a chain connecting two rings for enhanced flexibility. The Shang experimented with and gradually improved the horse-chariot associated items to improve functionality (Chang 2019).

Discussion and Future Directions

A "Prepared" Reception of Horses?

The change from almost zero to hundreds of horses seems, from an archaeological perspective, to have been rapid. Chronologically speaking, Pangeng (盘庚) is believed to have moved the Shang capital to Yinxu during his reign in about 1300 BCE (Xia-Shang-Zhou Chronology Project Team 2000:60). The earliest horse sacrificial pits were dated to Yinxu Phase II, which began during the late reign of King Wu Ding, according to the oracle bone inscription chronology (CASS IA 2003:284). Records of horse-related rituals on oracle bones seem to have begun during King Wu Ding's reign as well (CASS Anyang Team 1987:1068), which is dated to 1250 to 1192 BCE (Xia-Shang-Zhou Chronology Project Team 2000:57). Considering the oracle bone inscriptions about horses and that the earliest horses are believed to have arrived during the King Wu Ding's reign, the threshold of horses from zero to hundreds occurred during about fifty-nine years of King Wu Ding's time. Afterward, horses and chariots became increasingly popular among the elites of Yinxu and other Shang territories. Horse equipment was improved to efficiently control reins while better protecting wooden parts of the horse-controlling technological system (Chang 2019).

However, despite this seemingly rapid appearance, horses from the earliest documented period were treated with special care in both daily life and the afterlife during the Late Shang period. Horses at Yinxu seemed to suddenly enter the scene as a kind of valuable and prestigious animal that was instantaneously highly valued when compared to all the other domesticated animals. Given the archaeological contexts from which horse remains were unearthed, there is little doubt that access to horses belonged to kings and the royal elite. Knowledge of practical horse uses for hunting, pulling chariots, and in warfare was already established from the time of their arrival, as if they had always been a part of the lives of the Shang elites. In fact, many of the earliest horses found in Yinxu were buried with complete sets of horse equipment properly arrayed upon them, including forehead decorations that have no intrinsic functional use. A good example of such early and expertly outfitted horses is from grave M164 at Xiaotun, found along with bridle bits (Chang 2019). This suggests that horses and associated objects entered the Shang world in a form already well developed outside the Central Plain. Many horses of the Deer Stone Khirigsuur period in Mongolia, dated to about 1400 to 700 BCE, had unique dentition patterns that were probably associated with horse transport systems and even traditions of equid dental work (Taylor et al. 2021). This indicates an existing and contemporaneous version of developed horse practices to the north in the Shang dynasty.

The Shang could easily have acquired a great deal of knowledge and technology from the northern steppe groups. Perhaps a degree of existing knowledge among the Shang pre-dated the early arrival of horses. In opposition to such a proposal, Chang (2019:67) argues that the Shang elite clearly valued horses, but never buried horses directly inside their tombs. He goes on to suggest that the desire on the part of the Shang elites for exotic animals such as horses explains why they were valued but not integrated intimately into the core of Shang rituals. Chang points out that horses and chariots were supplementary symbols of prestige and wealth and always appear archaeologically in accompanying ritual pits near, but not within, the primary elite burial chambers. Horses at Yinxu were indeed exotic when they showed up within the Central Plain in large quantities; however, I argue that horses were not excluded from the ritual system of the Shang elites. On the contrary, horses in the Shang dynasty were managed only by the kings and high elites, used in royal hunting events, buried in special ritual contexts, and offered to male ancestors. They were introduced to Yinxu as agents through which the Shang kings and elites hoped to gain military power and ritual prerogative, rather than serving as simple exotic trophies. The Shang elites integrated horses into their belief and value systems, not only for ritual purposes, but in support of an entirely new system of horse care and husbandry to make horses more sustainable in the Central Plain environment. Significant and protracted interactions with communities that were knowledgeable about horses were the first steps in this adoption process, but Shang innovations transformed and embedded horses deeply in the value system and into the elite lifeways of the dynasty.

Contributions of the Yinxu Horse System
After the Shang elite at Yinxu adopted and modified the horse system to suit their environmental, ritual, and political context, the interesting question of whether they passed this system to the Shang territories outside Yinxu must be explored. Many sites of the Late Shang period with horses, chariots, and tack in archaeological contexts have been discovered beyond the precincts of Yinxu (see Wu 2002; Liu Y. 2010). For example, to the east of the Central Plain is the Qianzhangda (前掌大) site in Tengzhou, Shandong Province. Five horse-chariot pits were unearthed there, with each pit containing two horses and one chariot. Chariots from the Qianzhangda site share features with those found at Yinxu, but with a few unique objects and motifs. For instance, the horse bits form, a braided rod with a round ring on each end, is seen only in Qiangzhangda and not at Yinxu, but the U-shaped horse bits are exactly the same as the horse bit from burial M33:11 found at Hougang in Yinxu (Gu 2006). Rod-shaped bits with loops and rectangular cheek-pieces discussed above as possibly having analogs in the western regions of Eurasia were discovered at both Yinxu and at Laoniupo in Shaanxi Province.

Although more detailed comparison is needed, such as the provenance of horses, current evidence shows that horse and chariot systems during the Shang dynasty may have been developed and practiced using two different modes. One of these is primarily found to the west of the Central Plain at sites such as Laoniupo and Fushanqiao. These sites are along the geographical routes between Yinxu and the steppe frontiers to the north and west. These places may have directly acquired practices and technologies from the west, under the influence of both the central power in Yinxu and from frontier communities. A mode of horse and chariot use is located east of the Central Plain, represented mainly by the site of Qianzhangda. These sites may have received horse-related objects directly from the Shang state and subsequently may have contributed their own localized designs and motifs. Whether the people who had expertise in managing horses were sent directly from the Central Plain to assist in these regions or whether local people acquired training is an additional question of interest deserving further research.

Symbolic Meanings of Horses and Female Ancestors

Evidence of Yinxu horses reveals information about gender roles during the Late Shang. Even though oracle bone inscriptions record that the elite women in Shang, such as Lady Fu Hao, played a significant role in military affairs (Linduff 2002), they were buried with weapons and royal-style ritual bronzes, jades, pottery vessels, and even horse-related objects, but not with actual horses. For instance, a few pieces of bronze objects associated with horses, including two horse bits and two pieces of horse-shaped jades, were discovered from Yinxu M5, which is believed to be Lady Fu Hao's tomb, but there were no actual horse remains there (CASS IA 1980:110–111, 162). Moreover, as discussed, horses were not offered to female ancestors in rituals of veneration (Liu Y. and Cao 2004). Was this because the Shang elites had not fully accepted a symbolic system integrating horses as part of their core ritual system, as proposed by Chang (2019)? Clearly, the highly respected elite woman Lady Fu Hao, who was regarded as a warrior not unlike her male counterparts, did not receive the same level or kind of veneration as did her male contemporaries. Is this an indication that understanding of horses by the Shang elites comprised a gendered value system that linked horses and horse use with masculinity? If so, were these gendered understandings introduced along with the earliest horses or did they develop later independently within the Shang dynasty value system as a primary association for horses? These questions are also worthwhile for future consideration by scholars.

Conclusions

Horses suddenly appeared at Yinxu as highly valued goods in Yinxu Phase II during the reign of King Wu Ding. Because no comparable level of horse husbandry or similarly large numbers of horses were found anywhere else within China before the Shang period, these horses most likely were brought to the Central Plain via the western route through Xinjiang, or by the northern route through Mongolia and Inner Mongolia, or both. Horses were not only found in ritual contexts often with chariots, they also were likely a part of the daily lives of the kings and some high elites. Horse equipment and horse-related objects are widely distributed across the Yinxu site in prestigious settings. Rather than being acquired because of a simple desire for exotic prestige objects, I argue that the Shang elites sought from the beginning to integrate horses into their value system. The pursuit of success in warfare may have been one of the major reasons why the Shang kings adopted horses into their ritual system. The Shang elites kept experimenting with and improving horse equipment to better meet their needs in the Central Plain, a geographical area that was entirely different from the original habitat of horses on the Eurasian steppe. The earliest introductions may have occurred by way of varied processes, including horses captured in battle, given as tribute, or brought into the capital by those arriving from distant horse-keeping polities, as was possibly the case for Lady Fu Hao, the foreign bride of King Wu Ding.

As an inclusive, diverse and powerful polity, the Shang state accepted this new animal species —the domesticated horse—along with chariots, knowledge, and a range of novel skillsets. This imported "package," along with people having horse expertise, were successfully integrated into the Shang ritual and symbolic systems at the highest levels of esteem, value, and prestige. One question remains intriguing: What roles did people at Yinxu play in the transmission of horses, chariots, and associated objects and technologies afterward? Did Yinxu act as a distribution center for horses and chariots sent to other territories within the realm? Did a unique format of "horse culture" follow along with these gifts of animals and technology from the center? Were expert Yinxu horsekeepers also sent or did local people on the frontiers acquire such skills independently? These and many other salient questions about the Yinxu horse-chariot system still await answers.

Acknowledgments

I am grateful for the inspiring advice and suggestions from William Honeychurch and the anonymous reviewers, and for the great effort that Anne Underhill and Rosemary Volpe made to help me improve this paper.

References

ANTHONY, DAVID W. 2007. *The Horse, the Wheel and Language: How Bronze-age Riders from the Eurasian Steppes Shaped the Modern World*. Princeton: Princeton University Press. 553 pp.

BARBIERI-LOW, ANTHONY J. 2000. *Wheeled Vehicles in the Chinese Bronze Age (c. 2000–741 B.C.)*. Philadelphia: Department of Asian and Middle Eastern Studies, University of Pennsylvania. 98 pp. (Sino-Platonic Papers 99.) Available from https://sino-platonic.org.

BEIJING MUNICIPAL INSTITUTE OF CULTURAL RELICS. 1999. *Zhenjiangying and Tazhao—A typological and geological study of pre-Qin archaeological cultures in the Juma River valley*. Beijing: The Encyclopedia of China Publishing House. 574 pp. [in Chinese.]

CAMPBELL, RODERICK B., ZHIPENG LI, YULING HE, AND JING YUAN. 2011. Consumption, exchange and production at the Great Settlement Shang: Bone-working at Tiesanlu, Anyang. *Antiquity* 85(330):1279–1297. https://doi.org/10.1017/S0003598X00062050

CAO, DAZHI. 2018. Implications of "clan insignia" and the state structure of the Shang dynasty. *Gudai Wenming* 12:71–122. [in Chinese.]

[CASS ANYANG TEAM] CHINESE ACADEMY OF SOCIAL SCIENCES, ANYANG TEAM. 1975. Brief report of the excavation in the south locality of Xiaotun in 1973, Anyang. *Kaogu* 1:27–46. [in Chinese.]

—1987. Excavation of the Shang sacrificial pits in the north locality of Wuguancun, Anyang. *Kaogu* 12:1062–1145. [in Chinese.]

—2015. The Tiesanlu bone tool workshop site of the Yinxu cultural period, Anyang, Henan. *Kaogu* 8:38–62. [in Chinese.]

[CASS ^{14}C LABORATORY] ^{14}C LABORATORY OF THE CENTER FOR SCIENTIFIC ARCHAEOLOGY, INSTITUTE OF ARCHAEOLOGY, CHINESE ACADEMY OF SOCIAL SCIENCES. 2020. Radiocarbon date report (46). *Kaogu* 7:117–120. [in Chinese.]

[CASS IA] CHINESE ACADEMY OF SOCIAL SCIENCES, INSTITUTE OF ARCHAEOLOGY, ED. 1965. *Oracle Bone Inscription Corpus*. Beijing: Zhonghua Book Company. 976 pp. [in Chinese.]

—, ed. 1980. *Tomb of Lady Fu Hao at Yinxu in Anyang*. Beijing: Wenwu Press. 241 pp. [in Chinese.]

—, ed. 2003. *Chinese Archaeology: Xia and Shang volume*. Beijing: Zhongguo Shehuikexue Press. 730 pp. [in Chinese.]

[CASS IHS] CHINESE ACADEMY OF SOCIAL SCIENCES, INSTITUTE OF HISTORY STUDIES. 1981. Compilation of oracle bone inscriptions. *Zhonghua Shuju* 9(29415):3603. [in Chinese.]

CHANG, HUAIYIN. 2019. A supplementary discussion of Yinxu chariots. *Jianghan Kaogu* 5:59–70. [in Chinese.]

CHEN, ENZHI. 1987. Origins of horse physiognomy and the ancient cultures of raising horses. *Nongye Kaogu* 2:339–347. [in Chinese.]

CHEN, JIANXING. 2012. "Investigation of the Genetic Diversity, Phylogeny and Origins of Chinese Mongolian Horses" [dissertation]. Inner Mongolia Agricultural University. 68 pp. [in Chinese.]

CHEN, XIANG. 2021. "Animals and the Power Order of the Late Shang Dynasty" [dissertation]. Shandong University. 272 pp. [in Chinese.]

CHEN, XINGCAN. 2002. Discussion on the origin of domestic horses and other issues. In: Cultural Relics Press, ed. *Compilation of Essays by Chen Xingcan*. Beijing: Cultural Relics Press. First published in 1999. pp. 51–56. [in Chinese.]

CHEN, ZHIDA. 1994. Natural remains. In: Chinese Academy of Social Sciences, ed. *The Discoveries and Research of Yinxu*. Beijing: Kexue Press. pp. 415–418. [in Chinese.]

CURRY, ANDREW. 2023. Horse nations: After the Spanish conquest, horses transformed Native American tribes much earlier than historians thought. *Science* 379(6639):1288–1293. https://doi.org/10.1126/science.adh9893

DU, BORUI AND YULING HE. 2024. "A Large Sacrificial Site Discovered in the Southeast Corner of Huanbei Shang City." *Wenbo Zhongguo* [online public forum], edited by Xiaozhu Zhang, January 11, 2024. [in Chinese.]

FANG, XISHENG, DEXUAN SUN, AND LIANSHENG ZHAO. 1980. The Longshan cultural site of Baiying, Tangyin, Henan. *Kaogu* 3:193–202, 289. [in Chinese.]

FISKESJÖ, MAGNUS. 2001. Rising from blood-stained fields: Royal hunting and state formation in Shang China. *Bulletin of the Museum of Far Eastern Antiquities* 73:49–191.

FU, SINIAN. 1934. *The Black Pottery Cultural Site in Longshan Town, Licheng County, Shandong*]. Nanjing: Institute of History and Philosophy, Academia Sinica. 105 pp. [in Chinese.]

GU, FEI. 2006. Research on the chariot burials at the Qianzhangda site, Tengzhou, Shandong Province. *Sandai Kaogu* 2:483–503. [in Chinese.]

GUO, WU. 2004. *Affairs of the State: Chariots and War Horses in Ancient China*. Chengdu, China: Sichuan People's Publishing House. 190 pp. [in Chinese.]

HE, YULING. 2020. Research on the exogenous culture at Yinxu. *Zhongyuan Wenwu* 2:33–49. [in Chinese.]

HE, YULING, AND HONGBIN YUE. 2011. A review of ten-year on Huanbei City site at Anyang. *Journal of National Museum of China* 12:6–19. [in Chinese.]

HONEYCHURCH, WILLIAM. 2015. *Inner Asia and the Spatial Politics of Empire: Archaeology, Mobility, and Culture Contact*. New York: Springer. 321 pp.

JIA, PETER WEIMING, ALISON BETTS, PAULA N. DOUMANI DYPUY, DEXIN CONG, AND XIAOBING JIA. 2018. Bronze age hill forts: New evidence for defensive sites in the western Tianshan, China. *Archaeological Research in Asia* 15:70–81. https://doi.org/10.1016/j.ara.2017.10.005

JIA, XIAOBING, XIAOBING JIA, GELI NI, ZHAOLIN LIU, YAHUI HE, WEI GAO, AND CHAOCHAO QIN. 2016. Large scale complex of early Bronze Age settlement sites discovered at Wenquan, Xinjiang. *Zhongguo Wenwubao*, December 2, 2016, page 8. [in Chinese.]

KIKUCHI, HIROKI. 2019. Reevaluation of the ancient domesticated horses in China. *Nanfang Wenwu* 1:136–150. [in Chinese.]

LI, BOQIAN. 2006. The scope and policies of the Shang dynasty from the geographical distribution of the clans represented by the bronze emblems in Yinxu. *Kaoguxue Yanjiu* 6:119–153. [in Chinese.]

LI, YULIN, AND XIAOYAN SUN. 2013. Symphony of nature and life: Mongolian horse culture. *Education about Asia* 18(3):17–23. https://www.asianstudies.org/publications/eaa/archives/symphony-of-nature-and-life-mongolian-horse-culture/

LI, YUN, AND XIAOFEI WANG. 2023. National Cultural Heritage Administration reports on progress of "Archaeology of China" major projects—Four new archaeological discoveries reveal the societies in the north during the Shang dynasty. *Guangming Ribao,* May 31, 2013, page 9. [in Chinese.]

LI, ZHIPENG. 2018. 90 years of Yinxu zooarchaeology. *Zhongyuan Wenwu* 5:90–100. [in Chinese.]

LIN, YUN. 1998. A few issues on the bronze bow-shaped objects. In: Encyclopedia of China Publishing House, ed. *Scholastic Collections of Lin Yun*. Beijing: Encyclopedia of China Publishing House. First published in 1980. pp. 251–261. [in Chinese.]

LINDUFF, KATHERYN M. 1997. An archaeological overview. In: Emma C. Bunker, ed. *Ancient Bronzes of the Eastern Eurasian Steppes from the Arthur M. Sackler Collections*. New York: Arthur M. Sackler Foundation, distributed by Harry N. Abrams. pp. 18–98.

——2002. Women's lives memorialized in burial in ancient China at Anyang. In: Sarah Milledge Nelson and Myriam Rosen-Ayalon, eds. *In Pursuit of Gender: Worldwide Archaeological Approaches*. Walnut Creek, CA: Altamira Press. pp. 257–287.

—2003. A walk on the wild side: Late Shang appropriation of horses in China. In: Marsha Levine, Colin Renfrew, and Katherine V. Boyle, eds. *Prehistoric Steppe Adaptation and the Horse*. Cambridge: McDonald Institute for Archaeological Research. pp. 139–162. (McDonald Institute Monographs.)

LIU, LI, AND XINGCAN CHEN. 2012. *The Archaeology of China: From the Late Paleolithic to the Early Bronze Age*. Cambridge: Cambridge University Press. 498 pp.

LIU, YIMAN, AND DINGYUN CAO. 2004. The horses of Huadong H3's oracle bone inscriptions of the site the Yin dynasty. *Yindu Xuekan* 1:6–13. [in Chinese.]

LIU, YUNDONG. 2010. Discoveries and research on horse-chariot pits. *Wenwu Shijie* 1:16–19, 31. [in Chinese.]

LV, ZHIRONG. 2002. The Zhukaigou culture and relevant issues. *Huaxia Kaogu* 1:33–42. [in Chinese.]

MA, MINGZHI. 2009. Preliminary research on the Xicha culture. *Kaogu yu Wenwu* 5:38–45. [in Chinese.]

MENG, GUTUOLI. 2005. Calvary stimulated the horse raising industry—Analyses of horse sources for calvary. *Beifang Wenwu* 3:84–95. [in Chinese.]

MENG, XIANWU, GUICHANG LI, AND YANG LI. 2017. Chariots and horses in the Yinxu cemetery. *Sandai Kaogu* 7:403–418. [in Chinese.]

QIAOBEI ARCHAEOLOGICAL TEAM. 2006. The Shang and Zhou cemeteries in Qiaobei, Fushan, Shanxi Province. *Gudai Wenming* 5:347–394. [in Chinese.]

SHELACH, GIDEON. 2009. *Prehistoric Societies on the Northern Frontiers of China: Archaeological Perspectives on Identity Foundation and Economic Change during the First Millennium BCE*. London: Equinox. 222 pp.

SHELACH-LAVI, GIDEON, YITZCHAK JAFFE, AND GUY BAR-OZ. 2021. Cavalry and the Great Walls of China and Mongolia. *Proceedings of the National Academy of Sciences of the United States of America (PNAS)* 118(16):e2024835118. https://doi.org/10.1073/pnas.2024835118

SHI, ZHANGRU. 1972. Xiaotun Yinxu site in Anyang, Henan. No.1: The excavation of the site: Volume Bing-Yinxu cemetery no. 2: central group. Taipei: Institute of History and Philology, Academia Sinica. 352 pp. [in Chinese.]

SUN, JI. 2001. Bow-shaped objects from the Shang and Zhou periods. In: Ji Sun. *Chariots and Clothing of Ancient China*. Beijing: Cultural Relics Press. pp. 71–81. [in Chinese.]

TAKAHAMA, SHU. 2020. Two technical tradition of casting horse bits in China and their relationships with the steppe area. *Asian Archaeology* 3:47–57. https://doi.org/10.1007/s41826-019-00027-w

TAYLOR, WILLIAM T. T., JINPING CAO, WENQUAN FAN, XIAOLIN MA, YANFENG HOU, JUAN WANG, YUE LI, CHENGRUI ZHANG, HELENA MITON, IGOR CHECHUSHKOV, ET AL. 2021. Understanding early horse transport in eastern Eurasia through analysis of equine dentition. *Antiquity* 95(384):1478–1494. https://doi.org/10.15184/aqy.2021.146

TENG, MINGYU. 2011. Patterns of the bow-shaped objects and related issues. *Kaogu* 8:73–80. [in Chinese.]

TIAN, WEI. 2021. The confrontation between eastern and western regions in the Late Shang Dynasty. *Journal of National Museum of China* 2:18–32. [in Chinese.]

TIE, YUANSHEN. 2015. Research on the origins of domestic horses in northern China—focus on the Gansu and Qinghai region. *Nongye Kaogu* 1:241–248. [in Chinese.]

WANG, GEGE, AND JIE DONG. 2020. Knowledge of horse, domestic horse and horse in early China. *Qianyan* 6:118–124. [in Chinese.]

—2021. Hippology in Shang and Zhou dynasties. *Nongye Kaogu* 1:180–186. [in Chinese.]

WANG, GUIMIN. 1986. The Shang official systems and its characteristics in history. *Lishi Yanjiu* 4:107–119. [in Chinese.]

WANG, PENG. 2018. Interaction of Bronze and early Iron Age cultures in southern Siberia, Xinjiang, and northern China. Vestnik. NSU. History and Philology Series. *Oriental Studies* 17(4):16–29. https://doi.org/10.25205/1818-7919-2018-17-4-16-29 [in Russian.]

—2021. Usage and name of the bow-shaped objects. *Nanfang Wenwu* 5:98–105. [in Chinese.]

WANG, WEI. 1998. Studies on the origin of Shang chariots. In: Chinese Academy of Social Sciences, ed. *Compilation of Research Papers from the International Conference on Shang Culture*. Beijing: Encyclopedia of China Publishing House. pp. 380–388. [in Chinese.]

WANG, YONGQIANG, XIAO YUAN, AND QIURONG RUAN. 2019. Archaeological finds from the 2015–2018 excavation at the Jiurentaigoukou site and preliminary research in Nilike County, Xinjiang. *Xiyu Yanjiu* 1:133–138. [in Chinese.]

WANG, YUXIN. 1999. Discussion of horses, arrow-shooting in oracle bone inscriptions, and argument of horses, arrow-shooting and chariot assemblages. *Chutu Wenxian Yanjiu* 1:59–72. [in Chinese.]

WEI, JIAN, AND BAO FENG. 2020. On Zhukaigou culture. *Kaogu Xuebao* 4:461–484. [in Chinese.]

WU, XIAOYUN. 2002. Research on the typology of the bronze chariots in the Central Plain from the Shang to the Spring–Autumn period. *Gudai Wenming* 1:180–277. [in Chinese.]

—2011. The role of the transmission of chariots in early east-west interaction: 2,000–1,200 BCE. *Gugong Xueshu Jikan* 28(4):95–129. [in Chinese.]

XIA-SHANG-ZHOU CHRONOLOGY PROJECT TEAM. 2000. *The Xia-Shang-Zhou Chronology Project Report of the Results during 1996–2000 (brief version)*. Beijing: World Publishing Corporation. 118 pp. [in Chinese.]

—2022. *The Xia-Shang-Zhou Chronology Project Final Report*. Beijing: Science Press. 544 pp.

XIE, CHENGXIA. 1959. *The History of Horse Husbandry in China*. Beijing: Science Press. 284 pp. [in Chinese.]

YANG, BAOCHENG. 1984. The discovery and reconstruction of the chariots during the Yin dynasty. *Kaogu* 6:546–555. [in Chinese.]

YANG, HONG. 2008. Horses and military forces of ancient China. In: Hong Yang, Kan Hang, and Yan Zheng, eds. *The History of Horses in China*. Hong Kong: Shangwu Yinshuguan. pp. 6–24. [in Chinese.]

YUAN, JING. 2003. Research on the domesticated horse in ancient China. In: Shaanxi Cultural Relics Bureau, Shaanxi Provincial Institute of Archaeology, and Xi'an Banpo Museum, eds. *Research on Chinese Prehistoric Archaeology in China. Conference Proceedings for Congratulations to Mr. Shi Xingbang on the Half Century of Archaeological Work and His Eightieth Birthday*. Xi'an, China: Sanqin Press. pp. 436–443. [in Chinese.]

YUAN, JING, AND ROWAN FLAD. 2005a. New zooarchaeological evidence for changes in Shang Dynasty animal sacrifice. *Journal of Anthropological Archaeology* 24:252–270. https://doi.org/10.1016/j.jaa.2005.03.001

—2005b. Research on early horse domestication in China. In: Marjan Mashkour, ed. *Equids in Time and Space*. Oxford: Oxbow. pp. 124–131.

ZHAO, CHUNYAN, ZHIPENG LI, AND JING YUAN. 2015. Analyses and comparisons of the horse and pig teeth stable strontium ratios at the Yinxu site, Anyang, Henan Province. *Nanfang Wenwu* 3:77–80. [in Chinese.]

ZHAO, HUI. 2012. "The Analysis on Shang Dynasty Relics in Middle-Shanxi Province" [master's thesis]. Shandong University, School of History and Culture, Jinan, China. 65 pp. [in Chinese.]

ZHU, FENGHAN. 2013. The relationship between the Shang people and the ethnic groups in the northern frontier zone reflected by the northern style bronzes unearthed in Yinxu. *Kaogu Xuebao* 1:1–28. [in Chinese.]

CHAPTER SIX

Iron Age Sheep Management at Delgerkhaan Uul:
A Tale of Two Graves

Sarah PLEUGER-DREIBRODT,
Mandakh DAVAASUREN, and Sarah PEDERZANI

The Iron Age of Mongolia is widely regarded as a transformative period that resulted in the formation of the widespread and powerful nomadic Xiongnu state (Honeychurch 2014; Miller 2024). The unique Xiongnu confederacy has attracted the attention of researchers for decades. A lot of this attention has been focused on big picture questions which, given the widespread impact of the Xiongnu, is understandable. The highly mobile domestic livestock husbandry practiced intensively during this period facilitated extensive long-range relationships between people, nonhuman animals, and the steppe landscape itself, which in turn can all be regarded as functional parts of Xiongnu pastoral statehood (Wright, Honeychurch, and Amartuvshin 2009; Brosseder and Miller 2011; Honeychurch 2014). Local practices likely focused on communal needs, hence reflecting day-to-day subsistence as part of a larger conglomerate (Honeychurch and Amartuvshin 2006, 2007; Makarewicz 2011). With this study we provide some bioarchaeological insights from burial contexts located in Delgerkhaan Uul, Sükhbaatar Province. We aim to fill some of the remaining knowledge gaps by focusing on specific local variabilities in the archaeological manifestations of communal actions during the reign of the Xiongnu. In this context we compare two exemplary zooarchaeological funerary assemblages from a Late Bronze Age/Early Iron Age (around 1000–400 BCE) slab burial and an Iron Age Xiongnu (here around 250 BCE–200 CE) ring burial. The zooarchaeological and stable isotopic pilot data presented here are intended to provide a glimpse into local social relationships of human and nonhuman animals in Iron Age multispecies communities and within the larger context of known sociopolitical changes during this period. The spot-check comparison that was derived from stable isotopic oxygen and carbon analysis on tooth enamel sequences of two exemplary sheep groups of similar ages deposited in slab burials and Xiongnu burials showed little difference in husbandry practices. In turn, a difference in the in situ arrangement, as well as the assemblage demography (age group composition), was clearly observable.

Archaeological Background

The eastern Mongolian Gobi Desert steppe landscape (Figure 6.1) has been co-shaped by the presence of impressive stone-built monuments for roughly 3,500 years, some of which

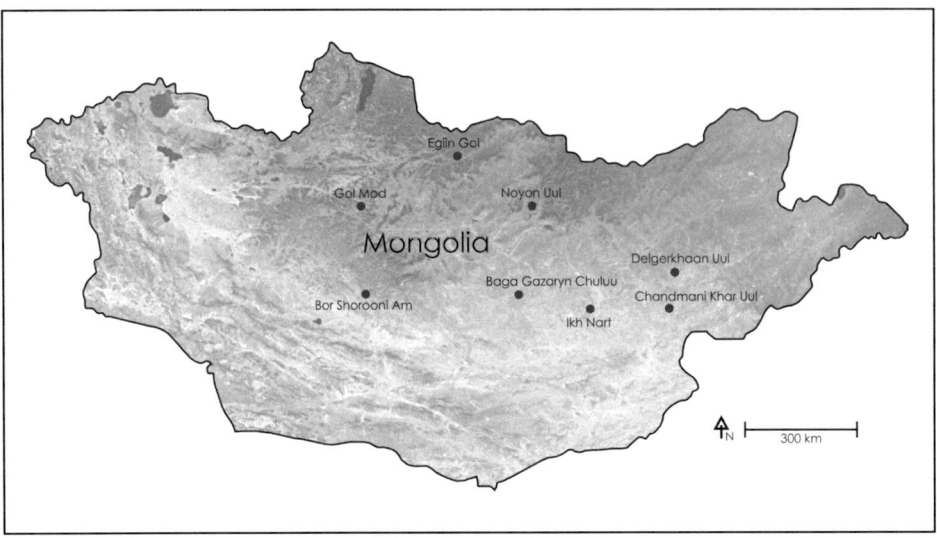

FIGURE 6.1. Map of Mongolia showing sites mentioned in the text. Base topography map Google Earth Pro, Version 7.3.6.9345 (2022), Mongolia, 46°57′51.09″N, 102°44′35.14″E. Data from SIO, NOAA, US Navy, NGA, GEBCO. Image Landsat/Copernicus, created December 2022.

still overlook the steppe surface today. Slab burials were constructed in a phase tentatively referred to as the Late Bronze Age/Early Iron Age between 1000 and 400 BCE, usually using large flat upright stone slabs fencing a central human burial underneath a layer of rocks (Honeychurch and Amartuvshin 2011; Burentogtokh, Honeychurch, and Gardner 2019). Such landmarks, which are within a reasonable distance to resources for building material, can be seen as places for expressions of "naturecultural" belief systems, as well as being practical signals of regional demarcation or orientation. Naturecultural belief systems here refers to a collection of spiritual and ritualistic traditions, such as the veneration of higher entities connected to the natural surrounding or the placement of sacred mounds and monuments into parts of the landscape holding special meaning (see, e.g., Davaa-Ochir 2008; Fijn 2011; Dal Zovo 2021).

Slab burials are often associated with a higher level of social differentiation and long-distance networking compared with, and gradually replacing, older traditions (Honeychurch 2014; Burentogtokh, Honeychurch, and Gardner 2019; Wright 2021). These monuments, of large stone slabs, are visible from a great distance, often crowning high above the landscape and containing comparatively large quantities of domestic livestock remains deposited alongside human interments. The regular incorporation of domesticated fauna into ritual practices in the form of comparatively standardized depositions presupposes an already long-established tradition of livestock management and circulation. The Iron Age in Mongolia brought a supraregional sociopolitical consolidation of mobile pastoralist lifeways that had been practiced for more than a millenium (Honeychurch, Wright, and Amartuvshin 2009; Shelach 2009).

During the last centuries of the first millennium BCE, the eastern Eurasian steppes saw the rise across Inner Asia of a new political and economic power, which is commonly regarded as the first Eurasian pastoral nomadic state—the Xiongnu. The economic foundation of this vast political network was built around pastoralism, which in turn likely influenced its extent, relations with neighboring realms, population mobility, and social hierarchies until around 200 CE (Rogers 2012; Honeychurch 2014; Brosseder 2016). Alongside the intensive herding of domesticated livestock, Xiongnu subsistence was quite diverse and regionally incorporated complementary crop cultivation and possibly hunting (Honeychurch and Amartuvshin 2007; Wright, Honeychurch, and Amartuvshin 2009; Ventresca Miller and Makarewicz 2019; Wilkin et al. 2020). The Xiongnu state largely sustained itself, but trade with adjacent regions, for example with the Han dynasty and Central Asia, was still an important part of the wider economy (Kradin 2011; Machicek 2012; Brosseder 2015). In some regions animal management strategies (e.g., foddering) and land-use practices (pasturing and penning) were comparatively intense during this period, as demonstrated through stable isotope analysis of livestock individuals from Baga Gazaryn Chuluu and Egiin Gol (Makarewicz and Tuross 2006; Makarewicz 2014, 2017; Cameron 2016). We do not know whether these practices were actually first picked up during this time or practiced prior to the formation of the Xiongnu state. While a more widespread and organized statehood likely contributed to the consolidation of pastoral social structures and the intensification of subsistence strategies, the specific practices concerning day-to-day subsistence and animal management were regionally variable.

Xiongnu mortuary contexts are usually divided by two comparatively standardized types, both demonstrating the high positions of interred individuals within a defined hierarchical sociopolitical structure. Large terrace tombs mark burials of the Xiongnu elite, mostly concentrated in Central Mongolia; for example, Noyon Uul (Polosmak et al. 2008; Miniaev and Elikhina 2009; Brosseder 2015) and Gol Mod I/II (Allard et al. 2002; Miller et al. 2006; Erdenebaatar 2012; Yeruul-Erdene 2014). More common, but nonetheless prestigous, are comparatively standardized Xiongnu ring graves, which can be found in concentrations in eastern Mongolia, such as at Chandmani Khar Uul (Amartuvshin et al. 2015) and Delgerkhaan Uul, located outside of the distribution areas of previously erected slab burials, a common phenomenon at multiperiod sites.

Faunal Depositions in Slab Burials and Xiongnu Ring Burials

Faunal depositions are an important and omnipresent part of funerary material culture in slab burials next to items related to horse riding, weaponry, and decorative artifacts (Volkov 1995; Johannesson 2011). It appears that depositional schemes are comparatively variable, including single horse heads, sets of multiple bovid skulls, or scapulae of domestic livestock placed in direct association with human interments (Erdenebaatar 1992; Törbat, Amartuvshin, and Erdenebat 2003; Gantulga et al. 2009; Enkhtör, Bemmann, and Brosseder 2018; Bayarsaikhan et al. 2019; see also "Excavations at Daram and Tevsh sites: A report on joint Mongolian-Japanese excavations in outer Mongolia," by Miyamoto et al., unpublished report, Faculty of Humanities, Department of Archaeology, Kyushu University, 2016). Scapulae are often carefully placed onto the interred individual and skulls are sometimes arranged in rows or by age groups (Enkhtör, Bemmann, and Brosseder 2018; Bayarsaikhan et al. 2019). The slab burial SG-2 at Bor Shorooni Am (800–550 cal BCE), for example, featured forty-one crania of sheep, goats, and horses arranged in several distinct rows. While no large stone slabs were used to construct the burial, it was ascribed to the slab burial culture because of its architecture, dating, and grave goods. Human remains were scattered within the context due to a disturbance interpreted as looting, but the faunal remains were found in situ (Bayarsaikhan et al. 2019; Lowry 2020). In eastern Mongolia the majority of known slab burials were disturbed through post hoc depositions dating to the Xiongnu and medieval periods or by later disruptions (Pleuger-Dreibrodt et al., in prep.), which makes a direct comparative quantification between animal depositions in mortuary contexts built in different time periods very difficult.

Depositions of osteological livestock remains in Xiongnu burials are usually comparatively rich in terms of quantities and demonstrate the deep sociocultural relationship between herders and herded (Makarewicz 2011; H. Martin 2011; Mandakh 2015; Miller 2023). Moreover, they regularly feature the same pattern of deposited skulls and extremities of horses, cattle, sheep, and goats in different Xiongnu burial types (Brosseder 2009; H. Martin 2011). These "heads and hooves" sets are often placed into special niches or on plateaus in the grave and have been interpreted as remains of feasting (Miller et al. 2008). Other researchers have pointed out that, from the zooarchaeological assemblages alone, it is equally possible that remains were collected and transported for the specific purpose of being deposited as grave goods (Johannesson 2015). In either case depositions certainly reflect the high social and economic status domestic livestock had within the Xiongnu society.

Delgerkhaan Uul

The greater region of Delgerkhaan Uul, Sükhbbatar Province, is located in the semiarid Gobi steppe desert of eastern Mongolia. In an area mostly south of the Delgerkhaan mountain, the Dornod Mongol Survey (DMS) team discovered and mapped thousands of archaeological features, including burial monuments from the Bronze Age to the Mongol period. Both slab burials and Xiongnu ring burials were found frequently in the region. An abundance of both landmark monuments and artifact scatters indicating habitation sites suggests that Delgerkhaan Uul was inhabited for thousands of years by pastoralist communities. Like other multiperiod sites, such as Baga Gazaryn Chuluu or Ikh Nart, Delgerkhaan Uul posed a sort of oasis in the wider area with favorable conditions for seasonal habitation activities, livestock husbandry, metal production, and the exploitation of an array of resources, including for the erection of monuments (also see Janz et al. 2015). For connecting Delgerkhaan Uul into a wider social network during the Early Iron Age and later as part of the Xiongnu state, horse riding (facilitating the long-distance transfer of information, goods, herd animals, and people) was certainly important, if not absolutely essential (Amartuvshin and Honeychurch 2010; Taylor et al. 2017; Wright et al. 2019).

Stable Isotope Ecology Background

The measurement of stable carbon and oxygen isotope ratios of incremental enamel samples taken along the crown of herbivore teeth can be used to capture seasonal records of climatic, environmental, and dietary changes that drive the isotopic systematics of these elements in the bio- and hydrosphere. Stable oxygen isotope delta values ($\delta^{18}O$) measured from enamel bioapatite reflect underlying isotopic variation in the respective animal's body water, which in turn is mostly driven by oxygen stable isotope variability of water ingested through drinking or food (Bryant and Froelich 1995; Pederzani and Britton 2019). The relative importance of oxygen inputs in shaping body water $\delta^{18}O$ depends on their respective amount contribution, with $\delta^{18}O$ of body water being strongly driven by drinking water in obligate drinkers. In herbivores that derive a larger proportion of water from plants, either from pronounced reliance on browse or from drought adaptation, $\delta^{18}O$ of body water is more strongly shaped by the consumption of leaf water. In mid to high latitudes, $\delta^{18}O$ of sequentially sampled herbivore tooth enamel shows higher values in summer and lower values in winter, as $\delta^{18}O$ of most available water sources such as precipitation, rain-fed water bodies, and leaf water are predominantly driven by changes in temperature and aridity (Pederzani and Britton 2019).

Stable carbon isotope delta values ($\delta^{13}C$) of herbivore enamel bioapatite reflect the proportions of isotopically distinct plant types in each animal's dietary intake. Specifically, plants following either the C3 or C4 photosynthetic pathway have different and nonoverlapping isotopic delta value ranges. Plant $\delta^{13}C$ values are additionally influenced by climatic environmental factors, such as temperature, aridity, salinity, and altitude, particularly in C3 plants (Körner, Farquhar, and Wong 1991; Tieszen 1991; Wittmer et al. 2008). Generally, C3 plants have $\delta^{13}C$ values ranging between approximately –35‰ and –22‰, while C4 plants have $\delta^{13}C$ values ranging between approximately –13‰ and –10‰ (van der Merwe 1982; Farquhar et al. 1989; Tieszen 1991). The ratio of C3 and C4 plants in an environment where both groups are present fluctuates based on seasonally changing factors, such as water availability and temperature, as C4 plants are more well adapted to higher temperatures and low water availability (Pearcy, Tumosa, and Kimberlyn 1981; Winslow, Hunt, and Piper 2003; Murphy and Bowman 2007).

Seasonally resolved isotopic records can be obtained from the high crowned teeth of terrestrial herbivores because their dental tissues form incrementally and dental enamel does not remodel after the initial growth period. Sampling horizontal bands along the teeth's growth axis therefore provides a time series (here of $\delta^{13}C$ and $\delta^{18}O$ measurements) reflecting the time period of tooth formation within an individual's lifespan (Fricke et al. 1998; Balasse 2002; Passey and Cerling 2002). For caprine M/2s this time span roughly captures the first year of life in terms of isotopic input (Milhaud and Nezit 1991; Balasse 2002; Hillson 2005). The method is not accurately sampling from biologically grown increments, thus single samples each do not represent actual points in time for isotopic intake. Instead, they can be regarded as artificial units representing relative, and partially homogenized, isotopic input signals within a known time frame (Balasse et al. 2003; Zazzo et al. 2005; Pederzani and Britton 2019).

Domesticated animals do not necessarily isotopically reflect the local plant baseline in a one-to-one relationship, as their diet may be shaped by herding practices. For example, herders of herbivorous livestock can counterbalance climatic or environmental aspects or changes by limiting access to certain pastures, by undergoing vertical transhumance, or by foddering livestock with vegetational material not naturally occurring in the environment at the time and place of ingestion (Makarewicz 2014; Hermes, Pederzani, and Makarewicz 2017; Makarewicz and Pederzani 2017). Isotopically some of these anthropogenic impacts can be detected by evaluating the relationship of carbon and oxygen stable isotope values on a seasonal basis (Balasse et al. 2009; Makarewicz and Pederzani 2017). In the Mongolian Gobi steppe desert both C3 and C4 plants are naturally present, but C4 plants are more abundant during the summer and almost completely absent in the winter. If livestock herders collect summer vegetation to provision their herds during the winter, $\delta^{13}C$ values of livestock tooth enamel will show a rise that is characteristic of C4 plant consumption during the winter months (as demarcated by low $\delta^{18}O$ values; Makarewicz and Pederzani 2017). Similarly, a provision with cultivated C4 plants, such as millet, will be reflected in higher $\delta^{13}C$ values as well (Hermes et al. 2019, 2022; Ventresca Miller et al. 2020).

Faunal Depositions and Stable Isotope Analysis

The faunal assemblages analyzed for this pilot study were recovered from two contexts, a slab burial and a Xiongnu ring burial, both located at different locales around Delgerkhaan Uul. They were discovered and recorded during extensive foot survey as part of the Dornod Mongol Survey Project and excavated in the 2018 expedition season. The slab burial DMS 1396A was dated to 916–816 cal BCE (95.4%) based on a sheep individual (2720 ± 20 BP, UGAMS 38777, Ind.18_07_013) used in this study and an additional cattle specimen dating to 916–826 cal BCE (95.4%) (2734 ± 18 BP, OxA 41517). The Xiongnu ring burial (DMS 777A) was dated to 51 cal BCE–61 cal CE (95.4%) based on a sheep specimen (2020 ± 20 BP, UGAMS 38773) (Pleuger-Dreibrodt et al., in prep.). Both of them yielded considerable quantities of faunal remains in clearly different arrangements.

The rectangular slab burial (DMS 1396A; Figure 6.2) measured about 6.3 by 5.8 m and was oriented toward the northeast. It contained both human interments, which were clearly disturbed, and a deposition of livestock, which was largely intact. These remains were mostly arranged in the southeastern corner of the burial. It is important to note that the burial was disrupted at some point. Because of this only a few bones from the human interment were preserved in the grave. It is possible that some of the original depositions of faunal remains were cleared out along with other grave goods close to the person interred. A partial cattle skull and equine tooth remains were found where the original funerary deposit was likely located. The elaborate sheep skull arrangement that is the basis for this study was found in situ and dated to the time of original usage of the monument.

The Xiongnu ring burial (DMS 777A; Figure 6.3) had a diameter of 8.5 m and contained a human skeleton as well as a rich assemblage of osteological livestock remains. All zooarchaeological remains were identified and recorded in the field by Pleuger-Dreibrodt and Mandakh. Age determinations were made via mandibular tooth wear analysis using ageing schemes for sheep and goats (Payne 1973) and for cattle (Grant 1982; Legge 1992). Age determinations on horse incisors were made according to Mongolian Indigenous knowledge and checked against American Association of Equine Practitioners guidelines (M. Martin 2002).

At habitation sites zooarchaeological findings are regularly analyzed demographically to infer subsistence modes through herd compositions. Payne (1973) and Vigne and Helmer (2007) have provided schemes to analyze the presence or absence and frequency of caprines of different age groups and sexes to narrow down the main mode(s) of production in a self-contained livestock management system. A high representation of age groups 6 to 24 months old, for example, resembles a subsistence focus on (tender) meat exploitation, while a high representation of age group 2 to 4 years represents a subsistence focus on dairy production. Zooarchaeological assemblages from burials do not directly reflect the actual demographic composition of a real-life herd. Instead, they reflect choices made and traditions carried on by the participants of funerary rites. Livestock individuals deposited in the case study graves underwent one or more selective processes. Those which were incorporated in feastings or offerings were selected and slaughtered for that purpose, after which it was decided to bury their remains alongside the deceased. Other individuals might have died of natural causes (e.g., neonates) and their remains kept for the purpose of depositing them. Some individuals might have been slaughtered or died previously independently from the funeral

FIGURE 6.2. Slab burial DMS 1396A in Delgerkhaan Uul. Drone photograph courtesy of the Dornod Mongol Survey Project. Photo credit: Batdalai Byambatseren, 2018.

FIGURE 6.3. Xiongnu ring burial DMS 777A in Delgerkhaan Uul. Drone photograph courtesy of the Dornod Mongol Survey Project. Photo credit: Batdalai Byambatseren, 2018.

and their remains kept and afterward deposited. In any case, the zooarchaeological remains recovered do reflect these decisions. We can use zooarchaeological methods normally applied to subsistence-related demographic questions on these assemblages to better understand selective processes that might have resulted in the selection at hand.

Sampling of teeth for stable isotope analysis was done in the field. A number of ten *Ovis* sp. second molars from the two selected radiocarbon-dated and in situ mortuary contexts were sampled for this study. Individuals were selected from two different age groups, 1 to 2 yea old ($n = 5$) and 2 to 3 years old ($n = 5$) respectively. All teeth had a total crown height higher than 34 mm with sampled lophs higher than 30 mm. Each sampled loph had a complete buccal portion and no cracks were visible before sampling. Increments were drilled every 3 mm along the tooth loph. The first increment was placed as close to the occlusal surface as possible, while the last was placed close to the enamel root junction. In the case of the individuals at age 1 to 2 years, the enamel root junction is not a clearly visible delineation as the teeth are still in formation. The lowest increment was placed as close to the zone of mineralization as possible, making sure the enamel layer was thick enough to obtain a full sample. While smaller distances between incremental samples would be optimal, particularly for smaller caprine teeth, sampling distances of 3 to 5 mm are commonly used in stable isotope archaeology to balance temporal resolution of isotopic time series with the time and cost constraints of processing large numbers of samples. Our sampling strategy was accordingly chosen as an appropriate compromise for the scope of a pilot study. Tooth enamel samples were taken using a diamond-coated cylindrical drill bit in a stationary Dremel rotary tool. Sampling and pretreatment were done following the protocol published by Ventresca Miller (2018).

The carbon and oxygen isotopic composition of the carbonate fraction of tooth enamel powders was determined by dual-inlet isotope ratio mass spectrometry at the Leibniz Laboratory for Radiometric Dating and Stable Isotope Research, Christian-Albrechts-University, Kiel, Germany, using a Kiel IV carbonate device coupled to a MAT 253 isotope ratio mass spectrometer (Thermo Fisher Scientific, Bremen, Germany; www.thermofisher.com). For each sample, within a range of 0.4 to 1.5 mg of tooth enamel powder was digested with 100% phosphoric acid (H_3PO_4) under vacuum at 75 °C for 4 minutes to release carbon dioxide (CO_2) gas. CO_2 gas was purified in the Kiel IV device using automated cryogenic distillation before transfer to the dual-inlet system of the MAT 253. Scale normalization to the VPDB (Vienna Pee Dee Belemnite) scale was achieved using two-point scale normalization with international reference standards NBS-19 (limestone, $\delta^{13}C = 1.95‰$, $\delta^{18}O = -2.20‰$) and IAEA-603 (calcite, $\delta^{13}C = 2.46 ± 0.01‰$, $\delta^{18}O = -2.37 ± 0.04‰$). Scale normalization was checked using two in-house enamel standards, CM1_E and ER1_D, which gave $\delta^{13}C$ values of $-14.5 ± 0.1‰$ ($N = 23$) and $-12.18 ± 0.06‰$ ($N = 27$), and $\delta^{18}O$ values of $-7.0 ± 0.1‰$ and $-7.8 ± 0.1‰$ ($N = 27$), respectively. Reproducibility was also checked using replicate measurements of samples. A total of sixteen samples were run in duplicate and gave an average standard deviation between replicates of 0.05‰ for $\delta^{13}C$ and 0.13‰ for $\delta^{18}O$. Together with the replicates of the in-house standards this suggests that analytical reproducibility is 0.1‰ or better for both $\delta^{13}C$ and $\delta^{18}O$.

Statistical tests were performed with R, Version 4.1.0 (R Core Team 2022), and PAST, Version 4.10 (Hammer, Harper, and Ryan 2001). For visualizations of the time series plots of $\delta^{13}C$ and $\delta^{18}O$ values we have used the R script by Hermes and colleagues (Hermes et al. 2022).

Results and Discussion

Zooarchaeological Observations

Livestock deposited in the slab burial (DMS 1396A) was entirely represented by elements of the skull region and articulated cervical vertebrae. A total of nineteen individuals, represented by crania and mandibles, were identified as *Ovis* sp. (Figure 6.4), *Equus* sp. and *Bos* sp. were represented by tooth fragments and a partial cranium, respectively. The *Ovis* sp. individuals were roughly arranged by age, with the youngest, including neonates, forming a little group to the south of the adult animals. The oldest was to the north, which seemingly creates the image of herd individuals advancing in age from top to bottom. Visually the "herd" was in a quite impressive arrangement, all facing outward to the east.

The sheep individuals in the slab burial represented three distinct age spans (Figure 6.5): 0 to 6 months ($n = 4$), including neonates; 1 to 3 years ($n = 8$); and 4 to 8 years ($n = 7$). Ages from 6 to 12 months, 3 to 4 years, and more than 8 years were not represented. If this pattern occurred in a death assemblage from a habitation site, a high kill-off of very young individuals (under 2 months) would be correlated with dairy surplus production (Payne 1973). In the context of subsistence production, dairying has been linked to a profile with moderate kill-off in all groups from 2 to 6 months and 3 to 4 years with a peak kill off of age group 6 to 12 months (Vigne and Helmer 2007). In turn, meat production has been linked with a moderate to high kill-off of age groups 2 to 6 and 6 to 12 months, to 1 to 2 and 2 to 4 years, respectively. The exploitation of herds for fleece is often represented by a comparatively high kill-off of older animals in the age groups 4 to 6 years and 6 to 10 years (Vigne and Helmer 2007). These models are based on the practical knowledge from livestock herding communities, in this case from Southwest Asia. Pastoralists, relying on their competence, employ different economically secure strategies to use their herds for different products. A key concern of pastoralists globally is the reliable production of subsistence goods from livestock herding and, in turn, the livelihood and prosperity of their herds, requiring careful risk management (Dyson-Hudson 1988; Roe, Huntsinger, and Labnow 1998). Consequently, pastoralists are constantly aware of sustaining herd compositions for their own and their herd's needs. It seems plausible that a prosperous and productive herd holds a high level of economic, but also symbolic, meaning.

Considering this, the selection of individuals for the skull arrangement in DMS1396A could symbolize the different aspects of sheep and goat herding and hence resemble a "herd in death" representing all different goods provided in life. The age groups absent from the deposition underline that the demographic composition of this "herd" is artificial and the individuals of certain age spans have been chosen representatively.

In the Xiongnu ring burial (DMS 777A), the majority of faunal remains was deposited in a ritual alcove structure on a rectangular pedestal to the northeastern side of the grave (Figure 6.6). The burial itself was possibly looted in later times, but apparently only the human burial was disturbed as the bones of the interred were partially scattered to the west. The deposit was not in direct spatial association with the human interment, but at a distance of at least 30 cm and spread across the pedestal structure. Three individual horse skulls, positioned in a row, formed the bottom foundation of the faunal deposit on the eastern wall, all facing north. The burial contained a total of 538 zooarchaeological remains from livestock animals (Figure 6.7). Approximately 76% ($n = 411$) were identified as a combined category of *Ovis/Capra*; 32% ($n = 170$) were identified as *Ovis* sp.; and 25% ($n = 136$) as tentative *Capra* sp. *Bos* sp. ($n = 64$) and *Equus* sp. ($n = 63$) were represented with 12% each. All

FIGURE 6.4. Sheep skull deposition in situ in slab burial DMS 1396A. Courtesy of the Dornod Mongol Survey Project. Photo credit: Batdalai Byambatseren, 2018.

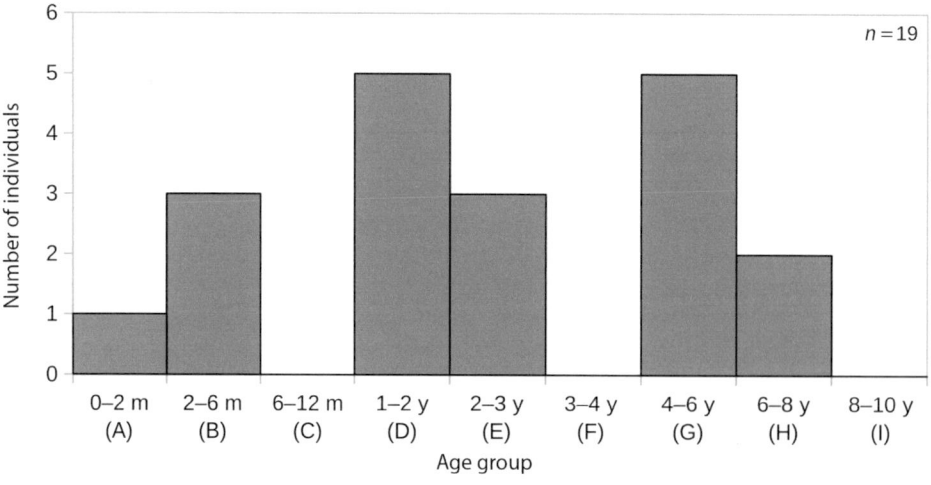

FIGURE 6.5. Age group distribution of sheep individuals from DMS 1396A based on age at death estimations from overall mandibular wear stages.

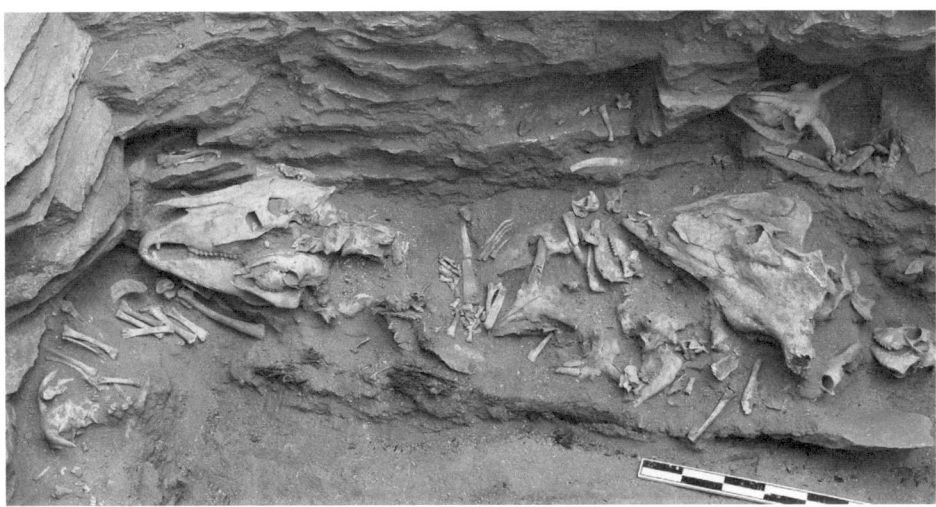

FIGURE 6.6. Faunal deposition in Xiongnu burial DMS 777A. Courtesy of the Dornod Mongol Survey Project. Photo credit: Batdalai Byambatseren, 2018.

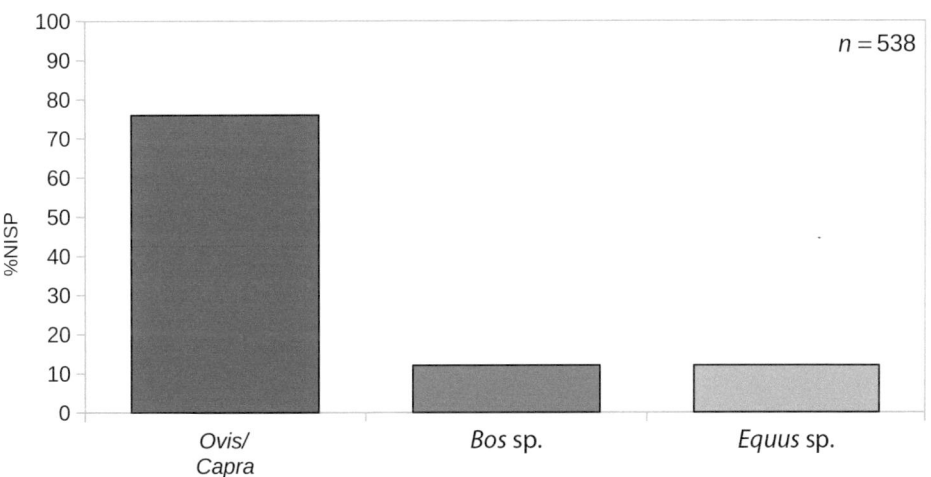

FIGURE 6.7. Distribution of taxa deposited in Xiongnu burial DMS 777A using the total number of identified bone specimens (NISP; $n = 538$).

taxa were largely represented by a similar set of skeletal elements (Table 6.1): the cranium (often with atlas and axis) and mandible, radius, and metacarpus, as well as phalanges 1, 2, and 3 were highly represented. Crania of *Bos* sp. and *Equus* sp. also had matching numbers of atlas bones represented. An additional pelvis fragment was identified as *Ovis/Capra*. What we find deposited in this grave is a typical set of "heads and hooves" plus elements of the lower forelimb and axial elements. Among the mandibles and radii, *Ovis* sp. and tentative *Capra* sp. were recorded with nine and eight individuals, respectively, which would

TABLE 6.1. Distribution of skeletal elements present in the Xiongnu ring burial (DMS 777A) by taxon.

Taxon	Cranium	Mandibula	Vertebrae	Pelvis	Radius	Ulna	Metacarpus	Phalange 1	Phalange 2	Phalange 3	Total
Ovis/Capra	15	15	28	1	30	30	29	112	101	100	461
Bos sp.	2	2	2		4	4	4	16	16	14	64
Equus sp.	3	3	3		6	6	6	12	12	12	63
Total	20	20	33	1	40	40	39	140	129	126	588

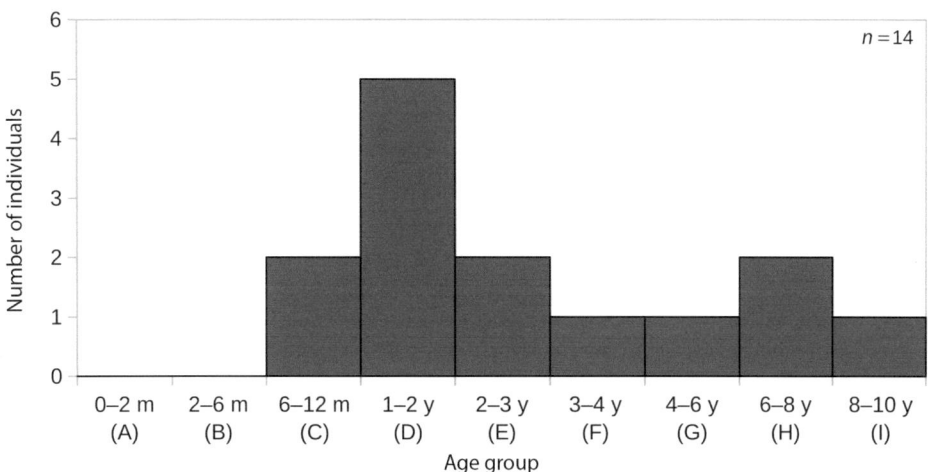

FIGURE 6.8. Age group distribution of sheep individuals from DMS 777A based on age at death estimations from overall mandibular wear stages.

add up to seventeen *Ovis/Capra* individuals. Since the *Capra* sp. specimens were tentative identifications, a more conservative count of fifteen *Ovis/Capra* individuals by mandibles alone seems more appropriate. *Equus* sp. and *Bos* sp. were represented with three and two individuals, respectively.

Age groups of sheep/goat individuals deposited in the Xiongnu ring burial (Figure 6.8) represent a more broadly distributed death assemblage older than 6 to 12 months. The largest number was killed at age 1 to 2 years ($n = 5$), followed by two individuals each from age groups 6 to 12 months, 2 to 3 years, and 6 to 8 years. Ages from 3 to 4, 4 to 6, and 8 to 10 years were represented with a single individual each. Individuals younger than 6 months were completely absent. This differs from the slab burial age distributions and does not mirror a pattern usually associated with dairy production. Instead, one could argue that this selection is the product of choosing prime meat individuals for a feasting event that took place in honor of the individual interred in DMS777A, complemented with a few older symbolic individuals. In a subsistence context a moderate kill-off of the latter is usually associated with a production mode involving exploitation for wool. But the high age of these individuals could be connoted with entirely different attributes in a ritual context (for example, long-living multispecies relationships and resilience). While most caprine individuals in this grave were probably associated with meat production, possibly for a feasting, the specific age structure of the assemblage might represent a more conservative approach to killing of individuals in a herd where the security strategy is to let young animals live at least until their first year. Of course, our pilot study focuses on a single assortment of osteological grave goods from only one grave each. However, if this was a regular pattern in Xiongnu ring burials this could be an indication of a systematic and conservative approach to herd and risk management, even at the occasion of a funeral feast.

Of the three horse individuals in the Xiongnu burials, only one (the individual placed in the front row) had a preserved premaxilla with incisors for proper age determination. According to the incisors and canine teeth, the individual was a stallion 5 to 7 years old. Of the other two we can say that one (last in the row) was of senile age, from the comparatively strong abrasion on all teeth. The individual in the middle was likely roughly around the age of 3 to 4 years, since the M/3s were still in the last stage of eruption. The three skulls were deposited with atlas bones still articulated; these show different stages of pathological exostoses on the cranial and dorsal margins, which would be in accordance with the different age groups assigned, assuming they were mostly used for riding. According to mandibular tooth wear stages, the two cattle individuals in the Xiongnu burial were comparatively old: 6 to 8 and 8 to 10 years of age, respectively. With a noticeable difference in size, it is possible that the two individuals are a male and a female. They might have been used for dairy, work, and breeding. Consistent with this, nine of the first and four of the second phalanges show moderate exostoses and lipping. Most of these (12 of 13) were larger than the others and likely belonged to an individual used for traction or work.

Our two exemplary contexts each represent the overall standard structural archetype burial for their respective time. For grave depositions, similar to findings from slab and Xiongnu burials in other regions of Mongolia, both put clear focus on the deposition of domesticated livestock remains, but clearly differ in their spatial arrangement, presentational framework, and the "demographic" composition of the assemblages. A focus on age groups of the deposited individuals revealed that the otherwise plausible explanation of feastings for depositing large amounts of domestic livestock remains might not suffice in all cases. The choice for sheep individuals of certain age groups, such as neonates, in slab burial DMS1396A seems to be deliberate and at least in part targeted at actually creating a particular herd assemblage rather than exclusively reflecting past ceremonial actions in the form of food consumption. A more detailed look at the herds-and-hooves-plus assemblage in the Xiongnu burial (DMS 777A) showed that, along with being the product of feasting, the depositions of both equine and bovine remains covered a comparatively large age span. This might be reflective of conservative meat consumption (as part of a feast), but could also possibly represent acknowledgment of the long service of aged animals used for riding, wool, and, in the case of cattle, possibly traction, or possibly individuals with special meaning for the deceased.

Stable Isotopic Carbon and Oxygen Pilot Study

Intratooth isotopic sequences were obtained from five sheep teeth (Table 6.2) each from the slab burial (DMS 1396A) and Xiongnu ring burial (DMS 777A). Ranges of $\delta^{13}C$ values were similarly narrow between individuals within one context as well as between the contexts themselves (Figure 6.9, Appendix 6.1). For individuals from the slab burial, $\delta^{13}C$ values ranged from −10.37 to −6.86‰ and from −10.63 to −5.97‰ for individuals from the Xiongnu burial. All individuals show relatively small amplitudes in $\delta^{13}C$ values, with on average 1.24‰ for the slab and 1.30‰ for the Xiongnu burial, and without a rise in $\delta^{13}C$ in the winter season. This is consistent with what is isotopically expected for the natural seasonal fluctuations of the plant biome. Thus, there is no indication that these individuals accessed pastures or fodder other than the naturally available mixed C3/C4 vegetation of the local Gobi steppe desert. Studies of $\delta^{13}C$ and $\delta^{18}O$ values of domestic caprine teeth from steppe and steppe desert environments (Makarewicz and Pederzani 2017; Hermes et al. 2019) have shown that comparatively high $\delta^{13}C$ values in the winter, indicated by lowest $\delta^{18}O$ values, can suggest management practices that make summer vegetation collected for foddering available to livestock during the cold period of the year. The foddering with summer vegetation, which includes relatively higher proportions of C4 plants, or even more so the foddering with cultivated C4 plants, such as millet, would result in higher $\delta^{13}C$ values

TABLE 6.2. Sampled M/2s from sheep individuals from mortuary contexts in Delgerkhaan Uul.

Burial type	Context number	Individual age (years)	Tooth number	Side	Sampled loph	Crown height total (mm)	Loph height sampled (mm)	Number of increments
Slab burial	DMS 1396A	1–2	18_7_05	Left	Posterior	34.9	24.0	6
	DMS 1396A	2–3	18_7_06	Right	Posterior	40.4	34.4	8
	DMS 1396A	2–3	18_7_10	Left	Anterior	38.8	34.5	6
	DMS 1396A	1–2	18_7_12	Left	Posterior	35.1	28.8	8
	DMS 1396A	2–3	18_7_13	Left	Posterior	40.7	30.5	8
Xiongnu burial	DMS 777A	1–2	18_2_40	Right	Posterior	41.6	32.8	7
	DMS 777A	2–3	18_2_41	Right	Anterior	42.1	27.8	7
	DMS 777A	1–2	18_2_46	Left	Posterior	46.8	34.6	8
	DMS 777A	2–3	18_2_49	Right	Posterior	41.4	32.5	7
	DMS 777A	1–2	18_2_51	Right	Posterior	40.6	30.0	7

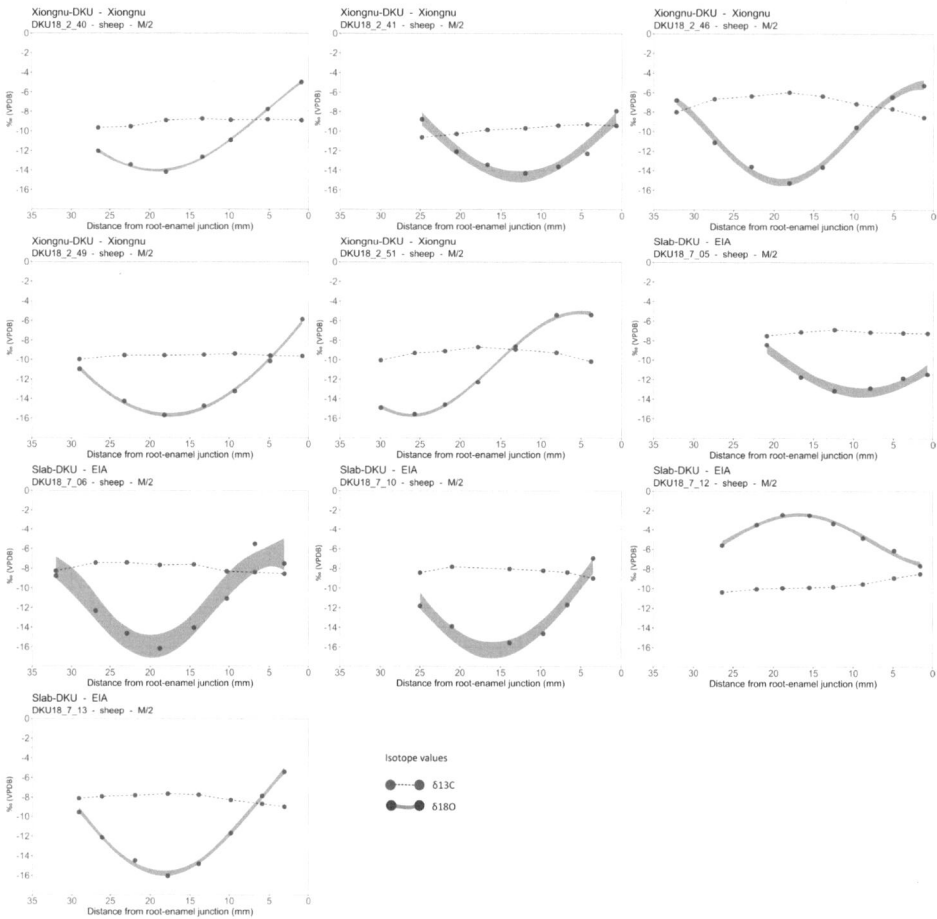

FIGURE 6.9. Time series plots of $\delta^{13}C$ and $\delta^{18}O$ of *Ovis* sp. using the Vienna Pee Dee Belemnite (VPDB) standard and the R script by Hermes et al. (2022). Individuals are from the slab burial DMS 1396A (specimens DKU18_7_05, 18_7_06, 18_7_10, 18_7_12, 18_7_13) and the Xiongnu burial DMS777A (specimens DKU18_2_40, 18_2_41, 18_2_46, 18_2_49, 18_2_51).

inversely correlating with lower winter $\delta^{18}O$ values. According to the intratooth isotopic variance in $\delta^{13}C$ in relation to $\delta^{18}O$ values, this does not seem to be the case for the sheep individuals at Delgerkhaan Uul.

To explore any differences in sheep diet between the slab burial and the Xiongnu burial, we statistically compared stable isotope results from the two burials. For this comparison it should be noted that most individuals (with the exception of individuals DKU18_7_12 from the slab burial and DKU18_2_51 from the Xiongnu burial) have truncated summer $\delta^{13}C$ and $\delta^{18}O$ values that do not capture a full seasonal cycle. Many tooth sequences do not capture the values coinciding with the warmest season, and the length of time recorded differs between teeth. Any comparisons between individuals or burials therefore need to be made using metrics that can be compared like-to-like across all individuals since, with the exception of the two mentioned individuals, no "true" seasonal maxima of $\delta^{18}O$ or $\delta^{13}C$, or full annual means, can be obtained. Because it was possible to obtain the "true" $\delta^{18}O$ minima (with the exception of one individual, which was likely an off-season birth) and to evaluate the composition of caprine winter diet at Iron Age Delgerkhaan Uul, we have compared the $\delta^{13}C$ values corresponding with the winter $\delta^{18}O$ minimum (referred to as "winter $\delta^{13}C$" in the following section). A Student's *t*-test shows no statistically significant difference between the mean winter $\delta^{13}C$ of individuals from the slab burial and the mean winter $\delta^{13}C$ value of individuals from the Xiongnu burial ($t = 1.4197$, df = 7, sed = 0.829, $p = 0.1987$). A second Student's *t*-test showed no statistically significant difference in winter $\delta^{18}O$ between the individuals from the slab burial and the individuals from the Xiongnu burial ($t = 0.5404$, df = 7, sed = 0.796, $p = 0.6057$). While this approach does not allow observations of changes in vegetational intake of sheep between summer and winter seasons, it might provide a reference point for a comparison of vegetational dietary intake or provision between the two groups from the slab and Xiongnu context in winter times.

Using work by Makarewicz and Tuross (2006), a range of –28.5‰ to –24.1‰ in $\delta^{13}C$ values was established for C3 plants and a range of –15.1‰ to –11.2‰ in $\delta^{13}C$ values for C4 plants at Baga Gazaryn Chuluu in an area of the steppe desert 350 km to the west of Delgerkhaan Uul. Zazzo et al. (2010) have established a fractionation of about 14‰ for a mixed C3/C4 diet and about 11.5‰ for a pure C4 diet measured in sheep enamel apatite. The sheep individuals from the slab burial and the Xiongnu burial dated around 800 years later gave mean winter $\delta^{13}C$ values of –7.5‰ and –8.7‰, respectively. Considering the isotopic signals for C3/C4, or even for a pure C4 diet, the winter diet of the Delgerkhaan Uul sheep was a C3/C4 mixed diet (19.0‰ to 23.2‰) and, more importantly, does not significantly change between the different time periods. Even though no "true" summer maxima are seen in the incremental tooth data, the $\delta^{13}C$ values along the $\delta^{18}O$ curves, with the exception of individual DKU18_2_46, are quite consistent, resulting in overall small amplitudes between 0.6‰ to 1.9‰ for the individuals from the slab burial and 0.6‰ to 1.3‰ for the other individuals (except DKU18_2_46 with 2.6‰). These values are also consistent between the two different time periods. With the exception of individual DKU18_2_4, none of the individuals' $\delta^{13}C$ curves show an inverse correlation with the $\delta^{18}O$ curve, which would be typical of access to plant fodder collected in the summer and provisioned in the winter.

Previous studies on bulk stable carbon and nitrogen isotopes from bone collagen of both livestock and humans so far show no indications of faunal or human millet consumption during the Bronze or Iron Age at Delgerkhaan Uul, or major shifts in dietary components between herbivores and consumers during these time periods (Pleuger-Dreibrodt et al., in prep.). From the carbon and oxygen isotopic data for incrementally sampled sheep molars presented here, it is possible that neither (millet) foddering nor a significant change of accessing different pastures were part of the Iron Age husbandry strategies at Delgerkhaan Uul. At the same time, this data indicates that winter environmental conditions and water sources for livestock were comparatively consistent between the early and later Iron Age. People at Delgerkhaan Uul likely continued to practice animal herding according to local needs and adapted to the particularly arid environment without potential or need for complementary crop farming. This could indicate that state interventions by Xiongnu rulers were either not impacting subsistence strategies in this part of the state or that there was a high level of acceptance of practical knowledge carried out by local herder families.

Conclusions

Both the slab burial tradition and even more so the Xiongnu state spanned wide territories of Mongolian Inner Asia during the Iron Age. Both traditions demonstrate unique patterns of burial structures and depositions of domestic livestock remains. Our study, albeit on only two archaeological contexts, showed that local variability of day-to-day practices did exist on the level of individual herding practice decisions. Strategies likely differed according to resources, communal decisions, environmental circumstances, and general practicability. The rise of the Xiongnu pastoral nomadic state facilitated stronger long-distance sociopolitical networks and the potential for more intensive livestock-management-based subsistence strategies. However, at Delgerkhaan Uul local communities likely retained autonomy over their day-to-day herding practices. Local variability might actually reflect social stability given that Xiongnu statehood relied heavily on horse mobility over vast distances to connect different habitation centers.

We have also shown that a detailed focus on context and composition of individual faunal burial depositions can provide us with a foundation for interpreting zooarchaeological remains in pastoralist mortuary contexts through various perspectives. The sets of nonhuman individuals deposited in the two exemplary graves discussed here, might carry a meaning that goes along with and beyond the remnants of feasting. Rather these remains of nonhuman members of a multispecies community carried symbolic meaning in part reflecting past pastoralist identities at the time. The datasets presented are preliminary and small, but might serve as a foundation for developing more refined approaches to similar research questions using differential methods with a particular focus on a thorough contextual analysis of individual contexts. While this is certainly only the "tale of two graves" applying this detail-oriented approach to the composition of a greater number of contexts will likely provide us with more substantial insights into the social dimension of livestock depositional patterns.

Acknowledgments

This study was kindly supported by many international colleagues and experts. First and foremost we would like to thank all colleagues of the DMS team, and in this particular context our three co-directors Chunag Amartuvshin, William Honeychurch, and Joshua Wright, as well as Batdalai Byambatseren and Ganbaatar Galdan for conducting crucial parts of the projects survey and excavation activities. We all had the opportunity and pleasure to work and spend precious time with Zeng Lingyi in the field. She was a wonderful team member and we cherish the memory of our experiences together. We would like to thank Anne Underhill for the opportunity to partake in remembering Lingyi through this volume.

This project would not have been possible without the generous collaboration of the Institute of Archaeology, Mongolian Academy of Sciences. We are most grateful to the families of Delgerkhaan Uul whose hospitality and knowledge helped us immensely. Fieldwork was supported in part by grants from the US National Endowment for the Humanities (grant RZ-249831-16) and the Wenner-Gren Foundation for Anthropological Research. Sarah Pleuger-Dreibrodt throughout the research design, data analysis, and writing of this paper was generously funded by the Gerda Henkel Foundation. Isotopic analyses were jointly (50:50) funded by the Gerda Henkel Foundation (Sachmittel Promotionsprojekt) and the Archaeological Research Support Fund (2021), School of History, Classics and Archaeology, University of Edinburgh. Sarah Pederzani was supported by a Leopoldina Postdoctoral Research Fellowship from the German National Academy of Sciences Leopoldina (Deutsche Akademie der Naturforscher Leopoldina–Nationale Akademie der Wissenschaften, LPDS 2021-13).

We would like to thank Nils Andersen of the Leibniz Laboratory at Kiel for his analytical work and support, as well as Alex Cherkinsky at the Center for Applied Isotope Studies at the University of Georgia, who produced two of the AMS dates reported here. The other date presented was kindly funded through a grant by National Environmental Isotope Facility (NF/2021/1/13) and run at the Oxford Radiocarbon Accelerator Unit at the University of Oxford. William Honeychurch, Robin Bendrey, and Taylor Hermes have supported different stages of this study through helpful comments and discussions.

APPENDIX 6.1. Oxygen and carbon isotope data from incrementally sampled sheep teeth at Delgerkhaan Uul. Duplicate measurements are included. Abbreviations: [RV1] ERJ, enamel root junction; VPDB, Vienna Pee Dee Belemnite standard.

Specimen number	Increment number	Distance to ERJ (mm)	δ13C (‰ VPDB)	Uncertainty (±)	δ18O (‰ VPDB)	Uncertainty (±)	Signal 44 (mV) Pr 1.Cycle	Percentage (%)
18_2_46	46_1	32.2	−8.02	0.01	−6.79	0.03	5006	1.1
18_2_46	46_2	27.4	−6.65	0.02	−11.12	0.04	8108	2.1
18_2_46	46_3	22.8	−6.35	0.02	−13.58	0.04	7653	1.1
18_2_46	46_4	18.1	−5.96	0.01	−15.34	0.03	9806	4.1
18_2_46	46_4	18.1	−5.97	0.02	−15.22	0.03	6779	1.3
18_2_46	46_5	13.9	−6.35	0.01	−13.65	0.02	5154	0.7
18_2_46	46_6	9.7	−7.20	0.01	−9.58	0.03	5138	1.7
18_2_46	46_6	9.7	−7.12	0.01	−9.51	0.03	9030	2.2
18_2_46	46_7	5.2	−7.67	0.02	−6.45	0.03	8232	0.9
18_2_46	46_8	1.2	−8.55	0.02	−5.25	0.03	4244	−1.2
18_2_40	40_1	26.5	−9.66	0.02	−12.03	0.04	8645	2.5
18_2_40	40_2	22.4	−9.53	0.02	−13.42	0.03	6735	−0.3
18_2_40	40_3	18	−8.90	0.02	−14.18	0.03	7275	2.4
18_2_40	40_4	13.4	−8.72	0.01	−12.62	0.03	9293	2.4
18_2_40	40_4	13.4	−8.74	0.02	−12.64	0.03	5738	1.7
18_2_40	40_5	9.8	−8.88	0.02	−10.97	0.04	5568	−2.2
18_2_40	40_5	9.8	−8.85	0.02	−10.85	0.04	5298	3.6
18_2_40	40_6	5.2	−8.81	0.02	−7.76	0.03	9801	3.4
18_2_40	40_7	0.9	−8.89	0.02	−4.97	0.04	9001	3.8

Continued

APPENDIX 6.1 CONTINUED.

Specimen number	Increment number	Distance to ERJ (mm)	δ13C (‰ VPDB)	Uncertainty (±)	δ18O (‰ VPDB)	Uncertainty (±)	Signal 44 (mV) Pr 1.Cycle	Percentage (%)
18_2_51	51_1	30	-10.04	0.01	-14.93	0.02	4379	2.2
18_2_51	51_2	25.7	-9.32	0.02	-15.56	0.03	5952	-0.8
18_2_51	51_3	21.9	-9.10	0.02	-14.64	0.03	5799	-3.2
18_2_51	51_3	21.9	-9.14	0.01	-14.54	0.02	5761	1.2
18_2_51	51_4	17.8	-8.70	0.01	-12.30	0.03	6845	-0.7
18_2_51	51_5	13.2	-8.95	0.01	-8.63	0.02	5823	-1.8
18_2_51	51_6	8.1	-9.36	0.02	-5.68	0.03	6831	0.1
18_2_51	51_6	8.1	-9.20	0.01	-5.13	0.03	10386	13.6
18_2_51	51_7	3.8	-10.17	0.01	-5.40	0.01	4696	-0.5
18_2_49	49_1	29	-9.98	0.01	-10.97	0.03	4716	-0.3
18_2_49	49_2	23.2	-9.56	0.01	-14.27	0.03	5138	-2.5
18_2_49	49_3	18.2	-9.60	0.01	-15.63	0.02	4150	0.4
18_2_49	49_3	18.2	-9.53	0.02	-15.75	0.03	6556	1.1
18_2_49	49_4	13.2	-9.51	0.02	-14.74	0.03	5327	0.5
18_2_49	49_5	9.3	-9.39	0.02	-13.26	0.05	6504	-3.6
18_2_49	49_6	4.9	-9.61	0.02	-10.10	0.03	8900	1.4
18_2_49	49_6	4.9	-9.58	0.01	-10.23	0.03	7327	-1.2
18_2_49	49_7	0.8	-9.63	0.02	-5.86	0.04	5145	-0.9

Continued

APPENDIX 6.1 CONTINUED.

Specimen number	Increment number	Distance to ERJ (mm)	δ13C (‰ VPDB)	Uncertainty (±)	δ18O (‰ VPDB)	Uncertainty (±)	Signal 44 (mV) Pr 1.Cycle	Percentage (%)
18_2_41	41_1	24.8	-10.63	0.02	-8.79	0.04	5816	0.1
18_2_41	41_2	20.5	-10.27	0.01	-12.09	0.03	6414	-1.4
18_2_41	41_3	16.7	-9.86	0.02	-13.42	0.04	3743	-1.3
18_2_41	41_4	12	-9.66	0.01	-14.02	0.02	6838	2.1
18_2_41	41_4	12	-9.73	0.02	-14.58	0.04	7649	-1.8
18_2_41	41_5	7.9	-9.41	0.02	-13.63	0.03	5171	-2.6
18_2_41	41_6	4.3	-9.30	0.01	-12.28	0.03	4563	-1.5
18_2_41	41_7	0.7	-9.42	0.02	-7.93	0.04	3691	-0.2
18_7_06	6_1	32	-8.27	0.02	-8.78	0.04	5543	-1.4
18_7_06	6_2	26.9	-7.44	0.02	-12.32	0.05	6528	0.6
18_7_06	6_3	22.9	-7.42	0.02	-14.63	0.04	5545	-1.9
18_7_06	6_4	18.8	-7.68	0.02	-16.16	0.03	6894	0.3
18_7_06	6_5	14.5	-7.62	0.02	-14.05	0.04	5600	-1.6
18_7_06	6_6	10.3	-8.37	0.01	-11.10	0.03	7174	2.2
18_7_06	6_6	10.3	-8.28	0.02	-11.08	0.03	4119	-0.7
18_7_06	6_7	6.8	-8.44	0.02	-5.60	0.03	5859	0.5
18_7_06	6_7	6.8	-8.36	0.01	-5.45	0.03	5845	-3.4
18_7_06	6_8	3.1	-8.56	0.02	-7.52	0.03	3918	1.1

Continued

APPENDIX 6.1 CONTINUED.

Specimen number	Increment number	Distance to ERJ (mm)	δ13C (‰ VPDB)	Uncertainty (±)	δ18O (‰ VPDB)	Uncertainty (±)	Signal 44 (mV) Pr 1.Cycle	Percentage (%)
18_7_13	13_1	29.1	-8.13	0.02	-9.57	0.04	8423	-1.5
18_7_13	13_2	26.1	-7.93	0.02	-12.14	0.05	5989	-1.7
18_7_13	13_3	21.9	-7.81	0.01	-14.48	0.03	5060	-1.8
18_7_13	13_4	17.8	-7.64	0.01	-16.14	0.02	3186	-0.2
18_7_13	13_4	17.8	-7.67	0.02	-15.97	0.03	7329	0.2
18_7_13	13_5	13.9	-7.75	0.02	-14.83	0.04	3908	-1.1
18_7_13	13_6	9.8	-8.31	0.02	-11.71	0.04	7218	0.6
18_7_13	13_7	5.9	-8.71	0.02	-7.87	0.04	6162	-2.4
18_7_13	13_8	3.1	-9.01	0.01	-5.42	0.03	3824	-1.6
18_7_05	5_1	20.9	-7.49	0.02	-8.42	0.03	4315	0.4
18_7_05	5_2	16.6	-7.10	0.02	-11.76	0.04	5951	-1.7
18_7_05	5_3	12.4	-6.90	0.01	-13.33	0.03	5202	0.9
18_7_05	5_3	12.4	-6.81	0.01	-12.99	0.02	10028	6.9
18_7_05	5_4	7.9	-7.17	0.01	-12.79	0.02	7870	-1.5
18_7_05	5_4	7.9	-7.06	0.01	-12.95	0.04	6612	-3.1
18_7_05	5_5	3.8	-7.19	0.01	-11.84	0.02	4447	-0.6
18_7_05	5_6	0.7	-7.22	0.01	-11.45	0.02	2242	-1.0

Continued

APPENDIX 6.1 CONTINUED.

Specimen number	Increment number	Distance to ERJ (mm)	δ13C (‰ VPDB)	Uncertainty (±)	δ18O (‰ VPDB)	Uncertainty (±)	Signal 44 (mV) Pr 1.Cycle	Percentage (%)
18_7_12	12_1	26.4	−10.37	0.01	−5.60	0.03	4011	1.6
18_7_12	12_2	22.1	−10.11	0.01	−3.55	0.03	5049	−2.3
18_7_12	12_2	22.1	−9.97	0.01	−3.40	0.03	8493	2.0
18_7_12	12_3	18.9	−9.94	0.01	−2.44	0.03	4711	−1.5
18_7_12	12_4	15.5	−9.89	0.01	−2.50	0.02	9530	1.2
18_7_12	12_5	12.5	−9.82	0.02	−3.35	0.03	9616	−0.5
18_7_12	12_6	8.8	−9.52	0.01	−4.86	0.03	4577	−0.8
18_7_12	12_7	4.9	−8.92	0.02	−6.13	0.04	7558	−2.1
18_7_12	12_8	1.6	−8.48	0.02	−7.66	0.03	5880	−1.8
18_7_10	10_1	25	−8.42	0.01	−11.81	0.03	6933	−2.8
18_7_10	10_2	21	−7.82	0.01	−13.88	0.03	8856	−1.2
18_7_10	10_3	13.9	−8.14	0.02	−15.43	0.04	7790	−1.8
18_7_10	10_3	13.9	−7.95	0.01	−15.68	0.02	4984	2.4
18_7_10	10_4	9.7	−8.21	0.01	−14.62	0.02	4733	−2.1
18_7_10	10_5	6.7	−8.39	0.02	−11.69	0.04	7751	−0.5
18_7_10	10_6	3.5	−8.99	0.02	−6.96	0.03	5338	1.6

References

Allard, Francis, Diimaajav Erdenebaatar, Natsagyn Batbold, and Bryan K. Miller. 2002. A Xiongnu cemetery found in Mongolia. *Antiquity* 76(293):637–639. https://doi.org/10.1017/S0003598X0009102X

Amartuvshin, Chunag, Natsagyn Batbold, Gelegdorj Eregzin, and Byambatseren Batdalai. 2015. *Archaeological Sites of Chandman Khar Uul*. Ulaanbaatar: Munkhiin Useg. 347 pp. [in Mongolian.]

Amartuvshin, Chunag, and William Honeychurch, eds. 2010. Survey and Bioarchaeology in the Middle Gobi: The Baga Gazaryn Chuluu Project. Ulaanbaatar: Mongolian Academy of Science, Institute of Archaeology. 456 pp. (Studia Archaeologica 27.) [in Mongolian.]

Balasse, Marie. 2002. Reconstructing dietary and environmental history from enamel isotopic analysis: Time resolution of intra-tooth sequential sampling. *International Journal of Osteoarchaeology* 12(3):155–165. https://doi.org/10.1002/oa.601

Balasse, Marie, Ingrid Mainland, and Michael P. Richards. 2009. Stable isotope evidence for seasonal consumption of marine seaweed by modern and archaeological sheep in the Orkney archipelago (Scotland). *Environmental Archaeology* 14(1):1–14. https://doi.org/10.1179/174963109X400637

Balasse, Marie, Andrew B. Smith, Stanley H. Ambrose, and Steven R. Leigh. 2003. Determining sheep birth seasonality by analysis of tooth enamel oxygen isotope ratios: The Late Stone Age site of Kasteelberg (South Africa). *Journal of Archaeological Science* 30(2):205–215. https://doi.org/10.1006/jasc.2002.0833

Bayarsaikhan, Jamsranjav, Tumurbaatar Tuvshinjargal, William Taylor, Zagd Batsaikhan, and Bryce Lowry. 2019. Archaeological discoveries at Bor Shoroonii am. *Nomadic Heritage Studies* 19(2):5–28.

Brosseder, Ursula. 2009. Xiongnu terrace tombs and their interpretation as elite burials. In: Jan Bemmann, Hermann Parzinger, Ernst Pohl, and Damdinsüren Tseveendorzh, eds. *Current Archaeological Research in Mongolia;* papers from the First International Conference on "Archaeological Research in Mongolia" held in Ulaanbaatar, August 19th–23rd, 2007. Bonn: Vor- und Frühgeschichtliche Archäologie, Rheinische Friedrich-Wilhelms Universität. pp. 247–280. (Bonn Contributions to Asian Archaeology 4.)

—2015. A study on the complexity and dynamics of inter-action and exchange in Late Iron Age Eurasia. In: Jan Bemmann and Michael Schmauder, eds. *Complexity of Interaction along the Eurasian Steppe Zone in the First Millennium CE*. Bonn: Vor- und Frühgeschichtliche Archäologie, Rheinische Friedrich-Wilhelms-Universität. pp. 199–332. (Bonn Contributions to Asian Archaeology 7.)

—2016. The Xiongnu Empire. In: Sitta von Reden, ed. *Handbook of Ancient Afro-Eurasian Economies*. Volume 1, Contexts. Berlin: De Gruyter Oldenbourg. pp. 195–204. https://doi.org/10.1515/9783110607741-007

Brosseder, Ursula, and Bryan K. Miller, eds. 2011. *Xiongnu Archaeology. Multidisciplinary Perspectives of the First Steppe Empire in Inner Asia*. Bonn: Vor- und Frühgeschichtliche Archäologie, Rheinische Friedrich-Wilhelms-Universität. 653 pp. (Bonn Contributions to Asian Archaeology 5.)

Bryant, J. Daniel, and Philip N. Froelich. 1995. A model of oxygen isotope fractionation in body water of large mammals. *Geochimica et Cosmochimica Acta* 59(21):4523–4537. https://doi.org/10.1179/1749631414Y.0000000055

Burentogtokh, Jargalan, William Honeychurch, and William Gardner. 2019. Complexity as integration: Pastoral mobility and community building in ancient Mongolia. *Social Evolution and History* 18(2):55–72. https://doi.org/10.30884/seh/2019.02.03

Cameron, Asa. 2016. "A Stable Isotopic (Carbon And Nitrogen) Evaluation of Regional Differences on Herded Animal Diet and Pastoral Risk Management Practices during The Xiongnu Period of Mongolia" [master's thesis]. Cornell University. https://doi.org/10.7298/X4RN35S5

Dal Zovo, Cecilia. 2021. *Ovoo*-cairns and ancient funerary mounds in the Mongolian landscape. Piling up a monumental tradition? Études mongoles et sibériennes, centrasiatiques et tibétaines 52. https://doi.org/10.4000/emscat.4925

Davaa-Ochir, Ganzorig. 2008. "Oboo Worship: The Worship of Earth and Water Divinities in Mongolia" [master's thesis]. University of Oslo.

Dyson-Hudson, Rada. 1988. Ecology of nomadic Turkana pastoralists: A discussion. In: Emily E. Whitehead, Charles F. Hutchinson, Barbara N. Timmermann, and Robert G. Varady, eds. *Arid Lands: Today and Tomorrow*; proceedings of an international research and development conference Tucson, Arizona, USA, October 20–25, 1985. Boulder, CO: Westview Press. pp. 701–703.

Enkhtör, Altangerel, Jan Bemmann, and Ursula Brosseder. 2018. The first excavations of Bronze and Iron Age monuments in the Middle Orkhon Valley, central Mongolia: Results from rescue investigations in 2006 and 2007. *Asian Archaeology* 1:3–44. https://doi.org/10.1007/s41826-018-0001-8

Erdenebaatar, Dimaadjav. 1992. Slab burials of Asgat. *Studia Archeologica Instituti Historiae Academiae Scientarum Mongolici Tomus* 13:1–8. [in Mongolian.]

—2012. Xiongnu king cemetery in Gol Mod-2. In: Russian Academy of Sciences, Institute of the History of Material Culture, ed. *Cultures of the Eurasian Steppe and Their Interaction with Ancient Civilizations*; Proceedings of the International Scientific Conference Dedicated to the 110th Anniversary of the Birth of the Outstanding Russian Archaeologist M. P. Gryaznova, Book 2. St. Petersburg, Russia: [n.p.]. pp. 463–468.

Farquhar, Graham, Kerry Hubick, A. Condon, and R. Richards. 1989. Carbon isotope fractionation and plant water-use efficiency. In: Philip W. Rundel, J. R. Ehleringer, and Kenneth A. Nagy, eds. *Stable Isotopes in Ecological Research*. New York: Springer. pp. 21–40. (Ecological Studies 68.) https://doi.org/10.1007/978-1-4612-3498-2_2

Fijn, Natasha. 2011. *Living With Herds: Human–Animal Coexistence in Mongolia*. New York: Cambridge University Press. 274 pp.

Fricke, Henry C., William C. Clyde, James R. O'Neil, and Philip D. Gingerich. 1998. Evidence for rapid climate change in North America during the latest Paleocene thermal maximum: Oxygen isotope compositions of biogenic phosphate from the Bighorn Basin (Wyoming). *Earth and Planetary Science Letters* 160(1–2):193–208. https://doi.org/10.1016/S0012-821X(98)00088-0

Gantulga, Jamiyan-Ombo, Jean-Jacques Grizeaud, Jérôme Magail, Makhbal Tsengel, and Chimiddorj Yeruul-Erdene. 2009. Report of the 2009 Monaco-Mongolia joint archaeological mission campaign. *Bulletin du Musée d'Anthropologie préhistorique de Monaco* 49:115–120. [in French with English abstract.] https://hal.science/hal-02554406

Grant, Annie. 1982. The use of tooth wear as a guide to the age of domestic ungulates. In: Bob Wilson, Caroline Grigson, and Sebastian Payne, eds. *Ageing and Sexing Animal Bones from Archaeological Sites*. Oxford: BAR Publishing. pp. 91–108. (BAR British Series 109.) https://doi.org/10.30861/9780860541929

Hammer, Øyvind, David A. T. Harper, and Paul D. Ryan. 2001. PAST: Paleontological statistics software package for education and data analysis. Palaeontologia Electronica 4(1):art. 4, 9 pp. https://palaeo-electronica.org/2001_1/past/issue1_01.htm

Hermes, Taylor R., Michael D. Frachetti, Paula N. Doumani Dupuy, Alexei Mar'yashev, Almut Nebel, and Cheryl A. Makarewicz. 2019. Early integration of pastoralism and millet cultivation in Bronze Age Eurasia. *Proceedings of the Royal Society* B 286(1910):20191273. https://doi.org/10.1098/rspb.2019.1273

Hermes, Taylor R., Sarah Pederzani, and Cheryl A. Makarewicz. 2017. Ahead of the curve?: Implications for isolating vertical transhumance in seasonal montane environments using sequential oxygen isotope analyses of tooth enamel. In: Alicia R. Ventresca Miller and Cheryl A. Makarewicz, eds. *Isotopic Investigations of Pastoralism in Prehistory*. 1st ed. New York: Routledge. pp. 57–76. (Themes in Contemporary Archaeology 4.) https://doi.org/10.4324/9781315143026

Hermes, Taylor R., Clemens Schmid, Kubatbek Tabaldiev, and Giedre Motuzaite Matuzeviciute. 2022. Carbon and oxygen stable isotopic evidence for diverse sheep and goat husbandry strategies amid a Final Bronze Age farming milieu in the Kyrgyz Tian Shan. *International Journal of Osteoarchaeology* 32(4):792–803. https://doi.org/10.1002/oa.3103

Hillson, Simon. 2005. *Teeth*. 2nd ed. New York: Cambridge University Press.

Honeychurch, William. 2014. *Inner Asia and the Spatial Politics of Empire: Archaeology, Mobility, and Culture Contact*. New York: Springer. 321 pp.

Honeychurch, William, and Chunag Amartuvshin. 2006. Survey and settlement in northern Mongolia: The structure of intra-regional nomadic organisation. In: D. L. Peterson, L. M. Popova, and A. T. Smith, eds. *Beyond the Steppe and the Sown: Proceedings of the 2002 University of Chicago Conference on Eurasian Archaeology*. Boston: Brill. pp. 183–201.

—2007. Hinterlands, urban centers, and mobile settings: The "new" Old World archaeology from the Eurasian steppe. *Asian Perspectives* 46(1):36–64. https://doi.org/10.1353/asi.2007.0005

—2011. Timescapes from the past: An archaeogeography of Mongolia. In: Paula L. W. Sabloff, ed. *Mapping Mongolia: Situating Mongolia in the World from Geologic Time to the Present*. Philadelphia: University of Pennsylvania Museum of Archaeology and Anthropology. pp. 195–219.

Honeychurch, William, Joshua Wright, and Chunag Amartuvshin. 2009. Re-writing monumental landscapes as inner Asian political process. In: Bryan K. Hanks and Katheryn M. Linduff, eds. *Social Complexity in Prehistoric Eurasia: Monuments, Metals and Mobility*. Cambridge: Cambridge University Press. pp. 330–357. https://doi.org/10.1017/CBO9780511605376.019

Janz, Lisa, James K. Feathers, and George S. Burr. 2015. Dating surface assemblages using pottery and eggshell: Assessing radiocarbon and luminescence techniques in Northeast Asia. *Journal of Archaeological Science* 57:119–129. https://doi.org/10.1016/j.jas.2015.02.006

Johannesson, Erik G. 2011. "Landscapes of Death, Monuments of Power: Mortuary Practice, Power, and Identity in Bronze-Iron Age Mongolia" [dissertation]. University of North Carolina at Chapel Hill. 320 pp. https://doi.org/10.17615/wja0-y124

—2015. Animals, identity, and mortuary behavior in Late Bronze Age–Early Iron Age Mongolia. In: P. Nick Kardulias, ed. *The Ecology of Pastoralism*. Boulder: University Press of Colorado. pp. 97–116.

Körner, C., G. D. Farquhar, and S. C. Wong. 1991. Carbon isotope discrimination by plants follows latitudinal and altitudinal trends. *Oecologia* 88:30–40. https://www.jstor.org/stable/4219750

Kradin, Nikolai N. 2011. Stateless empire: The structure of the Xiongnu nomadic super-complex chiefdom. In: Ursula Brosseder and Bryan K. Miller, eds. *Xiongnu Archaeology, Multidisciplinary Perspectives of the First Steppe Empire in Inner Asia*. Bonn: Vor- und Frühgeschichtliche Archäologie, Rheinische Friedrich-Wilhelms-Universität. pp. 77–96. (Bonn Contributions to Asian Archaeology 5.)

Legge, A. J. 1992. *Excavations at Grimes Graves, Norfolk 1972–1976*. Fasciule 4, Animals, Environment and the Bronze Age Economy. London: Published for the Trustees of the British Museum by British Museum Publications. 87 pp.

Lowry, K. Bryce. 2020. "Tracing a Transition: The Political Economy of Bronze and Iron Age Mongolia" [dissertation]. University of Chicago. 457 pp. ProQuest Dissertations and Theses Global (27833625). https://www.proquest.com/dissertations-theses/tracing-transition-political-economy-bronze-iron/docview/2449485143/se-2

Machicek, Michelle L. 2012. "Reconstructing Diet, Health and Activity Patterns in Early Nomadic Pastoralist Communities of Inner Asia" [dissertation]. University of Sheffield. https://etheses.whiterose.ac.uk/14581/1/569193.pdf

Makarewicz, Cheryl A. 2011. Xiongnu pastoral systems: Integrating economies of subsistence and scale. In: Ursula Brosseder and Bryan K. Miller, eds. *Xiongnu Archaeology: Multidisciplinary Perspectives of the First Steppe Empire in Inner Asia*. Bonn: Vor- und Frühgeschichtliche Archäologie, Rheinische Friedrich-Wilhelms-Universität. pp. 181–92. (Bonn Contributions to Asian Archaeology 5.)

—2014. Winter pasturing practices and variable fodder provisioning detected in nitrogen (δ^{15}N) and carbon (δ^{13}C) isotopes in sheep dentinal collagen. *Journal of Archaeological Science* 41:502–510. https://doi.org/10.1016/j.jas.2013.09.016

—2017. Winter is coming: Seasonality of ancient pastoral nomadic practices revealed in the carbon (δ^{13}C) and nitrogen (δ^{15}N) isotopic record of Xiongnu caprines. *Archaeological and Anthropological Sciences* 9:405–418. https://doi.org/10.1007/s12520-015-0289-5

Makarewicz, Cheryl A., and Sarah Pederzani. 2017. Oxygen (δ^{18}O) and carbon (δ^{13}C) isotopic distinction in sequentially sampled tooth enamel of co-localized wild and domesticated caprines: Complications to establishing seasonality and mobility in herbivores. *Palaeogeography, Palaeoclimatology, Palaeoecology* 485(1):1–15. https://doi.org/10.1016/j.palaeo.2017.01.010

Makarewicz, Cheryl A., and Noreen Tuross. 2006. Foddering by Mongolian pastoralists is recorded in the stable carbon (δ^{13}C) and nitrogen (δ^{15}N) isotopes of caprine dentinal collagen. *Journal of Archaeological Science* 33(6):862–870. https://doi.org/10.1016/j.jas.2005.10.016

Mandakh, Davaasuren. 2015. The result of the craniological measurements taken on dog bones from Xiongnu burial sites. *Studia Archaeologica* 35:544–554. [in Mongolian.]

Martin, Hélène. 2011. The animal in the Xiongnu funeral universe: Companion of the living, escort of the dead. In: Ursula Brosseder and Bryan K. Miller, eds. *Xiongnu Archaeology, Multidisciplinary Perspectives of the First Steppe Empire in Inner Asia*. Bonn: Vor- und Frühgeschichtliche Archäologie, Rheinische Friedrich-Wilhelms-Universität. pp. 229–242. (Bonn Contributions to Asian Archaeology 5.)

Martin, Michael T. 2002. *Official Guide for Determining the Age of the Horse*. 6th ed. Lexington, KY: American Association of Equine Practitioners. 39 pp. https://aaep.org/guidelines-resources/

Milhaud, G., and J. Nezit. 1991. Molar development in sheep: Morphology, radiography, microhardness. *Recueil de Medecine Veterinaire* 167(2):121–127. [in French.]

Miller, Bryan K. 2023. Consuming the herds: Animal sacrifice and offerings of the Xiongnu. In: Anke Hein, Rowan Flad, and Bryan K. Miller, eds. *Ritual and Economy in East Asia: Archaeological Perspectives*. Los Angeles: UCLA Cotsen Institute of Archaeology Press. pp. 181–198.

—2024. *Xiongnu: The World's First Nomadic Empire*. Oxford: Oxford University Press. 362 pp.

Miller, Bryan K., Francis Allard, Diimaajav Erdenebaatar, and Christine Lee. 2006. A Xiongnu tomb complex: Excavations at Gol Mod 2 cemetery, Mongolia (2002–05). *Mongolian Journal of Anthropology Archaeology and Ethnology* 2:1–21. https://journal.num.edu.mn/MJAAE/article/view/1672

Miller, Bryan K., Jamsranjav Bayarsaikhan, Tseveendorj Egiimaa, and Christine Lee. 2008. Xiongnu elite tomb complexes in the Mongolian Altai. *Silk Road* 5(2):27–35.

Miniaev, Sergei S., and Julia Elikhina. 2009. On the chronology of the Noyon uul barrows. *Silk Road* 7:21–35.

Murphy, Brett P., and David M. J. S. Bowman. 2007. Seasonal water availability predicts the relative abundance of C_3 and C_4 grasses in Australia. *Global Ecology and Biogeography* 16(2):160–169. https://doi.org/10.1111/j.1466-8238.2006.00285.x

Passey, Benjamin H., and Thure E. Cerling. 2002. Tooth enamel mineralization in ungulates: Implications for recovering a primary isotopic time-series. *Geochimica et Cosmochimica Acta* 66(18):3225–3234. https://doi.org/10.1016/S0016-7037(02)00933-X

Payne, Sebastian. 1973. Kill-off patterns in sheep and goats: The mandibles from Aşvan Kale. *Anatolian Studies* 23:281–303. https://doi.org/10.2307/3642547

Pearcy, Robert W., Nina Tumosa, and Kimberlyn Williams. 1981. Relationships between growth, photosynthesis and competitive interactions for a C_3 and C_4 plant. *Oecologia* 48:371–376. https://doi.org/10.1007/BF00346497

Pederzani, Sarah, and Kate Britton. 2019. Oxygen isotopes in bioarchaeology: Principles and applications, challenges and opportunities. *Earth-Science Reviews* 188:77–107. https://doi.org/10.1016/j.earscirev.2018.11.005

Polosmak, Natalia V., Evgeniy S. Bogdanov, Damdinsuren Tseveendorj, and Nasan-Ochir Erdene-Ochir. 2008. The burial construction of Noin Ula mound 20, Mongolia. *Archaeology, Ethnology and Anthropology of Eurasia* 34(2):77–87. https://doi.org/10.1016/j.aeae.2008.07.007

R Core Team. 2022. R: A language and environment for statistical computing [software]. Version 4.0.1. R Foundation for Statistical Computing, Vienna, Austria. https://www.R-project.org/

Roe, Emery, Lynn Huntsinger, and Keith Labnow. 1998. High reliability pastoralism. *Journal of Arid Environments* 39(1):39–55. https://doi.org/10.1006/jare.1998.0375

Rogers, J. Daniel. 2012. Inner Asian states and empires: Theories and synthesis. *Journal of Archaeological Research* 20(3):205–256.

Shelach, Gideon. 2009. Violence on the frontiers? Sources of power and socio-political change at the easternmost parts of the Eurasian steppe during the late second and early first millennia BCE. In: Bryan K. Hanks and Katheryn M. Linduff, eds. *Social Complexity in Prehistoric Eurasia: Monuments, Metals, and Mobility*. New York: Cambridge University Press. pp. 241–272.

Taylor, William T. T., Jargalan Burentogtokh, K. Bryce Lowry, Julia Clark, Tumurbaatar Tuvshinjargal, and Jamsranjav Bayarsaikhan. 2017. A Bayesian chronology for early domestic horse use in the Eastern Steppe. *Journal of Archaeological Science* 81:49–58. https://doi.org/10.1016/j.jas.2017.03.006

Tieszen, Larry L. 1991. Natural variations in the carbon isotope values of plants: Implications for archaeology, ecology, and paleoecology. *Journal of Archaeological Science* 18(3):227–248. https://doi.org/10.1016/0305-4403(91)90063-U

Törbat, Tsagaan, Chunag Amartuvshin, and Ulambayar Erdenebat. 2003. *Archaeological Monuments of Egiin Gol Valley*. Ulaanbaatar: Institute of Archaeology, Mongolian Academy of Science. 295 pp. [in Mongolian.]

van der Merwe, Nikolaas J. 1982. Carbon isotopes, photosynthesis, and archaeology: Different pathways of photosynthesis cause characteristic changes in carbon isotope ratios that make possible the study of prehistoric human diets. *American Scientist* 70(6):596–606. https://www.jstor.org/stable/27851731

Ventresca Miller, Alicia, Ricardo Fernandes, Anneke Janzen, Ayushi Nayak, Jillian Swift, Jana Zech, Nicole Boivin, and Patrick Roberts. 2018. Sampling and pretreatment of tooth enamel carbonate for stable carbon and oxygen isotope analysis. *JoVE Journal, Biochemistry* 138:e58002. https://doi.org/10.3791/58002. Online video, 7:57 min. https://doi.org/10.3791/58002-v

Ventresca Miller, Alicia R., Ashley Haruda, Victor Varfolomeev, Alexander Goryachev, and Cheryl A. Makarewicz. 2020. Close management of sheep in ancient Central Asia: Evidence for foddering, transhumance, and extended lambing seasons during the Bronze and Iron Ages. *STAR: Science and Technology of Archaeological Research* 6(1):41–60. https://doi.org/10.1080/20548923.2020.1759316

Ventresca Miller, Alicia R., and Cheryl A. Makarewicz. 2019. Intensification in pastoralist cereal use coincides with the expansion of trans-regional networks in the Eurasian steppe. *Scientific Reports* 9:8363. https://doi.org/10.1038/s41598-018-35758-w

Vigne, Jean-Denis, and Daniel Helmer. 2007. Was milk a "secondary product" in the Old World Neolithisation process? Its role in the domestication of cattle, sheep and goats. *Anthropozoologica* 42(2):9–40.

Volkov, Vitali V. 1995. Early nomads of Mongolia. In: Jeannine Davis-Kimball, Vladimir A. Bashilov, and Leonid T. Yablonsky, eds. *Nomads of the Eurasian Steppes in the Early Iron Age*. Berkeley, CA: Zinat Press. pp. 317–333.

Wilkin, Shevan, Alicia Ventresca Miller, Bryan K. Miller, Robert N. Spengler III, William T. Taylor, Ricardo Fernandes, Richard W. Hagan, Madeleine Bleasdale, Jana Zech, S. Ulziibayar, et al. 2020. Economic diversification supported the growth of Mongolia's nomadic empires. *Scientific Reports* 10:3916. https://doi.org/10.1038/s41598-020-60194-0

Winslow, Jerome C., E. Raymond Hunt Jr., and Stephen C. Piper. 2003. The influence of seasonal water availability on global C_3 versus C_4 grassland biomass and its implications for climate change research. *Ecological Modelling* 163(1–2):153–173. https://doi.org/10.1016/S0304-3800(02)00415-5

Wittmer, M. H. O. M., K. Auerswald, R. Tungalag, Y. F. Bai, R. Schäufele, and H. Schnyder. 2008. Carbon isotope discrimination of C3 vegetation in Central Asian grassland as related to long-term and short-term precipitation patterns. *Biogeosciences* 5(3):913–924. https://doi.org/10.5194/bg-5-913-2008

Wright, Joshua. 2021. Prehistoric Mongolian archaeology in the early 21st century: Developments in the steppe and beyond. *Journal of Archaeological Research* 29(3):431–479. https://doi.org/10.1007/s10814-020-09152-y

WRIGHT, JOSHUA, GALDAN GANBAATAR, WILLIAM HONEYCHURCH, BATDALAI BYAMBATSEREN, AND ARLENE ROSEN. 2019. The earliest Bronze Age culture of the south-eastern Gobi Desert, Mongolia. *Antiquity* 93(368):393–411. https://doi.org/10.15184/aqy.2018.174

WRIGHT, JOSHUA, WILLIAM HONEYCHURCH, AND CHUNAG AMARTUVSHIN. 2009. The Xiongnu settlements of Egiin Gol, Mongolia. *Antiquity* 83(320):372–387. https://doi.org/10.1017/S0003598X00098495

YERUUL-ERDENE, CHIMIDDORJ. 2014. Topographic study of Gol Mod Xiongnu aristocratic cemetery. *Studia Archaeologica* 34:236–244. [in Mongolian.]

ZAZZO, ANTOINE, MARIE BALASSE, BENJAMIN H. PASSEY, A. P. MOLONEY, F. J. MONAHAN, AND OFAF SCHMIDT. 2010. The isotope record of short-and long-term dietary changes in sheep tooth enamel: Implications for quantitative reconstruction of paleodiets. *Geochimica et Cosmochimica Acta* 74(12):3571–3586. https://doi.org/10.1016/j.gca.2010.03.017

ZAZZO, ANTOINE, MARIE BALASSE, AND WILLIAM P. PATTERSON. 2005. High-resolution $\delta^{13}C$ intratooth profiles in bovine enamel: Implications for mineralization pattern and isotopic attenuation. *Geochimica et Cosmochimica Acta* 69(14):3631–3642. https://doi.org/10.1016/j.gca.2005.02.031

CHAPTER SEVEN

Production and Distribution of Early Period Yue Wares in China in the Second through Sixth Centuries CE

WU Shuang, CHEN Hongbo, WANG Lei, and ZHENG Jianming

Yue-type (越) wares are the most celebrated kind of high-fired green glazed ceramics, or celadon, produced in Zhejiang from the second to sixth centuries CE. For a long time, Yue wares held a leading position among consumers of porcelains (*ci* [瓷]) in China before white porcelains were invented and gained popularity in northern China. Broadly speaking, the technological system of production of Yue wares greatly influenced later ceramic production in China, especially celadon production and use in southern China.

The most famous kind of Yue ware is Mi-se (秘色) ware, which was sent as tribute to the imperial court during the Tang (唐) dynasty (618–907 CE) and unearthed from the Famen Temple (法门寺) in the 1980s (Han et al. 1988). Although the Mi-se wares are so famous that many people think Yue wares were only produced during the Sui (隋) (581–618 CE) and Tang dynasties, the production of Yue wares actually dates from as early as the late Eastern Han dynasty (25–220 CE). Artisans also kept producing Yue wares until the end of the Song (宋) dynasty (960–1279 CE). On the basis of the chronology of different forms of Yue wares, Ren (1994) suggests that the whole history of Yue wares should be divided into three phases: the early period, the Tang dynasty, and the Southern Song (1127–1279 CE) dynasty. Lin (1999) subdivides the development of Yue wares further and proposes four phases: (1) the production of proto-porcelain, (2) the Eastern Han dynasty to the Sui dynasty (the early Yue ware), (3) the Tang and Song dynasties and the Northern Song dynasty, and (4) the imitation of the Yue ware (the Southern Song dynasty and the later period). Du (2007) proposes instead that Yue wares only have two developmental periods, early and late, with the Sui–Tang dynasties as the boundary. No matter how the development of Yue wares is regarded, there is now a common view among Chinese scholars that the early period of Yue wares was from the late Eastern Han dynasty to the Southern dynasties period (420–589 CE).

Compared with the Yue wares of the Sui and Tang dynasties, the early period of Yue wares has not been a hot topic of research among Chinese scholars, due to the lack of firsthand material and discovery of kiln sites. It was not until 1975 when celadon was unearthed from the burial at Fenghuabaidu (Wang L. and Lin 1981) that there was proof of celadon manufacturing beginning in Zhejiang Province as early as the late Eastern Han dynasty. Combining chronological and typological analysis in the 1980s, Zhu (1981) realized that some products from the Xiaoxiantan kiln site (Yu 1995) were made in the style of the Eastern Han dynasty. Afterward celadon production in Shangyu from the second to sixth century CE became a debated research topic. With the investigation and excavation of kiln sites in Shangyu, Niguposhan (Zheng J.L. 2007), Dayuanpin (Xu J.M. et al. 2009), Jinshan (Zheng J.M. 2015), and Fenghuangshan (Zheng J.M. 2016), researchers began to determine that, apart from Mi-se wares that circulated around Shanglin Lake (上林湖) in northern Zhejiang Province, there were other production centers in Zhejiang producing a variety of styles of early period Yue wares.

As for other types of ceramics, people often used Yue wares for daily life, burial, and ritual activities. During the earliest phase of production the shapes of early Yue wares seemed to mimic bronze vessels and lacquerware. But early period Yue wares include vessels vividly depicting the natural world. For example, animal shapes were used both as ornaments and for the main body of vessels. During the second through sixth centuries CE several political and social changes in China, notably the transition from unity to the division of the country, separated the north and south. The production and trade of early Yue wares must have been affected by such major social and culture changes, especially in southern China. Understanding the origin and the development of Yue wares requires a deeper analysis of the production process.

This essay aims to introduce archaeological remains that reveal patterns of production and distribution for early period Yue wares during the second through the sixth centuries CE in northern Zhejiang Province. We aim to increase understanding about production of early period Yue wares and discuss related issues about Yue wares and early celadon production in general. We analyze remains for 179 kiln sites and 140 tombs. We maintain that analysis of early period Yue ware production technology can help elucidate the relationship between proto-porcelain manufacture and the later production of celadon, in addition to other kinds of ceramic production among different regions. Last, but not the least, we also discuss how early period Yue wares continued to develop from the second through the sixth centuries CE. Analysis of changes in the early Yue wares, comparison of their production technology, along with analysis of the environmental and historical contexts, assist us in understanding changes in beliefs about aesthetics and behaviors in the use of these ceramics.[1]

Early Yue Wares as Celadon

People in early China distinguished different kinds of ceramics such as celadon and different kinds of porcelain by surface color from slip or glaze. As early as the Tang dynasty, the word "green" (*lu*) was used to describe Yue wares and the color of jade (Zhejiang Provincial Institute of Archaeology et al. 2002). For a long time people called green glazed ware *qing ci* (青瓷), translated into English as celadon. The term celadon is used instead to refer to high-fired green glazed wares from the Eastern Han dynasty to the Ming dynasty, with a production area including both south and north China.

To understand this better, we should discuss the meaning of celadon in more detail. The word celadon is defined as "a ceramic glaze originating in China that is greenish in color; also: an object with a celadon glaze" ("Celadon." Merriam-Webster.com Dictionary, Merriam-Webster, https://www.merriam-webster.com/dictionary/celadon; accessed 2 July 2024).

There is a more specific definition offered by archaeologist Wang Changsui (2004:91): "Celadon is a ware produced by using porcelain/china stone for the body, with the surface covered with high fired glaze, and fired at a temperature not lower than 1150 °C."

From the second to the sixth century CE, northern Zhejiang had the most advanced celadon producing technology in China. Li J.Z.'s (1978) scientific research on sherd samples from the Xiaoxiantan kiln site, H5, indicated that the quality of the ceramics had reached the standard of modern ceramics. As a result, Li J.Z. (1978) concluded that the successful production of mature celadon in China dates from the late period of the Eastern Han dynasty. Two years later, Guo, Wang, and Chen (1980) conducted a study on twenty-five celadon vessels from major eras of ancient China and concluded that high-quality celadon was already being made during the late period of the Eastern Han dynasty. After twenty-nine more years, Xu J.M. et al. (2009) tested another two samples from Dayuanping, a kiln site of the Eastern Han period. We have summarized the results of these analyses by porosity, absorbency, and firing temperature (Table 7.1). The definition offered by Xu J.M. et al. (2009) was then widely accepted. So, for a long time, Chinese scholars have regarded the invention of celadon, or fired, green glazed wares, as the beginning of Chinese *ci*, or porcelain, with the highest quality celadon wares the early period Yue wares.

In translations from modern Chinese into Western languages, the meaning of *ci* is equated to both stoneware and porcelain (Kerr and Wood 2004). Chinese and Western scholars also debate when porcelain originated in China. Scholars in China regard celadon as originating during the Eastern Han dynasty as *ci*, but Western scholars disagree. Henderson (2000) points out that celadon is a kind of stoneware and celadon is known in the West by that name because of its green glaze. Wood (1999) uses the word celadon instead to mean only the products of Longquan (龙泉) in southwestern Zhejiang, which was as famous as the Yue wares. However, he uses stoneware or green glaze ware to describe the ceramics from northern Zhejiang. It seems there is still no common view about celadon among scholars. We can next try focusing on other definitions.

Hobson (1976) noticed a new ceramic product that appeared in the Han dynasty and called it *tz'u* (*ci*), but it seems that he could not find a definitive word to describe it. Rice (2015) agrees with Hobson's idea but used the word celadon instead for those wares produced in the Longquan area from the eleventh through thirteen centuries CE. According to western researchers, starting with the Eastern Han dynasty one kind of ceramic product covered with green glaze appeared in Zhejiang, but they incorrectly describe it in different ways, such as proto-porcelain or stoneware.

The lack of understanding about the early phase of celadon production by Western scholars is due to challenges such as the lack of research materials and publications in different languages. But Chinese and Western scholars agree that there was one kind of new ceramic in China during the Han dynasty. Considering both the scientific analysis by all the Chinese scholars discussed above and the ideas of Rice (2015), we conclude that the celadon that developed during the second through the sixth centuries CE in China is one kind of high-fired green glazed ware, which uses porcelain stone as the material for the body, has a surface covered by green glaze, and is fired at temperatures from 1150 to 1310 °C. It therefore has the features of "porcelaneous" stoneware.

Distribution of the Early Period Yue Wares

The four hundred years from the late Eastern Han dynasty through the Six Dynasties period (六朝时期, from the second through the sixth centuries CE) in China was a time of political disunity, with different political powers in control across southern China (Table 7.2). Celadon appeared in the lower reaches of the Yangtze River as early as the second century CE, earlier than in other regions. It was not until the sixth century that people in northern China began to produce celadon (Henderson 2000).

TABLE 7.1. The porosity, absorbency, and firing range of ceramic samples from second- to sixth-century CE Zhejiang Province (Guo, Wang, and Chen 1980; Xu J.M. et al. 2009). *Abbreviations*: SHM, Shanghai Museum; ZJIA, Zhejiang Provincial Institute of Archaeology; ZJM, Zhejiang Provincial Museum. See Table 7.2 for era symbol definitions.

Form	Era	Location	Site number	Porosity (%)	Absorbency (%)	Firing temperature (°C)	Sample source
Lei (罍)	EH	Shangyu (上虞), Xiaoxiantan (小仙坛) kiln site	H4	0.66	0.32	1160 ± 20	ZJM
Lei (罍)	EH	Shangyu (上虞), Xiaoxiantan (小仙坛) kiln site	H5	0.62	0.28	1310 ± 20	ZJM
Guan (罐)	WJ	Shangyu (上虞), tomb	J4	0.92	0.42	About 1300	ZJM
Sherd	WJ	Shangyu (上虞), Zhangzishan (帐子山) 窑址	J5	1.31	0.60	1180 ± 20	ZJM
Guan (罐)	EJ	Shaoxing (绍兴) tomb	J6	2.68	1.22	1270 ± 20	ZJM
Bowl (碗)	SD	Shangyu (上虞), Zhangzishan (帐子山) 窑址	NB4	1.70	0.73	1190 ± 20	ZJM
Basin (盆)	EH	Shangyu (上虞), Xiaoxiantan (小仙坛) kiln site	SY8-5	0.36	0.16	1270	ZJM, ZJIA
Guan (罐)	EH	Shangyu (上虞),	SY8-7	0.49	0.22	1260	ZJM, ZJIA
Bowl (碗)	TK	Shangyu (上虞), Zhangzishan (帐子山) 窑址	SHT-12	1.06	0.45	1240	ZJM, ZJIA
Xi (洗)	EJ	Shangyu (上虞),	SY-16	1.06	0.5	1220	ZJM, ZJIA
Sherd	EH	Shangyu (上虞),	DYP5	0.57	—	1270 ± 20	SHM
Sherd	EH	Shangyu (上虞),	DYP6	0.75	—	1200 ± 20	SHM

TABLE 7.2. Major historical eras of Zhejiang Province and other areas of southern China.

Symbol	Era	Date (CE)
EH*	Eastern Han dynasty (东汉)	25–220
TK	Three Kingdoms (Sun Wu dynasty) (三国–孙吴)	229–280
WJ*	Western Jin dynasty (西晋)	280–316
EJ	Eastern Jin dynasty (东晋)	317–420
SD	Southern dynasties (南朝)	420–589
	Song (宋)	420–479
	Qi (齐)	479–501
	Liang (陈)	502–557
	Chen (陈)	557–589
S*	Sui dynasty (隋)	581–618

* Also relevant to areas of northern China discussed in this chapter.

In the past decades, excavation data shows that huge quantities of celadon have been uncovered from urban sites, smaller settlements, and burials. Tombs provide the most comprehensive data and many provide clear date information. When we compare the kinds of celadon excavated from burials with those from the kiln sites, it is evident that as early as the late Eastern Han dynasty, Yue wares were distributed in both southern and northern China. Some scholars have compared the burials that have celadon with celadon found at kiln sites, and with city sites for more information about this early period. Wei's (2011) research on the burials of the Six Dynasties period (220–589 CE) analyzed their structure, shape, and grave goods. He concluded that the lower reaches of the Yangtze River could be regarded as having a distinct burial culture, with Yue wares as the most distinguished kinds of celadon. At the same time, there is information on production areas for some kinds of early Yue wares. Since there is no other area with as many kiln sites with early Yue wares, it is commonly accepted that most of the celadons unearthed from sites in the lower reaches of the Yangtze River belong to the system of early Yue wares.

Using typological analysis combined with analysis of original reports, the following section uses data on tomb discoveries to interpret distribution patterns for the early period of Yue wares.

Tomb Sites of Southern China with Early Yue Wares
Jiangsu and Zhejiang Provinces were the political and economic centers of southern China from the second through the sixth centuries CE. Jiangsu Province has the most discoveries of tomb sites that include celadon. The published statistics, although incomplete, show that there are about 143 known tombs that contained celadon (Table 7.3). Except for the Three Kingdoms period (229–280 CE), the number of burials from each era is similar for Jiangsu and Zhejiang (Figure 7.1). Furthermore, most of the tombs are clustered in and around Nanjing, which had been the capital during the Six Kingdoms period. In Zhejiang almost all these tombs are located in the northeast area, where many kilns were discovered.

At the same time, archaeologists have found celadon in burials in other areas of southern China (for example, the tombs of Zhu Ran (朱然) [Ding 1986] in Anhui). Celadon wares also have been unearthed from Hubei, Fujian, and Guangdong Provinces. The number of tomb sites in those areas is less than that for Jiangsu and Zhejiang, and the quality of the celadon vessels is not as good as for those that were produced in Zhejiang. However, there has been no systematic research and at present there is not a common view about the production area for these celadon vessels. Therefore, our analysis here only includes tombs with clear information about the deceased individuals and dating.

Tomb Sites of Northern China with Early Yue Wares
Compared with southern China, celadon appeared later and was less common in northern China. The earliest tomb site in Luoyang, Henan Province, which yielded one kind of Yue ware dates to 287 CE (Jiang R. and Guo 1957). For now, there are thirteen known tomb sites in the north in Henan, Shanxi, and Jilin Provinces, with celadon vessels that were produced in Zhejiang (Figure 7.2). Overall, relatively few early celadons have been found in northern China. Accordingly, early celadon production was small in scale, even though it involved the most advanced production technology.

Functions and Production of Early Yue Wares

The earliest celadon excavated from southern China is a jar found in Anhui dated to 164 CE (Li C. 1978). By 175 CE, tombs in Zhejiang contain celadons, including *zao* (灶), jars, cups, and portable stoves or burners (Wang L. and Lin 1981). It was not until 219 CE (Gong and Zhou 2009) that people in the capital city of Nanjing placed celadon, including jars, bowls, and cups, in burials. Those early tombs show that the history of celadon production in China dates back as early as the middle and late phases of the Eastern Han dynasty. After that, celadon was one main kind of ceramic for use in daily life and for grave goods. However, even though celadon is a high quality and attractive kind of ceramic, large quantities of pottery vessels were still placed in tombs. In particular, sites in Zhejiang show that the granary jar was a common type of celadon and developed from an earlier pottery or earthenware form. Furthermore, given the era of political fragmentation, the style of early Yue wares was different than that for proto-porcelain; the styles of the early Yue wares seem intended to be more complex, innovative and diversified. During the early period of Yue ware production more than thirty kinds of decorative patterns are evident in Yue wares.

TABLE 7.3. The number of tomb sites with early Yue wares from different eras in Jiangsu and Zhejiang Provinces. See Table 7.2 for era symbol definitions.

Era	Jiangsu Province		Zhejiang Province	
	Location	Number of tombs	Location	Number of tombs
EH	Nanjing (南京)	1	Fenghua (奉化)	1
TK	Nanjing (南京)	13	Shengxian (嵊县)	2
	Jintan (金坛)	3	Shengzhou 嵊州)	1
	Suyang (溧阳)	1	Huangyanxiuling (黄岩秀岭)	1
			Chunan (淳安)	1
			Shangyu (上虞)	1
WJ	Nanjing (南京)	11	Shengxian (嵊县)	3
	Jurong (句容县)	1	Yuyao (余姚)	3
	Yixing (宜兴)	3	Ningbo (宁波)	2
	Yangzhou (扬州)	2	Anji (安吉)	2
	Liuhe (六合县)	1	Shaoxing (绍兴)	2
	Yutan (盱眙县)	1	Hangzhou (杭州)	2
	Wuxian (吴县)	1	Shangyu (上虞)	2
			Fenghua (奉化)	1
			Huangyan (黄岩)	1
			Zhuji (诸暨)	1
			Xinchang (新昌)	1
EJ	Nanjing (南京)	21	Xinchang (新昌)	6
	Zhenjiang (镇江)	5	Chuanan (淳安)	1
	Yangzhou (扬州)	1	Fenghua (奉化)	2
	Suyang (溧阳)	1	Huangyan (黄岩)	11
	Wuxi (无锡)	1	Shengxian (嵊县)	1
	Yixing (宜兴)	1	Shaoxing (绍兴)	1
			Linan (临安)	6
			Ruian (瑞安)	2
			Cixi (慈溪)	1
SD	Nanjing (南京)	5	Shengxian (嵊县)	1
			Linan (临安)	1
			Fenghua (奉化)	1
			Xinchang (新昌)	2
			Zhuji (诸暨)	1
			Huangyan (黄岩)	2

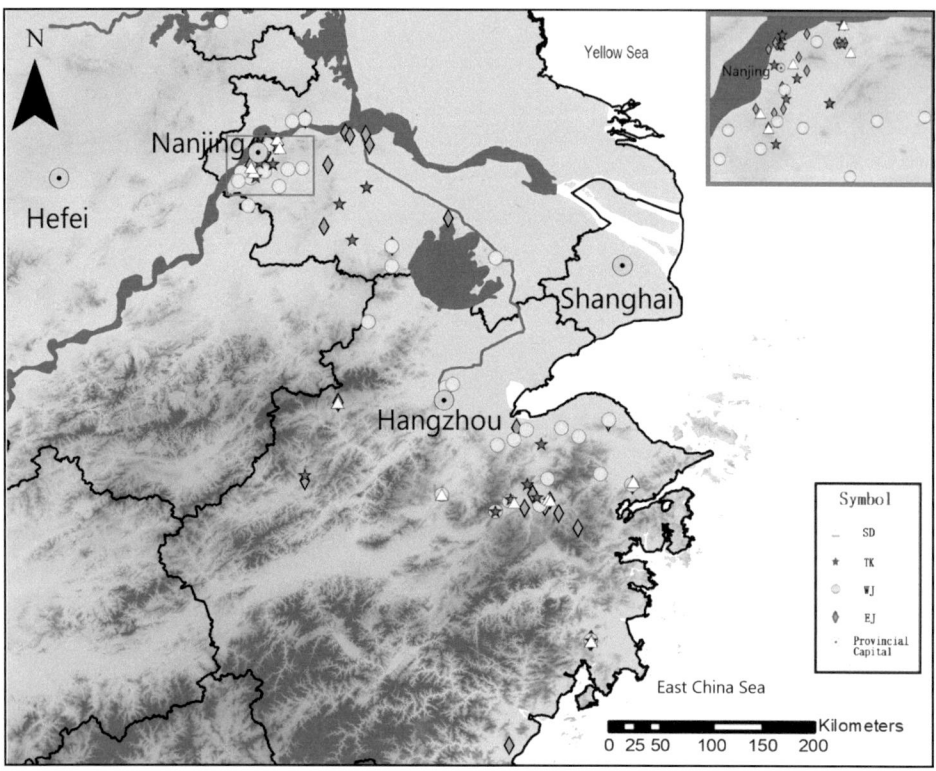

FIGURE 7.1. The location of tombs in southern China yielding early Yue wares. *Legend:* SD, Southern dynasties; TK, Three Kingdoms period; WJ, Western Jin dynasty; EJ, Eastern Jin dynasty.

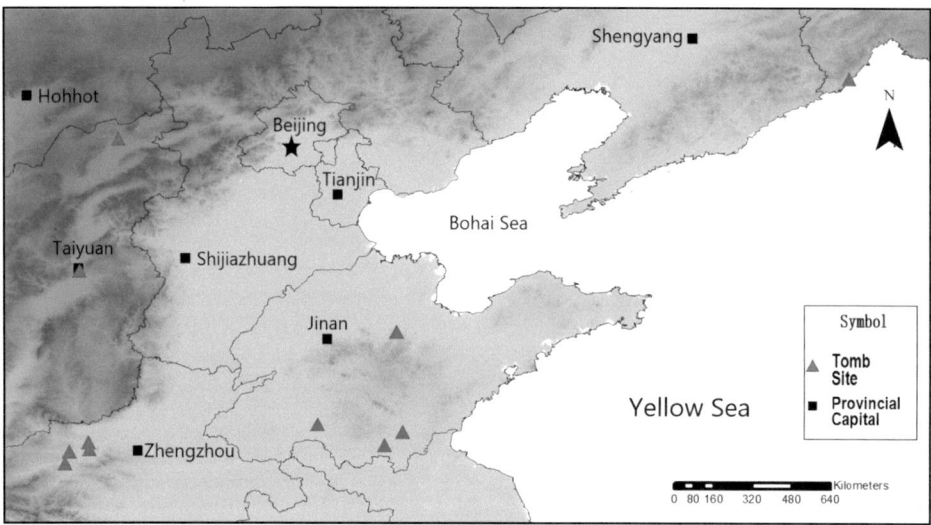

FIGURE 7.2. The location of tombs in northern China yielding early Yue wares.

Diverse Styles of Early Period Yue Wares

Benefiting from its favorable environment, Zhejiang Province has a long history of ceramic production from pottery to proto-porcelain and the successful production of early Yue wares, a technological achievement. The social and cultural contexts of the second through sixth centuries CE resulted in unique and diverse styles of early period Yue wares. First, in comparison with proto-porcelain, producers of early Yue wares imitated bronze vessels and lacquers less frequently. Even though some patterns are still regarded as imitating those on bronze vessels, early Yue wares are characterized more by innovation than imitation. But those vessels with patterns from bronzes are few and unearthed from upper class burials. Taking the flat kettle (扁壶) as an example, four flat kettles of celadon have been unearthed from burials. All are in Jiangsu Province, from tombs at Guojiashan (Museum of Nanjing 1998), Nonghuacun (Yue, Chen, and Tai 2013), Shizishan (Zhang Z. 1983), and Zhoumudun (Luo 1957). Research on burial practices by Wei (2011), Hsieh (1998), and Jiang Z. (2000) shows that those flat kettles were buried with the deceased of the upper class. Furthermore, even after huge changes and innovation in the patterns of early Yue wares, there are still obvious, basic characteristics with respect to the ornamentation of early Yue wares. One example of a kind of surface decoration is the use of the beast head, which is different from that on bronze vessels. The beast head for celadon wares lost its initial utility.

Early period Yue wares from southern China include whole vessels not only in the forms of animals such as sheep, lions, tigers (Figure 7.3A), and toads, but these also were used as ornaments. Feathers also were used as ornaments. In addition, Buddhist elements were another kind of ornaments (Figure 7.3B). Buddhism was introduced as early as the Eastern Han dynasty and during the Six Dynasties period (He and Ting 2023) and spread widely in southern China. Artisans produced early Yue wares in forms and with ornaments influenced by Buddhism. Furthermore, one of the most distinctive shapes of early Yue ware celadon for burials is the granary jar (Figure 7.3C). During the Three Kingdoms period celadon burial goods became more popular and included forms such as models of granaries, kitchen utensils, wells, and pigsties (Figure 7.3D). The granary jar developed from the five-tubed vase of the Han dynasty and its vivid effects made it one of the most distinct wares of the early Yue period. Tong (2006) argues from his systematic research on the granary jar that its function in tombs was significant for storage or sacrifice.

Yue Wares and Pottery Vessels in Tombs

It seems that early Yue wares, together with pottery vessels, became very popular tomb gifts and that potters occasionally invented new types of celadon. However, mourners usually did not put celadon and pottery vessels of the same form and function in tombs at the same time.

For the Three Kingdoms period, there are twenty-three tombs yielding celadon that have clear information about dating. Seventeen are located in Jiangsu and six in Zhejiang, but some tombs in both modern provinces were once within the state of Sun Wu. There are fifteen tombs in Jiangsu Province yielding both celadon and pottery vessels. In seven of these tombs there are more pottery vessels than celadon. For tombs in the Zhejiang area, one tomb contains only a single pottery jar. There are forty excavated tombs from the Western Jin dynasty in Jiangsu and Zhejiang. These show that the amount of pottery in tombs decreased over time; thirty-one of the tombs have more celadon than pottery. In addition, twenty-eight of those tombs only include celadon as ceramic gifts to accompany objects

FIGURE 7.3. Early celadon wares from southern China. **A.** Tiger-shaped vessel from Shengzhou (嵊州), Zhejiang Province. Photo credit: Zheng Jianming. **B.** *Zun* vessel with beast head and Buddhist stylistic elements unearthed at the Fenghuangshan (凤凰山) kiln site. Photo credit: Wu Shuang. **C.** Granary jar from Shengzhou, Zhejiang Province. Photo credit: Zheng Jianming. **D.** *Lanjuan* funerary (pigsty) model from Shengzhou, Zhejiang Province. Photo credit: Zheng Jianming.

made of other materials. From the Eastern Jin dynasty, there are sixty-one tombs yielding celadon, and for this period as well the use of pottery as grave goods continued to decrease. Eighteen of thirty tombs in Jiangsu yielded both celadon and pottery, while in Zhejiang only three tombs out of thirty-one did. During the Southern Song period, affected by the decline of celadon manufacture and changes in funeral customs, celadon no longer was one of the main tomb gifts. Only one excavated tomb in Jiangsu yielded celadon, whereas all eight tombs in Zhejiang contained celadon, with only one including pottery.

This shows that celadon did not replace pottery completely during the period from the second through the sixth centuries CE, even in the area with the most production and use of celadon. At the same time, the differences in use as seen from the tombs in Zhejiang and Jiangsu indicate that celadon became popular later in Jiangsu and declined earlier in Jiangsu than in Zhejiang (Figure 7.4).

The Distribution of Kiln Sites

Although the available information dating early celadon manufacture is scarce and not easy to interpret, there is a large quantity of excavated sherds and vessels from second- through sixth-century CE kiln sites in northeastern Zhejiang Province. Most of those remains are informative about celadon production.

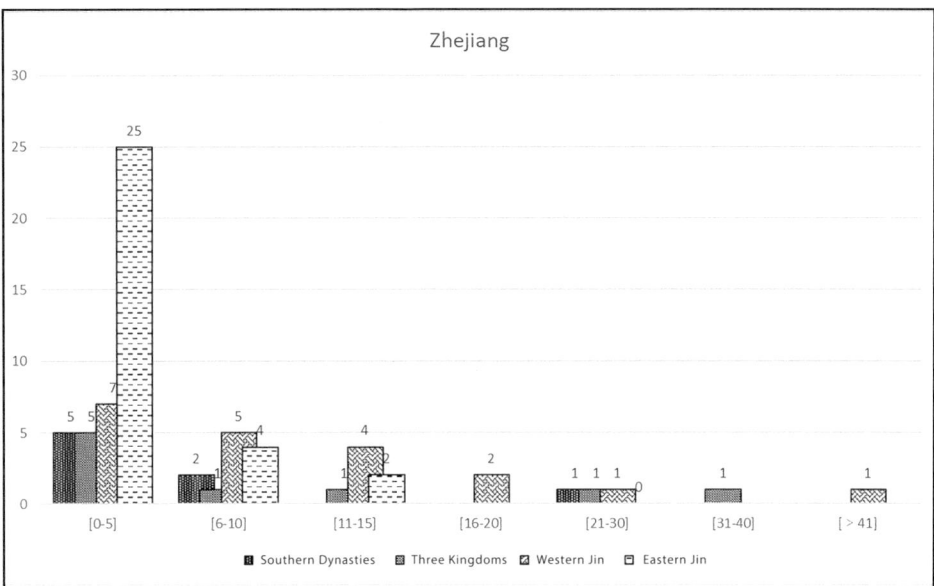
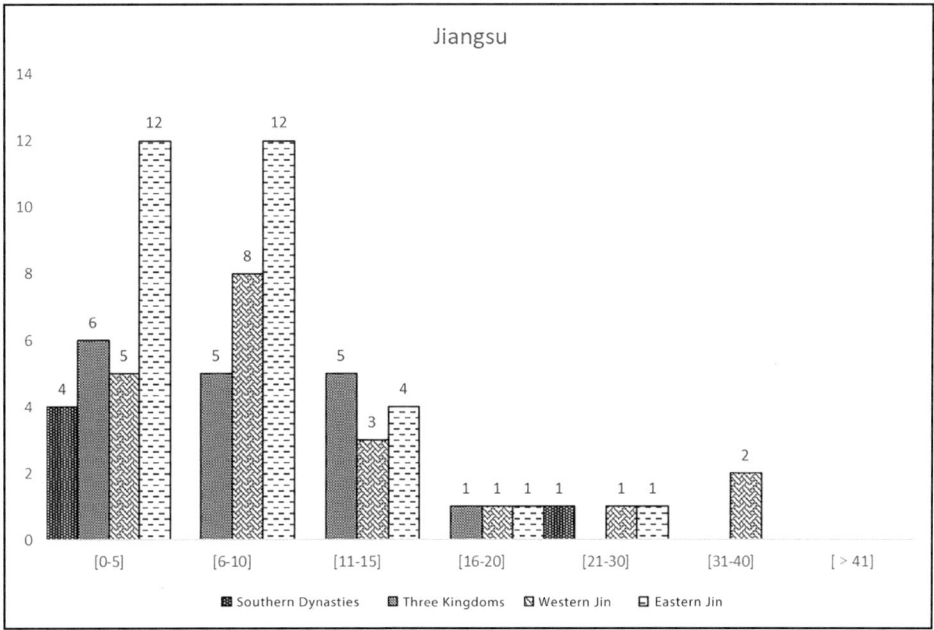

FIGURE 7.4. The number of early celadon wares excavated from tombs. **A.** Zhejiang Province. **B.** Jiangsu Province.

Details on Kiln Sites

Kiln sites for celadon production were first found in the 1930s. At that time, scholars thought that all dated to after the second through sixth centuries CE. It was not until the 1950s that earlier celadon-producing kiln sites were found and confirmed. Then, after three formal surveys to discover cultural artifacts and many investigations by the Archaeological Institute of Zhejiang, about 179 early kiln sites were confirmed. Since the 1990s, some of these kiln sites have been excavated. This fundamental work helped to map the distribution and the nature of celadon production over time (Table 7.4). Several kilns were used for more than one period, but we provide specific data for each period.

Diachronic Distribution of Kiln Sites

The number of kiln sites increased from the Eastern Han dynasty through the Western Jin dynasty (Figure 7.5). The diachronic distribution of kiln sites presents as a wave with an obvious curve. However, according to the data, most of those kiln sites dating to the Eastern Han dynasty were not used to produce only one kind of ceramic. Usually they produced earthenware, proto-porcelain, black glazed ware, and celadon. Since not all the kiln sites were excavated and published, and the survey data was made by different researchers, it is hard to distinguish clearly how many of the Eastern Han dynasty kiln sites produced only celadon. However, this does not affect the overall observation of changes in the number of kilns. Broadly speaking, the period from the Qin (221–206 BCE) to the Han (206 BCE–220 CE) dynasty involved transition between earthenware and stoneware (Chinese Ceramic Society 1982), with simultaneous production of pottery, proto-porcelain, and celadon.

Apart from the Eastern Han dynasty, the products of kiln sites from the other periods involve only celadon. For the Three Kingdoms period there are two categories of kiln sites. One type developed after the Eastern Han dynasty, which involved a change from production of multiple products to only celadon; the other type of kiln site only produced celadon over time. The later Western Jin (265–317 CE) dynasty was the peak of celadon production, achieving maximum production capacity from the second through the sixth centuries CE. From the beginning of the Eastern Jin (317–420 CE) dynasty the number of kiln sites decreased.

Early celadon manufacturing in Zhejiang from the Western Jin dynasty shows a trend of fast development followed by a period of stagnation (Figure 7.5B).

Regional Distribution

Because of the limited excavation of kiln sites, previous scholars considered the Shanglin Lake (上林湖) area to be the celadon production center of ancient Zhejiang. However, recent data show that the production center for the early period of celadon production, from the second through sixth centuries CE, was Shangyu (上虞), not Shanglin Lake (Figure 7.6). During the Eastern Han dynasty, 59% of the kiln sites in Zhejiang were in the Shangyu area. Later, in the Three Kingdoms period and Western Jin dynasty, after mature celadon wares appeared, 71% of the kiln sites were in Shangyu. Other areas in Zhejiang had fewer kilns for celadon production. During the Eastern Jin dynasty Shangyu lost the leading position with respect to the concentration of kiln sites in southern China. During the Southern dynasties period, even if we regard this to be a period of stagnation for celadon production as a whole, Shangyu still has the largest number of kiln sites.

TABLE 7.4. The number of kiln sites in second- to sixth-century CE Zhejiang Province. See Table 7.2 for era symbol definitions. A dash indicates not present.

Location	Eras				
	EH	TK	WJ	EJ	SD
Huzhou (湖州)	5	3	—	4	4
Shaoxing (绍兴)	4	3	5	2	1
Shangyu (上虞)	45	42	53	4	5
Cixi (慈溪)	10	2	—	6	4
Ningbo (宁波)	6	2	1	—	1
Taizhou (台州)	5	4	9	9	3
Yuyao (余姚)	1	3	6	2	1
Hangzhou (杭州)	—	—	1	5	1
Wenzhou (温州)	—	—	—	—	1
Total	76	59	75	32	21

Remains at Kiln Sites

Dragon Kilns

The dragon kiln (Figure 7.7) is one main kind of kiln from ancient China. At present, more than half of the kiln sites unearthed in China are dragon kilns and most are located in the lower reaches of the Yangtze River, particularly in Zhejiang Province (Xiong 1995).

A kiln was placed on the sloping side of a hill, forming essentially a tunnel on a gentle slope. The people who constructed dragon kilns made full use of the environmental resources, since the style and location helped create updrafts for firing that increased the temperature. The location on the hillside made it convenient to get wood and to avoid destruction from flooding and the drainage of water (Zhu 1984; Wood 1999). Southern China, especially Zhejiang, with its abundant forests, water, stone, and suitable clays, became the perfect area for the development of dragon kilns. At the same time, in a win-win situation, Zhejiang is abundant in another kind of essential raw material for celadon production—iron (Fe), the key element of the green glaze. The dragon kiln form enables both a reducing flame and rapid cooling (Ye and Cao 1979).

As early as the Shang and Zhou dynastic periods, the dragon kiln had been developed and used in the Shangyu area of Zhejiang. Some kilns of different periods in Zhejiang have been excavated (Zhejiang Provincial Institute of Archaeology 1987). These show that the dragon kiln was made of clay and organic material similar to the main structure. A sand layer on the floor stabilized the celadon when firing and protected wares from direct flames (Shen 2009). The excavation of the Qianshan kiln revealed traces of bamboo on the wall of the kiln (Zhejiang Provincial Institute of Archaeology 2005). Y. Wang (2010) and Shen (2009) supposed that the roof of the dragon kiln was made of bamboo and the structure was then covered by wet clay.

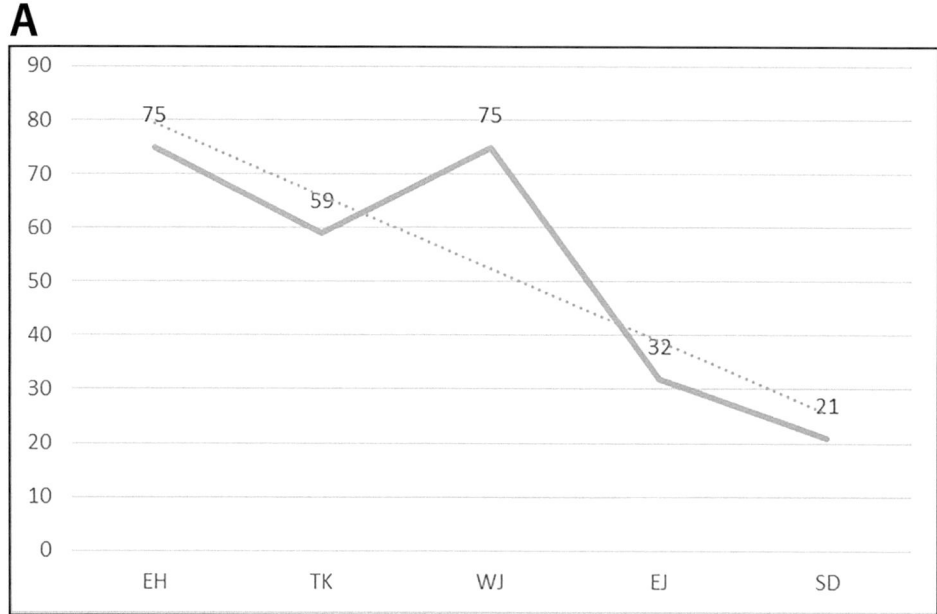

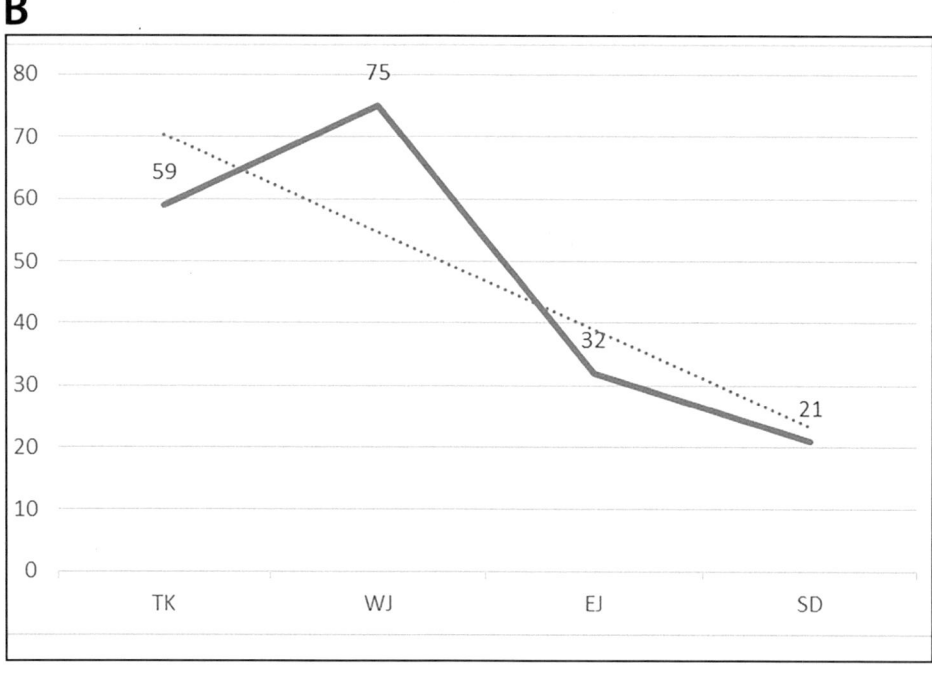

Figure 7.5. The number of kiln sites with celadon wares found in the Shangyu area of Zhejiang Province. **A.** From the Eastern Han dynasty (EH), Three Kingdoms period (TK), Western Jin dynasty (WJ), Eastern Jin dynasty (EJ), and Southern dynasties (SD) eras. Note that Eastern Han kilns fired black-glazed porcelain at the same time as celadon wares. **B.** From the Three Kingdoms period (TK), Western Jin dynasty (WJ), Eastern Jin dynasty (EJ), and Southern dynasties (SD) periods. Note that these kiln sites had exclusively celadon wares.

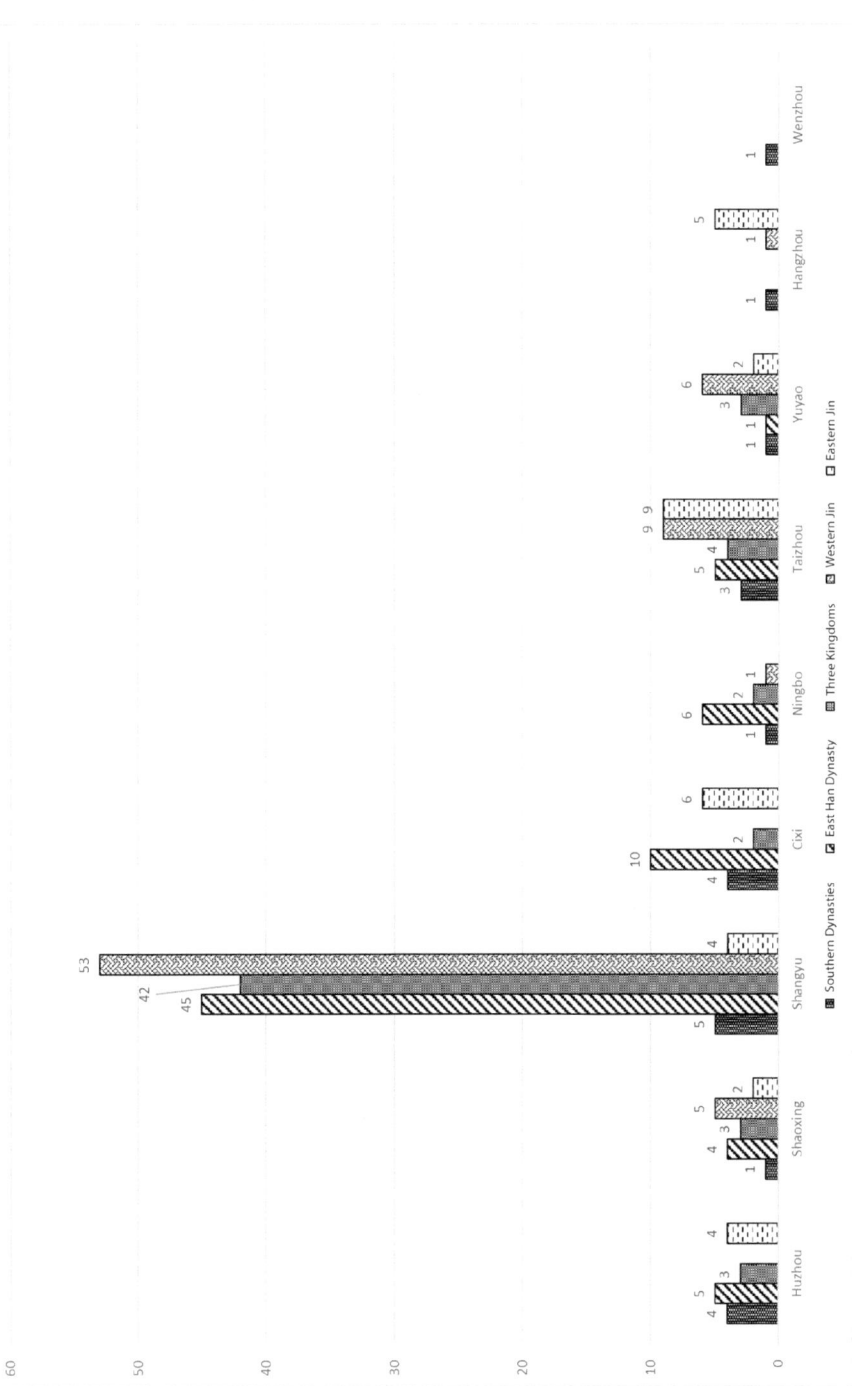

FIGURE 7.6. The number and distribution of kiln sites in different areas of Zhejiang Province from the second through sixth centuries CE.

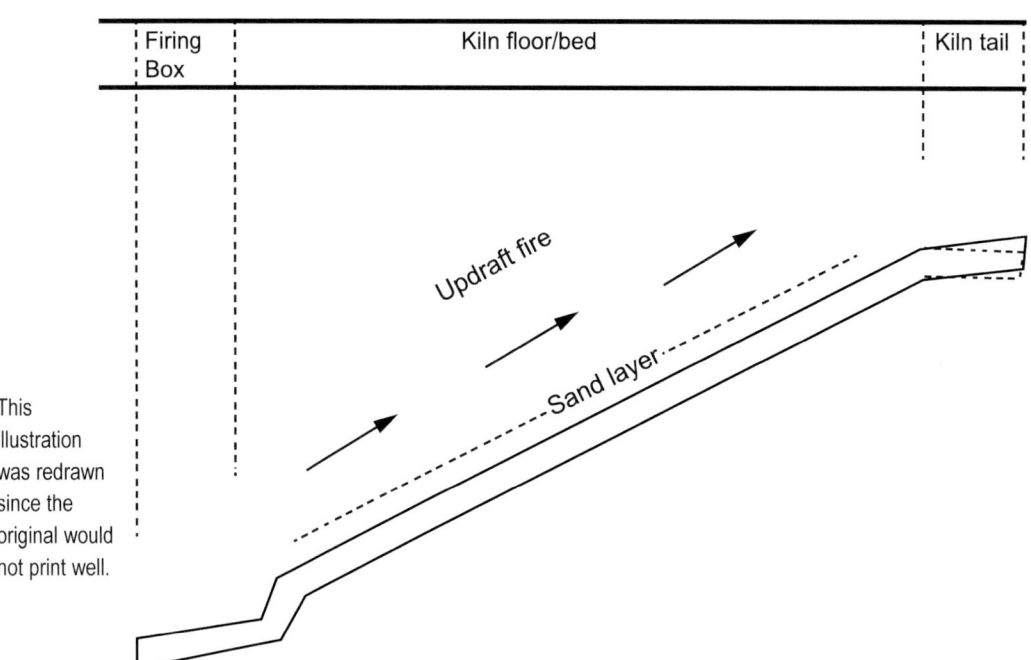

FIGURE 7.7. An exposed dragon kiln in Zhejiang Province. **A.** Evidence of the kiln internal structure. Photo credit: Wu Shuang. **B.** Plan of the dragon kiln floor.

In Shangyu from the second through the sixth centuries CE kiln building technology remained stable after a long period of experimentation (Table 7.5). In this period kilns were usually from 10 to 15 m long and about 2 to 2.5 m wide. The practice of making a hole or a door opening in the walls for adding wood had not been invented yet. Each time before firing vessels the potter needed to enter the kiln from the firebox, which was in the front of the kiln and at the lowest level, and then place the celadon wares in different places, depending on vessel size and the appropriate relative temperature for firing. Broadly speaking, compared with the early period kilns from the Eastern Han dynasty to the Southern Song dynasty, there are four main patterns. First, almost all the dragon kilns consisted of three parts: the firing box, kiln floor, and tail. Second, the kiln length was between 10 to 15 m, longer than in the earlier period. Third, to fire larger quantities of vessels the kiln furniture was often used for vessels of different forms and function. Fourth, most of the dragon kilns from this period included a chimney to provide a more stable firing temperature.

Workshops, Celadon Sherds, and Kiln Furniture

So far, few remains of workshops have been unearthed. On the one hand, even though Zhejiang Province was an economic center for thousands of years, workshops may have been destroyed, but on the other hand during the early period celadon production may have taken place inside and around the houses of individual potters. Compared with the kilns, there are few remains from workshops, such as equipment for clay handling and vessel forming.

Sherds are another very important category of remains from kiln sites. They were usually discarded with furniture and there are large quantities. Most of the sherds represent failed firing, broken vessels, or those with flaws. Their shapes and forms reveal all the products at individual kiln sites.

Kiln furniture is another important kind of equipment for celadon production in ancient Zhejiang. The different items described below were usually made of local clay. There were multiple forms and sizes of items that were used with the different style of celadon wares. Kiln furniture items were not used widely until the Eastern Han dynasty. As one of the most important technological innovations for ceramic production, the raw material use for furniture was low in cost, but the appearance and use of these items greatly helped to increase the quantity of vessels achieved from successful firings.

For any kiln excavation there are thousands of remains of furniture. Scholars assess the forms, sizes, and contexts of excavated pieces to make inferences about their functions. There are three main kinds: supporting furniture, propping furniture, and spacing furniture (Figure 7.8).

1. *Spacing furniture* was usually put between the celadon objects to make full use of space, to increase the total quantity of celadon products, and to reduce the breakage rate.

2. *Propping furniture* was usually put between the supporting furniture and the lowest level of the celadon wares in the kiln to play a stabilizing role, with their shapes and sizes decided by the bottom shape of the lowest level of ware.

3. *Supporting furniture* was usually put directly on the sand layer on the kiln floor to support the celadon ware, improve the firing atmosphere, and avoid destruction from the sand layer.

TABLE 7.5. Data for second- to sixth-century CE dragon kiln sites excavated in Shangyu District, Zhejiang Province (Shen Y. 2009; Wang Y. 2010). See Table 7.2 for era symbol definitions. A dash indicates no detailed data is available.

Kiln site	Era	Length (m)				Width (m)	Slope (°)				Chimney
		Total	Firebox	Floor	Tail		Total	Firebox	Floor	Tail	
Dayuanpin Y1 (大圓坪)	EH	>10	About 1.5	—	—	2.2	20	—	—	—	—
Xiaolu'ao Y1 (小陸岙)	EH	—	—	—	—	—	20	—	—	—	Present
Zhangzishan Y1 (帐子山)	EH	3	—	—	—	—	—	—	28	21	Present
Zhangzishan Y2 (帐子山)	EH	—	—	—	—	1.97–2.08	—	—	31	14	—
Anshan (鞍山)	TK	13	About 0.8	—	—	2.1–2.4	—	13	23	5	Present
Nigupo Y1 (尼姑婆)	TK–WJ	13	1.7	—	—	2.2	—	12	22	—	Present
Zhangzishan (帐子山) Jin dynasty (晋代)	WJ–EJ	—	—	—	—	2.4	—	—	10	<10	Present

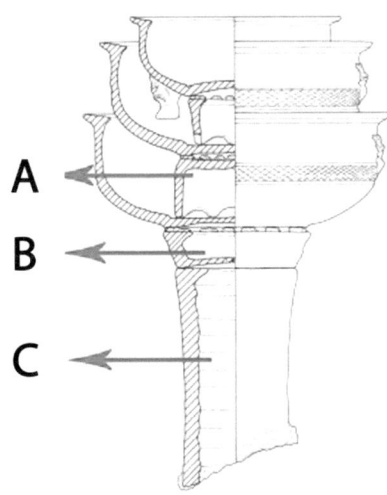
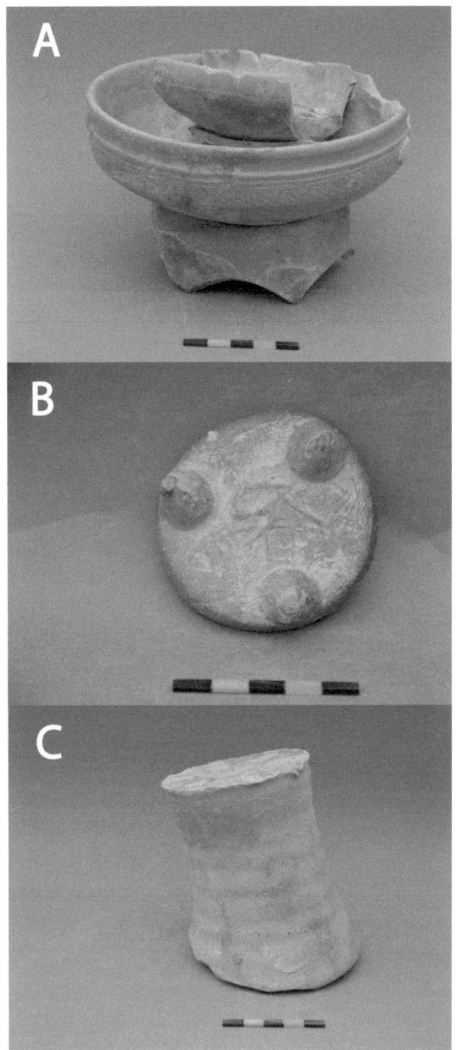

FIGURE 7.8. The three kinds of kiln furniture. Photo credits: Zheng Jianming.

It should be emphasized that individual items of furniture, such as items for propping up or spacing vessels, did not have a single function. Potters used them according to the individual situations they faced.

Moreover, the material used for clay furniture was affected by the intended specific function. To increase the quality of vessels and decrease the breakage rate as much as possible, potters during this period began to make furniture from different kinds of materials. Usually the spacing furniture was of porcelain stone, but the other kinds of furniture, which did not touch the celadon product directly, were still made with clay.

Discussion

Shangyu, the Production Center of Early Yue Wares

Our summary of the kiln sites and dated excavated celadon finds from Zhejiang identifies clear patterns that are worthy of discussion to better understand the early period of celadon production. The number of kiln sites found in Shangyu is higher than for other areas in Zhejiang, and in China as a whole, from the second through sixth centuries CE. During the Eastern Han period Shangyu had fifty-five kiln sites, 59% of the entire amount for all of Zhejiang. There are forty-three for the Three Kingdoms period and forty-five for the Western Jin dynasty. Even during the later period when celadon production began to decline, Shangyu still had five of the seven kiln sites dating to the Eastern Jin and Southern dynasties. The greater quantity of kiln sites indicates a higher celadon production capacity.

Apart from the number and scale of kiln sites, we should consider the quality of Shangyu celadon products. The Xiaoxiantan site is still regarded as representative of kiln sites for producing fully developed celadon. When we compare the celadon that was produced in other areas to celadon from Shangyu, it is clear that the quality of the glaze color and the body are better for the products from Shangyu. In addition, some celadons unearthed from tombs have clear information about the place of origin. The inscription of the surface of the green glazed tiger (*huzi*, 虎子) from the Nanjing Zhaoshigang (赵士岗) tomb (Museum of Nanjing 1980) says "257 CE made by Yuanyi (袁宜) in Shangyu." Another example is the bottle unearthed from Jintan, Jiangsu, with the inscription "this was made by Fanxiu (范休) in Shangyu" (Zhang M. and Huo 2008). Also, the inscription on the celadon tomb-guard unearthed in Wu country, Jiangsu, states "267 CE made in Kuaiji (会稽)." Shangyu was the center of the town of Kuaiji (Zhang Z. 1980). Those celadon vessels were rare in comparison to other kinds of celadons and made in special forms. However, there is little direct information about other production areas. The celadon ware from Shangyu is further evidence that Shangyu was an important producing center.

In northern China, there is no evidence for celadon production until the sixth century CE when some kiln sites appeared. In other areas of southern China, except Zhejiang, celadon production appeared later, with vessels of inferior quality and with fewer and scattered kiln sites. So it is logical to hypothesize that Shangyu was the celadon producing center of China with respect to scale and quality from the second through the sixth centuries CE.

Technological System: Dragon Kiln, Furniture, and Green Glaze

For about 1,300 years celadon was the most famous stoneware of southern China, a product of the most advanced ceramic technology that existed. During the Tang dynasty a common saying was that people like to use "green glazed wares in the south but white glazed wares in the north" (南青北白), reflecting the different kiln styles and consumer preferences of the north and south. As we have discussed, however, the technique of celadon production in Zhejiang originated much earlier. This had a big effect on other areas of China, as well as in Japan and Korea.

The name celadon mainly comes from its green color. Even though it is hard to say whether the popularity of green glaze ware promoted development of the dragon kiln building technique or not, it is true that there is a strong connection between the development of kiln building techniques and green glaze. From the perspective of kiln site remains, the early phase of celadon manufacture in the north of Zhejiang involved one common kind of dragon kiln with "dragon kiln plus furniture plus green glaze" factors (the varying amounts of iron oxide dissolved into the glazes during firing and the reducing atmospheres within the dragon kilns produced the greens). This is also the basic model of celadon production technology in southern China.

Almost all the celadon producing kilns found by archaeologists in Zhejiang Province are dragon kilns. As mentioned above, this type of kiln makes the most efficient use of local natural resources. Water, firing resources, and clay and porcelain stone resources are the three main factors affecting celadon production. Even though the dragon kiln was invented as early as the Shang and Western Zhou dynastic eras (around 1600–771 BCE), it was not until the later Eastern Han dynasty that the basic structure (which consists of a firing box, floor, and chimney) was used regularly. Different from the production of stamp stoneware or proto-porcelain, well-made celadon has a higher quality of glaze color and higher firing temperature. Locating the dragon type structure on the hill slope helps the fire updraft and the formation of the reducing flame, making the desired green color from the iron oxide (FeO) glaze. For this feature, the success and stability of the dragon kiln building technique is the fundamental feature of the development of celadon production. Tools or equipment are also important, but the furniture is essential to achieve the desired glaze. The system of furniture developed in Zhejiang made it possible to produce the green color that became famous in ancient China. This kiln furniture also made a large output and an increase in the quality of vessels possible. There are many kinds and types of furniture, as they were made according to type of object. At the very beginning, there were only some kinds of furniture, like clay bats or soil nails (*zhiding* [支钉], a kind of spacing furniture; see Figure 7.8). After the glaze was applied widely, more kinds of furniture were needed for the supporting or spacing function during the firings. So even though kiln furniture appeared during the Shang-Zhou (商–周) (around 1600–221 BCE) era (Zheng J.M. 2015:185–187), more effective kiln furniture was invented during the period from the second through sixth centuries CE.

As mentioned above, the technical system of celadon production, including the dragon kiln, furniture, and green color glaze, was completed during this period. It was later that there was production of Yue wares during the Sui and Tang dynastic periods, and the Longquan ware production from the Song period took the earlier model as its fundamental basis. Furthermore, the technology combining the dragon kiln, sophisticated kiln furniture, and production of special green glaze also had a great effect on ceramic production as a whole in China and areas beyond.

Conclusions

China has a long history of ceramic production and Yue wares constitute one of the most important kinds of glazed ceramics in ancient China. Wood (1999:37) states that the origin of Yue wares dates back to the Warring States period (481–221 CE) when yellowish-green stone wares were produced and used. Meanwhile, Chinese researchers documented the origin of celadon as the beginning of the third stage of Chinese ceramic history, affected by the invention of proto-porcelain, and early Yue wares produced in Zhejiang as one kind of the earliest porcelain-stoneware (*ci*) in China (Li J.Z. 1978). From this preliminary introduction and analysis of material about early period Yue wares, this chapter provides a synthesis of celadon production and transition to early period Yue wares.

First, early period Yue wares are one kind of celadon, with common styles of products, including the wares inspired by other factors (such as different materials as much as possible, with later inventions of patterns and ornamental styles). The innovation and changes in celadon production must have been affected by social and cultural changes from the second through sixth centuries CE.

Second, most of the celadon production kiln sites from the Eastern Han dynasty and Six Dynasties period are clustered in the middle reaches of the Cao'e River (曹娥江) in northeast Zhejiang. There is no doubt that the Shangyu area was the production center of early Yue wares. It can be seen from burials with celadon wares during this early period that celadon production was rather small in scale, with a consumer market near production centers, and with economic and political centers not far away. Furthermore, it is likely that the market price or value of celadon was higher than pottery, but lower than metal or jade products. At the same time, however, there were still some common forms of celadon, such as the flat kettles.

Last, but not least, after a long period of development, the fundamental and basic technological system of Chinese celadon production was established. The earliest celadon vessels– made from porcelain stone as the body material, bearing a surface covered by a green glaze, and produced at a firing temperature from 1150 to 1310 °C--had the features of "porcelaneous wares". In comparison with proto-porcelain, the Yue wares hold a more stable green glazed color. At the same time the technological system of early Yue wares took effect on celadon and porcelain production during later dynasties and in areas outside of China.

Notes
[1] Zeng Lingyi also conducted research about the production of ceramics in ancient China and published on the production of porcelain in Jingdezhen during the Yuan dynasty (1271–1368 CE); see Chapter 11.

References

CHINESE CERAMIC SOCIETY. 1982. *History of Ceramics in China.* Beijing: Cultural Relics Press. 127 pp. [in Chinese.]

DING, BANGJUN. 1986. Excavation report of the burial of Zhu Ran in Manshan, Anhui. *Wenwu* 3:1–15, 97–104. [in Chinese.]

DU, WEI. 2007. Investigation of the Yue kiln site in Shangyu. *Dongfang Wenwu* 24:6–15. [in Chinese.]

Gong, Juping, and Baohua Zhou. 2009. Longtaozhang tomb in Nanjing. *Kaogu* 2009(1):38–44. [in Chinese.]

GUO, YANYI, SHOUYING WANG, AND YAOCHENG CHEN. 1980. A study on the northern and southern celadons of ancient Chinese dynasties. *Guisuanyan Xuebao* 18(3):232–242. [in Chinese.]

HAN, WEI, ZANKUI WANG, XIANYONG JIN, WEI CAO, ZHOUFANG REN, JIANBANG HUAI, AND SHENGQI FU. 1988. Excavation report for the Femen temple of the Tang dynasty. *Wenwu* 10:1–28, 97–105. [in Chinese.]

HE, YUNAO, AND TING PAN. 2023. An overview of archaeological discoveries and research on early Buddhist remains in China. *Kaogu Yu Wenwu* 5:84–94. [in Chinese.]

HENDERSON, JULIAN. 2000. *The Science and Archaeology of Materials: An Investigation of Inorganic Materials.* New York: Routledge. 334 pp.

HOBSON, ROBERT L. 1976. *Chinese Pottery and Porcelain: An Account of the Potter's Art in China from Primitive Times to the Present Day.* New York: Dover Publications. Reprint of the 1915 edition originally published in 2 volumes by Funk and Wagnalls Co., New York.

HSIEH, MING-LIANG. 1998. Researching burial artifacts of the Six Dynasties from a class perspective. *Taiwan University Journal of Art History* 5:1–39. [in Chinese.]

JIANG, RUOSHI, AND WENXUAN GUO. 1957. The excavation of Jin tombs in Luoyang. *Acta Archaeologica Sinica* 1:169–185, 260–263. [in Chinese.]

JIANG, ZANCHU. 2000. Chronological analysis of Six Dynasties tombs found in the lower Yangtze River area. In: Jiang Zanchu, ed. *Treatises on the Archaeology and History of the Middle and Lower Valleys of the Yangtze River*. Beijing: China Science Publishing and Media, Ltd. pp. 74–84. [in Chinese.]

KERR, ROSE, AND NIGEL WOOD. 2004. Part 12, Ceramic technology. In: Joseph Needham, series ed. *Science and Civilisation in China*. Volume 5, Chemistry and Chemical Technology, edited by Rose Kerr. 1st ed. Cambridge: Cambridge University Press. pp. 709–711.

LI, CAN. 1978. Family tombs of Cao Cao in Bo country. *Wenwu* 8:12–16. [in Chinese.]

LI, JIANGZHI. 1978. A study on the emergence of porcelain in ancient China. *Guisuanyan Xuebao* 6:191–199. [in Chinese.]

LIN, SHIMIN. 1999. *Celadon and Yue Wares*. Shanghai: Rare Books Publishing House. 426 pp. [in Chinese.]

LUO, ZONGZHEN. 1957. Excavation report of the Jin tomb in Yixing, Jiangsu—about the unearthing of celadon. *Acta Archaeologica Sinica* 4:83–106, 143–151. [in Chinese.]

MUSEUM OF NANJING. 1980. *Celadon of the Six Dynasties in Jiangsu*. Beijing: Cultural Relics Press. 120 pp. [in Chinese.]

———1998. Three Kingdoms period tombs found in the north region of Nanjing, Jiangsu, by year. *Kaogu* 1998(8):21–26, 98. [in Chinese.]

REN, SHILONG. 1994. Yue wares and the Yue wares system. In: Ren Shilong, ed. *Life on the Porcelain Road—Practice and Understanding of Zhejiang Porcelain Kiln Site Archaeology*. Beijing: Cultural Relics Press. pp. 90–105. [in Chinese.]

RICE, PRUDENCE M. 2015. *Pottery Analysis: A Sourcebook*. 2nd ed. Chicago: University of Chicago Press. 561 pp.

SHEN, YUEMING. 2009. Some questions about the use of dragon kilns. *Wenwu* 9:55–64. [in Chinese.]

TONG, TAO. 2006. "A Comprehensive Archaeological Study on Five-linked Jar and Hun Ping in the Lower Reaches of the Yangtze River from the Han to Jin Period" [dissertation]. Sichuan University, Chengdu. 245 pp. [in Chinese.]

WANG, CHANGSUI. 2004. Rethinking a definition of proto-porcelain and the origin of celadon. *Kaogu* 2004(9):86–92. [in Chinese.]

WANG, LIHUA, AND SHIMIN LIN. 1981. Report on the Fenghuabaidu tomb of 175 AD. In: Zhejiang Provincial Institute of Archaeology, ed. *Collection of Essays. Zhejiang Provincial Institute of Archaeology*. Beijing: Cultural Relics Press. pp. 208–211. [in Chinese.]

WANG, YIFENG. 2010. Research on the early dragon kiln site as a celadon production center in ancient China. *Dongfang Wenwu* 1:27–39. [in Chinese.]

WEI, ZHENG. 2011. *An Archaeological Study of Six Dynasties Tombs*. Beijing: Peking University Press. 432 pp. [in Chinese.]

WOOD, NIGEL. 1999. *Chinese Glazes: Their Origins, Chemistry and Recreation*. London: A&C Black Publishers, Ltd. 280 pp.

XIONG, HAITANG. 1995. *Research on the Development and Transition History of Kiln Technology in East Asia*. Nanjing: Nanjing University Press. 83 pp. [in Chinese.]

XU, JIMING, WEIDONG LI, HONGJIE LUO, AND DONG ZHANG. 2009. A study on the body, glaze and manufacturing technique of celadon from the Dayuanping kiln site of the Eastern Han Dynasty. In: Hongjie Luo and Xinmiao Zheng, eds. *Technology of Ceramics: Proceedings of the International Seminar (ISAC '09)*. Shanghai: Shanghai Science and Technological Literature Press. pp. 135–143. [in Chinese.]

YE, HONGMING, AND HEMING CAO. 1979. Dragon kilns in ancient Zhejiang. *Hebei Ceramics* 3:10–15. [in Chinese.]

Yu, Zhinqin. 1995. Xiao Xiantan kiln sites in Shangyu, Zhejiang. *Nanfang Wenwu* (03):106–107. [in Chinese.]

Yue, Yong, Qinlong Chen, and Jiansheng Tai. 2013. Three Kingdom period tombs in Yuehuatai, Nanjing. *Kaogu* 2013(3):26–41, 1. [in Chinese.]

Zhang, Min, and Hua Huo, eds. 2008. *Complete Collection of Ceramic Art Unearthed in China*. Volume 7, Jiangsu, Shanghai. Beijing: Science Press. 224 pp. [in Chinese.]

Zhang, Zhixin. 1980. Excavation report of a Western Jin dynasty tomb in Wu country Jiangsu. *Wenwu Ziliao Congkan* 3:130–138. [in Chinese.]

—1983. Excavation report of tomb 4 of Western Jin dynasty in Wu country, Jiangsu. *Kaogu* 1983(8):707–713, 776. [in Chinese.]

Zhejiang Provincial Institute of Archaeology. 1987. Report of the stamped pottery kiln site from the Shang dynasty in Shangyu. *Kaogu* 1987(11):984–986. [in Chinese.]

—2005. Report of the Qianshan kiln site in Xiaoshan, Hangzhou. *Wenwu* 5:4–9. [in Chinese.]

Zhejiang Provincial Institute of Archaeology, School of Archaeology and Museology of Peking University, and Cixi Provincial Institute of Archaeology. 2002. *Excavation Report of Cilongkou Kiln Site of Yue Ware*. Beijing: Cultural Relics Press. 445 pp. [in Chinese.]

Zheng, Jiali. 2007. "Excavation of the Niguposhan kiln site of the Three Kingdoms to the Western Jin dynasty in Shangyu, Zhejiang." *Zhongguo Wenwu Bao*, June 20, 2015, page 2. [in Chinese.]

Zheng, Jianming. 2015. "The investigation and excavation of Jinshan kiln site in Shangyu, Zhejiang." *Zhongguo Wenwu Bao*, February 27, 2015, page 5. [in Chinese.]

—2016. "New type of kiln site from the Three Kingdoms period to the Western Jin dynasty in Shangyu." *Zhongguo Wenwu Bao*, May 6, 2015, page 2. [in Chinese.]

Zhu, Boqian. 1981. Discovery of Eastern Han kiln sites in Shangyu, Zhejiang. *Wenwu* (10):33–36. [in Chinese.]

—1984. Research on dragon kiln sites in ancient China. *Wenwu* 3:5–60. [in Chinese.]

CHAPTER EIGHT

Carnelian Beads during the Mongol Period of Mongolia

Asa CAMERON and Bukhchuluun DASHZEVEG

The Mongol period saw the creation of the largest contiguous land empire in history—uniting a roughly 23 million km² area of Eurasia from the Yellow Sea to Budapest. The conquest of such a vast territory brought with it violence and destruction, but also the "Mongol Peace" or *Pax Mongolica* (Kim 2009). The creation and maintenance of the *Yam* system (Vér 2016; Shim 2022), the installation of the *Yasa* law code (Aigle 2022), and the use of *qaraqchi* (guards) along trade routes all contributed to the increase in trade and greater movement of technology, ideas, and people across Eurasia that occurred under the Mongol rule (Allsen 2009; Ho 2022). Nowhere is this influx more evident than in Mongolia itself. Descriptions of the heart of the Mongol Empire by contemporary travelers such as William of Rubruck, excavations at the capital of Qaraqorum (Bemmann, Erdenebat, and Pohl 2010; Reichert 2019, 2020; Bemmann and Reichert 2021; Bemmann et al. 2022), and research on Mongol period mortuary sites (Erdenebat 2009a, 2016; Erdenebat, Burentogtokh, and Honeychurch 2022) provide a vivid picture of a multicultural society and a Mongolian populace with a taste for and access to a wide variety of craft items and trade goods.

One such material was carnelian, a red semiprecious stone used most commonly to make beads. In Mongolia carnelian beads have been recovered at Mongol mortuary and habitation sites and are one of the many types of personal adornment documented during this period, including: gold and silver rings and earrings; golden brocade and silk garments; glass, faience, amber, turquoise, serpentinite, and agate beads; metal brooches and belts inlaid with precious and semiprecious stones; and pearl necklaces and earrings (Tumen, Navaan, and Erdene 2006; Erdenebat 2009a; Oka 2009; Reichert 2020; Erdenebat, Burentogtokh, and Honeychurch 2022). What separates carnelian beads from these other artifacts is the history and length of their use prior to Mongol rule. This use dates back to the mid-second millennium BCE in Mongolia and the third millennium BCE in China.

This tradition uniquely positions research on carnelian beads to provide insights into how "exotic" or "prestige" items were incorporated into existing cultural practices and why certain precious materials became more prominent than others in the archaeological record during the Mongol period. This chapter provides an overview of the existing research on carnelian beads in Mongolia during the Mongol period, with a specific focus on the form, production, and geological origin of the beads. These data are discussed in relation to what is currently known about carnelian beads from earlier cultural periods in Mongolia and China. Finally, the frequency of carnelian bead finds at Mongol sites is compared against other types of Mongol personal adornment (e.g., glass beads). Inspired by the work and life of Zeng Lingyi, our hope is that this study pushes forward understandings of Mongol period craft production and pays respect to the woman we first met in 2015, when the three of us worked together on the Taravagtai Valley Archaeological Project in northern Mongolia.

Carnelian Beads in Mongolia during the Mongol Period

Carnelian is a folk taxonomic term for a red or reddish-yellow unbanded chalcedony classified as microcrystalline quartz. Beadmakers collect raw carnelian usually by mining it directly from exposed veins or in more opportunistic ways (Kenoyer, Vidale, and Bhan 1991), such as in the Gobi Desert where ancient nomadic communities in Mongolia made beads from carnelian gravels and geodes collected directly from the desert surface (Kenoyer et al. 2022). To prepare the carnelian, it next needs to be dried out. Artisans will leave it out in the sun, sometimes for months, before slowly heating the material to extract the intercrystalline moisture and make the carnelian easier to work (Kenoyer 2003). Once workable, beadmakers make "roughouts" and then "blanks" by chipping the carnelian down to the general desired shape and size of the bead they wish to produce (Francis 2000). The blanks are then perforated, either using a drill or through pecking. Finally, the perforated carnelian blank is ground, polished, and sometimes heated again to deepen the reddish hue—transforming it from chalcedony into carnelian.

Humans have a long history of shaping this semiprecious stone into beads. By the eighth millennium BCE in the Levant and by the Early Food Producing Era (7000–5500 BCE) in the Indus Valley, communities had already begun using carnelian beads (Groman-Yaroslavski and Bar-Yosef Mayer 2015; Kenoyer 2017). Archaeological and anthropological research into carnelian beads, particularly from Southwest and South Asia, has been fairly extensive (e.g., Gwinnett and Gorelick 1991; Kenoyer, Vidale, and Bhan 1991; Roux, Bril, and Dietrich 1995; Kenoyer 1997; Brunet 2009; Prabhakar 2016; Rabbani 2020).[1] In Mongolia, scholarship on carnelian beads is, at present, quite sparse. For the Mongol period, most of what is known comes from two studies: Susanne Reichert's (2020) book on craft production at Qaraqorum and Kenoyer et al.'s (2022) recent geochemical, scanning electron microscopy (SEM), and use-wear analyses of carnelian beads.

Since the late nineteenth century, research has been ongoing at Qaraqorum with several Mongolian and Mongolian international joint projects documenting different parts of the medieval capital (Radloff 1892; Tumen, Navaan, and Erdene 2006). The most recent excavations at the site began in 1999 as a Mongolian–German expedition. This project has extensively mapped the city and surrounding areas, documented the complex settlement history of the site, and excavated the Erdene Zuu Buddhist monastery (Bemmann, Erdenebat, and Pohl 2010; Reichert 2019, 2020; Bemmann and Reichert 2021; Bemmann et al. 2022). The other major contribution of the Mongolian–German project has been to record information about craft production and artisans at Qaraqorum. Reichert (2020) notes that ninety-four[2] objects of possible carnelian raw materials for gem-making and thirty-one stone blanks, semi-finished beads, or wasters were recovered from this site. Most come from occupation phases 6 to 7 at Qaraqorum, both associated with the Yuan dynasty (1271 to 1368 CE). The carnelian and chalcedony portion of the assemblage is made up of thirty-eight raw material pieces and twelve blanks, semi-finished beads, or wasters.

Gem production sites within Qaraqorum are small and localized to rooms. The raw materials, blanks, semi-finished beads, and wasters recovered from these contexts are all consistent with on-site carnelian beadmaking. However, the rooms are missing many of the other archaeological hallmarks of this type of craft production; namely, flaking debris, drills, and grinding stones (Maringer 1952; Kenoyer, Vidale, and Bhan 1991). There are also no complete carnelian or chalcedony beads at Qaraqorum, but Reichert (2020:149–150, pl. 69:19) notes that there is at least one carnelian waster (F.1212.1) with evidence of drilling. Because there are no finished artifacts, it is hard to comment on the shape of carnelian beads produced at Qaraqorum. However, from these blanks, semi-finished beads, and wasters (Reichert 2020:149–150, pl. 69), it seems that some of the would-be beads were spherical, circular oblate, and possibly long barrel (see Kenoyer 2017:157). These shapes can be seen more clearly in the glass beads recovered from the site (Reichert 2020, pl. 68).

For the Mongol period, Kenoyer et al. (2022) provide limited, albeit more detailed data on carnelian bead shape and production. This study looks at modern carnelian geodes collected from the Gobi-steppe of Mongolia and carnelian beads recovered from Late Bronze Age (around 1500–1000 BCE), Early Iron Age (around 1000–400 BCE), Xiongnu period (around 250 BCE–150 CE), and Mongol period graves. The researchers document bead shapes and use laser ablation inductively coupled plasma mass spectrometry (LA-ICP-MS) and SEM to document the geographical origin of the beads, the associated production technology, and use-wear. Kenoyer et al. (2022) examine two Mongol period beads: one from Gorzgoriin uvur (MG22) in Khentii Province (Batsaikhan and Erdenebaatar 1991) and one from Ereen (MG25) in Dundgovi Province (Erdene-Ochir and Gantulga 2013).

The Gorzgoriin uvur bead (MG22) is an irregular heptagonal-faceted, very short octagonal biconical bead (Figure 8.1). This artifact is single and double diamond drilled and crafted from a carnelian geode. The Ereen bead (MG25) is an irregular octagonal-faceted long octagon bead made from a piece of carnelian (Figure 8.2). The LA-ICP-MS data and canonical discriminant analysis show that both beads geochemically group with carnelian sources in Yemen. From the use-wear portion of the analyses, MG22 and MG25 show evidence of string wear and exterior polish. These are signs that the beads were likely part of a necklace and worn with some regularity against clothing—meaning that the objects were not made to be used just as adornments in funerary regalia.

One ongoing archaeological project made a notable Mongol carnelian bead find at Khalzan Shireg. Khalzan Shireg is a Mongol period settlement located in Govi-Altai Province. This site is mentioned in the *Yuan shi* (*Yuan History*)[3] as Zhenghai (or Chinhai) (Demchigdorzh, Gotov, and Baiaarsaikhan 2015). But the text fails to mention the site's specific location, only that Zhenghai was established in 1212 CE and occupied for a few centuries. Excavations at Khalzan Shireg began in 2004 (Ochir and Enkhtur 2004). The results document a walled enclosure that measures 190 m on the east, 220 m on the west, 190 m on the north, and 170 m on the south and holds the ruins of several buildings. On the surface of the site researchers recorded ceramic and porcelain (likely imported from China) fragments. In early excavations the team noted a large faunal assemblage as well as copious amounts of iron slag and bone tools. Accelerator mass spectrometry dating of organic residue on a porcelain fragment dates occupation of Khalzan Shireg to 1160 to 1255 CE (Nakata and Muraoka 2019). Archaeological test pits indicate that the cultural layer is 42 to 46 cm thick, consistent with long-term and sustained usage of the site (Delgermaa and Erdenebold 2022). The settlement is located at the crossroads of the Shargyn Gobi and was likely frequently visited by traders and military envoys.

FIGURE 8.1. Mongol period heptagonal-faceted carnelian long bead (MG22) from Gorzgoriin uvur in Khentii Province. Photo credit: Bukhchuluun Dashzeveg.

FIGURE 8.2. Mongol period octagonal-faceted carnelian short bead (MG25) from Ereen in Dundgovi Province. Photo credit: Bukhchuluun Dashzeveg.

FIGURE 8.3. Carnelian bead surface find from Khalzan Shireg in Govi-Altai Province. Photo credit: Amarbileg Chinbat.

The carnelian bead (Figure 8.3) from Khalzan Shireg is a surface find recorded by Turbat Tsagaan of the National University of Mongolia during the summer of 2022. This bead is unpublished and has yet to be studied. But, from pictures and measurements taken by Amarbileg Chinbat at the university's Archaeological Research Center, it is a heptagonal-faceted short octagonal biconical bead. The exact measurements (Beck 1928) are 14.1 mm in length and 20.2 mm in width (or diameter), with a hole that measures 2.6 mm in diameter. The bead appears drilled, but without SEM analysis the exact production technology is not clear. In turn, without LA-ICP-MS analysis, the geographical origin of the bead cannot be determined. From its multi-faceted octagonal shape, the bead does group well with the MG22 and MG25 beads. To date there is no evidence that multi-faceted octagonal beads appear among locally produced carnelian beads from Mongolia.

Since the discovery at Khalzan Shireg, a few additional examples of Mongol period carnelian beads have come to light from the newly opened Chinggis Khaan National Museum in the Mongolian capital of Ulaanbaatar. This includes: a bead (1.1 cm in diameter) recovered from a silver cup deposited within a ceremonial pit excavated from the ruins of Kheseg Baishin in Dornogovi Province (Chuluun and Enkhtuul 2018:37[4]); three beads (2.5 by 0.8 cm, 1.7 by 0.5 cm, and 1.5 by 0.8 cm) found in a woman's Yuan period grave (burial 9) at Ikh Oortsog Uul in Sukhbaatar Province (Bayarkhuu 2021[5]; Erdenebold et al. 2021:86[6]); beads from graves at Khorig Mountain in Khuvsgul aimag[7]; a multi-material hat ornament (or possible necklace) consisting of a carnelian bead, sixty-six pine nut seed pods, an amber bead, and glass beads in a cave burial of a high ranking man (1301–1410 CE) at Tsagaan Khanan in Umnugovi Province (Bayar and Erdenebat 2000; Erdenebat 2009c; Figures 8.4 and 8.5); and a necklace recovered from a female cave burial discovered at Ikh Nart in Dornogovi Province. Erdenebat and Khurelsukh (2007) have published images and a description of the Ikh Nart necklace. The authors report that seven beads threaded together with string were found in the grave and that the assemblage consists of two round beads (0.7 to 1 cm in diameter), one multi-faceted bead (0.7 cm in diameter), and four oblong hexagonal-faceted beads (1.8 cm in diameter).

Outside the reports of Reichert (2020) and Kenoyer et al. (2022), the surface find at Khalzan Shireg, and those beads currently on display at the Chinggis Khaan National Museum, the evidence of Mongol period carnelian beads is almost nonexistent. In two of the most thoroughly excavated and well-reported microregions of Mongolia, Baga Gazaryn Chuluu and Chandmani Khar Uul, no carnelian beads were recovered from Mongol period graves (Amartuvshin and Honeychurch 2010; Amartuvshin et al. 2015). Ulambayar

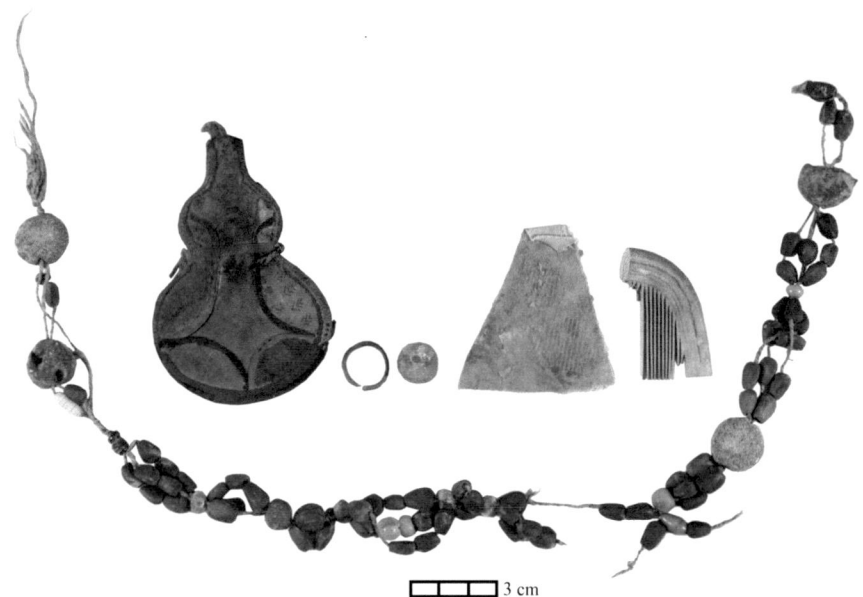

FIGURE 8.4. Necklace (or possible hat ornament) and associated fabric pouch, bronze ring, amber bead, fabric with hair brush imprints, and wooden hair brush from the elite cave burial at Tsagaan Khanan in Umnugovi Province. Photo credit: Chunag Amartuvshin.

FIGURE 8.5. Reconstruction of the Tsagaan Khanan beads as could be worn on a Mongol period man. Illustration by Bukhchuluun Dashzeveg and Asa Cameron.

Erdenebat's (2009a) dissertation, which provides a thorough review of Mongol burial practices and a catalog of known Mongol period cemeteries at that time, makes no mention of carnelian beads.[8] The overall dearth of evidence from site reports, combined with the data from Qaraqorum, Khalzan Shireg, the Chinggis Khaan National Museum, and the geochemical and SEM analyses, suggests that carnelian beads were likely not highly sought after during the Mongol period and, instead, were produced locally and obtained from foreign locals at a limited scale. The reason for this is best explained by the history of carnelian beads in Mongolia and China before the rise of the Mongol Empire and the Yuan dynasty.

Early Carnelian Bead Usage in Mongolia and China

Starting with the prone burial tradition (see Tumen, Khatanbaatar, and Erdene 2013; Amartuvshin 2016a; Wright et al. 2019) of the Late Bronze Age, carnelian beads first appear in Mongolia at sites such as Baruun Gyalat (Kovalev and Erdenebaatar 2009), Tsagaan Suvarga, Khuut, Delgerkhaan Uul (Amartuvshin et al. 2018), and Chandmani Khar Uul (Amartuvshin et al. 2015). These early beads were produced locally from carnelian geodes crafted using tapered cylindrical stone drills and pecking, and from naturally perforated geodes. So far, five bead shapes have been documented for this period: circular very short barrel, circular short barrel, oval short barrel, oval long barrel, and short circular bicone (Tsibiktarov 1998; Kenoyer et al. 2022).

During the Early Iron Age carnelian beads become more widespread in the archaeological record. Excavations of the Slab Grave Tradition (around 1100–400 BCE; Grishin 1975; Navaan 1975; Erdenebaatar 2004; Honeychurch 2015; Amartuvshin 2016b; Ma 2017) have produced carnelian beads from sites in Mongolia (Daram Uul, Javkhlant Uul, Khujirt, Emgent Khoshuu, Zaraa Uul, and Batshireet), Buriyatia (Astai II, Nilnii Boorgooltai, Pesterevo, Sayantoi, Tapkhar, Oolziit II, and Choolootii), and Zabaikal (Baroon-Kondoi, Boodoolan, Malii Bator, and Razezd no. 71) (Tsybiktarov 1998; Miyamoto and Obata 2016; Odsuren et al. 2018; Kenoyer et al. 2022). Carnelian beads have also been found in other regional Early Iron Age mortuary contexts, including Chandmani culture sites in northwestern Mongolia (Tseveendorj 1980, 2007, 2016; Kenoyer et al. 2022), Tagar culture sites in southern Siberia (Grishin 1975; Bokovenko 2006), Saka culture sites in Kazakhstan (Yablonsky 1995), and Scythian culture sites in Tuva (Bokovenko 1995). Similar to the prone burial artifacts, carnelian beads during the Early Iron Age were produced locally from geodes. However, by the Early Iron Age bead production technology and the variety of bead shapes had expanded. Naturally perforated geodes, pecked tapered cylindrical stone drilled beads, and straight cylindrical stone drilled beads have been documented for this period. The following are present among Early Iron Age bead shapes: circular short barrel, circular long barrel, circular very long barrel, oval short barrel, oval long barrel, short circular bicone, long circular bicone, and very long circular bicone (Tsybiktarov 1998; Kenoyer et al. 2022).

The Xiongnu period of Mongolia saw the rise of the first nomadic state in eastern Eurasia (see Rogers 2012; Honeychurch 2015) and an increase in the frequency of carnelian beads documented at archaeological sites. Carnelian beads are a common material find in ring graves of the local Xiongnu elite (Minyaev 2007; Eregzen 2011; Honeychurch 2015) and are well attested to from habitation sites, particularly in Transbaikalia (see Davydova 1995, 1996; Davydova and Minyaev 2003). Two notable developments in carnelian beads and related production technology occurred during this period. Geochemical analysis of an irregular octagonal-faceted long octogonal bead (MG31) from Delgerkhan Uul in Sukhbaatar Province seemingly shows that carnelian beads from India reached Mongolia by the Xiongnu period (Kenoyer et al. 2022:3). Using SEM, Kenoyer et al. (2022) also demonstrate that MG31 was double diamond drilled and MG26, a locally made circular short barrel bead from Oyu Tolgoi in Ömnögovi Province, was single and double diamond drilled. In addition, naturally perforated geodes, tapered cylindrical stone drilled beads, and the following bead shapes have also been documented for Xiongnu carnelian beads: circular long barrel, circular very long barrel, oval short barrel, oval very long barrel, short circular bicone, long square cylindrical, hexagonal faceted short barrel, septagonal faceted short barrel, and octagonal faceted short barrel (Kenoyer et al. 2022).

In China, the history of early carnelian bead usage begins several hundreds of years before the Late Bronze Age in Mongolia. Starting possibly as early as 2750 BCE (Hommel and Sax 2014), but definitely by the end of the third millennium BCE, carnelian beads appear at sites in the Qinghai and Gansu provinces of northern China. In some cases, such as at Xichengyi (Jaang 2015), these beads are found in direct concert with evidence of early metallurgy, the appearance of western plant (e.g., wheat) and animal domesticates (e.g., sheep), and other prestige items, such as pearls and cowrie shells. In the second millennium BCE, carnelian beads reached sites farther to the east, such as Dadianzi, a Lower Xiajiadian culture (around 2000 to 1500 BCE) site in Inner Mongolia (CASS IA 1996:xix; Rawson 2013). A comprehensive study of the Dadianzi carnelian beads does not exist, but pictures of the artifacts indicate that they are primarily short barrel beads. The images in the Dandianzi site report (CASS IA 1996:xix) do not give any indication of how the beads were perforated, but they do show the carnelian beads as part of a multi-material necklace or bracelet with long tubular jade beads and what appear to be steatite or limestone beads.

Within the Central Plain of China, carnelian beads have been identified at Shang dynasty (around 1600–1046 BCE) cemeteries, including at the late capital of Yinxu (around 1250–1046 BCE), where archaeologists recovered carnelian from the tomb of the royal consort Fu Hao (Hommel and Sax 2014, fig. 6.A; CASS IA 1980:xxxvi). A technical analysis of Shang period carnelian beads has not been done. However, the drawings and images of the Fu Hao beads show one long barrel and twenty-five short barrel beads, some of which appear to be pecked and drilled. During the subsequent Zhou dynasty (around 1046–256 BCE), mortuary customs incorporated carnelian beads directly into funerary attire and their use became widespread among elites (Rawson 2008; So 2019). Carnelian was one of several materials (including faience, turquoise, jet, jade, limestone, amazonite, serpentine, calcite, fluorite, gypsum, lignite, cowrie shells, and stone imitations of cowrie shells) that were used to fashion elaborate and ordered necklaces and wall hangings consisting of sometimes dozens of differently shaped and colored beads with accompanying pendants and plaques (Hommel and Sax 2014; So 2019). These magnificent ornaments also included long "bamboo-like" biconical drilled beads, which had no previous antecedents in carnelian beads from China.

At present, we do not know definitively about the geographical origins of the early carnelian beads documented in China. Using the documentation of long biconical beads, Rawson (2013) suggests that some of the Zhou carnelian could have come from the Indus Valley civilization, which has a long and well-documented history of carnelian bead production and is famous for its long biconical beads (Kenoyer 2017). Rawson (2013) also proposes that the early carnelian beads in China could be a local invention of communities occupying areas along the northern borders of Central China or that the beads originated from southern Siberia, the Urals, the Caucasus, or the Pontic Steppe. So (2019) and Janz et al. (2020) both note the abundance of workable chalcedony in the Gobi Desert and argue that a local origin for carnelian beads in China is quite probable. Given the accessibility of raw materials and the evidence of local carnelian bead production in Mongolia by the Late Bronze Age (Kenoyer et al. 2022), it seems likely that parts of northern China also produced carnelian beads by this time, if not earlier. In turn, because carnelian beads from India have been identified at a Xiongnu period cemetery in Mongolia, it also stands to reason that some of the novel bamboo-like beads from the Zhou period could be foreign imports.

For more than a millennium before the Mongol Empire, nomadic pastoral groups in Mongolia produced carnelian beads from local sources, adorned themselves with beads crafted thousands of kilometers away, and used carnelian beads in a wide variety of shapes as part of their funeral regalia. In China, carnelian beads appear even earlier in the archaeological record, eventually becoming part of the mortuary customs of Shang and Zhou elites. It is likely that many of the early carnelian beads were produced locally. Some Mongol period carnelian beads even have direct antecedents that date back to these periods. For instance, the Xiongnu bead from India (MG31) is the same shape and was perforated in the same manner as a Mongol period bead from Yemen (MG25). This long history of local carnelian bead production and usage in Mongolia and China could indicate that Mongols did not view carnelian as particularly prestigious or exotic and, thus, less desirable. While objects do not need to be foreign to be viewed as prestigious or desirable (Scarlett 2010), for forms of body adornment and funerary regalia the Mongol elite often had a strong preference for the exotic.

Carnelian Beads and Other Body Adornment during the Mongol Period

The Mongol desire for exotic goods can be seen clearly in the import and use of *nasīj*, the brocade woven from silk, golden and silver threads (Allsen 1997; Shea 2020; Eregzen 2023), pearls (Allsen 2019; Eregzen 2023), and glass beads (Erdenebat 2009a; Reichert 2020:123–132, pl. 68, 69). The Mongols used the exquisite textile in *bogtag* (headdresses) of women, to cover carts, to line their *gers* (yurts), and to make *deels* (robes) (Allsen 1997; Oka 2009; Erdenebat, Burentogtokh, and Honeychurch 2022; Eregzen 2023). Brocade was such an important commodity that during the Yuan dynasty the court had a Golden Brocade Office (Allsen 1997:39) and even Chinggis Khan mentioned the textile in one of his supposed maxims that the Ilkhanate historian Rashīd al-Dīn recorded (Allsen 1997:12). Under Mongol rule pearls held a similar and often congruent importance to brocade in displaying wealth and status (Allsen 2019).

The significance of pearls for body adornment and ornamentation during the Mongol period is readily attested to by the portraiture of the Yuan dynasty. Housed at the National Palace Museum of Taiwan[9] there exists a collection of paintings by an anonymous artist or artists[10] that depict the Khans with pearl-topped crowns and pearl earrings (Figure 8.6) and their consort empresses wearing royal attire adorned with brocade and covered in pearls (Figure 8.7). This royal costume was also replicated, although in a diminished fashion, by the Mongol elite outside the royal family. Apparently the desire for pearls and proper courtly clothing was so great that people went into debt just to acquire them, and often from great distances, particularly from the Persian Gulf (Allsen 2019).

FIGURE 8.6. Jayaatu Khan (Төвтөмөр), emperor of the Yuan dynasty (1329–1332 CE). Albums of Yuan Imperial Portraits, National Palace Museum, Taipei; Erdenebat and Törbat (2011:48).

FIGURE 8.7. Chabi (Чаби), empress and consort of Kublai Khan. Albums of Yuan Imperial Portraits, National Palace Museum, Taipei; Fong and Wyatt (1996:265).

The popularity of pearls at this time is also evidenced by the archaeological record, as pearl necklaces and earrings are a common find in Mongol graves (Halbertsma-Herold 2008; Erdenebat 2009a; Erdenebat, Burentogtokh, and Honeychurch 2022; Eregzen 2023). Allsen (2019) argues that the Mongol need for pearls is also visible in the white glass beads recovered from Qaraqorum, which he believes were manufactured at the site to be facsimiles for real pearls.

While Reichert (2020:124) comments on Allsen's idea of local faux pearl production, that "the published data did not provide convincing evidence or even arguments for this claim," she does note that ninety-one, or roughly one-third, of the glass beads excavated at Qaraqorum are white or off-white. The reason for Reichert's skepticism stems from the fact that the evidence for onsite glass bead production at the Mongol capital is similar to that of carnelian, very limited, and includes nothing to suggest that the white glass beads were definitively crafted there. However, unlike carnelian, excavations at Qaraqorum have documented numerous whole glass beads in a wide range of shapes and colors (see Reichert 2020, pl. 68, 69). A preliminary sourcing study of forty-five of the glass beads[11] was carried out using LA-ICP-MS. The results indicate that twenty-eight of the beads were made using Chinese recipes, ten beads likely came from West or Central Asia, and one could have been made in Europe or East Asia (Reichert 2020:130–132). Of the remaining glass beads, one is likely intrusive and modern, and the final three were made using an unknown recipe. The data from Qaraqorum suggest that glass beads were a commonly sought after craft item and that the majority recovered from sites in Mongolia were likely imported from foreign sources. Excavations of mortuary contexts have not shed more light on the geographic origin of glass beads for this period. However, the steady frequency of glass beads in graves does indicate that they were quite popular on necklaces and earrings among the Mongols (Erdenebat 2009a) and were sometimes used instead of pearls to decorate women's *bogtag* (Pozdnyakov et al. 2018).

Beyond popular Mongol forms of body adornment that are decidedly not carnelian, it is worth pointing out that the Mongol elite did use beads that could easily be confused as carnelian if not inspected closely. Five of the Yuan dynasty portraits in the National Palace Museum of Taiwan collection depict Khans wearing necklaces with red or reddish-brown beads (Figures 8.6, 8.8, 8.9, 8.10, and 8.11). It is impossible to tell what material these beads are made from, but by the color and shape most are likely either glass or carnelian, or possibly precious gems (e.g., rubies). Given the relative dearth of Mongol period carnelian finds, the depicted beads are probably not carnelian beads, but likely glass or precious stones. The Mongols certainly inlaid jewelry, clothing, and other objects with precious stones (Halbertsma-Herold 2008; Erdenebat, Burentogtokh, and Honeychurch 2022; Eregzen 2023), but the evidence for Mongol period ruby beads is less clear. There is better archaeological data to support the idea that these beads are glass. Erdenebat (2009b:259) reports a necklace from Tavan Tolgoi, consisting of seed pods and multi-colored glass beads, two of which are bright red or reddish-orange. These beads are close in appearance to the small beads displayed in the portraits of Rinchinbal Khan (Figure 8.8), Temür Khan (Figure 8.9), and Buyantu Khan (Figure 8.11). The longer dark red or reddish-brown faceted beads shown around the necks of Jayaatu Khan (Figure 8.6), Külüg Khan (Figure 8.10), and Rinchinbal Khan (Figure 8.8) are similar in color and shape to glass beads found at Qaraqorum (Reichert 2020, pl. 68, 11-F.4052.1), but are also similar in shape to the four oblong hexagonal-faceted carnelian beads recovered from the Ikh Nart cave burial (Erdenebat and Khurelsukh 2007, fig. 18). Regardless of what type of

Figure 8.8. Rinchinbal Khan (Ринчинбал), emperor of the Yuan dynasty (1332–1332 CE). Albums of Yuan Imperial Portraits, National Palace Museum, Taipei; Erdenebat and Törbat (2011:48).

Figure 8.9. Temür Khan (Төмөр), emperor of the Yuan dynasty (1294–1307 CE). Albums of Yuan Imperial Portraits, National Palace Museum, Taipei; Erdenebat and Törbat (2011:48).

Carnelian Beads during the Mongol Period of Mongolia 153

Figure 8.10. Külüg Khan (Хайсан), emperor of the Yuan dynasty (1307–1311 CE). Albums of Yuan Imperial Portraits, National Palace Museum, Taipei; Erdenebat and Törbat (2011:48).

Figure 8.11. Buyantu Khan (Аюурбарбад), emperor of the Yuan dynasty (1311–1320 CE). Albums of Yuan Imperial Portraits, National Palace Museum, Taipei; Müller and Pleiger (2005:306).

beads are actually depicted, the portraits illustrate that during the Yuan dynasty aspects of elite men's fashion could have allowed people to wear carnelian beads or at least use carnelian beads as substitutes for other materials, such as glass or precious stones. But neither seems to have occurred in any substantial way.

The contrast in finds between carnelian beads and other classes of body adornment in Mongolia during the Mongol period is both striking and telling. Brocade, pearls, and glass beads were undoubtedly highly sought after prestige items and likely came entirely from foreign locales. While these trade items may have been "exotic," they certainly were not alien to the Mongol populace. In 1195 CE, Chinggis Khan, then known as Temüjin, crushed the Tatar tribe and claimed a cache of golden brocade as part of the spoils (Allsen 1997:11). According to *The Secret History of the Mongols*, later when the Uyghur *Idu'ut* UyBarchu-art-tegin gained an audience with Chinggis Khan to pledge fealty, the Khan requested that UyBarchu-art-tegin bring "gold and silver, small pearls and large pearls, brocades, damasks, and silks" (Onon 2001:221–222). In addition to the pearls mentioned in *The Secret History of the Mongols* (Onon 2001), Allsen (2019) notes that the precursors to the Mongols, the Khitan Empire (916–1125 CE), were often gifted large pearls from the Abbāsid Caliphate. This idea is substantiated by the archaeological record. Excavations at the Khitan settlement of Chintolgoi Balgas[12] in north-central Mongolia have produced pearl-like glass beads and roof tiles with animal and flaming pearl designs (Kradin and Ivliev 2009; Ankhbayar and Erdenebold 2017). From the Khitan royal tomb of the Princess of Chen in Inner Mongolia, archaeologists also documented a double-dragon headdress crafted from amber and gold pendants, and three strands of pearls (Shen 2006:152–153). Of the three materials, glass beads have the longest history of use in Mongolia. By the Xiongnu period glass beads are well documented in the archaeological record (Eregzen 2011). LA-ICP-MS shows that these early glass beads were made using recipes associated with the Mediterranean and the Near East (Lankton et al. 2012).

Not only is there evidence that brocade, pearls, and glass beads were well known and held cultural significance in Mongolia prior to the Mongol Empire, but notably these materials were often used to accent existing endogenous material culture rather than adopted wholesale (Allsen 2009). For example, the *deel*, the traditional robe made with golden brocade (Oka 2009; Eregzen 2023), dates back to at least the Xiongnu period, and the cotton *deels* recovered from the royal tombs at Noyon Uul (Eregzen 2011:106). Adopting foreign goods or customs through an existing cultural lens is a widespread phenomenon across the globe (e.g., Dietler 2010; Liebmann 2015). For the Mongols, the agentive choices in how prestige goods were used by the royal and elite classes further highlight the difference between carnelian beads and brocade, pearls, and glass beads.

Conclusions

Beads and other forms of body adornment provide a lens into a wide variety of research topics, including wealth and status (e.g., Mainfort 1985; Coupland et al. 2016), marriage and funerary customs (e.g., Hughes-Brock 1999; Isla Cuadrado 2009), race and ethnicity (e.g., Nguru and Maina 2020; Allen 2021), gender (e.g., Davidson 2020), trade and exchange (e.g., Carter 2010), and the creation and maintenance of social networks (e.g., Malinowski 1922; Klehm 2021). For the Mongols, their elite costumes and choice in body adornment are tied directly to the wants and fashions of the royal court, the capacity of larger swaths of

Mongol society to replicate these costumes, and the relationship that the Mongols had with archaeologically assumed "exotic" materials such as brocade. These threads are pulled into even greater focus when specific materials are compared against one another, and we can unravel why seemingly valuable forms of body adornment, like carnelian beads, are not well attested to in the archaeological record.

The relative dearth of carnelian beads compared to other forms of body adornment shows that the royalty and elite of Mongol society often displayed their wealth and status by using familiar, yet foreign, materials to augment or complement existing "steppe" fashions and customs. It was through this process that the Mongols created many of their items and rituals associated with prestige. Carnelian beads do not fit this pattern and would have been difficult to implement in such a way. By the Mongol period the long history of carnelian bead use and local production in Mongolia and China, as well as the widespread availability of carnelian geodes across the Gobi (So 2019; Janz et al. 2020; Kenoyer et al. 2022), likely left carnelian without most of the cultural capital it once held. Even during the Yuan dynasty, when male courtly fashion might have allowed the wider populace to wear carnelian beads, the Mongol elite seemingly preferred other materials, such as glass.

Carnelian bead research in Mongolia and China is still in its early stages and the evidence for their use and production during the Mongol Period is currently lacking. To better understand the role carnelian beads played in Mongol society, LA-ICP-MS and SEM analyses are needed on additional carnelian beads and raw materials, such as those recovered from Khalzan Shireg, Ikh Nart, and Qaraqorum. In the archaeological literature, there also needs to be a greater emphasis on identifying the specific materials from which beads are made (e.g., Osanai et al. 2016) as well as describing the dimensions and shape of the beads. One of the difficulties in this type of research is that possible carnelian beads are sometimes just described as "stone beads" or the shape of beads needs to be interpreted from drawings or pictures. Lastly, the largest gap in knowledge of carnelian bead use in Mongolia and China comes from the time between the Xiongnu period and the Mongols. Research focused on this swath of time would help our understanding of why other forms of jewelry and body adornment were more valued by the Mongols. These data and changes in research practices would provide valuable insights into aspects of the agentive choices of Mongol royalty, Mongol burial customs, elite dress, and trade and exchange practices.

Acknowledgments

We would like to thank Turbat Tsagaan, Batdalai Byambatseren and Amarbileg Chinbat for providing data, photographs, and measurements of the carnelian bead recovered from Khalzan Shireg. We thank M. Sugar-Erdene for his assistance in tracking down recent unpublished excavation reports. We also would like to thank Chunag Amartuvshin for providing reports and sending us a figure to include.

Notes

1 See Society of Bead Researchers (2024) for extensive bibliographies of bead research from across the world.
2 Three of these samples are lost. One sample is flint, one sample is chalcedony, and the third was recorded as an unknown mineral.

3   See Fo Guang Shan Nan Tian Institute (2024) for a complete Chinese language version of the text.
4   See Хэсэг Байшин Тайлан 2018 at https://archive.org/details/2018_20200217_20200217_0518 for a digital copy of this report.
5   For a digital version of this article see Bayarkhuu (2021). The Chinggis Khaan National Museum's description of this burial, "Women's Burial in Great Yuan Period," can be found at https://qr.chinggismuseum.com/en/post/6367a30d5867c8390246ccbb.
6   In the original site report these beads are described as amber (Хув сувс).
7   Beads from Khorig Mountain are currently on display at the Chinggis Khaan National Museum. However, the recently published catalog of those excavations (Eregzen 2023) does not show the beads or describe them. In addition, photography and phones are not allowed in the museum, so we are unable to provide images.
8   Erdenebat references his own previously published work on the Tsagaan Khanan and Ikh Nart cave burials, but he does not mention the carnelian beads that were found in either context.
9   See "Age of the Great Khan," a digital museum theme website of the National Palace Museum in Taipei, Taiwan, available at https://theme.npm.edu.tw/khan/index.aspx?lang=2 for a virtual tour of the museum's collection of Yuan dynasty artwork.
10 Jing (1994) argues that the portraits of Khublai Khan and Chabi were painted by the Nepali artist Anige (1245–1306 CE).
11 Two beads in this analysis are faience.
12 A hexahedral biconical carnelian bead was also recovered from Chintolgoi Balgas. The bead is 17 mm long and 8 mm in diameter, and its hole is 2 mm in diameter (Kradin and Ivliev 2009:472).

References

AIGLE, DENISE. 2022. The Yasa. In: Timothy May and Michael Hope, eds. *The Mongol World*. London: Routledge. pp. 319–330. https://doi.org/10.4324/9781315165172-25

ALLEN, SHAONTA' E. 2021. Braids, beads, catsuits and tutus: Serena Williams' intersectional resistance through fashion. In: Rory Magrath, ed. *Athlete Activism: Contemporary Perspectives*. London: Routledge. pp. 132–143. (Routledge Research in Sport, Culture and Society.) https://doi.org/10.4324/9781003140290-13

ALLSEN, THOMAS T. 1997. *Commodity and Exchange in the Mongol Empire: A Cultural History of Islamic Textiles*. Cambridge: Cambridge University Press. 137 pp. (Cambridge Studies in Islamic Civilization.)

—2009. Mongols as vectors for cultural transmission. In: Nicola Di Cosmo, Allen J. Frank, and Peter B. Golden, eds. *The Cambridge History of Inner Asia: The Chinggisid Age*. Cambridge: Cambridge University Press. pp. 135–154. https://doi.org/10.1017/CBO9781139056045.011

—2019. *The Steppe and the Sea: Pearls in the Mongol Empire*. Philadelphia: University of Pennsylvania Press. 230 pp. (Encounters with Asia.)

AMARTUVSHIN, CHUNAG. 2016a. Hourglass-shaped graves and prone burials. In: Gelegdorj Eregzen, ed. *Ancient Funeral Monuments of Mongolia*. Ulaanbaatar: Institute of History and Archaeology, Mongolian Academy of Sciences. pp. 72–87. (Archaeological Relics of Mongolia 3.)

—2016b. Slab graves. In: Gelegdorj Eregzen, ed. *Ancient Funeral Monuments of Mongolia*. Ulaanbaatar: Institute of History and Archaeology, Mongolian Academy of Sciences. pp. 113–125. (Archaeological Relics of Mongolia 3.)

AMARTUVSHIN, CHUNAG, NATSAG BATBOLD, GELEGDORJ EREGZEN, AND BYAMBATSEREN BATDALAI. 2015. *Archaeological Sites at Chandman Khar Uul*. Ulaanbaatar: An Eternal Letter Press. [in Mongolian.]

Amartuvshin, Chunag, Zagd Batsaikhan, Ulambayar Erdenebat, Ganbaatar Galdan, Byambatseren Batdalai, Dalanjargalan Mandakh, Tsogtbayar Tselkhagarav, William Honeychurch, Joshua Wright, and Sarah Pleuger. 2018. 2018 fieldwork report by Mongol-American joint project "Eastern Mongolia: Archaeological survey, excavation." Ulaanbaatar: Institute of History and Archaeology, Mongolian Academy of Sciences. [in Mongolian.]

Amartuvshin, Chunag, and William Honeychurch. 2010. *Archaeological Research in Dundgovi Province: Bgaa Gazryn Chuluu*. Ulaanbaatar: Mongolian Academy of Sciences. [in Mongolian.]

Ankhbayar, Batsuuri, and Lkhagvasuren Erdenebold. 2017. *Settlements of Early Nomads*. Ulaanbaatar: National Museum of Mongolia. 454 pp. [in Mongolian.]

Batsaikhan, Zagd, and Diimaajav Erdenebaatar. 1991. *Eastern Mongolia Expedition*. Ulaanbaatar: Institute of History, Mongolian Academy of Sciences. [in Mongolian.]

Bayar, Dovdoi, and Ulambayar Erdenebat. 2000. A rare burial from the Mongol Empire. *Studia Archaeologica* 20(8):100–129. [in Mongolian.]

Bayarkhuu, J. 2021. The silence of the empire: Archaeological sites at Ikh Oortsog uul. *Newsletter from Chinggis Khaan Museum Journal* 1:36–40. [in Mongolian.]

Beck, Horace C. 1928. I.— Classification and nomenclature of beads and pendants. *Archaeologia* 77:1–76. https://doi.org/10.1017/S0261340900013345

Bemmann, Jan, Ulambayar Erdenebat, and Ernst Pohl, eds. 2010. *Mongolian–German Karakorum Expedition*. Volume 1, Excavations in the Craftsmen Quarter at the Main Road. Wiesbaden: Reichert Verlag. 337 pp. (Research into the Archaeology of Non-European Cultures 8.)

Bemmann, Jan, Sven Linzen, Susanne Reichert, and Lkh. Munkhbayar. 2022. Mapping Karakorum, the capital of the Mongol Empire. *Antiquity* 96(385):159–178. https://doi.org/10.15184/aqy.2021.153

Bemmann, Jan, and Susanne Reichert. 2021. Karakorum, the first capital of the Mongol world empire: An imperial city in a non-urban society. *Asian Archaeology* 4(2):121–143. https://doi.org/10.1007/s41826-020-00039-x

Bokovenko, Nikolay A. 1995. Tuva during the Scythian period. In: Jeannine Davis-Kimball, Vladimir A. Bashilov, and Leonid T. Yablonsky, eds. *Nomads of the Eurasian Steppes in the Early Iron Age*. Berkeley, CA: Zinat Press. pp. 265–283.

—2006. The emergence of the Tagar culture. *Antiquity* 80(310):860–879. https://doi.org/10.1017/S0003598X00094473

Brunet, Olivier. 2009. Bronze and Iron Age carnelian bead production in the UAE and Armenia: New perspectives. *Proceedings of the Seminar for Arabian Studies* 39:57–68. https://www.jstor.org/stable/41223969

Carter, Alison K. 2010. Trade and exchange networks in Iron Age Cambodia: Preliminary results from a compositional analysis of glass beads. *Bulletin of the Indo-Pacific Prehistory Association* 30:178–188. https://journals.lib.washington.edu/index.php/BIPPA/article/view/9966

[CASS IA] Chinese Academy of Social Sciences, Institute of Archaeology. 1980. *Tomb of Lady Hao at Yinxu in Anyang*. Beijing: Cultural Relics Publishing House. 288 pp. [in Chinese.]

—1996. *Dadianzi: Excavation Report of the Lower Xiajiadian Cultural Site and Cemetery*. Bejing: Science Press. 411 pp. [in Chinese.]

Chuluun, Sampildondov, and Chadraabal Enkhtuul. 2018. "17th century cities of Mongols": A report on archaeological excavation at Kheseg Baishin ruins in Ikh Khet soum, Dornogovi aimag. Ulaanbaatar: Institute of History and Archaeology, Mongolian Academy of Sciences. Available at https://archive.org/details/2018_20200217_20200217_0518 [in Mongolian.]

Coupland, Gary, David Bilton, Terence Clark, Jerome S. Cybulski, Gay Frederick, Alyson Holland, Bryn Letham, and Gretchen Williams. 2016. A wealth of beads: Evidence for material wealth-based inequality in the Salish Sea region, 4000–3500 cal B.P. *American Antiquity* 81(2):294–315. https://doi.org/10.7183/0002-7316.81.2.294

Davidson, James M. 2020. Black and white beads in the African diaspora. *Historical Archaeology* 54(4):681–737. https://doi.org/10.1007/s41636-020-00257-1

Davydova, Anthonyna V. 1995. *Ivolga Archaeological Complex.* Volume 1, Ivolga Settlement. Saint Petersburg: Asiatic Fund. 275 pp. (Archaeological Sites of the Xiongnu 1.) [in Russian.]

—1996. *Ivolga Archaeological Complex.* Volume 2, Ivolga Cemetery. Saint Petersburg: Centre for Oriental Studies. 176 pp. (Archaeological Sites of the Xiongnu 2.) [in Russian.]

Davydova, Anthonyna V., and Sergey Minyaev. 2003. *An Archaeological Complex Near Dureny.* Saint Petersburg: Asiatic Fund. 53 pp. (Archaeological Sites of the Xiongnu 5.) [inRussian.]

Delgermaa, Lhagvadorj, and Lkhagvasuren Erdenebold. 2022. Preliminary results of archeozoological research in Khalzan Shireg. *Studia Archaeologica* 41:129–147. [in Mongolian.]

Demchigdorzh, Chimed, Akim Gotov, and Magsarzhavyn Baiaarsaikhan. 2015. *History of the Yuan.* Ulaanbaatar: Soëmbo Printing KhKhK. [in Mongolian.]

Dietler, Michael. 2010. *Archaeologies of Colonialism: Consumption, Entanglement, and Violence in Ancient Mediterranean France.* Berkeley: University of California Press. 464 pp.

Erdenebaatar, Diimaajav. 2004. Burial materials related to the history of the Bronze Age on the territory of Mongolia. In: Katheryn M. Linduff, ed. *Metallurgy in Ancient Eastern Eurasia from the Urals to the Yellow River.* Lewiston, NY: Edwin Mellen Press. pp. 189–221. (Chinese Studies 31.)

Erdenebat, Ulambayar. 2009a. "Ancient Mongolian Burial Customs—Archaeological–Historical Investigations into Mongolian Burial Finds from the 11th to the 17th Centuries in Mongolia" [dissertation]. Rhenish Friedrich Wilhelm University, Bonn. 262 pp. [in German.]

—2009b. Cave burials of Mongolia. In: William W. Fitzhugh, Morris Rossabi, and William Honeychurch, eds. *Genghis Khan and the Mongol Empire.* Washington, DC: Dino Don, Mongolian Preservation Foundation; Arctic Studies Center, Smithsonian Institution; distributed by University of Washington Press. pp. 259–261.

—2009c. Cave burials: A unique burial tradition of the medieval nomads. *Mongolian Journal of Anthropology, Archaeology and Ethnology* 5(344):54–80. [in Mongolian.]

—2016. Graves with stone coverings of the Mongol period. In: Gelegdorj Eregzen, ed. *Ancient Funeral Monuments of Mongolia.* Ulaanbaatar: Institute of History and Archaeology, Mongolian Academy of Sciences. pp. 252–261. (Archaeological Relics of Mongolia 3.) [in Mongolian.]

Erdenebat, Ulambayar, Jargalan Burentogtokh, and William Honeychurch. 2022. The archaeology of the Mongol Empire. In: Timothy May and Michael Hope, eds. *The Mongol World.* London: Routledge. pp. 507–533. https://doi.org/10.4324/9781315165172-42

Erdenebat, Ulambayar, and Sosorbaram Khurelsukh. 2007. The cave burial of Nartyn Khad. *Studia Archaeologica* 4, 24(23):332–359. [in Mongolian.]

Erdenebat, Ulambayar, and Tsagaan Tòrbat. 2011. *Cultural Heritage of Ongon* [exhibition catalog]. Ulaanbaatar: Mongolian Academy of Sciences. [in Mongolian.]

Erdenebold, Lkhagvasuren, Erdene Jargalsaikhan, Ariunbold Ganbaatar, Bolormaa Sakhiya, and Gantogtokh Galsandovjoo. 2021. "Cultural Heritage of the Empire" project: A report on the archaeological excavation of the 2021 field season at Ikh Oortsog Uul in Tuvshinshiree soum, Sukhbaatar aimag. Ulaanbaatar: School of Humanities of the University of Science and Technology and Chinggis Khaan National Museum. [in Mongolian.]

Erdene-Ochir, Nasan-Ochir, and Jamiyan-Ombo Gantulga. 2013. A report on archaeological salvage excavation at mining licensed area "Ereen" of Taisheng Development, LLC, located in Bayanjargalan soum, Dornogovi Province. Ulaanbaatar: Institute of Archaeology, Mongolian Academy of Sciences. [in Mongolian.]

Eregzen, Gelegdorj, ed. 2011. *Treasures of the Xiongnu.* Ulaanbaatar: Institute of Archaeology, Mongolian Academy of Sciences. 277 pp. [in Mongolian and English.]

—ed. 2023. *Treasures of Khorig Mountain.* Ulaanbaatar: National Center for Cultural Heritage.

Fo Guang Shan Nan Tian Institute. 2024. "History of Yuan 元史." Chinese Notes. Updated March 24, 2024. https://chinesenotes.com/yuanshi.html

Francis, Peter, Jr. 2000. The stone bead industry of southern India. *BEADS: Journal of the Society of Bead Researchers* 12:49–62. https://surface.syr.edu/beads/vol12/iss1/8

Grishin, Yuri S. 1975. *Bronze and Early Iron Age of Eastern Zabaikal.* Moscow: Nauka. [in Russian.]

Groman-Yaroslavski, Iris, and Daniella E. Bar-Yosef Mayer. 2015. Lapidary technology revealed by functional analysis of carnelian beads from the early Neolithic site of Nahal Hemar Cave, Southern Levant. *Journal of Archaeological Science* 58:77–88. https://doi.org/10.1016/j.jas.2015.03.030

Gwinnett, A. John, and Leonard Gorelick. 1991. Bead manufacture at Hajar Ar-Rayhani, Yemen. *The Biblical Archaeologist* 54(4):187–196. https://doi.org/10.2307/3210280

Halbertsma-Herold, Ulrike. 2008. "Clothing Authority: Mongol Attire and Textiles in the Socio-Political Complex" [master's thesis]. Leiden University.

Ho, Colleen C. 2022. Overland trade in the Mongol world. In: Timothy May and Michael Hope, eds. *The Mongol World*. London: Routledge. pp. 484–504. https://doi.org/10.4324/9781315165172-40

Hommel, Peter, and Margaret Sax. 2014. Shifting materials: Variability, homogeneity and change in the beaded ornaments of the Western Zhou. *Antiquity* 88(342):1213–1228. https://doi.org/10.1017/S0003598X00115418

Honeychurch, William. 2015. *Inner Asia and the Spatial Politics of Empire: Archaeology, Mobility, and Culture Contact*. New York: Springer. 321 pp. https://doi.org/10.1007/978-1-4939-1815-7

Hughes-Brock, Helen. 1999. Mycenaean beads: Gender and social contexts. *Oxford Journal of Archaeology* 18(3):277–296. https://doi.org/10.1111/1468-0092.00084

Isla Cuadrado, Johny. 2009. From hunters to regional lords: Funerary practices in Palpa, Peru. In: Markus Reindel and Günther A. Wagner, eds. *New Technologies for Archaeology: Multidisciplinary Investigations in Palpa and Nasca, Peru*. Berlin: Springer. pp. 119–139. (Natural Science in Archaeology.) https://doi.org/10.1007/978-3-540-87438-6_8

Jaang, Li. 2015. The landscape of China's participation in the Bronze Age Eurasian network. *Journal of World Prehistory* 28(3):179–213. https://doi.org/10.1007/s10963-015-9088-2

Janz, Lisa, Asa Cameron, Dashzeveg Bukhchuluun, Davaakhuu Odsuren, and Laure Dubreuil. 2020. Expanding frontier and building the sphere in arid East Asia. *Quaternary International* 559:150–164. https://doi.org/10.1016/j.quaint.2020.04.041

Jing, Anning. 1994. The portraits of Khubilai Khan and Chabi by Anige (1245–1306), a Nepali artist at the Yuan court. *Artibus Asiae* 54(1/2):40–86. https://doi.org/10.2307/3250079

Kenoyer, Jonathan M. 1997. Trade and technology of the Indus Valley: New insights from Harappa, Pakistan. *World Archaeology* 29(2):262–280. https://www.jstor.org/stable/124951

—2003. Stone beads and pendant making techniques. In: James W. Lankton, ed. *A Bead Timeline: A Resource for Identification, Classification and Dating*. Volume 1, Prehistory to 1200 CE. Washington, DC: The Bead Museum. pp. 14–19.

—2017. Stone beads of the Indus tradition: New perspectives on Harappan bead typology, technology and documentation. In: Alok K. Kanungo, ed. *Stone Beads of South and Southeast Asia: Archaeology, Ethnography and Global Connections*. New Delhi: Aryan Books International in association with Indian Institute of Technology, Gandhinagar. pp. 149–164.

Kenoyer, Jonathan M., Asa Cameron, Dashzeveg Bukhchuluun, Chunag Amartuvshin, Byambatseren Batdalai, William Honeychurch, Laure Dussubieux, and Randall Law. 2022. Carnelian beads in Mongolia: New perspectives on technology and trade. *Archaeological and Anthropological Sciences* 14(1):1–38. https://doi.org/10.1007/s12520-021-01456-4

Kenoyer, Jonathan M., Massimo Vidale, and Kuldeep Kumar Bhan. 1991. Contemporary stone beadmaking in Khambhat, India: Patterns of craft specialization and organization of production as reflected in the archaeological record. *World Archaeology* 23(1):44–63. https://doi.org/10.1080/00438243.1991.9980158

Kim, Hodong. 2009. The unity of the Mongol Empire and continental exchanges over Eurasia. *Journal of Central Eurasian Studies* 1:15–42. https://cces.snu.ac.kr/data/publications/jces1_2kim.pdf

Klehm, Carla. 2021. Material histories of African beads: The role of personal ornaments in cultural change. In: Hannah V. Mattson, ed. *Personal Adornment and the Construction of Identity: A Global Archaeological Perspective*. Philadelphia: Oxbow Books. pp. 135–151.

Kovalev, Alexi A., and Diimaajav Erdenebaatar. 2009. Discovery of new cultures of the Bronze Age in Mongolia according to the data obtained by the International Central Asian Archaeological Expedition. In: Jan Bemmann, Hermann Parzinger, Ernst Pohl, and Damdinsüren Tseveendorzh, eds. *Current Archaeological Research in Mongolia*; papers from the First International Conference on "Archaeological Research in Mongolia" held in Ulaanbaatar, August 19th–23rd, 2007. Bonn: Vor- und Frühgeschichtliche Archäologie, Rheinische Friedrich-Wilhelms-Universität. pp. 149–170. (Bonn Contributions to Asian Archaeology 4.)

KRADIN, NIKOLAI N., AND ALEXANDR L. IVLIEV. 2009. The downfall of the Bohai state and the ethnic structure of the Kitan city of Chintolgoi Balgas, Mongolia. In: Jan Bemmann, Hermann Parzinger, Ernst Pohl, and Damdinsüren Tseveendorzh, eds. *Current Archaeological Research in Mongolia*; papers from the First International Conference on "Archaeological Research in Mongolia" held in Ulaanbaatar, August 19th–23rd, 2007. Bonn: Vor- und Frühgeschichtliche Archäologie, Rheinische Friedrich-Wilhelms-Universität. pp. 261–275. (Bonn Contributions to Asian Archaeology 4.)

LANKTON, JAMES W., CHUNAG AMARTUVSHIN, BERNARD GRATUZE, AND WILLIAM HONEYCHURCH. 2012. Glass and faience beads and pendants from Middle Gobi Xiongnu burials: New insight from LA-ICP-MS chemical analyses. *Ancient Cultures of Mongolia and Baikalian Siberia* 2012:683–694.

LIEBMANN, MATTHEW. 2015. The Mickey Mouse kachina and other "double objects": Hybridity in the material culture of colonial encounters. *Journal of Social Archaeology* 15(3):319–341. https://doi.org/10.1177/1469605315574792

MA, JIAN. 2017. The survey and study of slab burials in the Yinshan mountains. *Eurasian Studies* 5:54–84.

MAINFORT, ROBERT C., JR. 1985. Wealth, space, and status in a historic Indian cemetery. *American Antiquity* 50(3):555–579. https://doi.org/10.2307/280321

MALINOWSKI, BRONISLAW. 1922. *Argonauts of the Western Pacific*. London: Routledge and Kegan Paul. 527 pp.

MARINGER, JOHANNES. 1952. A Stone Age cave work site in the Gobi. *Anthropos* 47(5/6):891–896. [in German.] https://www.jstor.org/stable/41104366

MINYAEV, SERGEY. 2007. *Dyrestuj Burial Ground*. St. Petersburg: St. Petersburg University, Faculty of Philology Press. (Archaeological Sites of the Xiongnu. 3.) [in Russian.]

MÜLLER, CLAUDIUS, AND HENRIETTE PLEIGER, EDS. 2005. *Genghis Khan and His Heirs: The Empire of the Mongols*. Munich: Hirmer. [in German.]

MIYAMOTO, KAZUO, AND HIROKI OBATA, EDS. 2016. *Excavations at Daram and Tevsh Sites: A Report on Joint Mongolian–Japanese Excavations in Outer Mongolia*. Fukuoka, Japan: Department of Archaeology, Faculty of Humanities, Kyushu University. 87 pp.

NAKATA, YUKO, AND HITOSHI MURAOKA. 2019. *A God Statue of the Mongol Period Found in Altai, and its Significance*. Ulaanbaatar: Mongolian Academy of Sciences. [in Mongolian.]

NAVAAN, DORJPALAM. 1975. *The Bronze Age of Eastern Mongolia*. Ulaanbaatar: Mongolian Academy of Sciences. [in Mongolian.]

NGURU, MERCY MWIHAKI, AND SAMUEL MWITURIA MAINA. 2020. Social-cultural impact of bead work in East Africa: The nexus between the Dinka, Samburu and Masaai ethnicities. *International Journal of Innovative Research and Development* 9(7):87–94. https://doi.org/10.24940/ijird/2020/v9/i7/JUL20043

OCHIR, AYUDAI, AND ALTANGEREL ENKHTUR. 2004. *A Mongolian Report on Fieldwork by the Mongol–Japanese Joint Project "Inscription."* Ulaanbaatar: Library of National History Museum. [in Mongolian.]

ODSUREN, DAVAAKHUU, DASHZEVEG BUKHCHULUUN, LISA JANZ, AND ARLENE ROSEN. 2018. 2017 fieldwork report by Gobi Steppe Neolithic project. Ulaanbaatar: Library of Institute of Archaeology, Mongolian Academy of Sciences. [in Mongolian.]

OKA, ILDIKÓ. 2009. Three Mongolian coats from the 13th–14th century grave at Bukhiin Khoshuu. In: Jan Bemmann, Hermann Parzinger, Ernst Pohl, and Damdinsüren Tseveendorzh, eds. *Current Archaeological Research in Mongolia*; papers from the First International Conference on "Archaeological Research in Mongolia" held in Ulaanbaatar, August 19th–23rd, 2007. Bonn: Vor- und Frühgeschichtliche Archäologie, Rheinische Friedrich-Wilhelms-Universität. pp. 486–503. (Bonn Contributions to Asian Archaeology 4.)

Onon, Urgunge, trans. 2001. *The Secret History of the Mongols: The Life and Times of Chinggis Khan*. London: RoutledgeCurzon. 298 pp.

Osanai, Yasuhito, Tatsuro Adachi, Kazuhiro Yonemura, and Kazuo Miyamoto. 2016. Substance identification of the beads at the stone-slab grave from Daram site, Khentii province, Mongolia. In: Kazuo Miyamoto and Hiroki Obata, eds. *Excavations at Daram and Tevsh Sites: A Report on Joint Mongolian–Japanese Excavations in Outer Mongolia*. Fukuoka, Japan: Department of Archaeology, Faculty of Humanities, Kyushu University. pp. 73–75.

Pozdnyakov, Dmitri V., Sergey A. Pilipenko, Zhazgul Orozbekova, Olga L. Shvets, Lidiya O. Ponedelchenko, Zanna V. Marchenko, and Artem E. Grishin. 2018. A Mongolian era female headdress from the Upper Ob basin. *Archaeology, Ethnology and Anthropology of Eurasia* 46(4):74–82. https://doi.org/10.17746/1563-0102.2018.46.4.074-082

Prabhakar, V. Nandagopal. 2016. An overview of the stone bead drilling technology in South Asia from earliest times to Harappans. *Journal of Multidisciplinary Studies in Archaeology* 4:47–74.

Rabbani, Mubariz A. 2020. The typology, production and adornment of Gandharan beads during the mid-3rd century BCE–1st century CE: Preliminary results from Barikot, Swat, Pakistan. *Archaeological Research in Asia* 24:100228. https://doi.org/10.1016/j.ara.2020.100228

Radloff, Vasilii V. 1892. *Atlas of Antiquities of Mongolia.*. St. Petersburg: Imperial Academy of Sciences Press. 16 leaves. [in German.]

Rawson, Jessica. 2008. In search of ancient red beads and carved jade in modern China. *Cahiers d'Extrême-Asie* 17:1–15. https://www.jstor.org/stable/44171469

—2013. Ordering the exotic: Ritual practices in the late Western and early Eastern Zhou. *Artibus Asiae* 73(1):5–76. https://www.jstor.org/stable/24240768

Reichert, Susanne. 2019. *A Layered History of Karakorum: Stratigraphy and Periodization in the City Center*. Bonn: Vor- und Frühgeschichtliche Archäologie, Reinische Friedrich-Wilhelms-Universität Bonn. 347 pp. (Bonn Contributions to Asian Archaeology 8.)

—2020. *Craft Production in the Mongol Empire: Karakorum and Its Artisans*. Bonn: Vor- und Frühgeschichtliche Archäologie, Rheinische Friedrich-Wilhelms-Universität Bonn. 345 pp. (Bonn Contributions to Asian Archaeology 9.)

Rogers, J. Daniel. 2012. Inner Asian states and empires: Theories and synthesis. *Journal of Archaeological Research* 20(3):205–256. https://doi.org/10.1007/s10814-011-9053-2

Roux, Valentine, Blandine Bril, and Gilles Dietrich. 1995. Skills and learning difficulties involved in stone knapping: The case of stone-bead knapping in Khambhat, India. *World Archaeology* 27(1):63–87. https://www.jstor.org/stable/124778

Scarlett, Timothy J. 2010. What if the local is exotic and the imported mundane? Measuring ceramic exchanges in Mormon Utah. In: Carolyn D. Dillian and Carolyn L. White, eds. *Trade and Exchange: Archaeological Studies from History and Prehistory*. New York: Springer. pp. 165–177. https://doi.org/10.1007/978-1-4419-1072-1_10

Shea, Eiren L. 2020. *Mongol Court Dress, Identity Formation, and Global Exchange*. New York: Routledge. 206 pp. https://doi.org/10.4324/9780429340659

Shen, Hsueh-man, ed. 2006. *Gilded Splendor: Treasures of China's Liao Empire (907–1125)*. Milan: 5 Continents. 391 pp.

Shim, Hosung. 2022. The jam system: The Mongol institution for communication and transportation. In: Timothy May and Michael Hope, eds. *The Mongol World*. London: Routledge. pp. 382–393. https://doi.org/10.4324/9781315165172-30

So, Jenny F. 2019. Connecting friend and foe: Western Zhou personal regalia in jade and colored stones. *Archaeological Research in Asia* 19:100108. https://doi.org/10.1016/j.ara.2018.05.001

Society of Bead Researchers. 2024. "Researching the World's Beads: An Annotated Bibliography." Compiled by Karlis Karklins. Revised and updated July 1, 2024. https://beadresearch.org/resources/researching-the-worlds-bibliography/

Tseveendorj, Damdinsuren. 1980. Chandmani culture. *Studia Archaeologica*: 7(4):34–100. [in Mongolian.]

—2007. *Chandmani Culture*. Ulaanbaatar: Institute of Archaeology, Mongolian Academy of Sciences. [in Mongolian.]

—2016. Tombs of the Chandmani culture. In: Gelegdorj Eregzen, ed. A*ncient Funeral Monuments of Mongolia*. Ulaanbaatar: Institute of History and Archaeology, Mongolian Academy of Sciences. pp. 126–129. (Archaeological Relics of Mongolia 3). [in Mongolian and English.]

TSYBIKTAROV, ALEKSANDR D. 1998. *The Culture of Slab Graves in Mongolia and Transbaikalia*. Ulan-Ude, Russia: Buryat State University. [in Russian.]

TUMEN, DASHTSEVEG, DORJPUREV KHATANBAATAR, AND MYAGMAR ERDENE. 2013. Bronze Age graves in the Delgerkhaan Mountain area of eastern Mongolia. *Asian Archaeology* 2:40–49.

TUMEN, DASHTSEVEG, DORJPALAM NAVAAN, AND MYAGMAR ERDENE. 2006. Archaeology of the Mongolian period: A brief introduction. *Silk Road* 4(1):51–55.

VÉR, MÁRTON. 2016. "The Postal System of the Mongol Empire in Northeastern Turkestan" [dissertation]. University of Szeged, Hungary.

WRIGHT, JOSHUA, GALDAN GANBAATAR, WILLIAM HONEYCHURCH, BYAMBATSEREN BATDALAI, AND ARLENE ROSEN. 2019. The earliest Bronze Age culture of the south-eastern Gobi Desert, Mongolia. *Antiquity* 93(368):393–411. https://doi.org/10.15184/aqy.2018.174

YABLONSKY, LEONID T. 1995. The material culture of the Saka and historical reconstruction. In: Jeannine Davis-Kimball, Vladimir A. Bashilov, and Leonid T. Yablonsky, eds. *Nomads of the Eurasian Steppes in the Early Iron Age*. Berkeley, CA: Zinat Press. pp. 201–239.

CHAPTER NINE

HOUSEHOLD SCALE METALLURGICAL PRODUCTION IN MONGOLIA:
Implications for Local Community Independence

William R. GARDNER, Jang-Sik PARK, and Jargalan BURENTOGTOKH

Scholars commonly assumed that the mobile pastoralists of the Mongolian steppe, given their high level of household mobility, relied on trade with larger, settled manufacturing centers to acquire metal objects. This assumption was based on the notion that mobile households could not facilitate the workshop environment needed to produce more technologically advanced materials (e.g., McNeill 1963; Jagchid 1988; Jagchid and Symons 1989; Bentley 1998; Barfield 2001). Recent archaeological investigations, however, have established that large population centers, such as Karakorum, also functioned as centers of metal production (Amartuvshin et al. 2012; Sasada and Ishtseren 2012; Ishtseren and Sasada 2014; Sasada and Amartuvshin 2014; Park and Reichert 2015; Amartuvshin 2018). Archaeometallurgical investigations of metal objects recovered from these sites further suggest that mobile pastoralists developed distinct metallurgical traditions that supported a self-sufficient iron production industry (Park, Amartuvshin, and Eregzen 2008; Park, Eregzen, and Chimidorj 2010; Park, Erdenebaatar, and Eregzen 2018). For example, unlike the cast iron technologies predominant among settled communities in China (Wagner 1996), a bloomery iron-based technological tradition was established in Mongolia during the Xiongnu polity (around 200 BCE–100/150 CE) and consistently served as the primary method of iron production as late as the Mongol Period, from the thirteenth through the fourteenth centuries CE (Park, Eregzen, and Chimidorj 2010; Park, Honeychurch, and Amartuvshin 2019a).

While mounting evidence clearly indicates the presence of a distinct metallurgical tradition on the Mongolian steppe, one cannot help but question how a few large production centers could consistently supply highly dispersed communities of a mobile society with small, everyday items that had short functional durations but were crucial for completing important common tasks. Recent work on a small number of iron objects recovered from medieval campsites in the eastern grasslands of Mongolia has revealed microscale steelmaking through the recycling of small cast iron scraps conventionally viewed as waste metal of little practical or metallurgical value (Park, Honeychurch, and Amartuvshin 2019b). While the ability to produce steel at microscale is fascinating from a technological standpoint alone, the novel approach to manufacturing important household items from what could be considered waste material has many important implications that beg us to question the extent to which mobile communities of the greater Mongolian steppe relied on this practice.

In this chapter we aim to address this question by presenting the initial analysis of numerous small iron objects discovered during the excavation of the Tsagaan Ereg site, a Mongol period habitation in the mountainous Tarvagatai Valley of north-central Mongolia (Figure 9.1A). From this analysis we hope to determine whether there was a similar practice of use and re-use of what might have been considered waste material in a region of the country far removed from the eastern grasslands of the Mongolian steppe. We hope to determine whether a creative cast iron recycling process allowed steppe communities to successfully manufacture goods across a wide range of environments, including regions that may have lacked the natural resources needed for metal production, thereby giving dispersed local communities a level of self-reliance in the production of important everyday items.

Comments on the Tarvagatai Valley and the Tsagaan Ereg Archaeological Settlement

Formed by the Tarvagatai River, a tributary to the greater Egiin Gol River, the Tarvagatai Valley consists of approximately 120 km² of inhabitable land in the forest-steppe region of the Baikal Rift Zone in north-central Mongolia. The basal elevation of the east-to-west flowing Tarvagatai River is approximately 950 masl (meters above sea level). Physical relief in the valley is created by the Buteel Mountain Range to the north and east (1,850 masl) and the Khantain Mountain Range to the south (1,650 masl).

Over the last ten years the Tarvagatai Valley Project (TVP) has conducted an intensive pedestrian survey of over 86 km². These field efforts have identified multiple regions in the valley as locales preferred for habitation by both mobile pastoralists in antiquity and present-day herders. Dozens of such areas have undergone intensive auger testing, geophysical prospection, and small- and large-scale block excavations. For this study, we examine twenty iron and iron-related objects recovered from the excavation of a Mongol period habitation at the Tsagaan Ereg site (TVP-180; see Figure 9.1A).

The Tsagaan Ereg site was first identified during pedestrian survey because large amounts of cultural material have eroded from a bank incised by the Tarvagatai and Khujirt Rivers. The cultural material analyzed in this chapter comes from Dwelling 2 located along the edge of the cut bank created by the Tarvagatai River (Figure 9.1B). The rough extent of the dwelling was later confirmed by geophysical prospection conducted by Bryan Hanks of the University of Pittsburgh. The dwelling was excavated in the summer of 2019 by archaeologists from the Mongolian National University, Yale University, and the University of Wyoming.

Following methods used at excavations of Paleoindian dwellings (Kornfeld and Frison 2000; Stiger 2006), we placed a premium on in situ artifact identification and point-plot mapping. We paid specific attention to recovering highly accurate locational information of artifact types related to soil conditions to properly identify an artifact's position in stable versus disturbed soils, to ensure an accurate reconstruction of possible activity areas. To further ensure tight locational integrity of excavated materials, we excavated arbitrary 5 cm levels by trowel across a block divided into 1 by 1-m excavation units. These excavation units were further subdivided and excavated in 50 by 50 cm quadrants. By confining excavation to small compartments within the unit, attention was purposefully focused on identifying artifacts in situ. Additionally, this method of excavation provided tighter locational control over artifacts recovered from soils sieved through a 3 mm mesh screen. In total, 11 m² were excavated to a depth of approximately 1.3 m below ground surface, with excavations terminating at a sterile soil horizon consisting of loess deposits.

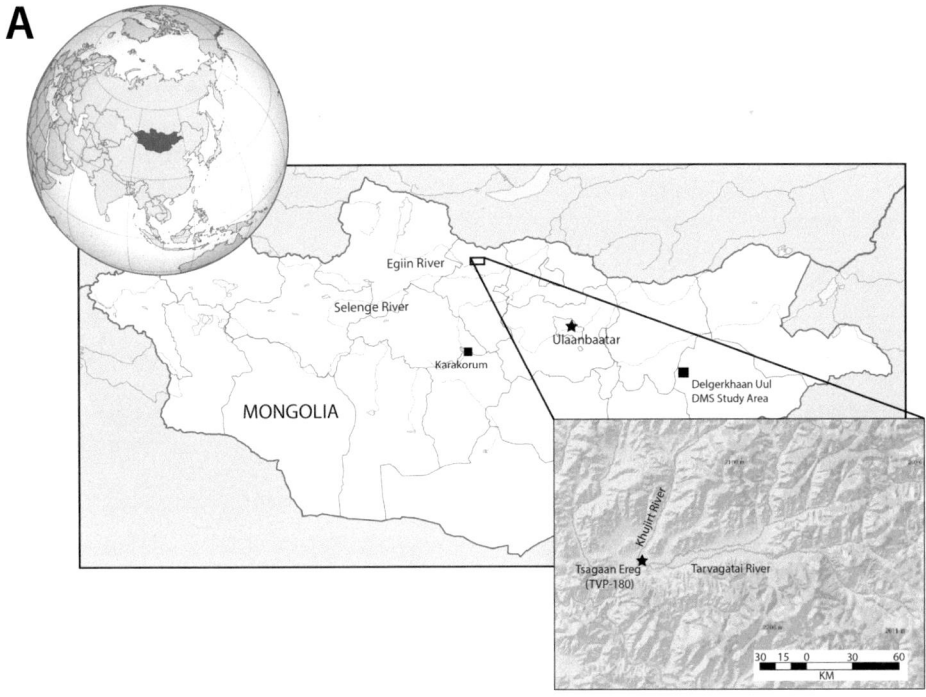

Figure 9.1. The archaeological site of Tsagaan Ereg (TVP-180). **A.** The site location in the Tarvagatai Valley of Mongolia, as well as Delgerkhaan Uul in the Dornod Mongol Survey (DMS) study area and the Karakorum site. **B.** An aerial photograph of the Tsagaan Ereg site taken by a drone camera, facing to the north toward the Khujirt River valley.

Radiocarbon dating of two separate bone collagen samples dated the habitation structure dates to 1290–1400 cal CE. The time-range of occupation is based on a bone collagen sample found in place, embedded into the original floor of the dwelling space (F.S. 2611, UGAMS 44800, 1298–1400 cal CE, 95.4% probability) and a second bone collagen sample in the fill material deposited after abandonment of the dwelling (F.S. 2487, UGAMS 46821, 1290–1395 cal CE, 95% probability). According to our current interpretation of the archaeological remains, we believe the occupants of the dwelling created a circular, semisubterranean habitation by excavating approximately 51 cm into the underlying loess deposit and then erecting a nonpermanent superstructure (of unknown material) supported by a series of wooden posts.

It also seems that, at some point, the structure was accidentally or intentionally burned; a birch bark floor was then laid over the subsequent ash lens and the structure was re-inhabited. On abandonment of the dwelling, loess sediment (possibly fill stockpile resulting from the original construction) and surrounding cultural debris were used to fill in the living area. All artifacts we discuss here were mixed with the loess sediment used to fill in the dwelling area. Given that radiocarbon dates from both the fill material and the living surface closely overlap, we are confident that the refuse material mixed with the fill was from the time of occupation of the dwelling space.

Lastly, during excavation of the dwelling space, we discovered a small iron-working feature in the southeast sector of the living area (Figure 9.2). This smelter consisted of two immediately adjacent rock-lined pits. Both pits had an opening on the western side and one pit was full of oxidized loess fill. The second pit contained small charcoal flecking, clinker, and slag materials. Two tunnels entered the pit from the south. These tunnels appear to be part of a flume that facilitated airflow. The clinker, slag fill, and presence of a potential flume seem to indicate that this feature functioned as a small work area for smelting iron ore.

Artifacts under Consideration

The iron objects under consideration here (Figure 9.3), selected for examination from the many metal fragments excavated, represent those relatively large in size. The weight of each, however, is 26.4 g or less (except object 4, which weighs 52.8 g); the majority of the objects are less than 10 g. Most of these artifacts are irregular and bounded by uneven surfaces suggestive of treatments applied at high temperatures, which is further supported by the small metal piece tightly welded to the larger block at the bottom (see arrows in Figure 9.3, objects 1 and 2).

For the benefit of later discussion, we arranged the objects (see Figure 9.3) according to the type of materials and treatments used, as determined by microscopic analysis, which is described in detail in the following sections. Objects derived from cast iron (Figure 9.3, 1–16) are placed ahead of those made of bloomery iron (Figure 9.3, 17–20). The fracture surface created when objects 14, 15, and 16 broke off the parent article is still readily identifiable, indicating that these subsequently underwent no significant thermal treatment. In contrast, the rest of the objects derived from cast iron have lost their initial shape as determined during the original casting operation. The thermal treatment given to them afterward was certainly responsible for this deformation. The deformation is particularly prominent in objects 1 through 9, which display features characteristic of a solidification reaction. The deformation in objects 11, 12, and 13 does not clearly define whether the

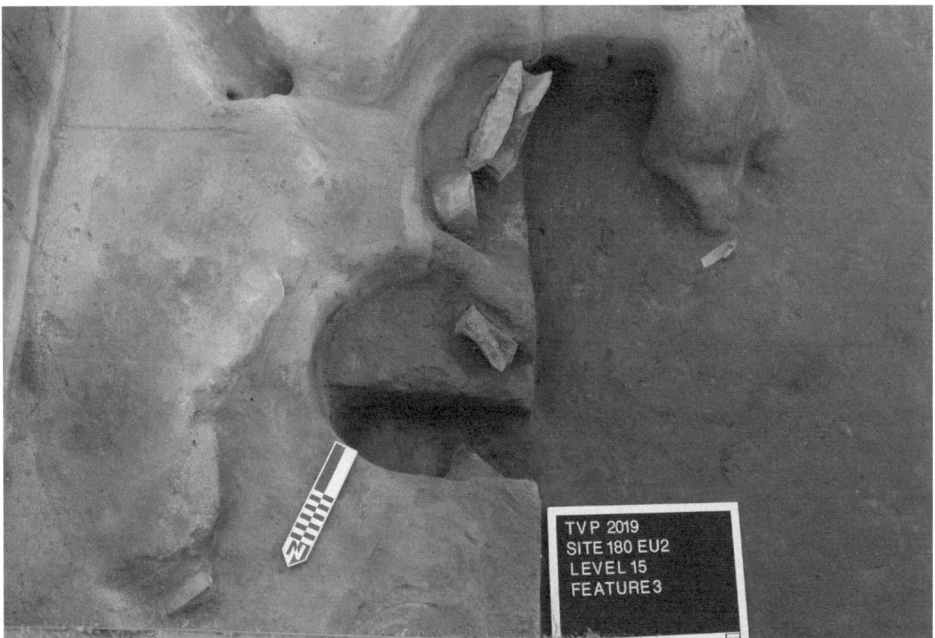

FIGURE 9.2. The two furnace structures installed in the southeast sector of the living area. The scale bar is 20 cm.

treatment was applied in the liquid state or not. Though not clearly visible here, object 10 takes the form of a thin plate with its cross section tapered as would be expected in a blade, which is a clear sign of the application of mechanical working. It is important to note that if the fragments labeled 14, 15, and 16 had been treated in the molten state, they would have then been deformed, resulting in the loss of their current shape, as was the case for objects 1 through 9.

Objects 17 through 20, of bloomery origin, were included for the sake of thoroughness, with the presentation of analytical results minimized (Table 9.1). In general, these samples have structures and chemical compositions qualitatively identical to those reported previously on the iron and iron-related assemblage derived from bloomery-based technology. Bloomery production was a contemporaneous technological practice evidenced at both Tasgaan Ereg and other nearby archaeological sites within the Tarvagatai Valley (Park, Honeychurch, and Amartuvshin 2020). However, bloomery production is substantially different from the technological process we identify in the objects made from cast iron scrap metal (Figure 9.3, 1–16) and discussed in detail below.

Interpretation of Artifacts

A thermal treatment involving cast iron in the molten state, apparently for decarburization, was evident in the external appearance of the objects under consideration. Visual inspection could therefore readily distinguish between those with (Figure 9.3, 1–9) and without (Figure 9.3, 15 and 16) the treatment. The latter represent fragments broken off from parent cast iron

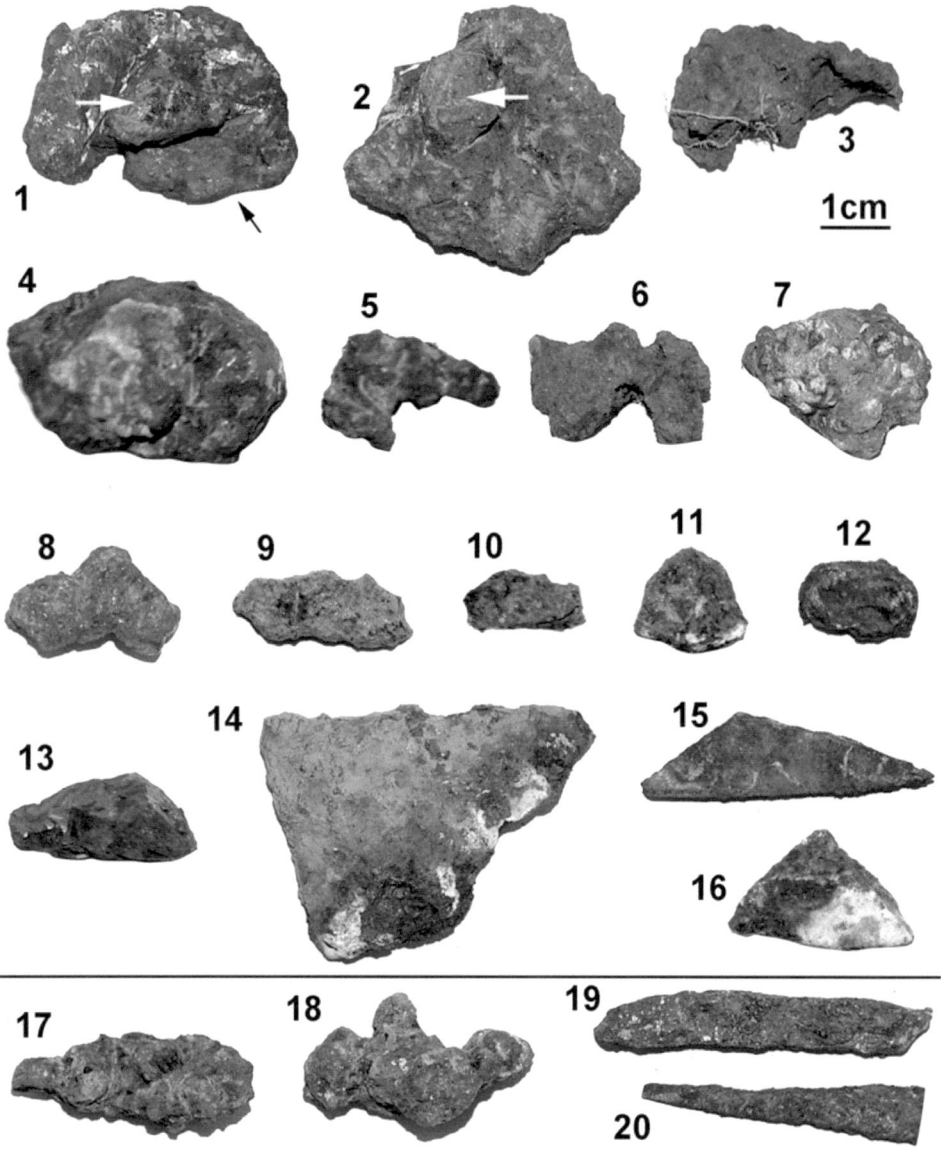

FIGURE 9.3. The general appearance of the iron objects under consideration. **1–9.** Fragments with an irregular surface profile characteristic of the solidification reaction from the partially molten state. **10.** A plate with the tapered cross section, as in a blade. **11–13.** Fragments with a shape displaying no hint of a treatment given in the molten state. **14–16.** Fragments in as-cast states. **17–20.** Bloomery products. Shown approximately to scale.

TABLE 9.1. The mass and chemical composition of metal fragments examined from the medieval site at Tarvagatai in north-central Mongolia. *Abbreviations*: HT, heat-treated in the solid state; NA, not applicable; ND, none detected; R, remelted; R-F, remelted, forged; R-Gr, remelted, graphite. The object numbers are consistent with the labels in Figure 9.3.

Object number	Field ID	Treatment	Find spot	Depth (cm)	Mass (g)	Composition (wt. %)				Comments
						C	Si	P	S	
Cast iron products										
1	44-P10#1	R	2242	80	20.0	1.0	0.8	0.5	0.9	2 pieces, welded
2	38-P6#2	R	2318	86.8	26.4	1.3	0.7	0.4	0.9	2 pieces, welded
3	33-P5#1	R	399	19.3	13.0	1.3	0.9	0.7	1.3	
4	47-P12#5	R	2091	80.3	52.8	1.3	0.8	0.4	0.8	
5	57b-P7#2	R	2552	95	9.8	1.3	0.3	0.4	0.8	
6	23-P3#1	R	740	25	6.5	1.3	0.3	0.3	0.6	
7	27-P3#9	R	2784	26.1	17.6	1.0–3.5	0.0–0.2	0.0	0.0	
8	43-P9#1	R	2576	104	5.2	1.5–3.5	0.0–0.2	0.4–0.6	0.5–0.9; 1.6	
9	55-P5#9	R	1369	16.7	2.5	0.8–1.0	0.6	0.0	0.0	
10	54a-P4#2	R-F	2415	97	1.6	0.8	0.2	0.0	0.2	Spherical cementite
11	57a-P7#2	R-Gr	2554	95	0.9	1.5	1.1	0.4	0.6	Blade

Continued

TABLE 9.1 CONTINUED

Object number	Field ID	Treatment	Find spot	Depth (cm)	Mass (g)	Composition (wt. %)				Comments
						C	Si	P	S	
Cast iron products										
12	62d-P17#1	HT	1902	73.4	1.4	1.3	0.5	0.6	2.1	
13	34-P5#2	As cast	313	16.7	10.7	2.5	0.5	0.3	0.7	
14	50-P19#1	As cast	1859	66.7	25.9	1.0	0.4	0.3	2.1	
15	49-P18#3	As cast	1823	65	7.8	2.5	0.8	0.4	1.8	
16	62b-P15#2	As cast	1303	51.2	7.3	2.8	1.1	0.5	1.2	
Bloomery products										
17	30P4#4	NA	2383	93.4	8.0	<0.02	ND	0.3	ND	Only ferrite
18	42P8#1	NA	2466	97.6	10.1	0.0–0.8	ND	ND	ND	Ferrite and pearlite
19	40P7#1	NA	2535	99	8.3	0.1–0.8	ND	ND	ND	Ferrite and pearlite
20	48P13#1	NA	905	36.7	2.5	0.0–0.5	ND	ND	ND	Ferrite and pearlite

articles and, in their present form, have little practical value. If treated for decarburization, however, they could be readily transformed into steel, an invaluable material for making highly functional items. The assemblage (see Figure 9.3) therefore consists of closely associated metal objects that are input and output materials for an engineering process intended for making steel from cast iron.

The unique microstructure, consisting of numerous spherical particles of pearlite with their boundaries filled with white cast iron eutectic, graphically illustrates the phase transition that occurs in cast iron when treated in the molten state for decarburization (Park, Honeychurch, and Amartuvshin 2019b). In this treatment the decreasing carbon level in the molten alloy drives the nucleation and growth of the proeutectic phase in spherical forms. If the treatment is terminated prematurely, the remaining liquid solidifies during the subsequent cooling stage to precipitate eutectic at the boundaries. As such, the fraction of eutectic in specimens thus treated may range significantly from zero to 100%. This variability was, in fact, confirmed in some of the samples examined, including objects 7 through 10. The structures observed in objects 1 through 6, however, were remarkably uniform and consistent, suggesting the existence of a technological guideline, though rudimentary, circulating as a reference for the process. The average carbon concentration inferred from these structures ranges from 1.0% to 1.3% (see Table 9.1), which was likely the target composition intended. This carbon level is well within the range of steel.

The major advantage of steel over cast iron is that it can accept substantial plastic deformation without breaking. In certain circumstances this valuable property justifies the investment required for such a small-scale decarburization process by which small pieces of metal can be individually treated. Object 10 provides an example of those items decarburized and then forged into a usable form, in this case a thin plate. Given the additional loss of carbon during the forging operation, its current carbon level of approximately 0.8% allows the original carbon concentration to be assessed at around 1.0% to 1.3%. This estimation agrees with what is inferred from objects 1 through 6, which were given a successful thermal treatment and were ready to be forged. By virtue of this technique, object 10 has enough carbon to ensure strength while its cementite phase precipitated in the form of spherical particles (see Figure 9.3) offers improved toughness. The tapered cross section of the object, weighing only 1.4 g, suggests that it was in the process of being made into a microblade.

By the time of the Mongol Empire, when these objects were produced, steelmaking by treating molten cast iron had long been practiced in the neighboring sedentary farming societies of eastern Asia. This technique, however, was primarily at an industrial scale and could not be applied to such a small-scale production effort as reflected in this assemblage (see Figure 9.3). In any case, the reduction of carbon concentration from 3.0% to 1.3%, as inferred from the data (see Table 9.1), requires the reaction temperature to be controlled within a relatively narrow range at around 1300 °C. This temperature control can only be achieved in a covered environment providing for thermal insulation. A proper means to supply oxygen is also necessary, whether for combusting fuels or for controlling the reaction atmosphere. The exact nature of the process and its infrastructure has yet to be documented in Mongolia. Considering the furnace features discovered at the Tsagaan Ereg settlement, it is important to note that these were likely used for bloomery smelting and are too large to support the steelmaking operation discussed here. However, the presence of these furnaces does indicate the practical knowledge and technological capacity required to carry out such metallurgical processes.

The equipment needed to implement steelmaking from individually treated cast iron fragments weighing mostly 10 g or less would not have been very large or complex. A small container, more like a crucible, with a means for supplying necessary oxygen would have sufficed. The irregular shape of most objects (see Figure 9.3) also shows that they were treated on a flat surface with nothing else to guide the shape formation during solidification. The reaction temperature, therefore, must have been set to have the molten metal confined by its own surface tension force. If the diffusion coefficient of carbon along the liquidus of the iron-carbon system is taken to be 10 to 4 cm^2/s, the distance of carbon diffusion for a hundred seconds is determined at approximately 1.0 mm. This distance is much larger than the microstructural scale observed in the treated samples. With the proper control of reaction temperature and atmosphere, therefore, it may have taken a few minutes for most of these objects to have their carbon level reduced to the target range.

According to our typological and radiocarbon periodization of sites with such steel-making remains across the two regions, most objects were recovered from Mongolian Empire contexts, from the thirteenth through fourteenth centuries CE, with some exceptions dating to the prior Khitan period, tenth through twelfth centuries CE. This chronological estimation is in line with the extremely high level of sulfur detected in most iron objects, which was derived from the use of mineral coal in smelting, begun in Mongolia during the Khitan period and carried forward into the period of the Mongol Empire. The successful implementation of this metallurgical process would not have been possible without a comprehensive understanding of the physical properties of iron-carbon alloys as determined by the various thermomechanical treatments applied. Moreover, the technique would not have been innovated if not appropriate for the needs and capabilities of daily life on the steppe. The fact that it was routinely practiced in several regions, like the Tarvagatai Valley of northern Mongolia as well as at Delgerkhaan Uul, 700 km to the southeast, underscores the uniformly high level of technological sophistication attained by mobile pastoralists. Evidently, the pertinent technological methods were widely shared by pastoralist groups across the expansive Mongolian steppe.

Discussion

As previously stated, prior investigation suggested a unique metallurgical tradition of Mongolian mobile pastoralists that included distinct methods of iron production and recycling of small cast iron scraps (which could have conventionally been deemed as waste) to produce crucial everyday items. Through analyzing small iron objects excavated from the Tsagaan Ereg site we aimed to determine the extent of this cast iron recycling process across the Mongolian steppe and to uncover whether it fostered self-reliance in local production, especially in areas lacking natural resources required for metal production. Analysis of artifacts from Dwelling 2 of the Tsagaan Ereg site shows visual differences based on whether they underwent a thermal treatment involving molten state manipulation, pointing to a small-scale, highly controlled decarburization process. The microstructure of the treated objects provides evidence of the phase transition that occurs in cast iron during the decarburization process, resulting in a unique structure of pearlite particles bounded by eutectic white cast iron.

Using an array of microscopy techniques, researchers investigated the microstructure and compositional variations in the treated and untreated objects. The average carbon concentration in successfully treated objects ranged from 1.0% to 1.3%, a range typical for steel, emphasizing the precision of the technique. From our findings we conclude that this technique was a practical and cost-effective method to create steel artifacts during the Mongol era. It allowed for transforming small fragments of metal into more functional and durable items, an advantage highlighted by a studied thin plate with a carbon level of approximately 0.8%, suggesting its original carbon concentration to be around 1.0% to 1.3%. The presence of spherical cementite particles implies increased toughness, reinforcing the merit of this technique.

The wider implications of the study suggest a high level of technological sophistication in these mobile pastoral societies. Despite the limited scale, the decarburization process required precise temperature control (around 1300 °C) and a particular atmosphere, reflecting the presence of advanced metallurgical knowledge. Moreover, the existence of these objects across vast regions, such as the Tarvagatai Valley and at Delgerkhaan Uul, highlights a widespread sharing of this advanced technique. Lastly, above and beyond the innovative techniques implemented to manufacture these items, recycling of cast iron scraps originally manufactured in distant production centers often provided communities across Mongolia with the ability to manufacture these items even in regions that lacked the natural resources necessary for the production of metal objects (Park, Honeychurch, and Amartuvshin 2019a).

Overall, the study underscores the innovative nature of the Mongol Empire's metallurgical practices and, specifically, the method of decarburizing cast iron into steel. These findings add nuance to our understanding of scientific and technological capabilities during this historical period, challenging the stereotypical portrayal of mobile pastoral societies as technologically inferior.

Conclusions

This chapter challenges the long-held assumption that the mobile pastoralists of the Mongolian steppe relied on trade with larger manufacturing centers for the acquisition of metal objects. Through archaeometallurgical investigations, we show the existence of distinct and self-sufficient metallurgical traditions among these societies, with a focus on recycling small cast iron scraps that were previously deemed waste into functional everyday items. The methodology includes excavating and analyzing iron objects from the Tsagaan Ereg site in the Tarvagatai Valley of north-central Mongolia. Detailed microscopy studies on these objects reveal evidence of a small-scale, highly controlled decarburization process that transformed cast iron into steel, requiring precise temperature control and specific atmospheres. The findings indicate that this technique was not only practical and cost-effective, but also allowed for the manufacture of more durable items, even in regions that lacked the natural resources necessary for metal production. The research reveals an advanced level of technological sophistication among the mobile pastoral societies of the Mongolian steppe, underscoring a broader dissemination of advanced metallurgical knowledge. The study significantly contributes to our understanding of the innovative nature of the Mongol Empire's metallurgical practices and calls for a reconsideration of the stereotypical portrayal of mobile pastoral societies as technologically inferior. It adds to the growing body of evidence showing how these societies adopted resourceful and sustainable practices to survive and flourish in challenging environments.

Acknowledgments

It has been a profound honor to participate in this volume dedicated to celebrating the life of the promising young scholar Zeng Lingyi. Lingyi's presence among us was tragically brief, but her impact and potential were nothing short of monumental, leaving an indelible mark on all who had the privilege of knowing her. Lingyi was a beacon of intellect and creativity, particularly shining in the field of Chinese archaeology. Her approach to her work was characterized by an unwavering passion and dedication, serving as a source of inspiration for all who crossed her path.

Beyond her scholarly pursuits, Lingyi was a beloved friend and colleague, known for her kindness, gentle spirit, and infectious laughter. Her warmth and compassion touched the lives of many and her absence has left a void that cannot be filled. As we come together to mourn the loss of Lingyi, let us also celebrate the extraordinary life she lived and the profound impact she had on each of us. Lingyi's memory will serve as a constant reminder to strive for excellence in all that we do and to cherish the moments we share with one another. Though Lingyi may no longer be with us, her legacy lives on in the hearts and minds of those who knew her.

References

AMARTUVSHIN, CHUNAG. 2018. History of Ancient Mongolian Craft Production [field report]. Ulaanbaatar: Mongolian Institute of History and Archaeology. [in Mongolian.]

AMARTUVSHIN, CHUNAG, TOMOTAKA SASADA, GELEGDORJ EREGZEN, I. USUKI, AND LOCHIN ISHEREN. 2012. Khustyn Bulagiin dursgalt gazart ilersen tomoriin khuder khai-luulakh bolon vaar shataakh zuukhny on tsagiin asuudald. *Arkheologiin Sudlal* 32:213–228.

BARFIELD, THOMAS J. 2001. The shadow empires: Imperial state formation along the Chinese–Nomad frontier. In: Susan E. Alcock, Terence N. D'Altroy, Kathleen D. Morrison, and Carla M. Sinopoli, eds. *Empires: Perspectives from Archaeology and History*. Cambridge: Cambridge University Press. pp. 10–41.

BENTLEY, JERRY H. 1998. Hemispheric Integration, 500–1500 CE. *Journal of World History* 9(2):237–254. http://www.jstor.org/stable/20078730

BURENTOGTOKH, JARGALAN, AND ADIYSUREN MOLOR. 2019. Archaeological and Paleoclimatic Research in Tarvagatai Valley of Teshig sum in Bulgan aimag 2019 [field report]. Ulaanbaatar: Mongolian Academy of Science, Institute of Archaeology. [in Mongolian.]

GARDNER, WILLIAM R. M., AND JARGALAN BURENTOGTOKH. 2018. Mobile domiciles of the Eurasian steppe: Archaeological evidence of possible dwelling space during the Early Iron Age. *Journal of Field Archaeology* 43(5):345–361. https://doi.org/10.1080/00934690.2018.1475994

ISHTSEREN, LOCHIN, AND TOMOTAKA SASADA. 2014. Research questions on the smelting furnaces of the Xiongnu state. *Arkheologiin Sudlal* 34:253–263. [in Mongolian.]

JAGCHID, SECHIN. 1988. Patterns of trade and conflict between China and the nomadic people of Mongolia. In: Sechin Jagchid. *Essays in Mongolian Studies*. Provo, UT: David M. Kennedy Center for International Studies, Brigham Young University. pp. 3–20.

JAGCHID, SECHIN, AND VAN JAY SYMONS. 1989. *Peace, War, and Trade Along the Great Wall: Nomadic-Chinese Interaction through Two Millennia*. Bloomington: Indiana University Press. 266 pp.

KORNFELD, MARCEL, AND GEORGE C. FRISON. 2000. Paleoindian occupation of the high country: The case of Middle Park, Colorado. *Plains Anthropologist* 45(172):129–153. https://www.jstor.org/stable/25669651

MCNEILL, WILLIAM H. 1963. *The Rise of the West: A History of the Human Community*. Chicago: University of Chicago Press. 829 pp.

Park, Jang-Sik. 2008. The key role of forging in ancient steel making from white cast iron. *Materials Characterization* 59(5):647–650. https://doi.org/10.1016/j.matchar.2007.03.013

Park, Jang-Sik, Chunag Amartuvshin, and Gelegdorj Eregzen. 2008. A technological transition in Mongolia evident in microstructure, chemical composition and radiocarbon age of cast iron artifacts. *Journal of Archaeological Science* 35(9):2465–2470. https://doi.org/10.1016/j.jas.2008.03.014

Park, Jang-Sik, Diimaajav Erdenebaatar, and Gelegdor Eregzen. 2017. Evolution of Mongolian bronze technology with the rise of the Xiongnu State. *Archaeological and Anthropological Sciences* 9:789–798. https://doi.org/10.1007/s12520-015-0304-x

—2018. The implication of the metallurgical traditions associated with Chinese style wagons from the royal Xiongnu tomb at Golmod 2 in Mongolia. *Archaeological and Anthropological Sciences* 10:1535–1546. https://doi.org/10.1007/s12520-017-0476-7

Park, Jang-Sik, Gelegdorj Eregzen, and Yeruul-Erdene Chimidorj. 2010. Technological traditions inferred from iron artefacts of the Xiongnu Empire in Mongolia. *Journal of Archaeological Science* 37(11):2689–2697. https://doi.org/10.1016/j.jas.2010.06.002

Park, Jang-Sik, William Honeychurch, and Chunag Amartuvshin. 2011. Ancient bronze technology and nomadic communities of the Middle Gobi Desert, Mongolia. *Journal of Archaeological Science* 38(4):805–817. https://doi.org/10.1016/j.jas.2010.11.003

—2016. Complicating the frontier: Armaments, fortifications, and identities beyond the Great Wall. *Journal of Archaeological Science: Reports* 6:475–487. https://doi.org/10.1016/j.jasrep.2016.03.024

—2019a. Novel micro-scale steel-making from molten cast iron practised in medieval nomadic communities of East Mongolia. *Archaeometry* 61(1):83–98. https://doi.org/10.1111/arcm.12413

—2019b. Iron technology and medieval nomadic communities of East Mongolia. *Archaeological and Anthropological Sciences* 11:555–565. https://doi.org/10.1007/s12520-017-0553-y

—2019c. The technological and chronological implication of ^{14}C concentrations in carbon samples extracted from Mongolian cast iron artifacts. *Radiocarbon* 61(3):831–843. https://doi.org/10.1017/RDC.2019.4

—2020. Technologies and complexities as reflected in small cast iron fragments recovered from medieval sites in eastern Mongolia. *Archaeological and Anthropological Sciences* 12:75, 13 pp. https://doi.org/10.1007/s12520-020-01030-4

Park, Jang-Sik, and Susanne Reichert. 2015. Technological tradition of the Mongol Empire as inferred from bloomery and cast iron objects excavated in Karakorum. *Journal of Archaeological Science* 53:49–60. https://doi.org/10.1016/j.jas.2014.10.005

Sasada, Tomotaka, and Chunag Amarthuvshin. 2014. Iron smelting in the nomadic empire of Xiongnu in ancient Mongolia. *ISIJ International* 54(5):1017–1023. https://doi.org/10.2355/isijinternational.54.1017

Sasada, Tomotaka, and Lochin Ishtseren. 2012. On the metallurgical industries at Chinngis khaan's Ikh Ord "site of Avargyn balgas." *Arkheologiin Sudlal* 32:268–277. [in Mongolian.]

Stiger, Mark. 2006. A Folsom structure in the Colorado mountains. *American Antiquity* 71(2):321–351. https://doi.org/10.2307/40035907

Surovell, Todd A., and Nicole M. Waguespack. 2007. Folsom hearth-centered use of space at Barger Gulch, Locality B. In: Robert H. Brunswig and Bonnie L. Pitblado, eds. *Frontiers in Colorado Paleoindian Archaeology: From the Dent Site to the Rocky Mountains.* Boulder: University Press of Colorado. pp. 219–260.

Verhoeven, John D. 1975. *Fundamentals of Physical Metallurgy.* New York: John Wiley and Sons. 567 pp.

Wagner, Donald B. 1996. *Iron and Steel in Ancient China.* 2nd impression with corrections. Leiden: E.J. Brill. First published in 1993. 573 pp.

CHAPTER TEN

A Translation of "Debating the Legitimate Succession of the Liao, Song, and Jin (辯遼宋金正統)" by Xiu Duan (修端), 1234 CE

KOH Choon Hwee

This essay devoted to the memory of Zeng Lingyi highlights the insights Lingyi had about the complexities of understanding relatively late historical polities that developed in China. Her path-breaking research on the multi-ethnic Mongol Empire (1206–1368 CE) was cut short by her untimely death in 2020. This essay is an effort to continue research inspired by Zeng Lingyi.

Lingyi advocated for research collaboration among scholars in China, who refer to this period as the Yuan dynasty, with scholars in Mongolia, Central Asia, and other areas. In her multidisciplinary dissertation research, Lingyi consulted the works of historians as well as archaeological units in China. I first met Lingyi in 2015 along with the art historian Yong Cho in Professor Valerie Hansen's Tang-Song-Yuan documents class. We worked together to translate Chinese texts and found that we shared an interest in China's connections with the Middle East and Inner Asia. We called ourselves the Turco-Mongols and organized several *quriltai* (assembly, council) where we exchanged tips about everything, from the travails of doing research in archives to the challenge of taking baths in the steppe (due to its flat terrain). Yong shared his experiences while on an archaeological dig in Mongolia and recounted how a group of Korean tourists came by and started taking photos of him when he was sitting on the ground outside his tent, thinking he was a local "nomad" resting in his natural surroundings. Yong then surprised them by speaking perfect Korean. He also shared that winters in the steppe were so cold that New Haven winters would probably feel more like spring to somebody like Chinggis Khan. I remember how Lingyi and I laughed all night at Yong's stories. We made plans for a real *quriltai* in the steppe, someday. Intellectually, it was clear to us even in those early days of graduate school that to properly understand China, we needed to uncover the kinds of exchanges—commercial, diplomatic, technical, artistic, and others—that took place between China and areas to the west.

Lingyi was not able to finish her planned analyses of the composition of various porcelain wares from the Mongol Empire with the goal of inferring production locations, exchange patterns, and preferences of consumers in different areas. She argued for the importance of new research on historical polities with origins outside of the Central Lands, the area commonly regarded as the heartland of China (*Zhongguo*, 中國) since the development

---

With additional translations, annotations, and analysis from Yang Shao-yun, *Denison University.*

of the earliest dynasties. As one historian inspired by Lingyi's creative research, in this essay I focus on debates regarding legitimate political succession that were written during the Yuan dynastic era (1271–1368 CE).

What is China—a word that does not exist in Chinese—and a term that refers to the modern nation-state (People's Republic of China) that is often assumed to have existed as a unified polity throughout centuries past (Wang 2012)? One way of thinking through this puzzle is to consider the twenty-four Standard Histories, which, as some scholars have observed, provide the ballast for the civilizational complex historical subjects called *Zhongguo*, or the "Central Lands."1 This historical practice, where a dynasty composed the Standard History of the preceding, vanquished dynasty, captures its quintessential "ontological continuity" (Thum 2014:136). In this vein and with this premise, the debates on legitimate succession (*zhengtong lun*, 正统论)—or, political genealogy— thus become fertile ground for uncovering just how (dis)continuous, contentious, and contingent this practice of historical relay was. There were newcomers who entered the Central Lands and competed for the baton. Amidst the exchanges of goods, of languages, of technologies, and of customs, the baton was not always passed cleanly from one dynasty to the next; sometimes the baton was dropped as civil war broke out, and sometimes interlopers snatched the baton from legitimate successors—or at least in the eyes of contemporary partisans. The peak of controversial baton-passing was arguably during the Yuan dynasty (1271–1368 CE). In his classic article, Chan (1981) provided a list of Yuan-era polemical tracts debating the issue of legitimate political genealogy. This paper translates and comments on one polemical tract from that list.2

"Debating the Legitimate Succession of the Liao, Song, and Jin" (辯遼宋金正統) is dated to 1234 CE and attributed to Xiu Duan (Xiu 1922), an official of the Jin dynasty (1115–1234 CE). There are two known versions of this primary text. I have translated the *Guochao wenlei* (國朝文類) version by Su Tianjue (蘇天爵, Su 1922), which is largely similar to the *Yutang jiahua* (玉堂嘉話) version by Wang Yun (王惲, Wang 1922). Translations of certain sections present in the latter, but not in the former, are provided in the footnotes courtesy of my generous senior colleague, the historian Yang Shao-yun. These two versions of the text have previously been translated into Japanese by Furumatsu (2003); his article also provided a synthesis and annotations.3

Very little is known about the author of this text, Xiu Duan. He was an official who served the Jurchen Jin (金). In 1234 CE he found himself at a gathering at the residence of Sun Hou with a group of friends from Shandong; 1234 was the year the Jin were destroyed at the hands of the Mongols, with some minor help from the Southern Song. This Southern Song–Mongol alliance against the Jin arguably repeated a pattern from over a century earlier in the 1120s. At the time, the Song had negotiated an alliance with the Jin against the Liao Khitans, with whom the Song enjoyed an expensive century of peace based on annual payments of silk and silver. This Song–Jin alliance led to the demise of the Liao in 1125 CE—but it also backfired on the Song. In 1125, the Jurchen Jin perceived an opportunity and invaded an ill-prepared Song, laying siege on and looting the Song capital Kaifeng. The Jin subsequently conquered much of north China. Song elites and subjects who managed to escape the Jin invasion fled to a new "Southern Song" state headed by Emperor Gaozong in the Yangzi delta. In 1141 CE, the Southern Song signed a peace treaty with the Jin that fixed their respective borders. In this treaty, the Southern Song emperor also submitted as a vassal to the Jin.4 The psychological impact of this defeat and of the Emperor Gaozong's submission as vassal was deep. Subsequent generations of Southern Song literati advocated warfare to regain the lost Song territory, arguing that there was a moral, even "filial," imperative to do so "to avenge the humiliation and death in captivity of the emperors Huizong and Qinzong" (Yang 2023:172). In 1234 CE, the Southern Song seemed to repeat a historical pattern from a century earlier by forging an alliance with the Mongols against the Jin, to vanquish the latter. Soon after, however, this Song-Mongol alliance would break down, with the Mongols beginning to raid Song territory just as the Jurchen Jin had done in 1125 CE. The Mongol-ruled dynasty known to scholars of China as the Yuan would take a few more decades to coalesce. In 1234, however, the Jin had just fallen; and Xiu Duan recounts in this text a lively conversation about legitimate political succession in the Central Lands.

What is significant about Xiu Duan's position on the topic is the irrelevance of ethnicity for determining legitimacy in the Central Lands. Instead, Xiu's main criterion for legitimacy is pragmatic: "If a dynasty lasted a long time, ruled a large amount of territory, and received tribute from many other countries, then it has to be recognized as legitimate. In other words, the best measure of legitimacy is sustained success."5 Thus, what is at stake for Xiu is the memory of actual historical events concerning the Jin and the Liao. It is this history of events that captures the Jin's "sustained success" that, in turn, justifies its legitimacy in the Central Lands. Yet, in Xiu's telling, the literati of the Central Lands were allegedly ignorant of the histories of the Liao and the Jin, and the Jin's achievements were at risk of being forgotten.

History and history writing had real stakes in establishing legitimate political genealogy. In relating the historical events of the Liao and the Jin, Xiu sought to legitimize the Jin's political lineage and succession. He also sought to critique the popular view of the renowned Song historian, writer, poet, and politician Ouyang (family name) Xiu (1007–1072 CE). Xiu agreed with Ouyang—and thus differing from many Southern Song literati—on the irrelevance of ethnicity for determining legitimacy. In Yang's analysis, Xiu disagreed with Ouyang fundamentally on two issues.6

First, Ouyang originally recognized all the Five Dynasties as legitimate, but eventually rejected them all as illegitimate on moral grounds. Xiu's held a different, more nuanced view. While he condemned Zhu Wen's (朱溫) usurpation as immoral—which led to the overthrow of the Tang and the establishment of the Later Liang (后梁)—he nevertheless recognized Later Liang as legitimate. For Xiu, Later Zhou (后周) is the only one of the Five Dynasties that was illegitimate. Instead, Xiu recognized the Northern Han (北漢) as a legitimate continuation of Later Han (后汉; see Table 10.1). He thus argues that the Song got its legitimacy not by replacing Later Zhou in 960 but by conquering Northern Han in 979 CE.

Second, Ouyang argued that in certain periods, like the Northern and Southern dynasties and the Five Dynasties, there was no legitimate dynasty and the dynastic succession was temporarily broken, because none of the contending dynasties was able to achieve the reunification of north and south. Xiu, on the other hand, seems to believe that parallel mandates of legitimacy existed in the Liao-Jin and Song. Liao got its mandate by conquering Later Chin (后晋) in 947 CE, and this mandate was inherited by Jin when it conquered Liao. The Song got its mandate by conquering Northern Han in 979 CE (see Table 10.1). This implies that in the collapse of the Later Chin in 947 CE, the Mandate of Heaven somehow split into two. One half of the Mandate was taken north by the Liao, and the other half remained in the Central Plains and was claimed by Later Han. The logic of this Two Mandate argument is never explained clearly, and it would seem to defeat the whole purpose of *zhengtong* discourse, in which there can only be one legitimate dynasty at a time. Although Xiu is adamantly sure that the Jin was legitimate, he also cannot bring himself to argue that the

TABLE 10.1. Historical timeline of China's dynasties. Modified from Standen (2007:4), Ebrey (2014:xxi–xxii), and Franke (1994). Note that 金 has been transliterated as "jin" and 晉 as "chin"

Jin (金)			Liao (遼)			Five Dynasties, Northern Song dynasty (五代, 北宋)			Ten Kingdoms (十國)	
Personal name	Temple name	Date (CE)	Personal name	Temple name	Date (CE)	Personal name	Temple name	Regime		Date (CE)
						Tang dynasty (唐)				
					888	Li Ye (李曄)	Zhaozong (昭宗)			
					904	Li Zhu (李柷)	Aidi (哀帝)	Wu (吳)		902–937
						Later Liang dynasty (后梁)				
			Abaoji (阿保幾)	Taizu (太祖)	907	Zhu Wen (朱溫)	Taizu (太祖)	Former Shu (前蜀)		901–925
					913	Zhu Yougui (朱友珪)	None	Wuyue (吳越)		907–978
					913	Zhu Youzhen (朱友貞)	Modi (末帝)	Min (閩)		909–945
								Southern Han (南漢)		917–971

Continued

TABLE 10.1 CONTINUED

Jin (金)			Liao (遼)			Five Dynasties, Northern Song dynasty (五代, 北宋)			Ten Kingdoms (十國)	
Personal name	Temple name	Date (CE)	Personal name	Temple name	Date (CE)	Personal name	Temple name	Date (CE)	Regime	Date (CE)
						Later Tang dynasty (後唐)				
						Li Cunxu (李存勗)	Zhuangzong (莊宗)	923	Nanping/Jingnan (南平/荊南)	924–963
			Deguang (德光)	Taizong (太宗)	926	Li Siyuan (李嗣源)	Mingzong (明宗)		Chu (楚)	927–951
						Li Conghou (李從厚)	Mindi (閔帝)	933		
						Li Congke (李從珂)	Modi (末帝)	934		
						Later Chin dynasty (後晉)				
						Shi Jingtang (石敬瑭)	Gaozu (高祖)	936	Later Shu (後蜀)	934–965
						Shi Chonggui (石重貴)	Chudi (出帝)	942	Southern Tang (南唐)	937–975

Continued

TABLE 10.1 CONTINUED

Jin (金)			Liao (遼)			Five Dynasties, Northern Song dynasty (五代, 北宋)		Ten Kingdoms (十國)	
Personal name	Temple name	Date (CE)	Personal name	Temple name	Date (CE)	Personal name	Temple name	Regime	Date (CE)
						Later Han dynasty (後漢)			
			Wuyu (兀欲)	Shizong (世宗)	947	Liu Zhiyuan (劉知遠)	Gaozu (高祖)		
					948	Liu Chengyou (劉承祐)	Yindi (隱帝)		
						Later Zhou dynasty (後周)			
			Yelü Jing (耶律璟)	Muzong (穆宗)	951	Guo Wei (郭威)	Taizu (太祖)	Northern Han (北漢) 951–979	
					954	Guo Rong (郭榮)	Shizong (世宗)		
					959	Chai (Guo) Zongxun (柴(郭)宗訓)	Gongdi (恭帝)		

Continued

"Debating the Legitimate Succession of the Liao, Song, and Jin (辯遼宋金正統)" 183

TABLE 10.1 CONTINUED

Jin (金)			Liao (遼)			Five Dynasties, Northern Song dynasty (五代, 北宋)			Ten Kingdoms (十國)	
Personal name	Temple name	Date (CE)	Personal name	Temple name	Date (CE)	Personal name	Temple name	Date (CE)	Regime	Date (CE)
						Northern Song dynasty (北宋)			Northern Han (北漢) 951–979	
					960	Zhao Kuangyin (趙匡胤)	Taizu (太祖)			
			Yelü Xian (耶律賢)	Jingzong (景宗)	969					
					976	Zhao Kuangyi (趙匡義)	Taizong (太宗)			
			Yelü Longxu (耶律隆緒)	Shengzong (聖宗)	982					
					997	Zhao Dechang (趙德昌)	Zhenzong (真宗)			
					1022	Zhao Zhen (趙禎)	Renzong (仁宗)			
			Yelü Zongzhen (耶律宗真)	Xingzong (興宗)	1031					
			Yelü Hongji (耶律洪基)	Daozong (道宗)	1055					
Ancestors of Wanyan Yingge and Jin Muzong have been omitted						Zhao Shu (趙曙)	Yingzong (英宗)	1063		
Jin Taizu is considered the first emperor of the Jin dynasty						Zhao Xu (趙頊)	Shenzong (神宗)	1067		

Continued

TABLE 10.1 CONTINUED

Jin (金)			Liao (遼)			Five Dynasties, Northern Song dynasty (五代, 北宋)			Ten Kingdoms (十國)	
Personal name	Temple name	Date (CE)	Personal name	Temple name	Date (CE)	Personal name	Temple name	Date (CE)	Regime	Date (CE)
						Zhao Xu (趙煦)	Zhezong (哲宗)	1085		
						Zhao Ji (趙佶)	Huizong (徽宗)	1100		
			Yelü Yanxi (耶律延禧)	Tianzuodi (天祚帝)	1101					
Wanyan Yingge (完顏盈歌)	Muzong (穆宗)	Reigned 1094–1103								
Wanyan Wuyashu (完顏烏雅束)	Kangzong (康宗)	Reigned 1103–1113								
Wanyan Aguda (完顏阿骨打)	Taizu (太祖)	1115								
Wanyan Cheng (完顏晟)	Taizong (太宗)	1123								
			End of the Liao dynasty in 1125 CE			Zhao Huan (趙桓)	Qinzong (欽宗)	1125		
						Jingkang period (靖康)		1126		
						Southern Song dynasty				
						Zhao Gou (趙構)	Gaozong (高宗)	1127		

Continued

TABLE 10.1 CONTINUED

Jin (金)			Liao (遼)			Five Dynasties, Northern Song dynasty (五代, 北宋)			Ten Kingdoms (十國)	
Personal name	Temple name	Date (CE)	Personal name	Temple name	Date (CE)	Personal name	Temple name	Date (CE)	Regime	Date (CE)
Wanyan Dan (完顏亶)	Xizong (熙宗)	1135								
Wanyan Liang (完顏亮)	Feidi (廢帝)	1150								
Wanyan Yong (完顏雍)	Shizong (世宗)	1161				Zhao Shen (趙昚)	Xiaozong (孝宗)	1162		
Wanyan Jing (完顏璟)	Zhangzong (章宗)	1189				Zhao Dun (趙惇)	Guangzong (光宗)	1189		
						Zhao Kuo (趙擴)	Ningzong (寧宗)	1194		
Wanyan Yongji (完顏永濟)	Weishao Wang (衛紹王)	1208								
Wanyan Xun (完顏珣)	Xuanzong (宣宗)	1213								

Continued

TABLE 10.1 CONTINUED

Jin (金)			Liao (遼)			Five Dynasties, Northern Song dynasty (五代, 北宋)			Ten Kingdoms (十國)	
Personal name	Temple name	Date (CE)	Personal name	Temple name	Date (CE)	Personal name	Temple name	Date (CE)	Regime	Date (CE)
Wanyan Shouxu (完顏守緒)	Aizong (哀宗)	1224				Zhao Yun (趙昀)	Lizong (理宗)	1224		
Wanyan Chenglin (完顏承麟)	Modi (末帝)	1234								
End of the Jin dynasty in 1234 CE						Zhao Qi (趙禥)	Duzong (度宗)	1264		
						Zhao Xian (趙㬎)	Gongdi (恭帝)	1274		
						Zhao Shi (趙昰)	Duanzong (端宗)	1276		
						Zhao Bing (趙昺)	Shaodi (少帝)	1278		
						End of the Southern Song dynasty in 1279 CE				

Song is illegitimate. What Xiu cannot abide is the notion that the Song alone is legitimate. For more information see Chan (1984), Liu (2004), and Xue (2022).

This translation of Xiu's account will hopefully contribute in a small way to existing discussions on non-Chinese empires in the Central Lands (Crossley 1999; Elliott 2001; Perdue 2009). In particular, historian Yang Shao-yun's notion of "ethnocentric moralism" is very generative as a juxtaposition to what Xiu Duan's text offers. According to Yang (2019), ethnocentric moralism was a rhetorical strategy among Tang and Song Classicist thinkers, in which those who followed "ritual propriety and moral duty" (*liyi*) were Chinese and those who did not were barbarians. In other words, neither "Chineseness" nor barbarism have an ontological existence in the world; they were fluid statuses that depended on an individual's actions. Ethnocentric moralism was particularly strong in the late eleventh and early twelfth centuries CE. Within the texts that elaborated on this position, "Chineseness" was further untethered from geographical location. This meant that a polity's observance of ritual propriety and moral duty could shift the location of the Central Lands (Yang 2019:64; see also Hansen 2018:214–215; Lorge 2018:158–159).

Yang's (2019) monograph is a generative text to think alongside Xiu's text. If "ritual propriety and moral duty" (*liyi*) were fluid statuses that depended on actions in the world, then it may be questioned whether later Classicist thinkers nevertheless distinguished some states' successes from others, and what criteria were used to evaluate different types of successes. The answers to these questions would, in turn, bear upon our understanding of which states were eligible to be "Chinese," how far this eligibility was tethered or untethered to the geographical space of the Central Lands, and the evolving relationship between the "Chineseness" and the legitimacy (*zhengtong*) of states.7 Further research will have to be conducted by other experts, given that I am not a specialist of this field. I only hope this translation may be a small contribution towards our collective understanding of the ontological essence known as "China."

Acknowledgements

It took me over two years to translate this text. I need to thank Richard Von Glahn and Wang Sixiang for sitting with me for hours as I checked my error-ridden translations with each of them, line by line. I thank them for their patience and generosity with their time and am also grateful for their scholarly ethic, since this particular text had little to do with their research interests. Yong Cho and Mai Huijun kindly gave feedback on a few sections of an early draft. Most unexpectedly, Yang Shao-yun gave my entire translation and introduction a thorough edit at the very end of 2023. In addition, without my asking, Yang strengthened the chapter with a translation of extra verses of the *Yutang jiahua* version of the text. His edits and annotations have improved this chapter immeasurably. Hong Cheng, Chinese Studies Librarian at the University of California, Los Angeles, taught me how to use the Erudition database and also answered my many questions. I thank all my fellow colleagues who accompanied me on this journey in parsing Xiu Duan's text written in classical literary style, which, in hindsight, was akin to an extended mourning ritual for an extraordinary friend and young scholar who left us too soon.

Notes

1. In this short introduction, I follow Yang Shao-yun in translating *Zhongguo* as the "Central Lands," which preserves the term's "plural character" (Yang 2019:8–9).
2. This text is also discussed in Zhao (1976:43–45, 50–51). For a translation and discussion of another text of a similar genre composed a century later, see Davis (1983).
3. According to Yang Shao-yun, Furumatsu's view is that the *Yutang jiahua* version is the original, while Su Tianjue edited the text and corrected some factual errors when anthologizing it in the *Guochao wenlei*.
4. I base my recounting of these historical events on Yang (2023). For a broader background, see also Lorge (2019), Hansen (2019), Hu (2019), and Foster (2019).
5. This is Yang Shao-yun's observation shared in my personal correspondence with him, December 16, 2023.
6. The specifics of Xiu Duan's text confounded me despite my repeated reading of it. The clear analysis expounded on here is Yang Shao-yun's. I thank Shao-yun for kindly outlining the two fundamental disagreements that Xiu Duan had with Ouyang and allowing me to reproduce his words verbatim in the paragraphs following this footnote.
7. In this vein, I have also found recent studies of Qing history, studies on Chinese Muslims, as well as what have been called "Critical Han Studies" generative to think with: Gladney (1998); Crossley (1999); Elliott (2001); Perdue (2009); Mullaney et al. (2012).

Debating the Legitimate Succession of the Liao, Song, and Jin (辯遼宋金正統)

Xiu Duan (脩端)

Chinese Text and Translation[1]

歲在甲午九月望日，東原諸友會于孫侯之第，語及前朝得失之事。

On the 15th day of the ninth month of the year Jiawu [1234 CE], a group of friends[2] from Dongyuan gathered at the residence of Sun Hou[3], and our conversation came to the topic of the achievements and failures of the previous [Jin] dynasty.

坐客問云：「金有中原百餘年，將來國史何如？」

One of the guests inquired, Jin possessed the Central Plains for over a hundred years—what should be done about its Official Standard History in the days to come?

或曰：「自唐巳降，五代相承，宋受周禪，雖靖康間二帝蒙塵，緣江淮以南，趙氏不絕，金於《宋史》中，亦猶劉、石、符、姚一載記爾。」

Somebody said, "After the Tang, the Five Dynasties succeeded each other [and] Song received the abdication of Later Zhou. Although two [Song] emperors went into exile during the Jingkang incident, to the south of the Yangtze and Huai rivers,[4] the Zhao line continues. Therefore, the Jin will be recorded in the *Official History of the Song* as a [mere] supplementary chronicle (載記), similar to how the rulers from the Liu, Shi, Fu, and Yao families [of the Sixteen Kingdoms] were recorded [in the *Official History of the Chin*]."[5]

眾頗惑焉。愚曰：「正閏之論，端雖不敏，請以本末言之。

Many of those gathered were misled by this opinion. I said, although I am slow-witted, please allow me to explain this subject of legitimacy and illegitimacy by getting to the root of things.

夫耶律氏，自唐以來，世為名族。延及唐末，朱溫篡唐，四方幅裂。

The Yelü were known as a prestigious clan for generations since the Tang. But at the end of the Tang, Zhu Wen usurped the Tang throne, and the empire was torn apart.

遼太祖阿保機乘時而起, 服高麗諸國, 并燕雲以北數千里, 與朱梁同年即位, 是歲丁卯。

Abaoji, the Liao emperor Taizu, took advantage of the times and rose up, subduing Goryeo and other kingdoms, conquering several thousand *li* of territory north of the Yan and Yun regions, and ascending to the imperial throne in the same year as Zhu Wen of Later Liang.[6] It was the year Dingmao [907 CE].

至丙子建元神冊, 在位二十年。其子德光嗣位, 是歲丁亥, 唐明宗天成二年也。

In the year Bingzi [916 CE] [Abaoji] inaugurated his first regnal era of Shence. He ruled for twenty years.[7] His son, Deguang, succeeded him in the year Dinghai [927 CE], which was the second year of the Tiancheng regnal era of Emperor Mingzong of the Later Tang.[8]

德光後號太宗, 當天顯十一年, 河東節度使石敬瑭爲清泰帝來伐, 遣使求救于遼, 奉表稱臣, 仍以父禮事之。

Deguang later received the temple name Taizong. In the eleventh year of the Tianxian regnal era [about 937 CE], the military governor of Hedong, Shi Jingtang, was under punitive attack by Emperor Qingtai [of Later Tang] and sent an embassy to the Liao to ask for military help.[9] In exchange, Shi Jingtang submitted a memorial that declared his vassalage to Taizong, whom he would serve with the ritual befitting a Father.

太宗赴援, 因以滅唐。石氏稱晉, 遂以燕雲十六州獻于遼, 仍歲貢帛三十萬疋。

Emperor Taizong came to [Shi Jingtang's] aid and destroyed the Later Tang; the Shi family then founded the Later Chin. [Shi Jingtang] then presented the Sixteen Prefectures of Yan and Yun to the Liao, and annually gave tribute of 300,000 bolts of silk.

天福七年晉高祖殂, 出帝嗣位, 大臣議奉表稱臣, 告哀於遼, 景延廣請致書稱孫而不稱臣, 與遼抗衡。

In the seventh year of the Tianfu regnal era [943 CE], Gaozu of Later Jin (Shi Jingtang) died. Emperor Chu [Chudi] succeeded him. High officials discussed the matter of submitting a memorial to the Liao [that would] accept vassal status and inform the Liao that they were in mourning. Jing Yanguang proposed to send a letter [in which Emperor Chu] would describe himself as [Taizong's] grandson but not [Taizong's] vassal, thereby seeking parity with the Liao.

太宗舉兵南下, 會同九年入汴, 以出帝爲負義侯, 遷黃龍府, 石晉遂滅。 大同元年, 太宗北還, 仍以蕭翰留守河南。 劉知遠在河東乘間而發, 由太原入汴, 自尊爲帝。

Taizong raised an army to attack southward and entered Kaifeng in the ninth year of the Huitong regnal era [946 CE]. He declared Emperor Chu to be the Ungrateful Duke and moved him to Huanglongfu.[10] The Shi family's Chin [Later Chin] dynasty was thus destroyed. In the first year of the Datong regnal era [947 CE], Taizong returned to the north, keeping Xiao Han behind to guard Henan. Liu Zhiyuan, based in Hedong, took advantage of the moment and set off from Taiyuan and entered Kaifeng, styling himself as emperor.

及乎宋受周禪, 有中原一百六十餘年。 遼爲北朝, 世數如之。 雖遼之封域褊於宋, 校其兵力而澶淵之戰, 宋幾不守, 因而割地連和, 歲貢銀絹二十萬兩疋, 約爲兄弟, 仍以世序昭穆, 降及晚年, 遼爲翁, 宋爲孫。

Including the time when it received Later Zhou's abdication, the Song controlled the Central Plains for over 160 years. The Liao was the northern dynasty for an equivalent number of generations. Although the Liao's dominion was less central than the Song's, in terms of military strength the Song nearly fell to Liao during the Chanyuan Campaign (of 1004–1005), with the result that they had to give up land for the sake of peace and pay an annual tribute of 200,000 taels of silver and 200,000 bolts of silk.[11] The two dynasties made a covenant establishing a relationship of brotherhood and ritual kinship. In later years, the Liao ruler was the grandfather, and the Song ruler was the grandson.

及至天祚, 金太祖舉兵, 平遼, 克宋, 奄有中原三分之二, 子孫帝王, 坐受四方, 朝貢百有餘年。

Coming to the reign of Emperor Tianzuo [of Liao], Jin emperor Taizu raised armies, pacified the Liao, defeated the Song, and extended his control over two-thirds of the Central Plains. His sons and grandsons reigned as emperors and received tribute from all four quarters of the world for over a hundred years.

今以劉石等比之, 愚故不可不辯也。 夫劉淵石勒皆晉之臣庶, 叛亂國家, 以臣伐君, 縱能盜據一隅, 僭至姚泓, 終爲晉將劉裕所虜, 斬建康市, 茲作載記, 理當然也。

I have no choice but to contest this idea of comparing the Jin with the Liu, the Shi and others [of the Sixteen Kingdoms period]. As for Liu Yuan, Shi Le and their ilk, they were all subjects of the Chin who treacherously rebelled against the ruling dynasty, a case of subjects attacking their lord.[12] Even though they could illegitimately occupy one corner [of the state], Yao Hong was finally captured and beheaded by the Chin general Liu Yu in the marketplace of [the Chin capital] Jiankang.[13] To record their reigns in supplementary chronicles [rather than an Official History] accords with reason.

完顏氏世爲君長, 保有肅慎, 至太祖時, 南北皆爲敵國, 素非君臣。 若如或者所言, 金爲載記, 未審遼史, 復如何爾。

[In contrast], the Wanyan family were rulers for generations over the territories of the ancient Sushen [in Manchuria].[14] Until the time of Taizu, the Northern and Southern [dynasties] [Liao and Song] were rival states [of equal standing] and were never lord and subject. If it is indeed as some say that the Jin should be relegated to a supplementary chronicle [as befits illegitimate rulers]--then I do not know what we are to do with the history of the Liao.

方遼太祖神冊之際, 宋太祖未生, 遼祖比宋前興五十餘年巳即帝位, 固難降就五十年之後, 包于《宋史》爲載記, 其世數相懸, 名分顛倒, 斷無此法。

During the time of Liao emperor Taizu, in the regnal era of Shence, Song emperor Taizu was not yet born. Liao emperor Taizu ascended to the throne more than fifty years before the Song was founded—it is thus difficult to skip over those fifty years and include the Liao as a [mere] supplementary chronicle for illegitimate dynasties in the *Official History of the Song*. This is a chronological mismatch and reverses their relative statuses—there cannot be such a logic.

既遼之世紀, 宋不可兼, 則金有中原, 尤難別議。

If the Song cannot equal the Liao [in longevity], then it is even harder to have a different opinion about the Jin, which controlled the Central Plains.

以公論處之, 據五代相因, 除莊宗入汴復讎伐罪, 理勢可觀外, 朱梁篡逆甚於王莽。

If we were to judge this impartially, [consider] the succession of the Five Dynasties. Apart from Zhuangzong[15] who was worth commending in terms of reason and circumstance because he marched into Kaifeng to avenge [the Tang dynasty] and punish those guilty [of usurpation], Zhu Wen of Later Liang was an even worse usurper than Wang Mang.[16]

石晉, 因遼有國, 終爲遼所虜。 劉漢自立, 父子四年, 郭周廢湘陰公而立。 以五代之君通作《南史》, 內朱梁名分, 猶恐未應。

As for the Shi family of Later Chin, they only had a state because of the Liao, and their emperor was captured by the Liao in the end. As for the Liu of Later Han, they established their own dynasty, and father and son ruled for four years [before] Guo Wei of Later Zhou deposed the Duke of Xiangyin[17] and claimed the throne. If we were to include all of the Five Dynasties within a *History of the Southern Dynasties*, that would be tantamount to recognizing Zhu Wen of Later Liang as legitimate, and one fears that would be inappropriate.

遼自唐末, 保有北方, 又非篡奪, 復承晉統, 加之世數名位, 遠兼五季, 與前宋相次而終, 當爲《北史》。

Since the end of the Tang, the Liao had controlled the northern region; moreover, it did not usurp power [from the Tang]. Moreover, [the Liao] inherited the Later Chin mandate [by conquering it]. In addition, its longevity and status far surpassed the Five Dynasties, and as it ended at the same time as the Former Song, [its history] should be compiled into a *History of the Northern Dynasties*.

宋太祖受周禪, 平江南, 收西蜀, 白溝迆南悉臣于宋, 傳至靖康, 當爲《宋史》。

Song emperor Taizu received the abdication of Later Zhou, pacified Jiangnan, and reclaimed Western Shu (the Sichuan Basin). All of the lands south of the Baigou River were subject to the Song until the Jingkang regnal era [1127 CE]. All of this should be included in the *Official History of the Song*.

金太祖破遼，克宋帝，有中原百餘年，當爲《北史》。自建炎之後，中國非宋所有，宜爲《南宋史》。」

Jin emperor Taizu vanquished the Liao, defeated the Song emperor, and controlled the Central Plains for over a hundred years—all this should be included in the *History of the Northern Dynasties*. After the Jianyan regnal era [1127–1130 CE], the Central Lands no longer belonged to the Song[18], and it is appropriate to record its history as the *Official History of the Southern Song*."

或曰：「歐陽氏宋之名儒也。定立五代，不云《南史》。當時想曾熟議，奈何今復有此論乎？」

Somebody said, Mr. Ouyang [Xiu] was a famous Confucian scholar of the Song.[19] He wrote a history of the Five Dynasties and did not call it the *History of the Southern Dynasties*. At the time, [it must have been] thoroughly discussed—why then are you making such arguments today?

愚曰：「歐陽氏作史之時，遼方全盛，豈不知梁晉漢周授受之由故？列五代者，欲膺周禪以尊本朝，勢使然爾。及作十國世家，獨曰『周漢之事，可謂難矣。』

I said, When Mr. Ouyang was penning his history, Liao was at the height of splendor. How could he have not known the reasons for the succession of the Later Liang, Later Chin, Later Han, and Later Zhou? The reason why he recognized all the Five Dynasties is because he wanted to recognize the abdication from the Later Zhou [to Song] as legitimate in order to respect his own state—this was due to the force of circumstances. But when compiling the Hereditary Houses[20] chapters on the Ten Kingdoms, he wrote, The matter of the relative statuses of Later Zhou and Northern Han is a difficult one indeed.[21]

歐陽公之爲是言，厥有旨哉！

Master Ouyang had good reason for saying what he did!

愚讀李屏山詠史詩, 詠五代郭周云:『不负先君持節死, 舉朝唯有一韓通。』蓋嘗驚哀此詩命意。宋自建隆以來, 名士大夫論議篇什不爲不多, 未嘗一語及此。非不能道也, 蓋禘之說也。故列五代者, 良可知矣。

I have read Li Pingshan's poems on history.[22] The poem on the Later Zhou of the Five Dynasties reads: Of those who did not betray their former ruler and held on to their integrity until death/ In all the court there was only Han Tong.[23] I have always been shocked and saddened by the message of this poem. Since the Jianlong regnal era of Taizu [960–963 CE], famous literati of the Song have composed a not inconsiderable number of argumentative essays, yet they have not written one word about this point. It is not the case that they were not capable of discussing it; rather, this is "the meaning of the Ancestral Sacrifice" [that commemorates the founding ancestor of the dynasty].[24] Therefore, we can understand the reason why Ouyang Xiu opted to recognize all the Five Dynasties.

隋季, 文中子作《元經》, 至晉宋已後, 正統在中原。而後大唐南北一統, 後至五代, 天下紛擾, 無由再議。

During the Sui, Wenzhongzi wrote the *Yuanjing* [saying] that after the Chin and Song [Liu-Song, 420–479 CE], political legitimacy was in the Central Plains.[25] After that, the Great Tang united the north and south. Later, during the Five Dynasties, the world was in chaos and there was no way to hold further discussions on these questions.

降及今日, 時移事改, 商確前人隱約之迹, 當從公論。」

Moving on to the present, circumstances have changed, so when we deliberate over the hidden meanings in writings by men of the past, we should strive to be fair and impartial.

或者又曰:「金有中原, 雖百餘年, 宋自建隆于今, 幾三百年. 況乎今年春正月攻陷蔡城, 宋復其雠, 固可以兼金矣。」

Then somebody said: Although the Jin controlled the Central Plains for over a hundred years, since the Jianlong regnal era the Song have been around for nearly three hundred years. Furthermore, the Song exacted vengeance by attacking and capturing Caicheng [Caizhou] in the first month of spring this year, [proving thus] that [the *Official History of the Song*] can encompass the Jin [as a supplementary chronicle].[26]

愚曰:「元魏、齊、梁, 世數已逺, 恐諸公不以爲然.請以五代周漢之事方之。

漢隐帝乾祐三年遇弒, 太后詔立河東節度使旻之子贇, 尋廢爲湘陰公, 旻遂即帝位于晉陽, 終旻之世猶稱乾祐, 旻係劉髙祖母弟, 其子承鈞孫繼恩繼元, 皆相繼立, 凡二十八年, 宋太宗太平興國四年始滅之。

夫東漢四主, 逺兼郭周, 則郭亦不當稱周, 固當爲閏, 宋太祖不當曰受周禪。

傳至太宗, 方承東漢之後, 歐陽不合作《五代史》, 合作《四代史》, 司馬光《通鑑》當列東漢爲世紀, 歐陽不宜作十國世家。

I said: "Since the Northern [Yuan] Wei, Southern Qi, and Liang are long past, I'm afraid you gentlemen will not agree with [my reading of their history].[27] [Hence] allow me to use the Later Zhou and [Northern] Han of the Five Dynasties as an analogy.

Emperor Yin [Yindi] of the Later Han was murdered in the third year of the Qianyou regnal era [951 CE].[28] The Empress Dowager issued an edict and made Liu Yun, son of the Hedong military governor Liu Min, Emperor Yin's successor.[29] [However, Guo Wei] later deposed Liu Yun and demoted him to Duke of Xiangyin.[30] Liu Min then ascended the throne in Jinyang, and continued using the regnal era Qianyou throughout his reign. Min was the younger brother of Emperor Gaozu [of Later Han, Liu Zhiyuan]. His son Chengjun and his grandsons Ji'en and Jiyuan all succeeded to the throne. [The regime of Northern Han] lasted 28 years in total, until Song emperor Taizong eliminated it in the fourth year of the Taiping Xingguo regnal era [979 CE].[31]

Now, since the Eastern [Northern] Han[32] had four rulers and outlasted the Later Zhou of the Guo family, the Guo regime should not be recognized with the dynastic name Later Zhou and should be seen as illegitimate. [In the same vein], Song Taizu should not be regarded as having received the Mandate via abdication from Later Zhou.

Only after Taizong [of the Song] succeeded Taizu did he receive the Mandate from the Eastern (Northern) Han. Ouyang [Xiu] should not have composed the *History of the Five Dynasties*, but rather a *History of the Four Dynasties*.[33] [Similarly], the *Zizhi tongjian* by Sima Guang should have used the Eastern [Northern] Han [not the Later Zhou] as the legitimate dynasty in its Annals.[34] It was also inappropriate for Ouyang to compose the Hereditary Households of the Ten Kingdoms.[35]

嗚呼!國家正閏, 固有定論, 不圖今日輕易褒貶, 在周則爲正, 在金則爲閏, 天下公論果如是乎?

Alas! Surely there is a settled consensus on the legitimacy and illegitimacy of dynasties. Who would have thought that now, some people would casually engage in promotions and demotions, making Later Zhou legitimate and Jin illegitimate? Would an impartial consensus really be like this?

況蔡城之亡, 蓋大朝征伐之力, 宋之邊將專權率意, 自撤藩籬, 快斯須之忿, 昧唇齒之理, 延引強兵深入.遵徽宗之覆轍, 媒孽後禍, 取笑萬世, 何復讎之有?

Furthermore, the destruction of [the Jin] at Caicheng was due to expeditionary armies from the Great (Mongol) State. The Song's border generals abused their power and engaged in unauthorized actions, dismantling their own border defenses in order to assuage their ire momentarily. They were blind to the principle of mutual codependence [between the Jin and Song],[36] with the result that they invited strong (Mongol) troops deep into [Jin] territory. Repeating the mistake of Huizong, they brought disaster upon themselves and will be ridiculed by future generations: what vengeance can we speak of?[37]

宋自靖康已來, 稱臣姪, 走玉帛, 歲時朝貢, 幾于百年。 豈期今日私論, 遽稱尊大, 復如是乎?

Ever since the Jingkang incident, the Song emperors have accepted the status of subjects and nephews [to the Jin emperors], and paid tribute in jade and silk every year at the appropriate time for nearly a hundred years. How could one have expected that today, some people would again be entertaining this partial opinion of honoring the Song as superior and great?[38]

金泰和間, 南宋寒盟, 起無名之師, 侵漁唐, 鄧, 宿, 泗。 章宗分遣應兵, 其淮、 漢、 川、 蜀之間, 大爲所破。 宋遣臣方信孺等卑辭告和, 請叔爲伯, 進增歲幣, 獻臣韓侂冑之首, 至于闕下。

During the Jin regnal era of Taihe [1201–1208 CE], the Southern Song violated the [Song–Jin] treaty, mobilized troops without cause and invaded and raided Tangzhou, Dengzhou, Suzhou, and Sizhou prefectures.[39] [Jin] Emperor Zhangzong dispatched his troops in a counterattack and captured numerous cities in the regions straddling the Huai and Han rivers and Chuan and Shu [Sichuan]. The Song sent their subject Fang Xinru and other officials to seek peace with humble words, accepting a junior status of ritual kinship to the Jin emperor, as well as an increase in the quantity of annual gifts.[40] [In addition,] the Song sent the decapitated head of Han Tuozhou[41] to the Jin imperial palace.[42]

是時中原連年蝗旱, 五穀不登, 山東尤甚。 章廟深用自責. 每以偃兵息民爲念。

At the time, the Central Plains were afflicted with years of locust infestation and drought, with poor harvests of the five cereals of rice, millet, and wheat, especially in Shandong. Emperor Zhangzong underwent deep self-reproach, and often thought of ceasing hostilities to bring relief to the people.

嘗詔百官議曰: 『朕聞海陵有言 : 『我國家雖受四方朝貢, 宋猶假息江左, 亦天下兩家邪?』故有親征之行。

He summoned his officials to discuss this, saying: I remember the Prince of Hailing[43] once said, "Although my state receives tribute from all four quarters of the world, the Song still lives on borrowed time to the south of the Yangtze River—how can the world be divided between two dynasties?" Therefore he personally led an invasion [of Southern Song].[44]

去歲宋人兵起無名, 搖蕩我邊鄙.今已敗衄, 哀懇告和。 朕思海陵之言, 宜如何爾?』

Last year, the Song attacked us illegitimately, disturbing our borders. Today [the Song] are defeated, plaintively pleading for peace. I ponder on the Prince of Hailing's words, wondering what I should do."

時臣下有希意者進曰:『向者靖康間, 宋祚已衰, 其游魂餘魄, 今雖據江左, 正猶昭烈之在蜀, 不能紹漢氏之遺統, 明矣。』

於是宋金和議遂定, 此乃當時繼好息民之大略, 非後世正閏之定論也。 夫昭烈之于漢, 雖云中山靖王之後, 其族屬疏遠, 不能紀錄。 高宗乃徽宗之子, 奄有江南, 似與昭烈頗異。

若以《金史》專依泰和朝議, 爲承宋統, 或從今日所論, 包爲載記, 二者俱非公論也。」

或者又曰:「遼之有國, 僻居燕雲, 法度不一, 似難以元魏北齊爲比。」

At that time an official, discerning [Zhangzong's] intentions, responded, saying: In the past, during the Jingkang era, the Song mandate had already declined. It is [today] no more than a wandering ghost and leftover spirit. Although it remains south of the Yangtze river, it is clear that the Song is like Emperor Zhaolie of Shu who was unable to continue the legacy of the Han dynasty's mandate.[45]

As a result, a new Song–Jin peace treaty was established. This was a grand policy to continue good relations and to give the people rest, not the basis for later generations to determine the legitimacy and illegitimacy [of dynasties]. As for Emperor Zhaolie and his connection to the Han, although it is said that he was a descendant of Prince Jing of Zhongshan, his kinship to [the last Han emperor] was distant, and that is why he could not be included in the basic annals of the Han emperors.[46] Song emperor Gaozong was the son of Huizong and controlled all of Jiangnan, so [his situation] seems quite different from that of Emperor Zhaolie.[47]

If, in [composing the] *Official History of Jin*, one relies solely on the court debates of the Taihe reign [to argue that] the Jin received the Song mandate, or if one follows the argument made today and records [Jin history] as a supplementary chronicle, neither of these would be an impartial approach."

Somebody else said, "The Liao state was located in the remote Yan and Yun prefectures. Its laws and institutions were not uniform, and it seems difficult to consider it as equal with the Northern [Yuan] Wei and Northern Qi [of the Northern Dynasties period]."

愚曰:「以此言之, 膚淺尤甚。若以居中土者爲正, 則劉、石、慕容、符、姚、赫連所得之土皆五帝三王之舊都也。若以有道者爲正, 符秦之量, 雄材英略, 信任不疑, 朱梁行事, 篡奪內亂, 不得其死, 二者方之, 統孰得焉? 夫授受相承之理, 難以此責。

況乎泰和初, 朝廷先有此論, 故選官置院刱修《遼史》。後因南宋獻馘告和, 臣下奏言靖康間, 宋柞已絕, 當承宋統。上乃罷修《遼史》, 緣此中州士大夫間不知遼金之興, 本末各異, 向使《遼史》早成, 天下自有定論, 何待余言?」

坐客愕然曰:「數百年隱顯之由, 何其悉也! 幸請書之, 以備它日史官採摭云爾。」

I said, "To speak thus is extremely shallow.[48] If we consider only those who occupy the Central Plains as legitimate, then [remember that] the land controlled by the Liu, Shi, Murong, Fu, Yao, and Helian families[49] encompassed all the old imperial capitals of the Three Sovereigns and Five Lords.[50] If we consider only those who possess the Way [of rulership] as legitimate, then Fu Jian of the Former Qin [r. 357–385 CE] was magnanimous, brilliant in strategy, and capable of trusting people unreservedly, [whereas] Zhu Wen of Later Liang usurped power [from the Tang] and engaged in incest, fully deserving his ignominious death.[51] If we compare the two, who was superior in terms of legitimacy? It is difficult to dispute the logic of transmission using such standards.

Furthermore, at the beginning of the Taihe regnal era, the court already had such a debate, and therefore selected officials to set up a committee to write the *Liao Official History*.[52] [However], due to the Southern Song's peace entreaties and presenting of [Han Tuozhou's] head, officials reported that during the Jingkang period, the mandate of Song had ended, and that it was more appropriate to inherit the mandate of Song. [Hence] the emperor abandoned the project to compose the *Liao Official History*, and it is based on this that all the literati of the Central Plains do not understand that the Liao and Jin arose differently. Suppose the *Liao Official History* had been completed, the world would have a consensus [on the matter of legitimacy], and there would be no need for me to speak on the matter."

The seated guests were stunned, and said, "How comprehensive is your understanding of both the subtle and the manifest in centuries of history! Please write all this down, so that someday, court historians may use it."[53]

Notes

1. See the primary text by Xiu Duan (修端) in 1992 book by Su Tianjue (蘇天爵); the original *Guochao wenlei* was first published in 1334 CE. An earlier version of Xiu's essay by Wang Yun (王惲) (1227–1304 CE) is found in "Fine Stories from the Jade Hall" and differs from the *Guochao wenlei* version in many places. This translation follows the *Guochao wenlei* version while indicating significant differences in the *Yutang jiahua* version (hereafter YTJH).
2. YTJH: "…a group of five or six friends" (五六友人).
3. Dongyuan was the area corresponding to modern Dongping in southwestern Shandong Province. Sun Hou could be a name or a rank, Marquis Sun. If the latter, then he could be one of several Chinese warlords enfeoffed by the Mongols during their invasion of north China, known historically as "hereditary marquises" (*shihou*, 世侯).
4. YTJH: "…to the south of the Yangtze River and Lake Dongting" (江湖以南).
5. The Liu, Shi, Fu, and Yao families were of Xiongnu, Jie, Di, and Qiang ethnicity, respectively. They respectively founded the states of Han-Zhao (or Former Zhao, 304–329 CE), Later Zhao (319–351 CE), Former Qin (351–394CE), and Later Qin (384–417 CE) in north China following the collapse of Chin dynasty rule in the north. Chin rule continued in south China and is known historically as Eastern Chin. Han-Zhao, Later Zhao, Former Qin, Later Qin, and eleven other regional states in north China and one state in the Sichuan basin are collectively known as the Sixteen Kingdoms or Sixteen States. The histories of these kingdoms are recorded in the supplementary chronicles section of the *Official History of the Chin*, compiled in the early Tang. Many of the kingdoms produced their own official histories, but these have all been lost.
6. The author seems to conflate Abaoji's conquest of Balhae (Bohai) in 926 CE with the Liao's first invasion of Goryeo in 993 CE, which resulted in Goryeo's submission as a Liao vassal and renunciation of vassalage to the Song.
7. The YTJH version erroneously implies that the Shence regnal era began in 907 CE and gives the length of his reign as nineteen years.
8. The YTJH version erroneously claims that Deguang succeeded Abaoji in 926 CE and adopted the new regnal era Tianxian. In fact, Abaoji adopted that regnal era five months before his death in 926, while Deguang only ascended the throne in 927 after a period of regency by Abaoji's empress.
9. Qingtai was the regnal era of the last Later Tang emperor, Li Congke (r. 934–936).
10. Huanglongfu was in the area of modern Siping City, Jilin Province.
11. Xiu Duan made an error here. Under the terms of the Chanyuan Covenant, this was technically a gift to the Liao and not tribute, as the two dynasties agreed to interact as equals. The amount of silk and silver was actually 200,000 bolts of silk and 100,000 taels of silver until 1042 CE. In 1042 this was increased to 300,000 bolts of silk and 200,000 taels of silver.
12. Liu Yuan and Shi Le were the founders of Han-Zhao and Later Zhao dynasties, respectively.
13. Yao Hong was the last ruler of Later Qin. Liu Yu led a military expedition that extinguished Later Qin in 417 CE, but he then usurped the throne from Chin in 420 and founded the Liu–Song dynasty.
14. The Sushen are a Manchurian people mentioned in ancient Chinese sources and were regarded as ancestors of the Jurchens.
15. The warlord Li Cunxu (885–926 CE), who captured Kaifeng and extinguished the Later Liang dynasty in 923. He then declared himself emperor of a restored Tang dynasty, but historians generally regard his Later Tang as a separate dynasty since he was a Shatuo Turk and not a descendant of the Tang emperors.
16. YTJH: "…worse than Youqiong and Xin" (甚於窮、新). Xin (New) was the name of the short-lived regime of Wang Mang (r. 9–23 CE), who usurped the throne from the Han dynasty but was later overthrown and killed by rebels. Youqiong was the clan name of Hou Yi, who is said to have usurped the throne from the third ruler of the legendary Xia dynasty.
17. Liu Yun, the adopted son of Liu Zhiyuan, founding emperor of the Later Han.

18 Jianyan was the first regnal era of the first Southern Song emperor Gaozong (r. 1127–1162 CE). Central Lands (*Zhongguo*) here refers to the North China Plain or Central Plain.

19 YTJH: "…was a famous minister of the Song" (宋之名臣也). Ouyang Xiu (1007–1072 CE) was one of the most accomplished Northern Song men of letters. He wrote *Historical Records of the Five Dynasties* privately during a period of exile, but it was later recognized as one of the official standard histories, effectively supplanting the *History of the Five Dynasties* produced by the Song court in 974 CE. The text was therefore commonly known as the *New History of the Five Dynasties* (see Ouyang 2004).

20 A category from the *Shiji* (史记) for chapters recording the history of ruling families that were not considered to have held the Mandate of Heaven. Xiu Ouyang used this convention for recording the history of nine regional states in tenth-century south China, as well as the Northern Han (see note 21).

21 This is a direct quote from Xiu's *New History of the Five Dynasties*. Northern Han was a regional regime in Shanxi founded by a member of the Later Han nobility after Later Han was usurped by Later Zhou in 951 CE.

22 Li Pingshan was Li Chunfu (1185–1231 CE), a prominent Jin man of letters.

23 Han Tong was the only Later Zhou general who opposed the 960 CE military coup in which general Zhao Kuangyin seized power and founded the Song dynasty. He and his entire clan were executed by Zhao's supporters.

24 The Ancestral Sacrifice (*di*) was offered triennially to the founding ancestor of the ruling dynasty. The author alludes here to *Analects* 3.11, where Confucius is asked about the meaning of this sacrifice and claims that he does not know. The author's insinuation is that Song literati avoided all praise of Han Tong's loyalism out of reverence for the dynastic founder.

25 Wenzhongzi was the Sui Confucian scholar Wang Tong (584–617 CE), who authored six texts modeled on the Confucian classics, including the *Yuanjing* (Primal Classic), which was modeled on the *Chunqiu* annals. All six are now lost. Wang was known for arguing that the Mandate of Heaven passed from the south to the north in 479 CE, on the usurpation of Liu-Song by Southern Qi (479–502 CE). He had personal reasons for this position (which was presumably reflected in the *Yuanjing*), as he was descended from a Liu-Song minister who had defected to the Northern Wei soon after the founding of the Southern Qi. However, his oral statements (collected in a text known as the *Zhongshuo*) show that he also justified it by arguing that the "Sinicizing" reforms introduced under Northern Wei emperor Xiaowen (r. 471–499 CE) had revived Chinese civilization in the north.

26 Caizhou was the last Jin capital and fell to a combined Mongol and Southern Song attack in 1234 CE. The speaker means that the Song proved its legitimacy by extinguishing the Jin despite having lost the Central Plains to the Jin.

27 Northern Wei was also known as Yuan-Wei because its Xianbei (Serbi) ruling clan changed its name from Tuoba (Tagbach) to Yuan in 494 CE. Liang was the southern dynasty that replaced Southern Qi in 502 CE; it was in turn replaced by Chen in 557 CE. The author implies here that he agrees with Wenzhongzi (Wang Tong) in recognizing Northern Wei, not Southern Qi and Liang, as legitimate.

28 Emperor Yin, named Liu Chengyou, was killed in a coup led by the general Guo Wei.

29 Liu Min was the younger brother of Liu Zhiyuan, founder of Later Han and father of Emperor Yin. His son Liu Yun was adopted by Liu Zhiyuan and was therefore Emperor Yin's brother by adoption.

30 This was a prelude to Guo Wei's founding of his own dynasty, the Later Zhou, in 951 CE.

31 YTJH: "[Northern Han] had four emperors and lasted twenty-nine years before being conquered by Song in the fourth year of the Xingguo regnal era of Song emperor Taizu" (四帝二十九年，至宋太祖興國四年歸宋). This is erroneous, as Taiping Xingguo was a regnal era of Taizu's successor Taizong and Northern Han lasted twenty-eight years (951–979 CE), not twenty-nine. *Taizu* may be a mistranscription of *Taiping*; if so, then 宋太祖興國四年 originally read 宋太平興國四年.

32 The author, following Xiu's *New History of the Five Dynasties*, terms Northern Han as "Eastern Han" because its founder had been military governor of Hedong (meaning "east of the Yellow River"). Hedong is today known as Shanxi (meaning "west of the Taihang Mountains") and it was in fact to the west of the Later Zhou capital Kaifeng.

33 That is, Later Liang, Later Tang, Later Jin, and Later Han.

34 The *Zizhi tongjian* (completed in 1084 CE) is a political history of the Chinese world from the Warring States to the end of the Five Dynasties and the founding of the Song. It is organized chronologically into Annals (*ji*) chapters, each named after the dynasty that Sima Guang considered to be legitimate during the corresponding period.

35 Because the Northern Han should have been considered a legitimate continuation of the Later Han, not one of the illegitimate Ten Kingdoms.

36 YJTH adds the line "and claimed to love their own kind and detest all others" (自謂愛己而惡佗).

37 The author likens the Song's alliance with the Mongols against the Jin to Song emperor Huizong's alliance with the Jin against the Liao, which led to the Jingkang disaster and the Jin conquest of the Central Plains. As a former Jin official, he evidently feels it would have been wiser for the Jin and Song to join hands to fend off the Mongol threat.

38 YTJH has, instead of 復如是乎, the line "If the spirits of the Song imperial ancestors were aware of this, even they would agree with me" (果使宋廟有靈，必可其議也).

39 In Song studies it is now conventional to include "*zhou*" (prefecture) in the transcription of prefecture names.

40 This was later referred to as the Taihe or Jiading Treaty of 1208 CE. Note that these were not officially classed as tribute, as the Song-Jin treaty of 1162 CE had allowed the Southern Song to change from the language of tribute to that of annual gifts and ritual kinship, similar to Song-Liao relations after 1005 CE.

41 Han Tuozhou was the chief minister who initiated the failed Song attack on Jin in 1206 CE. His political rivals assassinated him and used his severed head as a peace offering to the Jin. YTJH has "sent the decapitated heads of powerful officials" (獻權臣之首) and elaborates in a note: "These were Han Tuozhou and Hou Shidan. Their portraits were painted and their decapitated heads lacquered, and the portraits and heads put into boxes and sent to Youdu (the Jin capital, modern Beijing) (韓侂冑、侯師旦也。繪其容，漆其首，函送幽都). The name Hou Shidan is an error for Su Shidan (蘇師旦), Han Tuozhou's political ally and advisor, whose head was indeed sent to the Jin along with Han Tuozhou's. The portraits were presumably meant to aid the Jin court (who had never seen Han and Su) in identifying which head was whose.

42 YTJH follows this line by quoting a poem attributed to Fang Xinru:

> Xinru composed an ancient-style poem, which I can still roughly remember:
> Your Great Dynasty's ruler and chief minister are humane and compassionate;
> Even before the wheat had ripened, they stopped their army's attack.
> How could slaying one nefarious minister be enough to redeem the people's lives?
> Let bygones be bygones; we shall make up for our past offenses in the future.

This poem was written on the wall of the Shangyuan courier station [en route to Kaifeng], and when the [Jin] protocol officers arrived at [the Jin] court, they submitted a memorial quoting it. The emperor (Zhangzong) was greatly moved to sorrow and pity.

> 信孺有古調一篇，予能草畧記之：
> 『大朝君相仁且慈，小麥未熟休王師。姦臣豈足贖民命，既往不咎來可追。』
> 此詩書於上源驛壁間，館伴使入朝題奏，上頗哀憐。

43 The Prince of Hailing is Digunai, or Wanyan Liang (1122–1161 CE), who was Jin emperor from 1150 to 1161 CE, but was posthumously demoted to the status of a prince after his assassination.

44 This invasion failed disastrously and led to the discredited Wanyan Liang's assassination by members of the imperial guard.

45 Emperor Zhaolie was the posthumous title of the warlord Liu Bei (161–223 CE), who declared

himself emperor in Sichuan in 221 CE, claiming to be a member of the Han imperial clan and thus a legitimate successor to the Han Emperor Xian (Xiandi, r. 189–220 CE). Emperor Xian had been deposed five months earlier by Cao Pi (187–226 CE), who founded the Cao-Wei dynasty (220–266 CE). Liu Bei's regime was officially named Han, but is historically called Shu-Han or Shu, *Shu* being a traditional name for the Sichuan basin. Liu Bei's son Liu Shan succeeded him and ruled for forty years before surrendering to the Cao-Wei in 263 CE.

46 YTJH: "that is why his life and titles could not be included in the basic annals of the Han emperors" (不能紀録世數名位).

47 YTJH: "Gaozong of Southern Song was Huizong's son and Qinzong's younger brother, he lost no time in ascending the throne [after the capture of Huizong and Qinzong by the Jin], and he controlled all of Jiangnan, so [his situation] seems quite different from that of Emperor Zhaolie" (南宋高宗乃徽宗之子, 欽宗之弟, 歲月不易以即位, 奄有江南, 似與昭烈頗異).

48 YTJH: "I bowed twice (to show respect) and said, 'To dispute thus is extremely shallow.'" (僕再拜而言曰：「以此責之, 膚淺尤甚。…).

49 These were ruling families of the Sixteen Kingdoms. On the Liu, Shi, Fu, and Yao (see note. 5). The Murong were ethnically Xianbei (Serbi) rulers of four states called Yan: Former Yan (337–370 CE), Later Yan (384–409 CE), Western Yan (384–394 CE), and Southern Yan (398–410 CE). The Helian were ethnically Xiongnu rulers of the Xia state (407–431 CE).

50 The mythical sage-kings of antiquity.

51 According to historical records, Zhu Wen forced his daughters-in-law to have sexual relations with him. He was eventually assassinated by one of his sons in 912 CE.

52 YTJH adds: "Zhang Ji, the top candidate in the civil service examinations of 1194, was appointed to lead the project" (刑期榜狀元張槻預焉). *Xing qi bang* (刑期榜) was a reference to the 1194 examinations, in which the set topic for the palace examinations in literary composition was a quote from the *Shangshu* (尚書), "using punishments to eliminate the need for punishments" (*xing qi yu wu xing* [刑期于無刑]).

53 YTJH has a longer conclusion:

> The seated guests were stunned, and said, "How comprehensive is your understanding of both the subtle and the manifest in centuries of history! We asked one question and obtained the answers to three. This is truly more than we hoped for. We are fortunate to have heard you speak on this." I therefore took up brush and paper and wrote down my ignorant blather, in the hope that some inquisitive person will edit it and that someday, court historians may use it. Xiu Duan of Yanshan humbly wrote this.
>
> 坐客愕然曰：「數百年隱顯之由, 何其悉也! 問一得三, 寔出望外, 幸謂言之。」僕因就毫楮録狂斐, 以俟意事者刪之, 庶備他日史官之採摭云爾。燕山脩端謹記。
>
> This passage supplies the only extant biographical information on Xiu Duan, identifying his place of origin as Yanshan, the area corresponding to modern Beijing. This was the location of the Jin capital, Zhongdu, from 1153 to 1214 CE. However, the text begins with Xiu as one in a group of friends from southwestern Shandong. He may have taken refuge in Shandong during the prolonged twenty-year period of warfare and instability between the Jin court's flight from Zhongdu to Kaifeng in 1214 CE and the fall of the last Jin capital at Caizhou in 1234 CE. During this time, Shandong was divided between various warlords, some of whom were aligned with the Mongols and others with the Southern Song.

References

Primary Sources from Early China

Su, Tianjue (蘇天爵 [1294–1352]). 1922. *Guochao Wenlei* 國朝文類 [Categorized anthology of literature from our (Yuan) dynasty]. Shanghai: Shanghai Commercial Press.

Wang, Yun (王惲 [1227–1304]). 1922. *Yutang Jiahua* 玉堂嘉話, *juan* (卷)100 [Fine Stories from the Jade Hall, 100 chapters]. In: *Qiujian Xiansheng Daquanji* 秋澗先生大全集 [Collected works of Master Qiujian]. Shanghai: Shanghai Commercial Press. pp. 1a–5b.

Xiu, Duan (修端). 1922. Bian Liao Song Jin Zhengtong 辯遼宋金正統 [Debating the legitimate succession of the Liao, Song, and Jin]. In: Tianjue Su (蘇天爵 [1294–1352]). *Guochao Wenlei* 國朝文類 [Categorized anthology of literature from our (Yuan) dynasty]. Shanghai: Shanghai Commercial Press. pp. 1974–1984.

Secondary Sources

Chan, Hok-Lam. 1981. Chinese official historiography at the Yuan court: The composition of the Liao, Chin, and Sung histories. In: John D. Langlois, Jr., ed. *China Under Mongol Rule*. Princeton, NJ: Princeton University Press. pp. 56–106.

—1984. *Legitimation in Imperial China: Discussions under the Jurchen-Chin Dynasty (1115–1234)*. Seattle: University of Washington Press. 267 pp. (Publications on Asia of the Henry M. Jackson School of International Studies, University of Washington 38.)

Crossley, Pamela Kyle. 1999. *A Translucent Mirror: History and Identity in Qing Imperial Ideology*. Berkeley: University of California Press. 403 pp.

Davis, Richard L. 1983. Historiography as politics in Yang Wei-Chen's "Polemic On Legitimate Succession." *T'oung Pao* 69(1):33–72. https://doi.org/10.1163/156853283X00045

Ebrey, Patricia Buckley. 2014. *Emperor Huizong*. Cambridge, MA: Harvard University Press. 661 pp.

Elliott, Mark. 2001. *The Manchu Way: The Eight Banners and Ethnic Identity in Late Imperial China*. Stanford: Stanford University Press. 580 pp.

Franke, Herbert. 1994. The Chin dynasty. In: Denis C. Twitchett and Herbert Franke, eds. *The Cambridge History of China*. Volume 6, Alien Regimes and Border States, 907–1368. Cambridge: Cambridge University Press. pp. 215–320. https://doi.org/10.1017/CHOL9780521243315.005

Foster, Robert. 2019. The Southern Song dynasty. In: Victor Cunrui Xiong and Kenneth J. Hammond, eds. *Routledge Handbook of Imperial Chinese History*. London: Routledge. pp. 197–212.

Furumatsu, Takashi. 2003. Xiu Duan's essay "Distinguishing the Legitimate Succession of the Compilation on Liao, Song and Jin Dynasties," Jin and Song histories under the Yuan dynasty. *Journal of Oriental Studies* 75:123–200. [in Japanese.] https://doi.org/10.14989/66867

Gladney, Dru C. 1998. *Ethnic Identity in China: The Making of a Muslim Minority Nationality*. Orlando, FL: Harcourt Brace. 195 pp.

Hansen, Valerie. 2019. The Kitan-Liao and Jurchen-Jin. In: Victor Cunrui Xiong and Kenneth J. Hammond, eds. *Routledge Handbook of Imperial Chinese History*. London: Routledge. pp. 213–228.

Hu, Yongguang. 2019. The Northern Song. In: Victor Cunrui Xiong and Kenneth J. Hammond, eds. *Routledge Handbook of Imperial Chinese History*. London: Routledge. pp. 182–196.

Liu, Pujiang. 2004. Debates over the Five Phases Cycle and the question of the legitimacy of the Liao and Jin dynasties. *Social Sciences in China* 2:189–203. [in Chinese.]

Lorge, Peter. 2019. The Five Dynasties and Ten Kingdoms. In: Victor Cunrui Xiong and Kenneth J. Hammond, eds. *Routledge Handbook of Imperial Chinese History*. London: Routledge. pp. 157–172.

Mullaney, Thomas S., James Leibold, Stéphane Gros, and Eric Vanden Bussche, eds. 2012. *Critical Han Studies: The History, Representation, and Identity of China's Majority*. Berkeley: University of California Press. 410 pp.

Ouyang, Xiu. 2004. *Historical Records of the Five Dynasties*. Translated by Richard L. Davis. New York: Columbia University Press. 669 pp.

Perdue, Peter. 2009. *China Marches West: The Qing Conquest of Central Eurasia.* Cambridge, MA: Harvard University Press. 725 pp.

Standen, Naomi. 2007. *Unbounded Loyalty: Frontier Crossings in Liao China.* Honolulu: University of Hawaii Press. 279 pp.

Thum, Rian. 2014. China in Islam: Turki views from the nineteenth and twentieth centuries. *Cross-Currents: East Asian History and Culture Review* 12:118–142.

Wang, Gungwu. 2012. Thoughts on four subversive words. *The Asia Pacific Journal of Anthropology* 13(2):199–210.

Xue, Chen. 2022. From the "Five Dynasties" 五代 to the "Ten States" 十國: Interpreting post-Tang identities in Northern Song (960–1127) historiography. *T'oung Pao* 108(5–6):646–695. https://doi.org/10.1163/15685322-10805003

Yang, Shao-yun. 2019. *The Way of the Barbarians: Redrawing Ethnic Boundaries in Tang and Song China.* Seattle: University of Washington Press. 229 pp.

—2023. The Song–Jurchen conflict in Chinese intellectual history. In: Yannis Stouraitis, ed. *War and Collective Identities in the Middle Ages: East, West, and Beyond.* Leeds: Arc Humanities Press. pp. 169–190. (War and Conflict in Premodern Societies.)

Zhao, Lingyang. 1976. *Regarding the Legitimacy Debates of Past Dynasties.* Hong Kong: Xuejin Publishing House. 172 pp. [in Chinese.]

CHAPTER ELEVEN

浮梁磁局大使和督陶官
"Commissioner of the Fuliang Porcelain Bureau" and "Officials that Oversee Porcelain Production" [during the Yuan Dynasty of China]

ZENG Lingyi (曾令怡)
Translated and annotated by SHEN Dewei

In the fifteenth year of the Zhiyuan (至元) era (1278 CE) [under the reign of Kublai Khan (r. 1264–1294 CE)], the Yuan government established the *Fuliang ciju* (浮梁磁局, Fuliang Porcelain Bureau) to manage various aspects of porcelain production. However, very little information about this crucial bureau has survived due to the loss of detailed records over time. Why did the Yuan government create this bureau, specifically in Fuliang? Were there similar institutions in other parts of the Yuan territory? How did the bureau function, and what issues did it regulate? Did the bureau oversee any state-sponsored porcelain factories, and what was its relationship with the official kilns (官窑) of the Yuan? These questions require further examination. This article aims to reinvestigate the section of the Yuan bureaucracy responsible for regulating porcelain production, with a particular focus on its institutional change over time. By closely analyzing Yuan historical documents, I argue that this institutional change reflects the shifting attitudes of the Yuan ruling class towards porcelain production, the reasons for which I will discuss below.

The Administrative Status of Fuliang

As documented in the *Yuan shi* (元史, *Yuan History*), Fuliang (浮梁, in modern northeastern Jiangxi) was raised in administrative status from being a county to a prefecture in the early Yuan (*Yuan shi* 62.1501). It is known that during his southward conquest of China, Kublai Khan applied differentiated policies to gradually integrate different regions into the Great Yuan territory:

Translator's note: The translations of the Yuan dynasty official titles and bureaucracy follow Farquhar (1990), thanks to the recommendation of the reference by Professor Ruth Dunnell. All endnotes in the original article have been converted to conform to the format of this volume. Section information is given for specific passages in the *Yuan shi* (元史, *Yuan History*) and *Da Yuan shengzheng guochao dianzhang* (大元圣政国朝典章, *Statutes and Precedents of the Sacred Administration of the Great Yuan Dynastic State*). Annotations are in brackets. This translation provides a modified version of the original Figure 1 in Zeng (2012).]

Originally published as "Fuliang Ceramics Bureau Officer and Governor (浮梁磁局大使和督陶官)" in the *Journal of the National Museum of China*, 2012. Coutesy of the National Museum of China Editorial Department.

> In the fifth year of the Zhongtong (中统) era (1264), [the two systems of] counties and prefectures existed side-by-side with no differences [in administrative status between them] delineated…. (*Yuan shi* 91.2317)

However,

> in the twentieth year [of the Zhiyuan era] (1283), it was further decided that in the south of the Huai River, that which owned 30,000 households or above belonged to the category of *shangxian* (上县, upper county), that which owned 10,000 households or above *zhongxian* (中县, middle county), and that which owned less than 10,000 households *xiaxian* (下县, lower county). [The magistrate of] an upper county was ranked Class 6B;… [that of] a middle county was ranked Class 6A;… [that of] a lower county was ranked Class 7B. (*Yuan shi* 91.2318)

In other words, before the year 1283, Fuliang as a county was still under the administrative regime typically adopted by the former Tang and Song governments. Yet after 1283, counties were classified into "upper," "middle," and "lower" categories by the Yuan government. Although, constrained by limited sources, we do not know exactly which category Fuliang falls in, it is reasonable to infer that the rank of Fuliang should not have surpassed Class 6B regarding its administrative status.

In the first year of the Yuanzhen era (1295), Fuliang County became *Zhongzhou* (中州, Zhong Prefecture). Correspondingly, the number of households under its jurisdiction increased from 50,000 to 100,000 (*Yuan shi* 62.1501, 18.393). It is documented that *daluhuachi* (达鲁花赤, Daruhachi Overseer) and *zhizhou* (知州, Prefect of Zhongzhou) were ranked Class 5A, whereas *tongzhi* (同知, Associate Prefect) was ranked Class 6B and *panguan* (判官, Administrative Assistant) Class 7B (*Yuan shi* 91.2317). Obviously, after the promotion of its administrative status as a prefecture, the rank of the chief administrator of Fuliang was raised significantly by three steps from Class 6B to Class 5A.

Regardless of the status change, Fuliang was subordinate to the governance of *Raozhou lu* (饶州路, Raozhou Circuit) both before and after 1295 (*Yuan shi* 91.1500; Figure 11.1). According to "Dili zhi" (地理志, "Treatise on Geography") in the *Yuan History*, Rouzhou Circuit, regarded as *shanglu* (上路, upper circuit), was promoted as *Raozhou zongguanfu* (饶州路总管府, Directorate-General for Raozhou Circuit) in the fourteenth year of the Zhiyuan era (1277), leading *lushi si* (录事司, Administration Office), the three counties of Poyang (鄱阳), Dexing (德兴), and Anren (安仁), and the three prefectures of Yugan (余干), Fuliang, and Leping (乐平) (*Yuan shi* 62.1500). "Baiguan zhi" (百官志, "Treatise on Officialdom") in the *Yuan History* points out that the highest office of Raozhou Circuit, *Daruhachi* Overseer and Director-General, belonged to Class 3A in rank (*Yuan shi* 91.2316). Equally noteworthy is the superior administrative unit that oversaw the Raozhou Circuit, which also changed in history. Although Raozhou was put under Jiangxi Province (江西行省) since Ming and Qing, it was subordinate to Jiangzhe Province (江浙行省) during the Yuan (*Yuan shi* 91.2304).

To sum up, for the period under question, Fuliang was subordinate to the Raozhou Circuit in Jiangzhe Province; it was a county before its promotion to Zhong Prefecture. Fuliang's status as a Yuan administrative unit began no later than 1277 (*Yuan shi* 62.1500) and ended in 1361 at the latest, when generals of Zhu Yuanzhang (朱元璋) (the would-be Ming emperor, reigning from 1368 to 1398 CE) conquered the Raozhou Circuit (*Yuan shi* 42–46.896, 909, 928, 957).

浮梁磁局大使和督陶官 "Commissioner of the Fuliang Porcelain Bureau"   209

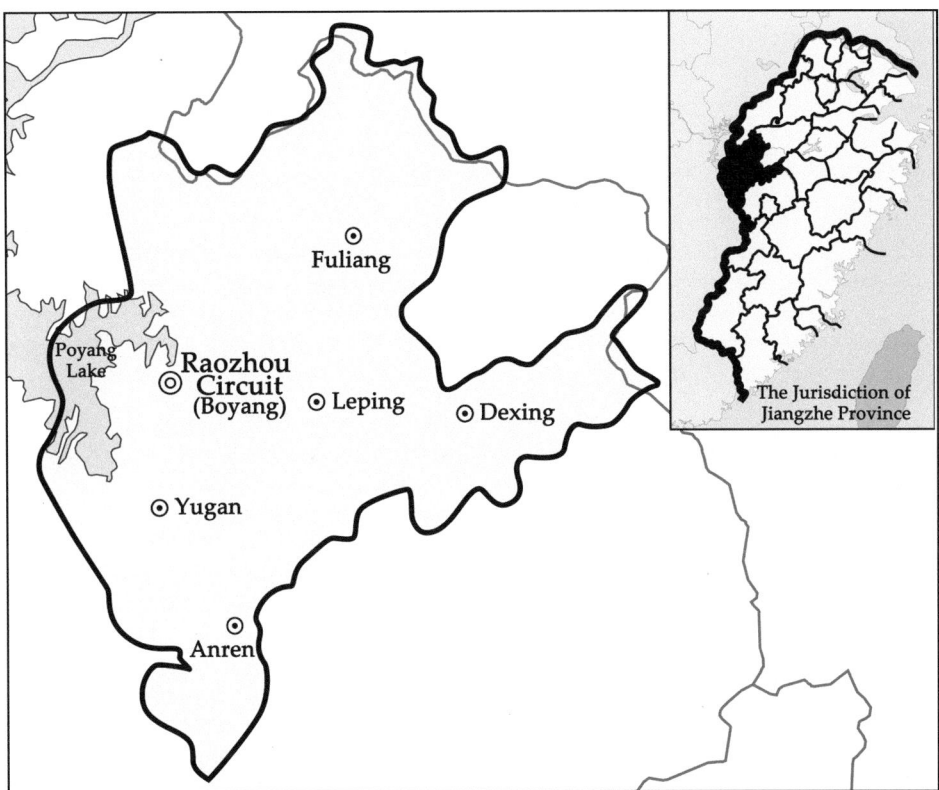

FIGURE 11.1. The jurisdiction of Jiangzhe Province, Raozhou Circuit, and Fuliang in the first year of the Zhishu era (1330 CE) of the Yuan dynasty (Tan 1982:27–28).

Institutions Related to the Fuliang Porcelain Bureau

Overall, the official system of the Yuan dynasty was complex and cannot be easily summarized. That said, in the section entitled "Libu" (吏部, "Ministry of Personnel") in the *Da Yuan shengzheng guochao dianzhang* (大元圣政国朝典章, *Statutes and Precedents of the Sacred Administration of the Great Yuan Dynastic State*; hereafter YSP), it is evident that in principle Yuan offices are divided into the *neiren* (内任, internal offices) and *wairen* (外任, external offices) halves. "External offices" is further subdivided into categories that include *minzhi* (民职, civil offices), *junmin zhi* (军民职, military-civil offices), *zhuzhi* (诸职, various offices), *junzhi* (军职, military offices), and *jiangzhi* (匠职, artisan offices). The way the Yuan offices are classified in the "Treatise on Officialdom" in the *Yuan History*—which groups offices in accordance with three rules: by categories, by ranks, and by subordinate relationships—is not all the same with that seen from the YSP. Indeed, in both sources, Yuan offices are introduced in the order of six ministries and respective commissions, courts, superintendencies, and directorates, as well as ranks from high to low. Comparatively, the text of "Treatise on Officialdom" seems to lend more primacy to an overall description of the duties assumed by an office and its relationship to other offices under its administration. The treatise thus presents offices as small units with relatively clear institutional boundaries. This characteristic is crucial for us to elucidate the bureaucratic relations that defined Fuliang Porcelain Bureau (FLPB) below.

In the *Yuan History*, information about FLPB is recorded under the entry of "*Jiangzuoyuan*" (将作院, Imperial Manufactories Commission):

> Imperial Manufactories Commission: It was ranked Class 2A, and responsible not only for manufacturing headgears, decorative accessories, implements, and vessels made from gold, jade, pearls, kingfisher feathers, rhinoceroses' horns, elephant tusks, jewels, and cowries; but also for making embroidered satin bolts and gauzes: all things of different patterns and various kinds as such. In the thirtieth year of the Zhiyuan era (1293), the office of *yuanshi* (院使, Director) was inaugurated and presided by one person, and the offices of *jingli* (经历, Registrar) and *dushi* (都事, Office Manager) with one person to fill in each. In the thirty-first year (1294), the personnel for the office of Director were increased to two persons. In the first year of the Yuanzhen (元贞) era (1295), two more persons were added to the Director's office. In the seventh year of the Yanyou (延祐) era (1320), [however,] two persons were cut back from the Director's office....
>
> Directorate-General for Precious Metal and Jewel Artisan in Various Circuits (诸路金玉人匠总管府): It was ranked Class 3A, and responsible for manufacturing crowns and hats decorated with jewels, cowries, gold, and jade, as well as waist belts, and golden and silver implements and vessels. It oversaw affairs from [related] various supervisorates and bureaus. In the second year of the Zhongtong era (1261), Bureau of Gold and Jade (金玉局) was initially established, ranked Class 5A. In the third year of the Zhiyuan era (1266), this bureau was rearranged into Directorate-General, presided by one person as Director-General, and two persons as Registrar and Record Keeper respectively....
>
> Fuliang Porcelain Bureau: It was ranked Class 9A. Installed in the fifteenth year of the Zhiyuan era (1278), it was responsible for firing and making porcelain, as well as making hats from lacquered horse tails, palm leaves, rattan, and bamboo, with offices of one Commissioner and one Assistant Commissioner.

Although the above passage is brief, we can know that from the day of its foundation, FLPB was ultimately administered by Jiangzuoyuan, even though it belonged to Directorate-General for Precious Metal and Jewel Artisan in Various Circuits. Some scholars infer that since Jiangzuoyuan was created as late as 1293 CE, FLPB (created in 1278) was likely to have been free from Jiangzuoyuan's supervision for fifteen years. They hence further argue that before 1293, the administrative body that governed FLPB should have been the Ministry of Works or certain Executive Branch of Ministry of Works (Li 1994; Jiang and Jiang 2008). However, this line of argument was refuted by a few Taiwanese scholars ten years ago, who pointed out that the crux of the problem rests on the misunderstanding of the founding year of Jiangzuoyuan. This misunderstanding was derived from the erroneous punctuation of the sentence "至元三十年始置院使一员" (from the above-cited passage; Shih 2003). There were records dated as early as 1278 about this institution, documenting that Araniko (or Anige [阿尼哥] in Chinese; 1244–1306 CE) "concurrently supervised Jiangzuoyuan" (*Yuan shi* 10.198). Another entry from the *Yuan History* reveals that in 1280, "[the Yuan emperor] awarded the artisan from Jiangzuoyuan, Lü Hela (吕合剌), silver, paper cash, and silk bolts" (*Yuan shi* 11.227). It is apparent that Jiangzuoyuan had existed no later than the year 1278, although such an institution may have been inchoate at the time and thereby in need of concurrent supervision by Araniko, whose major position was Grand Minister of Education (大司徒). It was not until 1293 that Jiangzuoyuan *shizhi* (始置, "inaugurated") the offices of Director, Registrar, and Office Manager. Its composition of personnel seems to have been stabilized only after the era of Yanyou (1314–1320 CE).

As for the end date of Jiangzuoyuan, its latest documentation in the *Yuan History* is seen in the biography of Zhang Yong (张庸, fl. 1559 CE) in "Memoir 83." The memoir mentions that when the heir apparent of Emperor Shun of Yuan (r. 1333–1368 CE) was planning to establish the Bureau of the Master of Cavalry (大抚军院), he "commanded that Zhang Yong lead the militia in Fangshan (房山) and promoted him to the position of Deputy Junior Assistant Director of Jiangzuoyuan (同佥将作院事)" (*Yuan shi* 196.4435). Since Emperor Shun instated his heir apparent in 1367 (the twenty-seventh year of Zhizheng [至正]) (*Yuan shi* 47.980), we can infer that Jiangzuoyuan was still at work around the time. In conclusion, a minimalist estimate is that Jiangzuoyuan operated from 1278 to no earlier than 1367. FLPB was overseen by Jiangzuoyuan from the very first day of its foundation.

The Rank of the Commissioner of Fuliang Porcelain Bureau

The rank of the Commissioner of FLPB has caused much controversy. The *Yuan History* only records that "Fuliang Porcelain Bureau was ranked Class 9A," with "offices of one Commissioner and one Assistant Commissioner." According to the convention of recording the rank of official titles in the *Yuan History*, "Class 9A" in this context ought to refer to the rank of the top office of the bureau, that is, the Commissioner of FLPB. Using common sense, since the text distinguishes "Commissioner" from "Assistant Commissioner," the rank of the two official positions must be different from each other in level. Accordingly, the rank of the Assistant Commissioner of FLPB should be lower than Class 9A. This, however, contradicts one record in the YSP, which documents that the Assistant Commissioner of FLPB was ranked Class 9A (YSP 7.225). Even if both the Commissioner and Assistant Commissioner of FLPB belonged to Class 9A, it still contradicts another historical record in the YSP under the entry of "Ranks of the Offices in the Artisan Bureaus" (in the "Bureaus and Commissioner" part of the "Ministry of Personnel" section): "(In the twenty-fourth year of Zhiyuan [1287]) The rank of artisans in Jiangnan was determined by the number of artisan households that entered such a bureau for work…. Commissioner and Assistant Commissioner of an artisan bureau: if the number of artisan households exceeds 1,000, the Commissioner is to be ranked Class 7A, whereas the Assistant Commissioner Class 8B; if the number exceeds 500, the Commissioner is to be ranked Class 7B, whereas the Assistant Commissioner Class 9A." If these records in the YSP are trustworthy, then the Assistant Commissioner of FLPB should be ranked Class 9A. Although the YSP does not specify the rank of the Commissioner of FLPB, according to the above-cited entry of "Ranks of the Officials in the Artisan Bureaus," the rank of the Commissioner of FLPB was Class 7B. Following this logic, we can infer that the number of artisan households working for FLPB was between 500 and 1,000.

The YSP was written in the seventh year of the Yanyou era (1320). It records various statutes and institutions formulated and promulgated between 1260 and 1320 under the reign of Kublai Khan. The records are recognized as largely reliable. In comparison, the compilation of the *Yuan History* was started as late as the early Hongwu (洪武) period (1368–1399 CE) of the Ming dynasty and finished hastily. It mainly referenced the Yuan official records, including the YSP, to complete the part regarding the Yuan official positions. It was very likely that its compilers simply cited from the YSP the record of the Assistant Commissioner of FLPB being ranked Class 9A, without further examining the rank of the Commissioner. As for why there is no record of the rank of Commissioner of FLPB in the YSP, it is probably because a section is made in the YSP that specifies the ranks of the artisan bureaus, which is taken as a convention for determining the ranks of Jiangnan artisan groups overall. It would thus be redundant to further list the ranks of the Commissioner and Assistant Commissioner of those bureaus.

Scholars have also proposed another possibility, that "if there were no omissions in these texts, we can infer that before 1320, Fuliang Porcelain Bureau had only an Assistant Commissioner ranked Class 9A but no Commissioner" (Wang 2000:13). However, I argue that this theory is not plausible. Because according to this theory, the Yuan government could have simply appointed a Commissioner ranked Class 9A for FLCB without bothering to even appoint an Assistant Commissioner in the first place. Not a few Yuan bureaus and commissions had only one Commissioner. For instance, the Jade Bureau (瑾玉局), Picture Bureau (画局), Bindery Bureau (装订局), Large and Small Woodcarving Bureau (雕木局), and Rhinoceros-horn and Tortoise-shell Bureau (温犀玳瑁局), all of which, just like FLPB, were all under the jurisdiction of Directorate-General for Precious Metal and Jewel Artisan in Various Circuits (*Yuan shi* 88.2225). In short, it was very unusual for these bureaus to have only Assistant Commissioner but no Commissioner.

On the other hand, by comparing the settings of offices in various Yuan institutions, we can observe an obvious correlation patterned between the number and the rank of these offices, and both were determined by the importance of these institutions to the Yuan ruling class. For instance, all those aforementioned bureaus that had only one Commissioner were ranked relatively low, equal to Class 8B. On the contrary, institutions such as Superintendency of the Jade Bureau (玉局提举司) and Gold and Silver Utensils Superintendency (金银器盒提举司), which were responsible for manufacturing objects from gold and precious jade as favored by the Yuan ruling elites, had significantly more offices and the highest rank of these offices was equal to Class 5B (*Yuan shi* 88.2225). By the same token, the top office of FLPB, which had one Commissioner and one Assistant Commissioner, should have enjoyed a rank higher than bureaus that installed just one Commissioner—that is, higher than Class 8B. It is, therefore, consistent with this inference that the Commissioner of FLPB was of Class 7B and Assistant Commissioner was of Class 9A. Although the rank of FLPB was not as high as those institutions that made artifacts from gold and precious jade, it was not as low as previously assessed, either. The two tables (Tables 11.1 and 11.2) demonstrate the relationship between FLPB and related offices, and their respective ranks.

Status Changes of the Yuan Officials Who Managed Porcelain Production

Although the Yuan government established FLPB in the Raozhou Circuit in 1278, the managerial operations over porcelain production was not limited to this institution. The official titles of those in charge of this task underwent changes from "Commissioner" and "Assistant Commissioner" of FLCB in the Zhiyuan era to supervisory officials of porcelain production *dutao guan* (督陶官) who were higher-ranking and dispatched by the metropolitan government in the middle and late period of Yuan.

浮梁磁局大使和督陶官 "Commissioner of the Fuliang Porcelain Bureau"

Table 11.1. Offices of the Fuliang Prefecture (or County) and their ranks.

Civil Office	Top Official of the Office	Rank
Jiangzhe Province	Chief Councillor and Privy Councillor	Class 1B *
Raozhou Circuit	Director-General	Class 3B
Fuliang Prefecture (Fuliang County)	Prefect (District Magistrate)	Class 5A (Class 6B)

* *Yuan shi* 91.2316

Table 11.2. Offices of Fuliang Porcelain Bureau and their ranks.

Artisan Office	Top Official of the Office	Rank
Jiangzuoyuan	Director	Class 2A
Directorate-General for Precious Metal and Jewel Artisan in Various Circuits	Director-General	Class 3A
Fuliang Porcelain Bureau	Commissioner	Class 7B

The historical records related to these *dutao guan* include:

1. In the older preface composed by Tu Jiheng (涂济亨) (in 1325) appended to the 1682 version of the *Fuliang County Gazetteer* (浮梁县志), compiled in the twenty-first year of the Kangxi (康熙) reign of the Qing dynasty, it records: "In the third month since I had arrived to administer this prefecture, the commandery governor, Mr. Duan from the Qingquan (清泉) County, was ordered to oversee porcelain-making in this prefecture" (Chengwen Publishing Company 1989:113). This "Mr. Duan" may refer to Duan Tinggui (段廷珪), the Director-General of the Raozhou Circuit at the time (Chengwen Publishing Company 1989:599; Li 1994).

2. In the nineteenth fascicle of the *Zhengjiang Gazetteer of the Zhiyuan Era* (至顺镇江志), it records: "Du Run 堵闰…was transferred one more time to the positions of Gentleman of the Fourth Class (承务郎) and Legal Officer of the Directorate-General of the Raozhou Circuit (饶州路总管府推官). He went to court when summoned and was excused from service due to his elderly mother. For this, he was appointed per se as Superintendent of Rice Paddies (稻田提举) in Zhenjiang (镇江) and other places. A gold treasury was further bestowed on him to show the imperial

favor. In the seventh month of the second year of the Zhishun (至顺) era (1331 CE), he was ordered to oversee porcelain production in Raozhou. He died of illness while traveling at Changshan (常山) in Sanqu (三衢)" (ZJG 1999:762).

3. In the second fascicle of *Straightforward Records of the Zhizheng Era* (至正直记) written by Kong Qi (孔齐, fl. ca. 1367 CE), it records: "The imperial soil in Raozhou shines a white color like chalk. Officials are sent every year to oversee the making of porcelain vessels for tribute, which are called imperial soil kilns (御土窑)" (Shanghai Ancient Books Publishing House 2001:6616).

4. In the seventh fascicle of *Great Gazetteer of the Jiangxi Province* (江西省大志) compiled by Lu Wangai (陆万垓, 1533–1599 CE) during the Wanli (万历) reign of the Ming dynasty, it records: "During the Song dynasty, (Jiangxi) oversaw (porcelain) production per request of the court. During the Taiding (泰定) era of Yuan, General-Director of this (Raozhou) Circuit monitored the pottery-making process. Porcelain was always in supply on imperial orders and the production would stop if otherwise" (Xiong and Xiong 2007:47).

5. In the 1783 version of the *Fuliang County Gazetteer* (compiled in the forty-eighth year of the Qianlong reign of the Qing dynasty), it is written: "After the Taiding era of Yuan, the General-Director of this (Raozhou) Circuit supervised porcelain production. Porcelain was always in supply on imperial orders and the production would stop if otherwise" (Lu 2000:22).

From the above records, it can be seen that by the beginning of the second year of the Taiding era (1325) at the latest, the Yuan government had already appointed high-level officials (such as the General-Director of the Raozhou Circuit) to oversee porcelain production. A consensus has been reached on this point, which will not be further discussed here. However, there are still several points worth noting.

First, it is not clear yet when the Yuan metropolitan government began appointing supervisory officials of porcelain production (*dutao guan*). Although historical records indicate that instances of General-Director of the Raozhou Circuit overseeing porcelain production all occurred after the Taiding era, this cannot be taken as an absolute dividing line, but only an indicator that the practice of appointing officials to oversee porcelain-making became more common in the middle and late period of Yuan.

Second, the officials appointed to oversee porcelain-making in Raozhou during the middle and late periods of Yuan was not necessarily the General-Director of the Raozhou Circuit. This can be reasoned from the record of Du Run, the *dutao guan* (supervisory official of porcelain production). Before that appointment, he served positions as Legal Officer of the Directorate-General of the Raozhou Circuit and Superintendent of Rice Paddies in Zhenjiang and other places. He never served as General-Director of the Raozhou Circuit, however. This reveals that errors exist in the Ming and Qing documents regarding the record that "the General-Director of this (Raozhou) Circuit supervised porcelain production." Records from the Yuan are more reliable.

Third, both Tables 11.1 and 11.2 show that the Commissioner of FLPB was ranked Class 7B, whereas the General-Director of the Raozhou Circuit was ranked Class 3A. According to the YSP, Du Run, the Legal Officer of the Directorate-General of the Raozhou Circuit mentioned above, was ranked Class 6B (YSP 7.202). When he was later sent to oversee porcelain production in Raozhou, he was promoted to Class 5B (*Yuan shi* 89.2271), which was higher than the rank of the Commissioner of FLPB. Since "[a] gold treasury was further bestowed upon him to show the imperial favor," we can tell that Du Run's status (as *dutao guan*) was high and his treatment was generous. In short, regardless of whether the officials appointed in the middle and late periods of Yuan to oversee porcelain production were General-Director of the Raozhou Circuit or not, there is no doubt that their status was higher than that of the Commissioner of FLPB.

Fourth, regarding FLPB's responsibilities when its operation began to be overseen by the supervisory officials of porcelain production (*dutao guan*) during the middle and late Yuan dynasty, a few scholars infer that "at least by the second year of Taiding (1325 CE), FLPB, despite a former standing institution, had already been taken over by the General-Director of the Raozhou Circuit to temporarily make *guanyaoqi* (官窯器, imperial kiln-vessels). In other words, although FLPB no longer existed, thanks to the General-Director of the Raozhou Circuit, porcelain for the imperial government could still be produced" (Wang 2000:13–14). Other scholars, however, argue that "this does not mean the abolition of FLPB because it seems unlikely to abolish a standing institution that controlled porcelain production when more imperial porcelain was in demand. For sure, it is possible to abolish a standing institution and establish a new one, but viewed from the situation at the time, there was no evidence of either abolition or establishment" (Lu 2000:22). I support the latter view for the following reasons: based on the above-cited record "[p]orcelain was always in supply on imperial orders and the production would stop if otherwise," *dutao guan*, the supervisory official of porcelain production, should have been a temporary office created by the Yuan government. On the contrary, FLPB was a standing institution in charge of firing porcelain, which was unlikely to be established or dismissed on short notice to meet the imperial demand of porcelain. Rather, my understanding is that, the Commissioner of FLPB stuck to his duties; but when there was an imperial order, he would assist and obey the temporary *dutao guan* sent by the superior to complete the given task. When there was no imperial order, the *dutao guan* would return and the Commissioner of FLPB would continue to perform his routine duties of overseeing porcelain production.

Conclusions

Through the analysis of the ranks of the offices in charge of porcelain production in Raozhou across different periods of the Yuan dynasty, we can conclude that at the beginning of the establishment of FLPB, only lower-ranking *jiangzhi guan* (匠职官, artisan officials), such as Commissioner and Assistant Commissioner, were in charge of the making of porcelain. However, in the middle and late period of Yuan, higher-ranking *minzhi guan* (民职官, civil officials) were appointed by the metropolitan government to supervise the production of porcelain, which was "in supply on imperial orders and would stop if otherwise." These reflect two characteristics of the Yuan government's demand for porcelain.

On the one hand, the overall trend was an increase in the demand for porcelain and a growing emphasis on its production. People like Duan Tinggui and Du Run, who served either as the General-Director of the Raozhou Circuit or other higher-ranking civil offices, were trusted by the Yuan emperor. Nevertheless, they were all ordered to participate in the supervision of porcelain production, a task related to the Commissioner of FLPB, whose rank was far below the formers. Undoubtedly, this contrast reveals the heightened attention of the Yuan metropolitan government to porcelain. The increased demand for porcelain is mainly reflected in two aspects: an increase in the demand for official porcelain (such as sacrificial vessels and wine vessels) and an increase in the demand for trade porcelain. These two aspects are confirmed by both historical documents and unearthed artifacts (Chinese Ceramic Society 1982:354; *Yuan shi* 140.3366).

On the other hand, with the change of imperial power, the demand for sacrificial porcelain vessels by the Yuan government experienced periodic fluctuations, as intimated by the record that porcelain production "was in supply on imperial orders and would stop if otherwise." Its peak of demand appeared when the emperor ascended to the throne and held sacrificial ceremonies (*Yuan shi* 74.1847).

In my opinion, these characteristics are mainly related to the following factors: the implementation of austere financial policies in the middle and late period of Yuan, due to the gradual decline of its state capacity; the deepened Sinicization of the Yuan rulers; and the recovery of handicraft industry and the development of commerce.

References

Primary Sources from Pre-modern China

Song, Lian 宋濂 [1310–1381]), ed. 1976. *Yuan shi* 元史 [*Yuan history*]. Beijing: China Book Company Press. 15 volumes.

[YSP] *Da Yuan shengzheng guochao dianzhang* 大元聖政國朝典章 [*Statutes and precedents of the sacred administration of the great Yuan dynastic state*]. 1998. Beijing: China Radio and Television Press. 3 volumes.

Yu, Xilu (俞希魯 [fl. 1333]), ed. 1999. *Zhishun Zhengjiang zhi* 至順鎮江志 [*Zhengjiang gazetteer of the Zhishun era*]. Nanjing: Jiangsu Ancient Texts Press. 2 volumes.

Secondary Sources

Chengwen Publishing Company. 1989. *Compendium of Chinese Local Gazetteers*. Taipei: Chengwen Publishing Company. [in Chinese.]

Chinese Ceramic Society. 1982. *History of Chinese Ceramics*. Beijing: Cultural Relics Press. 462 pp. [in Chinese.]

Farquhar, David M. 1990. *The Government of China under Mongolian Rule: A Reference Guide*. Stuttgart, Germany: Franz Steiner Verlag. 594 pp. (Münchener ostasiatische Studien 53.)

Jiang, Jianxin, and Jianmin Jiang. 2008. Investigation of the Fuliang Porcelain Bureau, its kiln sites, and products. *Cultural Relics from the South* 2008(1):57–61. [in Chinese.]

Li, Minju. 1994. Fuliang Porcelain Bureau and the vessels from the imperial soil kilns. *Cultural Relics from the South* 1994(3):47–50. [in Chinese.]

Lu, Minghua. 2000. Issues related to the firing of egg-white glazed porcelain from Jingdezhen during the Yuan dynasty. In: Qingzheng Wang, ed. *The Complete Works of Chinese Ceramics*. Volume 11, Yuan (part 2). Shanghai: Shanghai People's Fine Arts Press. pp. 21–28. [in Chinese.]

Shanghai Ancient Books Publishing House. 2001. *A Survey of Song and Yuan Note-style Fictions*. Shanghai: Shanghai Ancient Books Publishing House. 6671 pp. [in Chinese.]

Shih, Ching-fei. 2003. A preliminary study of the use of porcelain in the Mongol–Yuan Court. *Compilation of Essays on Art History* 15(2003):169–203, 299. [in Chinese.]

Tan, Qixiang, chief ed. 1982. *The Historical Atlas of China*. Volume 7, The Yuan Dynasty Period, the Ming Dynasty Period. Beijing: Maps of China Press. 838 pp. [in Chinese.]

Wang, Qingzheng. 2000. Yuan dynasty porcelain from Jingdezhen. In: Qingzheng Wang, ed. *The Complete Works of Chinese Ceramics*. Shanghai: Shanghai People's Fine Arts Press. 311 pp. [in Chinese.]

Xiong, Liao, and Xiong Wei, eds. 2007. *Compendium of Classical Chinese Ceramic Literature*. Shanghai: Shanghai Chinese Culture Press. 743 pp. [in Chinese.]

Zeng, Lingyi. 2012. Fuliang Ceramics Bureau Officer and Governor. *Zhongguo Guojia Bowuguan Guankan* 4:63–71. [in Chinese with English abstract.]

CHAPTER TWELVE

Porcelain in the Yuan Period of the Mongolian Empire:
Moving from Portable X-ray Fluorescence Analysis toward Political Economy Insights

ZENG Lingyi, WANG Qingzhu, Mandakh DAVAASUREN, Chunag AMARTUVSHIN, and Ellery FRAHM

Empires are expansive, incorporative polities composed of diverse communities and ethnic groups (e.g., Areshian 2013; Khatchadourian 2016; Boozer, Düring, and Parker 2020). The creation and maintenance of empires necessitates administering (and exploiting) this diversity during the incorporation of new territories and peoples who are ethnically or socially distinct, or both, from the political leadership (Barfield 2001). Vexing issues for understanding empires include the nature of their political economies as well as elite legitimation processes and infrastructural power (Yoffee 2016). Investigating how empires controlled the production and distribution of prestige goods is a crucial way to elucidate these issues through material culture. Different patterns and strategies in the processes of political economy—including control of labor, raw materials, iconography, and value—have been recognized in the Roman Empire (Alcock et al. 2001; Mattingly 2013; Hoffman and Brody 2014), Inka Empire (D'Altroy and Bishop 1990; Burger and Salazar 2004), Aztec Empire (Smith and Sergheraert 2012), Persian Empire (Khatchadourian 2016), and Vijayanagara Empire (Sinopoli 2000), as well as in the dynasties of imperial China (Ledderose 2000; Barbieri-Low 2007; Pines et al. 2014; Shelach-Lavi 2015; Yao 2016). Within these empires there was a tendency for the elites to establish their political legitimacy by creating "internationalizing" styles and new systems of value as part of a symbolic infrastructure (Baines and Yoffee 1998; Honeychurch 2014, 2015). Inka elites, for example, appropriated the traditional Andean gender and transformational associations of three metals—gold, silver, and copper—and incorporated them into an imperial organizational framework in which each of these substances represented a particular social segment, as a means to establish a new structural hierarchy within the empire (Lechtman 2014).

In contrast, relatively little is known about the political economy of the nomadic and steppe empires (Allsen 1996; Rogers 2012; Honeychurch 2014). The scale, variability, and mobility of these polities pose considerable challenges to scholars. In the beginning of the thirteenth century CE, Chinggis Khan (Genghis Khan) conquered much of the Eurasian steppe and East Asia and, in doing so, built the largest contiguous land empire in history. By 1260 CE, a civil war and the difficulty of maintaining centralized control across the entire Eurasian region resulted in a subdivision of the empire into four independent states that could be considered scaled-down empires in their own right. In the east, central authority passed into the hands of Kublai Khan and the Yuan dynasty (1271–1368 CE) in what is now modern China and Mongolia (Rogers 2012). The Mongols' strategies in controlling the political economy and the changes that they brought about are especially instructive for understanding the process of elite legitimization issues that are shared by many empires; however, as the largest of the steppe empires, the Mongol Empire also had its own unique challenges. A critical question is how the Mongol elites, seen as nomadic foreign rulers, engaged with material culture in ways that supported their legitimacy in a political environment in which they would have had a low probability of being recognized as legitimate by the sedentary peoples of China. Studying the production, distribution, and consumption of white-glazed and blue-and-white porcelain is one approach toward clarifying the political economy of the Mongol Empire and, in turn, understanding the legitimization process of rulers who, in all likelihood, would have been regarded as foreign in many parts of this extensive empire.

The application of anthropological approaches to studies of production, distribution, and consumption has a long history (Kopytoff 1986; Rice 1987; Costin 1991; Sinopoli 1991; among others), but the application of such ideas in Chinese archaeology is comparatively recent (e.g., social change and mortuary practices in northern China in Underhill [2002]; salt production along the Yangzi River in Flad [2011]; prestige goods from northern China in Liu L. [2003]). Ceramics from the Mongol Empire provide a window to investigate the roles of the government in the production, distribution, and consumption of goods in the ethnically diverse communities of a large political territory. Here we consider these phenomena through the elemental analyses of two ceramic wares that emerged and saw increasing demand during the Mongol period: blue-and-white and egg-white glazed porcelains.

Blue-and-white porcelain is one of the most renowned products during the Mongol Yuan period (1271–1368 CE). Although porcelain with blue-and-white patterns was initially produced in the Gongyi kiln during China's Tang dynasty, the quantity was small, and the production soon ceased (Ma 2010; Zhao 2013). The production of blue-and-white porcelain in the Yuan period was thus unrelated to Tang blue-and-white porcelain. Many scholars (e.g., Liu X.Y. 1981; Jiang 1991; Wang 2000; Lin 2009) propose that blue-and-white porcelain was invented during the Yuan dynasty to serve as gifts for the Mongolian western khans. Others (Hang 2020) suggest that the origin of blue-and-white porcelain reflects the Islamization of northeast China. The expansion of the Mongol empire across Eurasia made the invention and spread of blue-and-white porcelain possible, as these highly valued products were most likely commissioned by the Mongol khans in China as a means to boost the economy and increase revenue during the Yuan period (Liu X.Y. 1981; Jiang 1991).

Egg-white glazed porcelain is another new product initiated during the Yuan period in China. The egg-white glazed porcelain can be regarded as an innovation derived from earlier bluish-white glazed porcelains, a popular type of porcelain in Jingdezhen and Longquan kilns since the Song dynasty in China (960–1276 CE). Scholars (Ming et al. 2014; Wu et al. 2014) have noted the chemical differences between bluish-white and egg-white glazed porcelains, and it has been widely thought, from the inscriptions found on certain vessels, that the egg-white porcelains were ordered by the Mongol government for military or ritual uses.

For craft production and distribution, it seems that the Mongol regime took care to exert more control over artisan households than the rest of the population (Oshima 1983). Once the Mongols had created an orderly administration in China, "they gathered the artisans from the known world, assembled them at the capital, classified and distributed them to local offices and bureaus" (Su 1967:19, translated). Scholars have widely assumed that Jingdezhen, in Jiangxi Province of southern China, was the only place where blue-and-white and egg-white glazed porcelains were made during the Mongol period (e.g., Liu X.Y. 1981; Jiang 1991; Wang 2000). This is based on one record in the *Yuan shi* (*History of Yuan*) stating that, in 1278 CE, the Yuan government established an organization termed the Fuliang Ceramics Bureau to take charge of ceramics-related issues and that the bureau was headed by two commissioners. This reflects involvement of the Mongol government in ceramics production, but a multitude of questions remain. For example, why did the government establish such an agency at Jingdezhen and were there similar organizations in other regions of the empire during that period? This bureau's responsibilities and functions (e.g., whether it was operated as a production facility run by the government, a coordinating body, or a storage and distribution center) are unknown. Whether all blue-and-white or egg-white glazed wares were produced in Jingdezhen during the Mongol period is also a mystery. Unlike the highly controlled Ming and Qing imperial kilns and their sophisticated labor systems found in later historical records, few written accounts about production were kept during the Mongol period. Therefore, it is unknown to what degree the Mongol elites controlled ceramic production and how their control changed over time.

Past research into historical porcelains has principally (although not exclusively) focused more on creating typologies and chronologies based on vessels' decorative patterns and inscriptions than attempting to relate vessels to the societies and polities that produced and used them. Some scholars have even relied heavily on indirect evidence in historical records without studying porcelain vessels directly (e.g., Pope 1981; Lin 2009). There have been relatively few scientific analyses of porcelains from the Mongol Yuan period in China, and most of this work has focused on museum collections that reflect only the best-known production site at Jingdezhen. Little is known of Yuan porcelains from archaeological contexts beyond Jingdezhen. It should, though, be noted that of late there have been more scientific studies along these lines. For example, Fischer and Hsieh (2017) used elemental analysis and reflectance spectroscopy to distinguish blue-and-white porcelain sherds made in Jingdezhen and Zhangzhou, but recovered in Indonesia and the Philippines. Dennison (2023) used mass spectrometry to analyze porcelain sherds made at various kiln sites in southern China and then sent to and used by three Philippine polities. While these researchers have focused on the south, there has still been no research looking to the northern regions under the Yuan dynasty.

Our purpose here is to demonstrate how routine, nondestructive compositional analyses of historical porcelain sherds can shed light on topics of anthropological significance. Specifically, we have used portable X-ray fluorescence spectrometry (pXRF, sometimes known as handheld XRF) and, to a lesser degree, scanning electron microscopy (SEM) with energy-dispersive X-ray spectrometry (EDS) for elemental analyses of blue-and-white and egg-white glazed porcelains. Others previously have analyzed historical porcelains with pXRF; however, their focus has most commonly been conservation, authentication, and dating (e.g., Bezur and Casadio 2012; Casadio et al. 2012). For example, a Royal Society of Chemistry technical brief (Domoney 2017) largely focuses on simple pigment identification (e.g., distinguishing eighteenth-century British copper-based green enamels from nineteenth-century chromium-based ones) within museum settings. In contrast, the methods that we describe here with a small collection of sherds could, when eventually applied to a much larger corpus of archaeological sherds, yield elemental data that highlight otherwise invisible spatiotemporal trends in porcelain production and use and, when coupled with historical frameworks, elucidate strategies of porcelain production and distribution used by governmental and local agents.

Hypotheses and Expectations

The ultimate goal, using the methods discussed here, is to analyze porcelains from various parts of the Mongol Empire to identify the underlying sociopolitical factors that affected their consumption, production, and distribution at the local, regional, and interregional levels. Earlier scholars have approached the production and use of porcelain in the Mongol Empire from the angle of acculturation, arguing that, by the late Mongol era, Mongols had been profoundly assimilated by the Han Chinese people whom they ruled (Wang 2000; Shi 2001). More recently, this view has been challenged by historians who offer compelling evidence against the concept of sinicization and instead identify this as a trope stemming from a pervasive sino-centrism in historical research on eastern Asia (Munkh-Erdene 2023). It is our working hypothesis that Mongol elites purposefully enabled the production of blue-and-white and egg-white glazed porcelains as prestige goods during the building of the empire in support of their burgeoning political economy.

We propose that, in the early phase of the Mongol Yuan period (around 1270–1320 CE), Mongol elites sought to organize and control production of porcelains formerly controlled by Chinese authorities as a way of establishing political legitimacy. The production of these two porcelain wares was a specialized craft under control of the central government and, as the primary consumers, the Mongol rulers took an active role in the creation and staffing of production facilities, bringing raw materials (e.g., fine white kaolinite from southern China, cobalt from Central Asia), specialists, and technologies together from different areas. Private potters lacked the requisite amounts of capital and raw materials in quantities that only the government could supply. In addition, colors had great symbolic significance for the Mongols (e.g., white was associated with good fortune and had a clear political association, as did blue, which had—and still has—ritual importance; Allsen 1997) and the glazed surfaces of porcelain vessels were ideally suited to the eating and drinking habits of the Mongol elites (Carswell 2000). Thus, the Mongol rulers could have tried to control the production and distribution of these prestige goods to display their political power and legitimize their rule of the empire through gifting and feasting.

In contrast, during the later Yuan phase (around 1320–1370 CE), we hypothesize that these two types of porcelains became more available to intermediate elites who were pursuing a higher social status. The consumption of these products supported and reinforced the initial legitimacy of higher elites, through their acceptance of this material symbolism and their participation in an imperial system of value. The Mongol central government played a key role in stimulating the production of porcelains in more locations, given that this would increase revenue. In response to greater demand for porcelains across the empire, the central government could have started to loosen control over these types of porcelain and local elites could also have participated in their production.

Given these hypotheses, we would expect particular patterns to be evident by means of our analyses. First, during the early phase of the empire, if indeed Mongol rulers controlled production and distribution of these two porcelain types as new kinds of prestige goods, we would expect to see centralized and attached production (sensu Costin 1991) ordered by the imperial government and made in official kiln(s). Intended for elite use, these earlier porcelains should be of higher quality (e.g., made of finer clays with fewer impurities and additives). With access to a diachronic sample, it would be insightful to investigate the degrees of standardization and quality control for each type of porcelain produced by the Mongol government over time. Ideally one could distinguish official wares from civilian wares by assessing the amount of skill and labor involved in their production using objective criteria (e.g., clay purity and color, pigment source and complexity, and size standardization). In addition, a high degree of similarity in elemental compositions of bodies, glazes, and pigments of porcelain from different regions would suggest that there were only a few production centers or even a single center. Specifically, following our hypothesis, we would expect to find little compositional difference between porcelain artifacts from the suspected Jingdezhen production sites and those from archaeological sites to the north in Mongolia, for example, and elsewhere across the empire. This, in turn, would indicate that these porcelains were specially made within Jingdezhen ("official kilns") and were distributed to different parts of the empire. If there was a specific glaze composition for each porcelain type from a given kiln site, it could indicate highly controlled production. Variation in glaze composition, though, may suggest that the production of glazes was not closely controlled.

Our hypothesis for the later phase, in contrast, is that there were one or more local agencies producing these porcelain types, driven by social demand among different communities for a wider variety of vessels. Given this scenario, we would expect to see both official and civilian kilns operating at the same time with more variable outcomes and different levels of quality control. For example, we would anticipate greater compositional variability from different sites in the later phase, suggesting that there were multiple production sites or sources for the clays and pigments. In addition, we expect that there may have been local imitations of elite styles (such as vessels similar in design and shape, but made using local clay). Furthermore, there might have also been various approaches to the application of the glazes and pigments across the empire. Such variation among porcelain sherds from different areas would support the existence of different workshops and imitations.

Excavations in Inner Mongolia in northern China have revealed several important hoards and residential areas with both blue-and-white and egg-white porcelains dating to the Mongol period. Chen (2023) hypothesized that sites in Inner Mongolia with these vessels likely functioned as trading depots between the production center in Jingdezhen and settlements in Mongolia. If sites in all three areas have porcelains with similar chemical compositions, it would suggest that the vessels were likely made in the same production center, whereas chemical variability would suggest the possibility of multiple centers of production. Ideally such research would include fieldwork at excavated production sites in Jingdezhen from the Mongol period (Jiang 1991). The site of Luomaqiao, for example, is a recently excavated Mongol porcelain production area with the richest materials so far (see, for example, the recent book by Weng and Li [2021]). Initial observations noted the presence of both high- and low-quality porcelains at this site (Zeng, personal observation); however, it remains unknown if this difference in production quality was synchronous (that is, two distinct production units) or instead reflects a change over time. Stratigraphic evidence from these kiln sites (and others) will be crucial for making this distinction.

Previous Studies

Various scientific studies of Chinese porcelains have focused on elemental analysis of bodies and glazes from the Tang (618–907 CE), Song (960–1279 CE), Ming (1368–1644 CE), and Qing (1644–1911 CE) dynasties (e.g., Guo 1987; Yap and Hua 1992; Pollard and Hatcher 1994; Yu and Miao 1998; Wood et al. 2007; Wood and Tite 2009; Li et al. 2017).

Most of these studies did not attempt to relate porcelain chemical compositions to specific geological sources (although there has since been more work that has endeavored to do so; e.g., Dennison 2023). Instead these researchers focused on trying to establish compositional criteria for distinguishing porcelains made in different locations and time periods. Because of the limited data for the Yuan dynasty, it has been proposed that these porcelains were produced using a distinctive tradition involving the use of "porcelain stone," a fine aggregate of quartz (silica), muscovite (potash mica), and albite (sodium feldspar), to which kaolinite (a white clay mineral) was subsequently added at times (Tite, Freestone, and Bimson 1984). This has been considered a Yuan period development, but it is not yet certain when the addition of kaolinite initially occurred. For making the glaze, "glaze ash" (lime, or CaO) was added, potentially in different amounts (Tite, Freestone, and Bimson 1984). For example, a low lime content would result in an opaque glaze, probably due to the development of silica crystals, and a high lime content results in crazing (a network of fine cracks along the surface). Consequently, it seems likely that the glaze compositions of elite porcelains would show little chemical variation as a result of careful control to avoid opacity and crazing so that the underglaze decorations were best displayed. Regarding the pigments themselves, researchers have largely focused on the cobalt-rich blue colorants and suggested that there was a change from Persian low manganese arsenical cobalt ores to local Chinese manganiferous ones (e.g., Wen et al. 2007; Wen and Pollard 2014). Wen et al. (2007) also investigated elemental fingerprints for cobalt ores used during the Yuan and subsequent dynasties using manganese-to-cobalt (Mn/Co) and iron-to-manganese (Fe/Mn) ratios.

Materials

Here we consider only a small sample of the porcelain sherds that were analyzed by Zeng (unfortunately, almost all of her data remain inaccessible). That is, instead of considering her full sample of hundreds of sherds, here we are restricted to a set of only eleven sherds, exported with permission of the Institute of Archaeology, Academy of Sciences, Mongolia. This sample, however, still enables insights into porcelain variation in the period of interest. The sample includes three blue-and-white sherds: one from Bayankhongor Province (MNP-1986) and two from the site of Dushiin Dorvoljin in Khanbogd District of Ömnögovi Province. There are also eight white porcelain sherds from Avraga in Khentii Province: six sherds from one surface scatter (AV05a–AV05f) as well as two individual sherds (AVN L2-10 E3.P1 and AV14 L2-10 D4). For this work we did not distinguish between egg-white glaze and other potentially similar wares (for example, the green-white glazes of Qingbai ware), given the lack of any other diagnostic features (for example, vessel shape) on the small sherds.

Avraga is a well-known palace and ceremonial site that spans the Mongol imperial period, from the late twelfth through fourteenth centuries CE (Shiraishi and Tsogtbaatar 2009), whereas the two other sites have received minor attention from archaeologists. The Bayankhongor collection site is a surface scatter, where the sherds were recovered in 1986, in the southwestern Mongolian Gobi. The Khanbogd collection site, Dushiin Dorvoljin, is a walled settlement dated to the Manchu period (fifteenth through sixteenth centuries CE) in the southern Gobi (Amartuvshin, Batzorig, and Byambatseren 2019). That is, the two Khanbogd sherds date to a later period than the others, but we retain them here for the sake of comparison.

Analytical Methods

Major elements within the sherd bodies were measured using SEM-EDS. This was done with the Thermo Scientific Phenom XL G2 Desktop scanning electron microscope (Thermo Fisher Scientific, Inc.; https://www.thermofisher.com) housed in the Yale University Archaeological Laboratories. The measurements were made on lightly polished sherd edges. When operated at a low vacuum this microscope can image and analyze specimens without the need to apply a thin layer of gold, carbon, or other conductive substance. This instrument has a high-brightness CeB_6 electron source and was operated with an accelerating voltage of 15 kV and an emission current of 40 µA. Its silicon drift detector has an area of 25 mm^2 and a spectral resolution of ≤132 eV (for the Mn Kα characteristic X-ray peak). Each analysis collected 200,000 X-ray counts over an area of approximately 0.5 mm^2 on a polished section, averaging out microscopic heterogeneities. Element identification and analysis made use of Thermo Scientific's Element Identification (EID) software package for automated peak recognition and quantification. These data were calibrated using a series of twelve certified microanalysis reference materials: Juan de Fuca basalt glass (NMNH 111240-52/VG-2), Makaopuhi basalt glass (NMNH 113498-1/VG-A99), Indian Ocean basalt glass (NMNH 113716-1), Yellowstone rhyolite glass (NMNH 72854/VG-568), synthetic tektite glass (USNM 2213), and Amelia albite (Harvard Mineralogical Museum 131705), as well as Corning Glasses IR-V (NMNH 117083), IR-W (NMNH 117084), IR-X (NMNH 117085), A (NMNH 117218-4), B (NMNH 117218-1), and C (NMNH 117218-2). Consequently, our SEM-EDS measurements of the sherd sections should be considered fully quantitative elemental data.

Our focus with SEM-EDS was identifying elemental differences that reflect variations in the mineral proportions, following an approach from Tite, Freestone, and Bimson (1984). Quartz (SiO_2) is one of the primary mineral components, as are various aluminosilicate minerals (e.g., kaolinite, albite, and muscovite), so a scatterplot of the amount of silicon (Si) against aluminum (Al) can highlight the abundance of quartz to aluminosilicates within a corpus of sherds. Albite [$Na(AlSi_3O_8)$], one end-member of plagioclase feldspar minerals, is another common component, but the actual minerals used as porcelain ingredients in the past were unlikely to have been pure albite. Instead, such minerals were likely somewhere compositionally between albite and anorthite [$CaAl_2Si_2O_8$]. Thus, a scatterplot comparing the amount of sodium (Na) and calcium (Ca) can reveal the amount of albite and anorthite in porcelains and their relative proportions. Muscovite [$KAl_2(AlSi_3O_{10})(OH)_2$], one end-member of mica minerals, is also common in porcelain, but the actual micas may have skewed geochemically toward other end-members, such as biotite [$K(Mg,Fe)_3(AlSi_3)O_{10}(OH)_2$]. Therefore, a scatterplot comparing potassium (K) and Mg + Fe can indicate differences in the micas present. Lastly, sherds with the highest concentrations of Al should correspond to those with the most kaolinite [$Al_2(Si_2O_5)(OH)_4$], the key ingredient in porcelain manufacturing. Accordingly, X-ray spectrometric data can enable us to draw some conclusions about the nature of the porcelain components and their variations and, in turn, we can consider our topics of interest, such as strict manufacturing control versus local imitations.

The sherd glazes were measured by pXRF in the Yale University Archaeological Laboratories. In particular, we used an Olympus (formerly Olympus Scientific Solutions, now Evident; https://www.evidentscientific.com/) Vanta VMR (M-series) instrument outfitted with a 4 W X-ray tube, a rhodium (Rh) anode, and a large-area silicon drift detector capable of high spectral resolutions (approx. 134 eV). When this instrument is operated in the two-beam "GeoChem" mode, its X-ray tube current and voltage automatically change (in combination with the built-in beam filters) to optimally fluoresce the heavier and lighter periodic table elements; these mode settings are: (1) tube voltage 40 kV, current 65.8 µA, filter 2000 µm thick Al, count rate approximately 70,000 cps (counts per second); and (2) tube voltage 10 kV, current 76.4 µA, no filter, count rate approximately 70,000 cps. Each measurement took 40 s (30 s for the heavier elements, 10 s for the lighter elements). The resulting data were corrected using Olympus fundamental parameters implementation to adjust for varied phenomena that affect the relationships between raw X-ray intensities and element concentrations (e.g., fluorescence and absorption edges, mass attenuation coefficients, and Rayleigh and Compton cross sections). This instrument's initial factory calibration, which is based on a set of reference standards from organizations such as the United States Geological Survey (USGS; https://www.usgs.gov/) and the US National Institute of Standards and Technology (NIST; https://www.nist.gov/), was augmented specifically for quantitative elemental analyses of archaeological ceramics using a Yale-developed calibration set. Two or three measurements were taken on each surface feature (e.g., plain white glaze and blue pigment).

Some authors (e.g., Bezur and Casadio 2012:276–284) have expressed concerns that, because of variable penetration depths of X-rays emitted from different elements, pXRF measurements of glazes might also contain contributions from the porcelain bodies beneath. Indeed, the penetration depths of X-rays depend on (1) their energies (and, in turn, the corresponding elements) and (2) the density and composition of the specimen. For example, the measured Ca X-rays (Kα, 3.7 keV) primarily (90%) escape from depths of approximately 12 µm in a clear porcelain glaze versus approximately 3 µm in a high-lead glaze (Bezur and Casadio 2012). In contrast, the measured yttrium (Y) X-rays (Kα, 14.9 keV) primarily escape from depths of approximately 570 µm in a clear glaze and approximately 34 µm in a high-lead glaze. Thus, glaze thickness and composition both affect which elements are only measured from the glaze and which include contributions from the underlying porcelain. Consequently, Bezur and Casadio (2012:259) suggest that, when conducting pXRF "on a relatively thick (about 150 to 200 µm) section of clear or white glaze," one should restrict measurements to elements from magnesium (Mg) to Fe to ensure there is no contribution from the underlying porcelain. For example, Bezur and Casadio (2012:293) focus on K, Ca, Ti (titanium), and Fe to discern Böttger and Du Paquier (eighteenth-century European) porcelain vessels.

It should be noted that the depths reported by Bezur and Casadio (2012) are mathematical determinations based entirely on the solutions to a series of nonlinear equations. This issue, thanks to seredipity, can be tested experimentally for the porcelains considered in this chapter, meaning that we were able to determine the suitability of heavier elements (rubidium [Rb] through niobium [Nb]) for our study. One of the sherds (Figure 12.1) has a thicker (800 µm) glazed exterior and a thinner (200 µm) glazed interior, as observed and measured by SEM. This permitted us to directly compare measurements from thin and thick glazes. Conducting Student's t-tests for elements such as Rb (thick: 230.4 ± 2.1 ppm; thin: 230.2 ± 2.5 ppm; $p = 0.894$), Y (thick: 16.0 ± 1.2 ppm; thin: 17.2 ± 0.4 ppm; $p = 0.067$), and Nb (thick: 24.8 ± 0.4 ppm; thin: 25.2 ± 0.8 ppm; $p = 0.347$) show that the measurements do not have statistically significant differences between the two sherd sides. This suggests, therefore, that the 200 µm glaze encompasses the analytical depth for these X-rays as well as an 800 µm glaze does. Consequently, we felt confident in using these heavier elements in our interpretations.

FIGURE 12.1. Backscattered electron image of a lighly polished edge of a white-glazed porcelain sherd (AV05) from Avraga in Khentii Province. The outer glaze layer (top, which contains abundant bubbles) is 800 μm thick, whereas the inner glaze layer (bottom) is 200 μm thick, allowing us to test the emission depth of characteristic X-rays of interest.

Results and Interpretation

Plots of the SEM-EDS elemental data for the body paste reveal differences and similarities in the porcelain components. Our plots of SiO_2 and Al_2O_3 measurements (Figure 12.2) show the relative abundance of quartz compared with aluminosilicate minerals, especially kaolinite. Our plots of Na_2O and CaO measurements (Figure 12.3) reveal the relative amounts of albite and anorthite. Our plots of K_2O and FeO + MgO (Figure 12.4) show the relative amounts of muscovite and biotite, whereas plots for FeO and MgO (Figure 12.5) highlight differences in the biotite compositions. These plots enable us to make observations about the porcelain compositions. For instance, the Bayankhongor blue-and-white porcelain has more quartz, whereas the Khanbogd blue-and-white porcelain has more kaolinite (see Figure 12.2). As another example, the Avraga white-glazed porcelain sherds show differences in their plagioclase feldspar components. The six sherds from the AV05 scatter have albite, while the other two sherds instead have anorthite (see Figure 12.3). Futhermore, the Khanbogd blue-and-white porcelain contains little plagioclase feldspar at all, but the Bayankhongor blue-and-white porcelain sherd has the most albite and the least anorthite in our sample, highlighting variations in the mica minerals present (see Figures 12.4 and 12.5).

Regarding the cobalt blue pigments, Wen and colleagues (Wen et al. 2007; Wen and Pollard 2014) noted elemental differences between imported Persian cobalt ores (low manganese [Mn] and high arsenic [As]) and the Chinese ones (high Mn and As free). Our plots (Figure 12.6) of Mn and As pXRF measurements on the blue pigments—specifically, two measurements on each of the three blue-and-white sherds—shows that the Bayankhongor cobalt blue

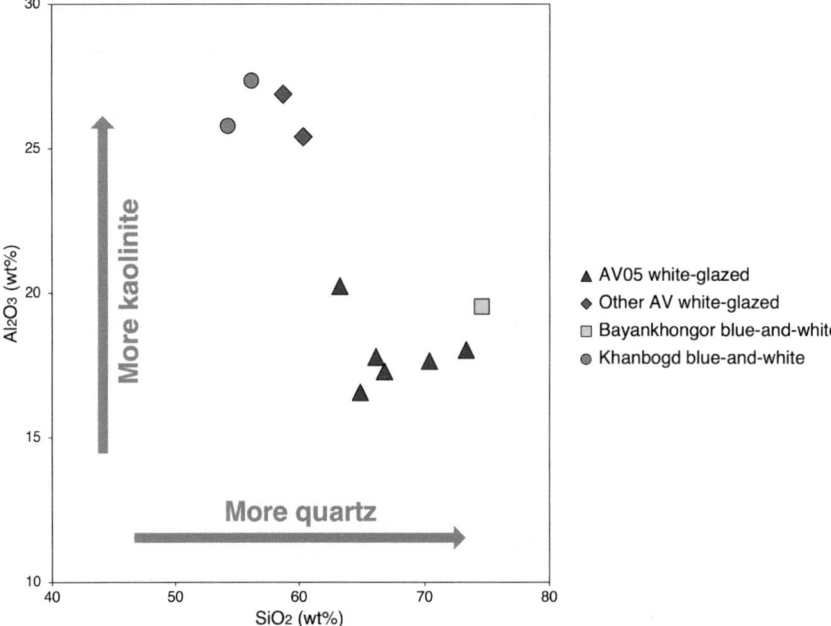

FIGURE 12.2. SEM-EDS measurements of silica (SiO$_2$) versus alumina (Al$_2$O$_3$) for the body pastes of the porcelain sherds.

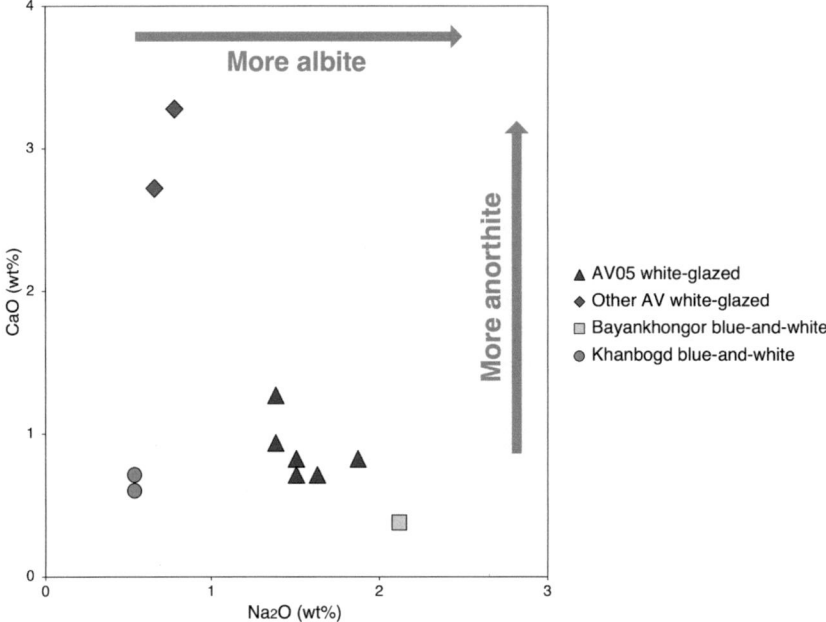

Figure 12.3. SEM-EDS measurements of sodium oxide (Na$_2$O) versus calcium oxide (CaO) for the body pastes of the porcelain sherds.

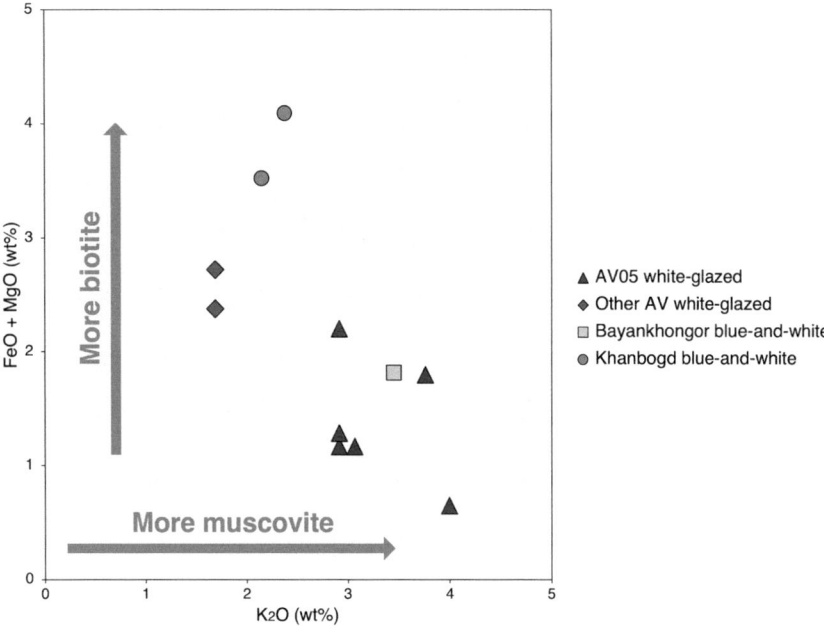

Figure 12.4. SEM-EDS measurements of potassium oxide (K$_2$O) versus FeO + MgO for the body pastes of the porcelain sherds.

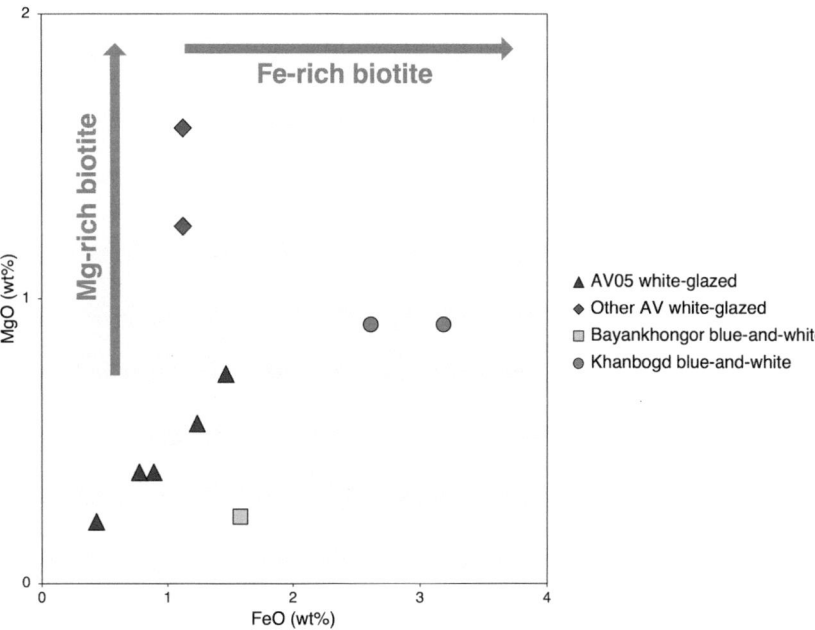

Figure 12.5. SEM-EDS measurements of iron oxide (FeO) versus magnesium oxide (MgO) for the body pastes of the porcelain sherds.

pigment is low As (although not As free) and high Mn, whereas the Khanbogd cobalt blue is low Mn and high As (and, accordingly, apparently an imported Persian ore). Wen et al. (2007) also differentiated various cobalt ores by Mn/Co and Fe/Mn ratios, and here we use their data to consider potential matches to the blue pigments on the Bayankhongor and Khanbogd sherds. There are no matches for the Khanbogd cobalt blue (Figure 12.7). For the Bayankhongor blue, our Fe/Mn and Mn/Co ratios are similar to those measured using synchrotron radiation XRF by Wen et al. (2007) for porcelain sherds from the Yongle period, a transitional time between the Yuan and Ming dynasties. Such an outcome is consistent with the findings from Wen et al. (2007), who proposed that Yongle craftspeople, like those in the Yuan, used pigments imported from Persia (specifically the cobalt pigment known as "Sumali blue"). Thus, it seems that not only is the Bayankhongor blue imported from Persia, but also, more specifically, it might be the Sumali blue mentioned in late Ming literature. Indeed, analyses by other researchers (Cowell and Zhang 2001) also support the conclusion that Sumali blue was used on Yuan blue-and-white porcelain. Consequently, we propose that the Khanbogd and Bayankhongor pigments are both imported Persian cobalt and that the latter, specifically, may be Sumali blue.

Regarding the glazes, we analyzed two or three areas on the white-glazed sherds as well as the white areas on the blue-and-white sherds. Our pXRF analyses measured more than twenty elements in the glazes, but here we focus on the patterns observed in a subset of those elements. As discussed above, "glaze ash," or lime (CaO), is a key ingredient that, to achieve the desired outcome, requires its addition in the right amounts (too little yields opaque glaze, too much yields crazing). Potassium oxide (K_2O), included in some form, is also important to lower the melting point (i.e., as a flux) and it can enhance characteristics such as viscosity and luster. Therefore, in a scatterplot of our K and Ca measurements (Figure 12.8), although the blue-and-white sherds have a fairly consistent Ca content, there is a bimodal distribution among the eight white-glazed Avraga sherds, even among those from the AV05 scatter—half of them have a higher lime content than the blue-and-white sherds, while half have a lower one. This is consistent with our visual observations: the sherds with a low lime content have a whiter, more opaque glaze (due, it is thought, to the formation of silica crystals), whereas the sherds with a higher lime content have a more transparent glaze (and sometimes a slight blueish tint). It is unclear, though, if these were desired or coincidental appearances (e.g., was an opaque white glaze the intended result, or does it instead reflect a lack of technical know-how?).

The trace elements in the glazes, which tend to reflect raw material differences rather than technological choices, also offer insights about the porcelains. Taken together, our scatterplots of Rb and Y (Figure 12.9) and Zr and Nb (Figure 12.10) suggest that these porcelain sherds had a variety of raw material sources, including at least two or three among the AV05 sherds. In addition, strontium (Sr) and Ca, which occur in the same column (or period) on the periodic table, behave alike as elements, which means that Sr atoms can chemically substitute for Ca atoms in lime. In our scatterplot of our Ca and Sr measurements (Figure 12.11), for sherds that lie along or near the dotted line, Sr correlates with Ca and, as a result, likely corresponds to the lime content of the glaze. This is the case for the Bayankhongor blue-and-white porcelain as well as for five out of the six AV05 white-glazed sherds. For sherds that lie to the right of the dotted line, Sr abundance reflects more than just the lime content. We also observed trends in other elements, such as copper (Cu) and zinc (Zn); however, we suspect that the consistently higher Cu and Zn levels in the blue-and-white porcelain (relative to the white-glazed porcelain) correspond to trace impurities in the cobalt ores and, thus, blue pigments. Ultimately, our element data suggest that the glaze ingredients were rather variable instead of tightly controlled.

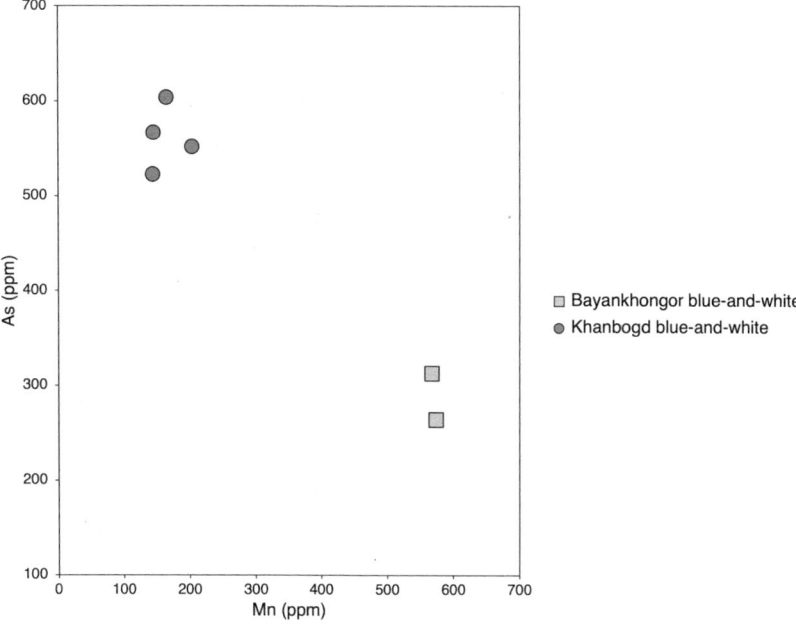

FIGURE 12.6. pXRF measurements of manganese (Mn) versus arsenic (As) for the cobalt blue pigments on the sherds.

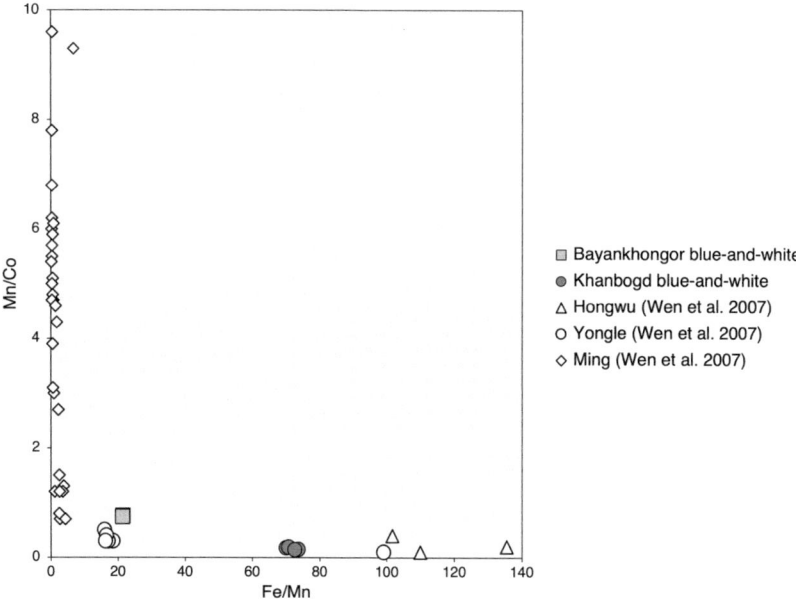

FIGURE 12.7. pXRF measurements of Fe/Mn versus Mn/Co ratios for the cobalt blue pigments on the sherds in comparison with the SR-XRF dataset for Hongwu, Yongle, and Ming wares from Wen et al. (2007).

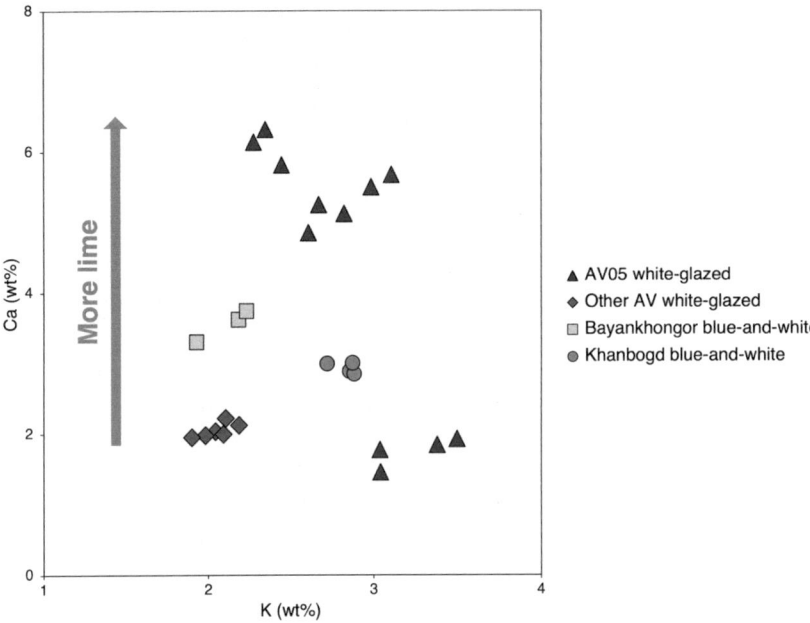

FIGURE 12.8. pXRF measurements of potassium (K) versus calcium (Ca) for the glaze on the porcelain sherds.

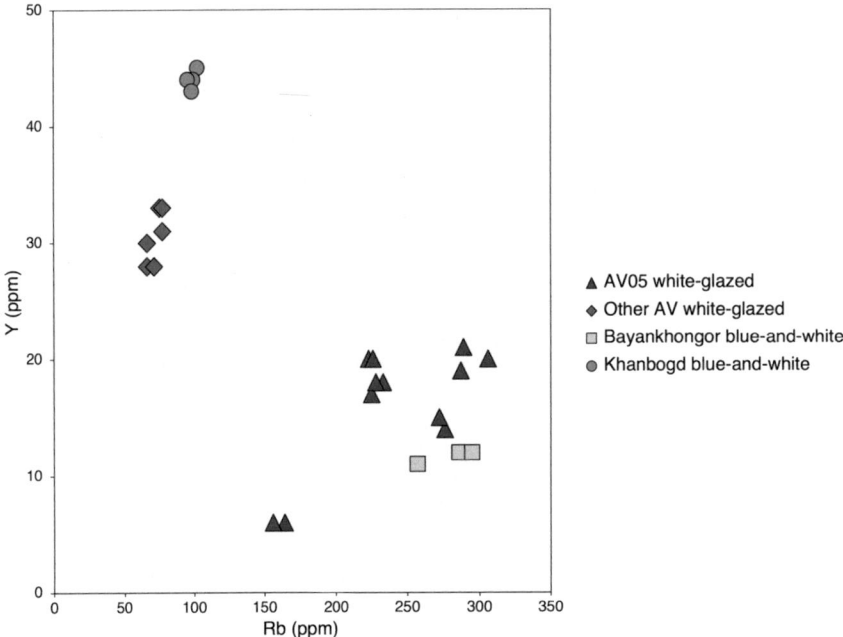

FIGURE 12.9. pXRF measurements of rubidium (Rb) versus yttrium (Y) for the glaze on the porcelain sherds.

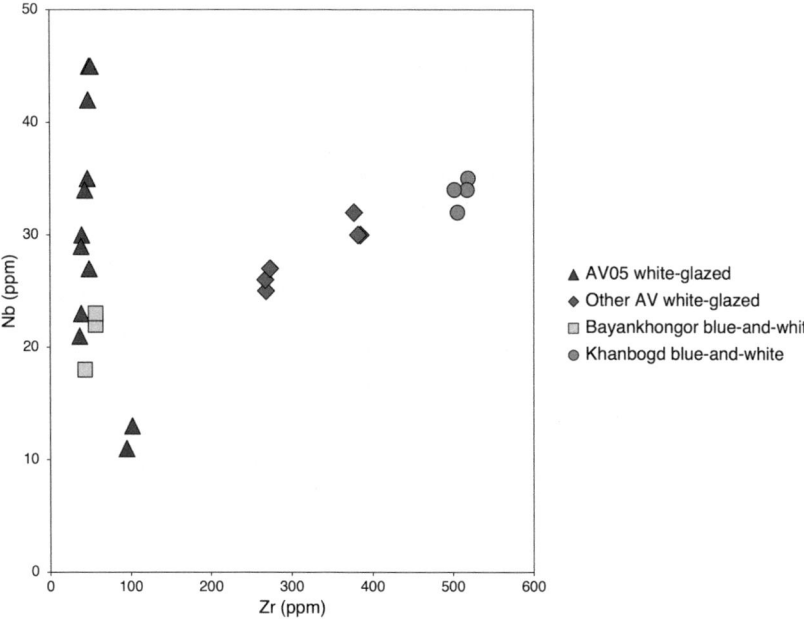

FIGURE 12.10. pXRF measurements of zirconium (Zr) versus niobium (Nb) for the glaze on the porcelain sherds.

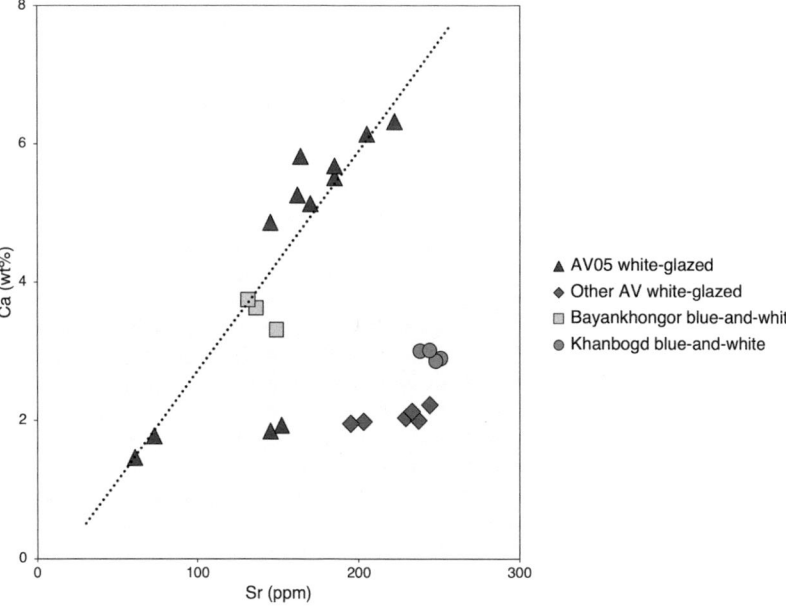

FIGURE 12.11. pXRF measurements of strontium (Sr) versus calcium (Ca) for the glaze on the porcelain sherds. Sherds on or near the dotted line contain Sr, we propose, principally due to the lime in the glaze.

Discussion

Even for such a small sample size, we can discuss our findings within the framework of some of our overarching research questions. Our data are consistent with these blue-and-white porcelain sherds having cobalt blue pigment from two different Persian sources; one of those sources may be the origin of Sumali blue, mentioned in historical documents. The importation of a particular blue pigment from a distant region has potentially relevant implications. It is possible, for example, that the distant origin of the pigment was symbolically significant, potentially linked to its rarity and the economic forces necessary to organize expansive trade networks. Alternatively, the use of imported cobalt blue could reveal limits to the technological know-how required to create such brilliant blue decorations on porcelains. Without the knowledge of how to produce such a pigment, it might have been necessary to import it until craftspeople learned, whether through experimentation or training, how to produce such colors for themselves. Clearly a much larger sample size is needed to parse these issues, but here we have at least shown that the requisite measurements can be taken quickly and nondestructively using pXRF instruments.

Regarding the body pastes, our data show that there is variation in all of the key ingredients of porcelain. For example, some sherds have more kaolinite, whereas others have more quartz. Not only does the amount of feldspar differ among the sherds, but also the feldspars differ in composition from albite to anorthite. The mica contents also differ from muscovite to biotite, and furthermore, the biotite minerals differ in their Fe and Mg concentrations. Again, for a small sample size, it is difficult to derive significant patterns in these data. At this point, we can propose that some of these observed differences are more likely to reflect deliberate choices with technical relevance (i.e., the amount of quartz relative to kaolinite), while other differences are more likely to reflect differences in the raw materials available to potters (i.e., albite versus anorthite). Hence, there are apparent elemental signals that likely reflect either technological choices or material origins. With a larger sample it should be possible to consider whether control was exerted over technology or material.

Like the body pastes, the glazes provide similar elemental clues about technological choices and raw material origins. Measuring Ca and K, for example, offers insights into the amounts of lime and potash used to create the glazes, while variation in trace elements from Rb to Nb instead reflect variation in the geological sources of the ingredients. One advantage of measuring these elemental signals in the glazes is that such measurements can be taken nondestructively using pXRF, enabling much larger datasets to be collected. More importantly, collecting such data from porcelain vessels, which typically cannot be destructively sampled for SEM-EDS or other analytical techniques, permits additional observations for hypothesis testing. Consider that vessels with elaborate decorations and inscriptions (e.g., names, indications of official use, or functional clues) are more likely to be housed in art museums and intact vessels are superior for identifying standardized dimensions, mass, or other features. These types of observations for vessels can help to disentangle issues related to status and control, and their nondestructive analysis will almost always be necessary.

Ultimately these sherds show variation in body pastes, glazes, and pigments; however, we cannot address at this point, given the limitations of this sample (e.g., with a small sample size and from surface scatters) whether the observed variation is concurrent or sequential—that is, is the variation geographical or diachronic (or something else, like sociopolitical) in nature? Addressing this issue will be key to the larger research questions related to political economy of the Mongols. It will require porcelains with known dates (or, at least, relative ages) to test whether the organization of porcelain production changes from the early to the late Yuan period, and contexts (e.g., mortuary versus residential) to investigate the variation of the sociopolitical roles that the blue-and-white and egg-white glazed porcelain played throughout the Yuan dynasty. Inscriptions and decorations can offer insights into the vessels' quality and the consumers' social status. Ideally, these investigations could also be carried out in different parts of the empire, which might indicate a difference on how porcelains were valued, especially in relation to other materials or objects. Our research demonstrates the possibility of applying pXRF for nondestructive compositional analysis for porcelains. Research along these lines could enable us to tease out which patterns are linked to production, distribution, and consumption and their changes through time across the empire.

Conclusions

Here we share one approach to the investigation of porcelain production, distribution, and consumption using archaeological methods, exploring how economic strategies changed over time in more than one part of the Mongol Empire. The goals of such an investigation are (1) understanding better how Mongol rulers produced and supported their legitimacy and, in turn, (2) contributing to wider cross-cultural studies of imperial political economy around the world (e.g., how social relations and cultural values can underlie ceramic consumption as well as intertwine with anthropological theories concerning ethnicity, cultural hybridity, and chosen identities). Rather than focusing on the typical lens of acculturation, there is value in comparative studies of percelain production, distribution, and consumption in more than one region of the Mongol Empire. Such a line of research could, we hope, ultimately enable scholars to gain a more detailed understanding of the diverse areas that politically, economically, and culturally interacted as a result of the Mongol Empire.

Acknowledgments

Portions of this chapter (opening introduction, Hypotheses and Expectations, Previous Studies, and Conclusions) are largely derived—nearly word-for-word in most sentences—from Zeng Lingyi's National Science Foundation proposal titled "Imperial Political Economy: Ceramic Production, Distribution, and Consumption in the Mongol Empire" and adapted here by her colleagues, friends, and dissertation committee members. The Discussion section offered here is, where possible, based on ideas from this proposal (ultimately awarded as grant BCS-1746779). Lingyi had already completed her data collection, but it was impossible to finish all of her analyses. She had done surveys of relevant porcelain collections in China at Jingdezhen in Jiangxi Province, Yunnan, and Inner Mongolia, in addition to participating in two excavations in Mongolia, thanks to Mandakh Davaasuren, Chunag Amartuvshin, and dissertation committee member William Honeychurch. The original analytical methods for the study (using SEM-EDS, EDXRF, and pXRF) were developed by Lingyi, but the compositional analyses were necessarily completed with different instruments, by dissertation committee member Ellery Frahm. Former fellow PhD student Wang Qingzhu made several contributions during his time in the United States and after he began a postdoctoral fellowship in China. As Lingyi's advisor, Anne Underhill provided guidance on the overall research plan. This chapter builds on Lingyi's work as much as possible, presenting new results and interpretations. We all miss her very much.

References

Alcock, Susan E., Terence N. D'Altroy, Kathleen D. Morrison, and Carla M. Sinopoli, eds. 2001. *Empires: Perspectives from Archaeology and History.* Cambridge: Cambridge University Press. 523 pp.

Allsen, Thomas T. 1996. Spiritual geography and political legitimacy in the Eastern steppe. In: Henri J. M. Claessen and Jarich G. Oosten, eds. *Ideology and the Formation of Early States.* New York: E. J. Brill. pp. 116–135.

—1997. Ever closer encounters: The appropriation of culture and the apportionment of peoples in the Mongol Empire. *Journal of Early Modern History* 1(1):2–23.

Amartuvshin, Chunag, Otgonjargal Batzorig, and Batdalai Byambatseren. 2019. *Archaeological Sites of Khanbogd.* Ulaanbaatar: Institute of Archaeology, Mongolian Academy of Sciences. 273 pp. [in Mongolian.]

Areshian, Gregory E. 2013. *Empires and Diversity: On the Crossroads of Archaeology, Anthropology, and History.* Los Angeles: The Cotsen Institute of Archaeology Press. 256 pp. (Ideas, Debates, and Perspectives 7.)

Baines, John, and Norman Yoffee. 1998. *Order, Legitimacy, and Wealth in Ancient Egypt and Mesopotamia.* Santa Fe: School of American Research Press. 178 pp.

Barbieri-Low, Anthony J. 2007. *Artisans in Early Imperial China.* Seattle: University of Washington Press. 394 pp.

Barfield, Thomas J. 2001. The shadow empires: Imperial state formation along the Chinese–nomad frontier. In: Susan E. Alcock, Terence N. D'Altroy, Kathleen D. Morrison, and Carla M. Sinopoli, eds. *Empires: Perspectives from Archaeology and History.* Cambridge: Cambridge University Press. pp. 10–41.

Bezur, Anikó, and Francesca Casadio. 2012. The analysis of porcelain using handheld and portable X-ray fluorescence spectrometers. In: Aaron N. Shugar and Jennifer L. Mass, eds. *Handheld XRF for Art and Archaeology.* Leuven, Belgium: Leuven University Press. pp. 249–312. (Studies in Archaeological Sciences 3.)

Boozer, Anna Lucille, Bleda S. Düring, and Bradley J. Parker, eds. 2020. *Archaeologies of Empire: Local Participants and Imperial Trajectories.* Albuquerque: University of New Mexico Press. 344 pp. (School for Advanced Research Advanced Seminar Series.) https://muse.jhu.edu/book/78106

Burger, Richard L., and Lucy C. Salazar, eds. 2004. *Machu Picchu: Unveiling the Mystery of the Incas.* New Haven: Yale University Press. 230 pp.

Carswell, John. 2000. *Blue & White: Chinese Porcelain around the World.* London: British Museum Press. 208 pp.

Casadio, Francesca, Anikó Bezur, Kelly Domoney, Katherine Eremin, Lynn Lee, Jennifer L. Mass, Andrew Shortland, and Nicholas Zumbulyadis. 2012. X-ray fluorescence applied to overglaze enamel decoration on eighteenth- and nineteenth-century porcelain from central Europe. *Studies in Conservation* 57(Supp. 1):S61–S72. https://doi.org/10.1179/2047058412Y.0000000047

Chen, Kai Jun. 2023. *Porcelain for the Emperor: Manufacture and Technology in Qing China.* Seattle: University of Washington Press. 211 pp.

Cline, Eric H., and Mark W. Graham. 2011. *Ancient Empires: From Mesopotamia to the Rise of Islam.* Cambridge: Cambridge University Press. 368 pp.

Costin, Cathy L. 1991. Craft specialization: Issues in defining, documenting, and explaining the organization of production. *Archaeological Method and Theory* 3:1–56. https://www.jstor.org/stable/20170212

Cowell, M., and Fu-kang Zhang. 2001. Analyses and source of the cobalt blue pigment employed on Chinese ceramics. In: Jessica Harrison-Hall, ed. *Catalogue of Late Yuan and Ming Ceramics in the British Museum.* London: British Museum Press. pp. 601–605.

D'Altroy, Terence N., and Ronald L. Bishop. 1990. The provincial organization of Inka ceramic production. *American Antiquity* 55(1):120–138. https://doi.org/10.2307/281498

Dennison, Rory A. 2023. "Firing and Feasting: Examining Porcelain Production and Consumption of Early Second Millennium East Asia" [dissertation]. University of Illinois at Chicago. 435 pp. ProQuest Dissertations & Theses Global (30603431). https://www.proquest.com/dissertations-theses/firing-feasting-examining-porcelain-production/docview/2830127662/se-2

Domoney, Kelly. 2017. X-ray fluorescence (XRF) analysis of porcelain: Background paper. *Analytical Methods* 9(16):2371–2374. https://doi.org/https://doi.org/10.1039/C7AY90044A

Fischer, Christian, and Ellen Hsieh. 2017. Export Chinese blue-and-white porcelain: Compositional analysis and sourcing using non-invasive portable XRF and reflectance spectroscopy. *Journal of Archaeological Science* 80:14–26. https://doi.org/10.1016/j.jas.2017.01.016

Flad, Rowan K. 2011. *Salt Production and Social Hierarchy in Ancient China: An Archaeological Investigation of Specialization in China's Three Gorges*. Cambridge: Cambridge University Press. 285 pp.

Guo, Yanyi. 1987. Raw materials for making porcelain and the characteristics of porcelain wares in north and south China in ancient times. *Archaeometry* 29(1):3–19. https://doi.org/10.1111/j.1475-4754.1987.tb00393.x

Hang, K. 2020. My opinion on the origin of the Yuan blue-and-white porcelains. *Chinese Cultures* 51:267–279. [in Chinese.]

Hoffman, Gail L. and Lisa R. Brody, eds. 2014. *Roman in the Provinces: Art on the Periphery of Empire*. Boston: McMullen Museum of Art, Boston College. 352 pp.

Honeychurch, William. 2014. Alternative complexities: The archaeology of pastoral nomadic states. *Journal of Archaeological Research* 22(4):277–326. https://doi.org/10.1007/s10814-014-9073-9

—2015. *Inner Asia and the Spatial Politics of Empire: Archaeology, Mobility, and Culture Contact*. New York: Springer. 321 pp.

Jiang, Jianxin. 1991. A summary of ceramic kilns at Jingdezhen. *Cultural Relics from Jiangxi* 1991(3):44–50. [in Chinese.]

Khatchadourian, Lori. 2016. *Imperial Matter: Ancient Persia and the Archaeology of Empires*. Oakland: University of California Press. 332 pp. https://doi.org/10.1525/luminos.13

Kopytoff, Igor. 1986. The cultural biography of things: Commoditization as process. In: Arjun Appadurai, ed. *The Social Life of Things: Commodities in Cultural Perspective*. Cambridge: Cambridge University Press. pp. 64–92. https://doi.org/10.1017/CBO9780511819582.004

Lechtman, Heather. 2014. Andean metallurgy in prehistory. In: Benjamin W. Roberts and Christopher P. Thornton, eds. *Archaeometallurgy in Global Perspective*. New York: Springer. pp. 361–422. https://doi.org/10.1007/978-1-4614-9017-3_15

Ledderose, Lothar. 2000. *Ten Thousand Things: Module and Mass Production in Chinese Art*. Princeton: Princeton University Press. 272 pp. (The A.W. Mellon Lectures in the Fine Arts.)

Li, Weidong, Xiaoke Lu, Hongjie Luo, Xinmin Sun, Lanhua Liu, Zhiwen Zhao, and Musen Guo. 2017. A landmark in the history of Chinese ceramics: The invention of blue-and-white porcelain in the Tang dynasty (618–907 A.D.). *STAR: Science and Technology of Archaeological Research* 3(2):358–365. https://doi.org/10.1080/20548923.2016.1272310

Lin, Meicun. 2009. The powerful Yuan dynasty official Zhang Gui and Yuan dynasty court wine vessels unearthed in Baoding. *Palace Museum Journal* 143(3):24–41. [in Chinese.]

Liu, Li. 2003. "The products of minds as well as of hands": Production of prestige goods in the Neolithic and early state periods of China. *Asian Perspectives* 42(1):1–40. https://doi.org/10.1353/asi.2003.0025

Liu, X. Y. 1981. Research on some problems of manufacture of Jingdezhen porcelain in Yuan Period I—to Sir John Addis. *Journal of Jingdezhen Ceramic Institute* 2(1):67–78. [in Chinese.]

Ma, Wenkuan. 2010. Re-discussion of the Chinese blue-and-white porcelains and the Islamic blue-and-white ceramics (I). *Collector* 11:19–24. [in Chinese.]

Mattingly, David J. 2013. *Imperialism, Power, and Identity: Experiencing the Roman Empire*. Paperback edition. Princeton: Princeton University Press. 376 pp. (Miriam S. Balmuth Lectures in Ancient History and Archaeology 1.)

Ming, Chaofang, Yimin Yang, Jian Zhu, Li Guan, Changsheng Fan, Changqing Xu, Zhengquan Yao, Jonathan M. Kenoyer, Guoding Song, and Changsui Wang. 2014. Archaeometric investigation of the relationship between ancient egg-white glazed porcelain (*Luanbai*) and bluish white glazed porcelain (*Qingbai*) from Hutian Kiln, Jingdezhen, China. *Journal of Archaeological Science* 47:78–84. https://doi.org/10.1016/j.jas.2014.04.005

Munkh-Erdene, Lhamsuren. 2023. *The Nomadic Leviathan: A Critique of the Sinocentric Paradigm*. Leiden: Brill. 524 pp.

Oshima, Ritsuko. *1983*. The Chiang-hu in the Yuan. *Acta Asiatica* 45:69–95.

Pines, Yuri, Gideon Shelach, Lothar von Falkenhausen, and Robin D. S. Yates, eds. 2014. *Birth of an Empire: The State of Qin Revisited*. Berkeley: Global, Area and International Archive, University of California Press. 408 pp. (New Perspectives on Chinese Culture and Society 5.)

Pollard, A. M., and H. Hatcher. 1994. The chemical analysis of Oriental ceramic body compositions: Part 1: Wares from North China. *Archaeometry* 36(1):41–62. https://doi.org/10.1111/j.1475-4754.1994.tb01064.x

Pope, John A. 1981. *Chinese Porcelains from the Ardebil Shrine*. 2nd ed. London: Sotheby Parke Bernet. 194 pp.

Rice, Prudence M. 1987. *Pottery Analysis: A Sourcebook*. Chicago: University of Chicago Press. 559 pp.

Rogers, J. Daniel. 2012. Inner Asian states and empires: Theories and synthesis. *Journal of Archaeological Research* 20(3):205–256. https://doi.org/10.1007/s10814-011-9053-2

Shelach-Lavi, Gideon. 2015. *The Archaeology of Early China: From Prehistory to the Han Dynasty*. Cambridge: Cambridge University Press. 373 pp.

Shi, Jingsong. 2001. Archaeology in China. *Acta Archaeologica* 72(2):55–90.

Shiraishi, Noriyuki, and Batmunkh Tsogtbaatar. 2009. A preliminary report on the Japanese–Mongolian joint archaeological excavation at Avraga site: The Great Ordu of Chinggis Khan. In: Jan Bemmann, Hermann Parzinger, Ernst Pohl, and Damdinsüren Tseveendorj, eds. *Current Archaeological Research in Mongolia*; papers from the First International Conference on "Archaeological Research in Mongolia" held in Ulaanbaatar, August 19th–23rd, 2007. Bonn: Vor- und Frühgeschichtliche Archäologie, Rheinische Friedrich-Wilhelms-Universität. pp. 549–562. (Bonn Contributions to Asian Archaeology 4.)

Sinopoli, Carla M. 1991. *Approaches to Archaeological Ceramics*. Boston: Springer. 238 pp.

—2000. From the Lion Throne: Political and social dynamics of the Vijayanagara Empire. *Journal of the Economic and Social History of the Orient* 43(3):364–398. https://doi.org/10.1163/156852000511330

Smith, Michael E., and Maëlle Sergheraert. 2012. The Aztec Empire. In: Deborah L. Nichols and Christopher A. Pool, eds. *The Oxford Handbook of Mesoamerican Archaeology*. New York: Oxford University Press. pp. 449–458.

Su, Qingbin. 1967. *Research on the Clans of the Foreign People Who Settled in China from the Han Dynasty to the Five Dynasties: Records of Foreign Surnames from the Han Dynasty to the Five Dynasties*. Hong Kong: New Asia Research Institute. 367 pp. [in Chinese.]

Tite, Michael S., I. C. Freestone, and M. Bimson. 1984. A technological study of Chinese porcelain of the Yuan dynasty. *Archaeometry* 26(2):139–154. https://doi.org/10.1111/j.1475-4754.1984.tb00329.x

Underhill, Anne P. 2002. *Craft Production and Social Change in Northern China*. Boston: Springer. 346 pp.

Wang, Qingzheng. 2000. Yuan dynasty porcelain from Jingdezhen. In: Qingzheng Wang, ed. *The Complete Works of Chinese Ceramics*. Shanghai: Shanghai People's Art Press. 147 pp. [in Chinese.]

Wen, Rui, and A. Mark Pollard. 2014. The pigments applied to Islamic Minai wares and the correlation with Chinese blue-and-white porcelain. *Archaeometry* 58(1):1–16. https://doi.org/10.1111/arcm.12143

Wen, Rui, C. S. Wang, Z. W. Mao, Y. Y. Huang, and A. Mark Pollard. 2007. The chemical composition of blue pigment on Chinese blue-and-white porcelain of the Yuan and Ming Dynasties (AD 1271–1644). *Archaeometry* 49(1):101–115. https://doi.org/10.1111/j.1475-4754.2007.00290.x

Weng, Yanjun, and Baoping Li. 2021. *New Finds of Yuan Dynasty Blue-and-White Porcelain from the Luomaqiao Kiln Site, Jingdezhen: An Archaeological Approach*. London: Unicorn Publishing Group. 176 pp.

Wood, N., and Michael S. Tite. 2009. Blue and white—the early years: Tang China and Abbasid Iraq compared. In: Stacey Pierson, ed. *Transfer: The Influence of China on World Ceramics: Held November 5–7, 2007*. London: University of London, Percival David Foundation of Chinese Art, School of Oriental and African Studies. pp. 21–45.(Colloquies on Art and Archaeology in Asia 24.)

Wood, N., Michael S. Tite, C. Doherty, and B. Gilmore. 2007. A technological examination of ninth–tenth century AD Abbasid blue-and-white ware from Iraq, and its comparison with eighth century AD Chinese blue-and-white *Sancai* ware. *Archaeometry* 49(4):665–684. https://doi.org/10.1111/j.1475-4754.2007.00327.x

Wu, Juan, Tiejun Hou, Maolin Zhang, Qijiang Li, Junming Wu, Jiazhi Li, and Zequn Deng. 2014. A technical comparison of three Chinese white porcelains: Ding, Shufu, and Dehua. *Studies in Conservation* 59(5):341–349. https://doi.org/10.1179/2047058413Y.0000000121

Yao, Alice. 2016. *The Ancient Highlands of Southwest China: From the Bronze Age to the Han Empire*. New York: Oxford University Press. 270 pp. (Oxford Studies in the Archaeology of Ancient States.)

Yap, C. T., and Younan Hua. 1992. Raw materials for making Jingdezhen porcelain from the Five Dynasties to the Qing dynasty. *Applied Spectroscopy* 46(10):1488–1494. https://doi.org/10.1366/000370292789619386

Yap, C. T., and S. M. Tang. 1985. Zn Kα/Rb Kβ Ratio of Ch'ing, Republic and Modern Chinese Porcelains. *X-Ray Spectrometry* 14(4):157–158. https://doi.org/10.1002/xrs.1300140404

Yoffee, Norman. 2016. The power of infrastructures: a counternarrative and a speculation. *Journal of Archaeological Method and Theory* 23(4):1053–1065. https://doi.org/10.1007/s10816-015-9260-0

Yu, K. N., and J. M. Miao. 1998. Multivariate analysis of the energy dispersive X-ray fluorescence results from blue and white Chinese porcelains. *Archaeometry* 40(2):331–339. https://doi.org/10.1111/j.1475-4754.1998.tb00841.x

Zhao, L. 2013. The use of cobalt blue in West Asia and China before the 14th century: A discussion of the origin of the Yuan blue-and-white porcelains. *Cultural Relics in Southern China* 3:60–65. [in Chinese.]

Index

Locators in *italic* refer to figures and tables

A

Allsen, Thomas T., 149, 151, 154, 222
Andersson, Johan G.: excavation of Neolithic and Bronze Age sites for the Geological Survey of China, 30–31; quartzite lithic artifacts recognized by, 12; Zhoukoudian localities studied by, 10–11
Araniko (or Anige [阿尼哥] in Chinese): Jiangzuoyuan supervised by, 210–211; portraits of Khublai Khan and Chabi, 149, *150,* 156n10

B

Barbieri-Low, Anthony J., 73
Bayankhongor Province. *See* Mongolia—Bayankhongor Province
Bellwood, Peter, 62
Bentsen, Silje Evjenth, 9
Bezur, Anikó, 221, 226
Bhan, Kuldeep Kumar, 142, 143
Bimson, M, 224, 225
Binford, Lewis R., 13, 16, 17
Black, Davidson, 11, 12–13, 16–17
Boaz, Noel T., 13
Bonomo, Michael F., 36
Bray, Lois M., 33
Breuil, Henri (or Abbé Breuil), 16–17
Brittingham, Alex, 20
Bylin-Althin, Margit, 30–31

C

carnelian bead research—in China: "bamboo-like" biconical drilled beads from the Zhou period, 148, 149; Dadianzi carnelian beads, 148; early carnelian beads produced in northern China, 148–149; Shang period carnelian beads, 148
carnelian bead research—Mongol period: bead from Gorzgoriin uvur, 143, *144*; beads produced from local sources by nomadic pastoral groups (over a millennium before the Mongol Empire), 149; biconical carnelian bead recovered from Chintolgoi Balgas, 156n12; carnelian beads as prestige goods in Mongol society, 141–142, 154–155; carnelian beads from Khalzan Shireg, 145, *145,* 147, 156; early carnelian bead usage traced to before the Late Bronze Age, 148; irregular octagonal-faceted bead (MG31) from Delgerkhan Uul, 148, 149; necklace (or possible hat ornament) from Tsagaan Khanan, 145, *146*; reddish-brown beads easily confused with carnelian featured on Yuan dynasty portraits, 8.9, 8.10, *150, 151, 152–153,* 154, and 8.11}; short bead from Ereen, 143, *144*
Casadio, Francesca, 221, 226
ceramic production and exchange. *See also* Fengbitou painted pottery; Huangguashan painted pottery; Jingdezhen; Longshan/ Lungshan culture (龙山, about 2400–1800 BCE)—ceramics; petrography; Taiwan Strait—Neolithic pottery; Yuan dynasty (1271–1368 CE)—porcelain techniques; Yue-type (越) wares; Zeng Lingyi—study of porcelain: Bronze Age pottery production in the Chengdu Plain, 36; global connections revealed by, 1, 3; Inka ceramic production, 219; kiln furniture, 133, 135, *135,* 137; Majiayao pottery, 31, 35–36; similarities between pottery from southeast mainland China and western Taiwan, 47–49, 60, 62, 63, 64; social role of porcelain during the Mongol Empire, 7, 220, 222–223, 235; terracotta warriors of Qin Shi Huangdi, 32–33, 37–38
ceramic production and exchange—dragon kilns: celadon production associated with, 136–137; kilns traced to the Shang and Zhou dynastic periods, 129; in Shangyu District, 133, *134*; structure and construction of, 129, *132,* 133

ceramic production and exchange—paste: common minerals found in pottery paste categorized by Druc, 49; for Huangguashan and Fengbitou pottery, 50, *51–52, 53, 54, 56, 59,* 60, *60,* 62, 64; petrographic studies of regional paste recipes, 29–33, 35, 39–40; shift in paste recipes in the Middle Bronze Age, 36; variation in body pastes of porcelain, 227, *228–229,* 230, 234

Chan, Hok-Lam, 178

Chang, Huaiyin: argument that horses were not integrated into Shang rituals, 81, 82; on horse bridle parts and chariot parts at Yinxu, 69, *71*; on horse mouthpieces at Yinxu, 70, *72, 79,* 80

Chang, Kwang-chih: the concept of the Chinese interactive sphere introduced by, 63–64; Fengbitou culture identified with fine-cord-marked ware culture, 64; on the fine red ceramic wares from the "Lungshanoid culture", 48–49, 63; pottery in western Taiwan was categorized into horizons by, 60; sherds from the Fengbitou site collected by, 49, 58–59, *59*; on trade as a motivation to navigate from southeast China to Taiwan, 62

Chastain, Matthew L., 37

Chen, Chun, 34, 39

Chen, Enzhi, 76

Chen, Kai Jun, 223

Chinbat, Amarbileg, 145

Chinese Academy of Social Sciences Institute of Archaeology (CASS IA): Dadianzi site report, 148; on forty-nine characters of horses recorded in the oracle bone inscriptions, 76; horse sacrificial pits dated to Yinxu Phase II in the oracle bone inscriptions, 99; on Lady Fu Hao's tomb, 82, 148; on Shang territory during the Late Shang period, 73–74

Chinggis Khaan National Museum, 145, 147, 156

Cho, Yong, 177

Cui, Wei, 35

D

Dammer, Evgenia, 35

Da Yuan shengzheng guochao dianzhang 大元聖政國朝典章. *Statutes and precedents of the sacred administration of the great Yuan dynastic state* (YSP): "Libu" (吏部, "Ministry of Personnel"), 209

Dennison, Rory A., 221, 224

Di, Nan, 36

Druc, Isabelle C., 49

Duan, Tianjing, 34

E

Eastern Jin (317–420 CE; [EJ]): kiln sites with celadon wares, 128, *130*; as a major historical era,121

Erdenebat, Ulambayar, 145, 147, 156n8

exchange. *See also* ceramic production and exchange; prestige goods: impact of nonlocal materials on locally produced objects, 3–4; role of horses, 3, 73; trade as a motivation for interregional migration between mainland China and Taiwan, 47, 62–63; translocal objects as markers of sociopolitical status or group identity, 2–3; Zeng Lingyi's work on, 1–2, 177–178

F

fabric—brocade: brocade as an "exotic" material in Mongol Society, 155; consort empresses depicted wearing brocade, 149, *150*; *deel* made with golden brocade traced to the Xiongnu period, 154; golden brocade claimed by Chinggis Khan as war spoils, 154; Golden Brocade Office at the Yuan dynasty court, 149; golden brocade recovered at Mongol mortuary and habitation sites, 141; import and use of *nasīj* (golden brocade), 149

fabric—silk: bolts of silk gifted to the Liao by Shi Jingtang of the Later Chin, 190; bolts of silk gifted to the Liao under terms of the Chanyuan Covenant, 191, 201n11; requested by Chinggis Khan according to *The Secret History of the Mongols,* 154; silk and jade paid in tribute to the Jin by the Song after the Jinkang incident, 178, 197; silk garments recovered at Mongol mortuary and habitation sites, 141

Fen, Wang, 34, 39

Fengbitou painted pottery: coiling features in painted pottery paste, 58, *60*; location of the archaeological site, *50,* 58; painted pottery from southern China compared with, 60, 62, 63; painted pottery sherds examined, 58, *59*; pottery vessel types, 58–59, *61*; use of a slow-wheel technique, 58

fire use by humans. *See also* Zhoukoudian Locality 1—fire produced at: in Africa, 9, 20, *20,* 22; cultural transmission hypothesized by Katharine MacDonald et al., 8–9, 13–14, 20, 22; independent discovery across hominin populations, 2, 8–9, 20, 22; investigations involving polycyclic aromatic hydrocarbons (PAHs), 20; sites with evidence of, 20, *21,* 22

Fischer, Christian, and Ellen Hsieh, 221

Five Dynasties: Ouyang Xiu's *Historical Records of the Five Dynasties,* 202n19; Xiu Duan on Ouyang's views of the legitimacy of the Five Dynasties, 179, 187, 194–195, 196

Five Dynasties—Later Liang (907–923): in Ouyang's history, 179; Zhu Wen, 179, *180,* 189–190, 193, 200, 204n51

Five Dynasties—Later Tang (923–936): Li Congke (Qingtai) as the last Later Tang emperor, *181,* 190, 201n9; Li Cunxu's establishment of, *181,* 201n15; Mingzong, *181,* 190; Zhuangzong, *181,* 193

Five Dynasties—Later Chin (937–947): Chudi (Emperor Chu), *181,* 190–191; collapse of (947 CE), 179, 191, 193; in

Ouyang Xiu's history, 194; Shi family's founding of, 190, 191, 193; Shi Jingtang, *181,* 190

Five Dynasties—Later Han (947–951): Emperor Yin (Liu Chengyou) killed in a coup led by Guo Wei, 196, 202n28; Liu Min, 196, 202n29; Liu Zhiyuan's founding of, 191

Five Dynasties—Later Zhou (951–960): Guo Wei's founding of, 193, 196, 202n28, 202n30; Han Tong, 195, 202nn23–24; Li Pingshan's poem on, 195; viewed as illegitimate by Xiu Duan, 179, 193

Freestone, I. C., 224, 225

Fu Hao (Yinxu, Shang): carnelian beads from the tomb of, 148; horse-related objects found in her tomb, 81–82

Fuliang: location in the jurisdiction of Jiangzhe Province, Raozhou Circuit, 208, *209;* offices of, 212, *213;* during the Tang and Song dynasties, 208

Fuliang ciju (浮梁磁局, Fuliang Porcelain Bureau [FLPB]): administration by the Jiangzuoyuan, 210–211; establishment of (1278 CE), 207, 212, 215; in the YSP, 209–210; in the *Yuan Shi*, 210, 211

Fuliang ciju (浮梁磁局, Fuliang Porcelain Bureau [FLPB])—Commissioner and Assistant Commissioners of: ranks of, 211–212, *213,* 214–215, 216; supervision of the production of porcelain, 216–217

Furumatsu, Takashi, 178, 188n3

G

Gansu Province: horse remains unearthed in, 68; horses in the daily life of contemporary pastoralists, 67; Majiayao pottery from, 35

Gao, Xing, 12, 19

Geological Survey of China, 17, 30

Goldberg, Paul, 16, 18, 19

Goodenough, Ward, 62

Guo, Meng, 36

Guo, Yanyi, 119

Guo, Yi, 37

H

Han dynasty (汉代; 206 BCE–220 CE): granary jar developed from the five-tubed vase of, 125; painted pottery from Han tombs in Shanxi and Shandong Provinces, 33, 38; trade with the Xiongnu state, 89; varieties of ceramics, 128

Han dynasty (汉代; 206 BCE–220 CE)—Eastern Han (25–220 CE; [EH]): Emperor Zhaolie of Shu, 199, 203–204n45, 204n47; kiln furniture used during, 133, 137; kiln sites with celadon wares, 128, *130,* 136, 138; as a major historical era, *121;* the term Northern Han used as "Eastern Han," 203n32; viewed as a legitimate continuation of the Later Han, 203n35; Yue ware production traced to, 117, 118–119, 136

He, Yuling, 73

Hein, Anke, 36

Helmer, Daniel, 92, 95

Henderson, Julian, 119

Ho, Chuan Kun, 13, 17

Hobson, Robert L., 119

Honeychurch, William: on the introduction of horses to Yinxu, 70

horses: in the daily life of contemporary pastoralists, 67; horse incisors used for age determinations, 92, 99; horse skeletons in Xinjiang predating the Late Shang, 68, 70–71; role in facilitating exchange, 3; as symbols of prestige, 67, 69, 76, 79, 80–81, 82

horses and chariots: chariot-packages found at the Qiaobei (桥北) site in Shanxi, 73, 74; horse bridle parts and chariot parts at Yinxu, 69–70, *71;* introduction to the Shang from Inner Mongolia as a hypothesis, 70, 72–74, 82; introduction to the Shang from Mongolia as a hypothesis, 73, 82; introduction to the Shang from Xinjiang as a hypothesis, 73, 82; mobility and military potency provided by horses and chariots during the Warring States period, 67; in the Shang royal hunt, 78, 81

horses in the Shang dynasty: introduction to Yinxu (Anyang), 3, 67–68; in the ritual system of the Shang elites, 80–81, 82

Hsieh, Ming-Liang, 125

Huang, Weiwen, 10

Huangguashan painted pottery: coiling features in painted pottery paste, 50, *54;* decorations on the interior of rims, 50, 53, *54,* 60; evidence of firing, 54, *56;* excavation site in Fujian Province, 49, *50;* painted pottery in western Taiwan compared with, 60, 62, 63; painted pottery sherds examined, 49, *51–52;* painting tools used for painted lines, 54, *55;* pottery vessel types, 55–56, *57, 58;* selection of raw materials for, 50, *53, 54,* 60; use of a slow-wheel technique, 50, 60

I

Inner Mongolia: carnelian beads from Dadianzi, 148; horses in the daily life of contemporary pastoralists in, 67; introduction of horses and chariots to the Shang as a hypothesis, 70, 72–74, 82; Khitan royal tomb of Princess Chen, 154; porcelains dating to the Mongol period excavated from, 223; pottery from Xinglongwa (兴隆洼; 6000–5000 BCE) and Haminmangha (哈民忙哈; 3500–3000 BCE), 36

isotopic time series plots of $\delta^{13}C$ and $\delta^{18}O$ of Ovis sp.: as a method, 90–91, 94; sampling of individuals for Xiongnu burial sites, 94, 102–103, *102, 106–110*

J

Janz, Lisa, 149, 155

Jia [Chia], Lanpo, 10, 13

Jiang, Jianxin, 220, 221, 223

Jiang, Zanchu, 125

Jiao, Tianlong: on Huangguashan culture as a the source of painted pottery in western Taiwan, 49; on maritime adaptation facilitating migrations across the Taiwan Strait, 62; on painted pottery of Yuanshan, 48, 55; on the term Fengbitou culture, 64

Jin dynasty (1115–1234 CE). *See also* Xiu Duan: Jin Taizu, *183, 184,* 191, 194; Li Pingshan (Li Chunfu, 1185–1231 CE), 195, 202n22; Prince of Hailing, 198, 203n42; Xiu Duan on the *Official History of Jin* (金史), 199

Jing, Anning, 156n10

Jingdezhen: blue-and-white and egg-white glazed porcelains made during the Mongol period associated with, 220–221; scientific analysis of porcelains from the Mongol Yuan period, 221; Zeng Lingyi's studies at Jingdezhen Ceramic University, 1, 4

K

Kenoyer, Jonathan M., 142– 143, 147–149, 155

Khitan Empire (or Kitan Liao, 916–1125 CE): mineral coal used in smelting during, 172; petrography used to study earthenware pottery from, 38; royal tomb of Princess of Chen, 154; settlement of Chintolgoi Balgas, 154, 156n12; Song–Jin alliance against the Liao Khitans (1120s), 178; Xiu Duan on the legitimacy of its political lineage and succession, 179, 187, 190–193; Yelü clan of, *183–184,* 189

Kirch, Patrick V., 62

Kivi, Nicholas, 38

L

Li, Chi (Li Ji), 11
Li, Feng, 13
Li, Guichang, 79
Li, Jiangzhi, 118–119
Li, Yang, 79

Liao dynasty. *See* Khitan Empire (or Kitan Liao, 916–1125 CE)

Lin, Kuei-chen, 36
Lin, Meicun, 220, 221
Lin, Shimin, 117

lithic technology: Acheulean (Mode 2) lithic technology, 8; independent emergence of Levallois lithic technology, 7–8, 9, 22; lithic artifacts from Zhoukoudian Locality 1, 10, 11–12, 14, 15, 19; lithic technology in association with use of fire by MacDonald et al., 8–9, 13–14, 22; lithic tolls found at Huangguashan, 49

Liu, Li, 36
Liu, Nani, 36
Liu, X. Y., 220, 221
Li Wenjing, 39

local traditions: early carnelian beads produced in northern China, 148–149; impact of nonlocal materials on locally produced objects, 3–4; Late Bronze Age carnelian beads crafted from carnelian geodes in Mongolia, 147; translocal objects incorporated into, 2–4; Zeng Lingyi's research on porcelain production, distribution, and use in different locales of the Mongol Empire, 2, 223, 235

Longshan/Lungshan culture (龙山, about 2400–1800 BCE)—ceramics: egg-shell black pottery, 35, 64; homogenization of ceramic styles in the Chinese interactive sphere, 63–64; locally produced pottery from Guowan, 37; Neolithic Fengbitou wares viewed as Lungshanoid, 48, 63–64

Lu, Minghua, 214, 215
Lu, Qingyu, 34, 35, 39

M

MacDonald, Katharine, et al., 8–9, 13–14, 20, 22

Majiayao (马家窑; 3200–2000 BCE) culture: analyses of the technological aspects of ceramics from, 31, 35–36; circulation of the pottery of, 36

Makarewicz, Cheryl A., and Noreen Tuross, 103

Meng, Gutuoli, 74
Meng, Xianwu, 79

Ming dynasty (1368–1644): cobalt blue pigments on sherds from, 230, *231*; Raozhou Circuit placed under Jiangxi Province, 208; scientific studies of porcelains from, 223–224

Mongol Empire (1206–1368 CE). *See also* Chinggis Khan (Genghis Khan or Temüjin); Yuan dynasty (1271–1368 CE): demand for metal and metal products during, 4; diversity and size of, 7, 141, 219; Southern Song-Mongol alliance against the Jin, 178, 179; symbolic significance of colors for the Mongols, 222

Mongol Empire (1206–1368 CE)—Khalzan Shireg: carnelian beads on display at the Chinggis Khaan National Museum, 145, 147, 156; carnelian bead surface find from, 145, *145*; ceramic and porcelain fragments dating to, 143; location of, 143

Mongol Empire (1206–1368 CE)—Qaraqorum (Karakorum): as the capital of the Mongol Empire, 141; carnelian beads recovered from, 142, 147, 155; as a center of metal production, 4, 163, *165*; craft production at, 142; gem production sites, 143; local faux pearl production at, 151

Mongolia. *See also* Baga Gazaryan Chuluu; Xiongnu period (around 250 BCE–150 CE); Xiongnu ring burial (DMS 777A); Xiongnu slab burial (DMS 1396A): Chinggis Khaan National Museum, 145, 147, 156; introduction of horses and chariots to the Shang from, 73, 82; isotope analysis of livestock individuals from Baga Gazaryn Chuluu and Egiin Gol, 89, 103; Khitan settlement of Chintolgoi Balgas, 154, 156n12

Mongolia—Baga Gazaryn Chuluu: carnelian beads not recovered from Mongol-period graves in, 145; Delgerkhaan Uul compared with, 90; isotope analysis of livestock individuals from, 89, 103; location of, *88*

Mongolia—Bayankhongor Province: blue-and-white porcelain sherds from, 224, 227, *228–229*, 230, *231–233*; collection site location, 224

Mongolia—Bor Shorooni Am: location of, *88*; slab burial SG-2 at, 89

Mongolia—Chandmani Khor Uul: carnelian beads found in Early Iron Age culture sites, 147; carnelian beads not recovered from Mongol-period graves in, 145; carnelian beads produced locally found in Late Bronze Age sites, 147; location of, *88*; Xiongnu ring graves found in, 89

Mongolia—Delgerkhaan Ulu. *See also* Xiongnu period—mortuary practices—slab burial (DMS 1396A): animal herding practiced during the Bronze or Iron Age at, 103–104; irregular octagonal-faceted bead (MG31) from, 148, 149; location in eastern Mongolia, *88, 90*; slab burials and Xiongnu ring burials found in, 90, 92; steel making at, *165*, 172, 173

Mongolia—Dundgovi Province: Mongol period carnelian short bead from Ereen, 143, *144*

Mongolia—Egiin Gol: isotope analysis of livestock individuals from, 89; location of, *88*

Mongolia—Gol Mod: location of, *88*; terrace tombs of the Xiongnu elite, 89

Mongolia—Ikh Nart: Delgerkhaan Uul compared with, 90; location of, *88*; necklace recovered from a female cave burial, 145, 151, 155

Mongolia—Khentii Province: Mongol period bead from Gorzgoriin uvur, 143, *144*; white porcelain sherd from, 224, 226, *227*

Mongolia—metallurgical tradition: Qaraqorum (Karakorum) as a center of metal production, 4, 163, *165*; self-sufficient iron production by mobile pastoralists, 162–164, 173

Mongolia—Noyon Uul: cotton *deels* recovered from the royal tombs at, 154; location of, *88*; terrace tombs of the Xiongnu elite, 89

Mongolia—Ömnögovi Province: Khanbogd blue-and white porcelain, 224, 227, *228–229*, 230

Mongolia—Tsagaan Ereg: location of the Tarvagatai Valley Project (TVP) in, 164, *165*; time-range of occupation, 166

Mongolia—Tsagaan Ereg (TVP-180)—metallurgical production during the Mongol period, 4, 171, *172–173*; furnace structures in, 166, *167*, 171; general appearance of iron objects studied, 166–167, *168*, 171, 172; microscopy of iron objects from, 166–167, *169–170*, 171, 172–173

O

Ouyang Xiu (1007–1072 CE): *Historical Records of the Five Dynasties* written by, 196, 202n19; the legitimacy of the Five Dynasties rejected on moral grounds, 179; on the statuses of the Later Zhou Northern Han, 194, 202n20; Xiu Duan on Ouyang's views of the legitimacy of the Five Dynasties, 179, 187, 194–195, 196

P

Payne, Sebastian, 92, 95
pearls: Khans depicted with pearl-topped crowns and pearl earrings, 149, *150*; local faux pearl production at Qaraqorum, 151; pearl-like glass beads recovered from excavations at Chintolgoi Balgas, 154; pearl necklaces and earrings recovered at Mongol mortuary and habitation sites, 141, 151

Pei, Wen-Chung (Pei Wenzhong), 11, 12, 16, 19

petrography: as a method for the study of ceramic production and circulation, 3, 29, 35–38

political history and genealogy. *See also* Standard Histories; Xiu Duan—"Debating the Legitimate Succession of the Liao, Song, and Jin": *Historical Records of the Five Dynasties* by Ouyang Xiu, 196, 202n19; Yuan-era polemical tracts debating legitimate political genealogy, 178; *Zizhi tongjian* of Sima Guang, 196, 203n34

Pollard, Mark A., 224, 227

prestige goods, carnelian bead research—Mongol period. *See also* carnelian bead research—in China; fabric—brocade; fabric—silk; pearls; control of their production and distribution by empires, 219; horses and chariots as symbols of, 67, 69, 76, 79, 80–81, 82; sociopolitical role of carnelian beads in Mongol society, 141–142, 149, 154–155; sociopolitical role of porcelain during the Mongol Yuan period, 7, 220, 222, 235

Q

Qi, Wang, 34, 39

Qin dynasty (秦代; 221–206 BCE): role of horses in its conquest of neighboring states, 67; terracotta warriors, 32–33, 37–38; transition from earthenware during the Qin to stoneware during the Han, 128

Qing dynasty (1644–1911 CE): scientific studies of porcelains from, 223–224

Qinghai Province: carnelian beads found at third-millennium BCE sites in, 148; horse remains predating the Shang found in, 68; Majiayao pottery from cemetery sites in, 35, 36; as part of the Chinese interactive sphere, 63–64

Qiu, Zhenwei, 37

Quinn, Patrick S., 29, 30, 38

R

Rawson, Jessica, 148–149
regional perspective: empire- or state-focused perspective contrasted with, 4
Reichert, Susanne, 142, 143, 151
Ren, Mei'e, 14, 15
Ren, Shilong, 117
Rice, Prudence M., 119
Roebroeks, Wil, 8
Roman Empire: petrography used to analyze ceramics from, 29; production and distribution of prestige goods by, 219

S

Schlosser, Max, 10
Shang dynasty (around 1600–1046 BCE). See also Yinxu period: horses in the ritual system of the Shang elites, 80–81, 82; petrographic analysis of ceramics, 31; territory of, 73–74
Shao, Jing, 36
Shelach, Gideon, 72
Shen, Guanjun, 12, 15, 19
Shen, Yueming, 129
Shepard, Anna O., 29
Shimelmitz, Ron, 9
Six Dynasties period (六朝时期, 220–589 CE): Buddhism introduced to China during, 125; celadon production kiln sites from, 138; Yue wares produced during, 121
Sixteen Kingdoms, 192, 200, 201n5, 204n49
So, Jenny F., 148, 149, 155
Song dynasty (960–1279 CE). See also Ouyang Xiu (1007–1072 CE); Xiu Duan: Chanyuan Covenant signed with the Liao, 191, 201n11; Emperor Taizong (Zhao Kuangyi), 38, 183, 190–191, 196, 202n31; Emperor Taizu (Zhao Kuangyin), 183, 193, 195, 196, 202n31; Northern Han (Later Han dynasty) conquered in 979 CE, 179; the Official History of the Song criticized by Xiu Duan, 189, 192, 193, 194, 195, 202n26; petrographic study of porcelain from, 31–32; scientific studies of porcelains from, 38, 223–224
Song dynasty (960–1279 CE)—Southern Song (1127–1279 CE): decline of celadon manufacture, 126; Han Touzhou's failed attack on the Jin (1206), 198, 200, 203n41; imitation of Yue ware during, 117; the Jin attacked and captured at Caicheng [Caizhou], 195, 197; Longquan (龙泉) ware produced during, 119, 137, 220; peace treaty signed with the Jin (1141 CE), 178, 199; on Song emperor Gaozong, 199, 204n47; Song-Jin treaty, 178, 198, 199, 203n40; Song-Mongol alliance (1234 CE), 197, 203n37
Sorby, Henry C., 29
Southern dynasties (420–589 CE; [SD]): early Yue wares produced during, 117; kiln sites with celadon found in the Shangyu area, 128, 130, 136; as a major historical era, 121; tombs in southern China yielding Yue wares, 122, 124; Xiu Duan on including the Five Dynasties within a History of the Southern Dynasties, 193, 194
Spataro, Michela, 35
Standard Histories. See also Yuan shi (元史, Yuan History): the Official History of the Song criticized by Xiu Duan, 189, 192, 193, 194, 195; on the "ontological continuity" of vanquished dynasties captured in, 178; Xiu Duan on the Official History of Jin (金史), 199
Stilborg, Ole, 36
Stoltman, James B., 30, 33, 37
Stone, Nancy M., 13, 17
Su, Qingbin, 220
subsistence practices. See also Xiongnu period—livestock-management-based subsistence strategies: reflection in human-animal interactions, 3, 87, 95
Sui dynasty (581–618 CE; [S]): as a major historical era, 121; Yuanjing (Primal Classic) written by Wang Tong (Wenzhongzi), 195, 202n25; Yue ware produced during, 117, 137
Sun, Zhouyong, 36
Sundius, Nils, 31
Sung, Wenxun, 63

T

Taiwan Strait: maritime adaptation facilitating migrations across, 47, 62; spread of millet and rice agriculture from mainland China to Taiwan, 47, 62; trade as a motivation for interregional migration, 47, 62–63
Taiwan Strait—Neolithic pottery. See also Fengbitou painted pottery; Huangguashan painted pottery: homogenization during the Longshan cultural period in the Chinese interactive sphere, 63–64; similarities between pottery from southeast mainland China and western Taiwan, 47–49, 60, 62, 63, 64
Tang dynasty (618–907 CE): blue-and-white porcelain, 220; Mi-se (秘色) ware unearthed from the Famen Temple, 117; saying about glazed ware preferences, 136; scientific studies of porcelains from, 38, 223–224; Zhu Wen's (朱温) usurpation, 179, 180, 189–190, 193, 200, 204n51
technological innovations. See also ceramic production and exchange—dragon kilns; fire use by humans; horses and chariots; lithic technology; Mongolia—metallurgical production; Mongolia-Tsagaan Ereg (TVP-180)—metallurgical production during the Mongol period; wheel-made pottery: of early Yue wares, 122, 125, 137–138; impact of canoe-making techniques on seafaring, 47; independent emergence of Levallois lithic technology, 7–8, 9, 22; kiln furniture for ceramic production, 133, 135, 135, 137; social roles impacting the transmission of innovations, 7, 220, 222–223, 235
Teilhard de Chardin, Pierre, 12, 16, 17, 18

Ten Kingdoms—Northern Han (951–979): Song conquering of (979 CE), 179; viewed as a legitimate continuation of the Later Han by Xiu Duan, 179, 194, 196, 202n21
thin section petrography: barriers to the application of ceramic petrography, 30; ImageJ software, 30; PETROG digital petrography system, 30
Three Kingdoms period (229–280 CE; [TK]): kiln sites with celadon wares, 128, *130*; as a major historical era, *121*; popular celadon burial goods, 125, *126*; tomb sites with early Yue wares dating to, 122, *123*
Thum, Rian, 178
Tite, Michael S., 224, 225
Tsagaan, Turbat, 145
Tsang, Cheng-Hwa, 62, 64

V

Vidale, Massimo, 142, 143
Vigne, Jean-Denis, 92, 95
Villa, Paola, 8

W

Wang, Changsui, 118
Wang, Chuan-Chao, 47
Wang, Meng, 34
Wang, Peng, 73, 79
Wang, Qingzheng, 212, 215, 220, 221, 222
Wang, Wei, 73
Wang, Yifeng, 129
Warring States period (481–221 CE): mobility and military potency provided by horses and chariots during, 67; origin of Yue wares dated to, 137
Wei, Lu, 38
Wei, Zheng, 121, 125
Weidenreich, Franz: crania of *Sinanthropus pekinensis, 10,* 11
Weiner, Steve, 18–19
Wen, Rui: on cobalt ores used during the Yuan and subsequent dynasties, 224; imported Persian cobalt ores compared with Chinese cobalt ores, 227; on Sumali blue pigment used by Yongle craftspeople, 230

Western Jin (265–317 CE; [WJ]): kiln sites with celadon wares, 128, *130*; as a major historical era, *121*
wheel-made pottery: research on raw materials from Shang pottery from Anyang, 33; spiral lines on Huangguashan pottery produced with a slow-wheel technique, 50; vessel rims of Huangguashan and Fengbitou pottery finished using a slow wheel technique, 58, 60; vessels at Shimao (石峁; 2300–1800 BCE) in Shaanxi, 36
Whitbread, Ian K., 30
Womack, Andrew, 35, 36, 40
Wood, Nigel, 119, 137
Wu, Rukang, 14, 15
Wu, Shuang, 34, 38, 39
Wu, Weihong, 37

X

Xia, Yan, 33
Xinjiang: horses in the daily life of contemporary pastoralists in, 67; horse skeletons predating the Late Shang, 68, 70–71; introduction of horses and chariots to the Shang as a hypothesis, 73, 82
Xiongnu period (around 250 BCE–150 CE): carnelian bead usage during, 147–148, *149,* 155; glass beads, 154; iron-based technological tradition established during, 163; rise of the nomadic state in eastern Eurasia, 104, 147
Xiongnu period—livestock-management-based subsistence strategies: herd compositions, 92, 94; local variability of, 3, 89, 103, 104
Xiongnu period—mortuary practices: faunal depositions in, 89–90; slab burial construction, 88; slab burials and ring graves in the sociopolitical hierarchy, 87, 89; terrace tombs of Xiongnu elite in Noyon Uul and Gol Mod I/II, *88,* 89
Xiongnu period—mortuary practices—slab burial (DMS 1396A): age groups of sheep,

95, *96,* 100; intratooth isotopic sequences of sheep teeth from, 100, *101,* 102–103, *106–110*; isotopic time series plots of $\delta^{13}C$ and $\delta^{18}O$ of Ovis sp., 102–103, *102*; size and location in Delgerkhaan Uul, *88, 92, 93*; skull deposition, *95,* 95
Xiongnu period—mortuary practices—Xiongnu ring burial (DMS 777A): age groups of sheep/goat individuals, 99, *99*; distribution of skeletal elements, 97, *98,* 99; faunal deposition, 95, *97*; intratooth isotopic sequences of sheep teeth from, 100, *101,* 102–103, *106–110*; isotopic time series plots of $\delta^{13}C$ and $\delta^{18}O$ of Ovis sp., 102–103, *102*; size and location in Delgerkhaan Uul, *88, 93,* 95; zooarchaeological remains identified and recorded, 92, 95–96, *97*
Xiu Duan: biographical details, 178–179, 204n53; as a former Jin official, 178, 203n37; on the irrelevance of ethnicity for determining legitimacy in the Central Lands, 179; on Ouyang's views of the legitimacy of the Five Dynasties, 179, 187, 194–195, 196
Xiu Duan—"Debating the Legitimate Succession of the Liao, Song, and Jin": on the Chanyuan Covenant, 191, 201n11; on Han Touzhou's failed attack on the Jin (1206), 198, 200, 203n41; on the Liao's political lineage and succession, 179, 187, 190–193; on the Liu, Shi, Murong, Fu, Yan, and Helian families controlling the Central Plains, 189, 192, 200, 201n5, 204n49; the Northern Han viewed as a legitimate continuation of the Later Han by Xiu Duan, 179, 194, 196, 202n21; on the *Official History of Jin* (金史), 199; the *Official History of the Song* criticized in, 189, 192, 193, 194, 195; on Ouyang's views of the legitimacy of the

Five Dynasties, 194–195, 196; on the Song-Mongol alliance (1234 CE), 197, 203n37; versions of the texts, 178, 188n3, 201n1; on Zhu Wen's (朱溫) usurpation, 179, *180*, 189–190, 193, 200, 204n51

Xu, Jiming, 119

Xu, Wenting, 37

Y

Yang, Shao-yun: notion of "ethnocentric moralism," 187; translations of sections of "Debating the Legitimate Succession of the Liao, Song, and Jin," 178, 188nn1–5; on Xiu Duan's disagreement with Ouyang Xiu, 179, 188n6

Yang, Zhenzhen, 36

Yinxu period (c. 1300–1046 BCE): horses and chariots in the Shang royal hunt, 78, 81; horses at the center of ritual acts, 78–79; horses used in rituals throughout, 74, *75,* 76, 78; petrography used to study proto-porcelain from, 38

Yinxu period (c. 1300–1046 BCE)—Wuguancun North Locality: elephants found at, 69, 70; horses from sacrificial pits at, 68, 74, *75*; rituals held at, 69

Yinxu period—Phase I: horse remains in a sacrificial trench at Huanbei Shang possibly dated to, 79; integration of horses into the Shang system during, 76; interactions with the northern steppe during, 71–73; northern style objects from burials dated to, 71; Shang capital moved to Yinxu, 80

Yinxu period—Phase II: chariot-packages found at the Qiaobei (桥北) site in Shanxi, 73, 74; earliest horse sacrificial pits dated to, 68, 90; horse bit dating to, *72*; horse husbandry associated with King Wu Ding's reign, 69, 76–77, *77,* 80–81, 82–83; Lady Fu Hao, 81–82,

148; northern style objects with horse depictions dated to, 71

Yinxu period—Phase III: horse remains in a sacrificial trench at Huanbei Shang possibly dated to, 79

Yinxu period—Phase IV: horse bits dating to, *72*

Young, C. C., 16, 17, 18

YSP. *See Da Yuan shengzheng guochao dianzhang* 大元 聖政國朝典章. *Statutes and precedents of the sacred administration of the great Yuan dynastic state* (YSP)

Yuan dynasty (1271–1368 CE): cobalt Yuan porcelain, 224; jurisdiction of Fuliang County during, 208, *209*; offices overseeing gold and precious jade, 212; official system of, 209–210, 212; reddish-brown beads easily confused with carnelian featured on Yuan dynasty portraits, 8.9, 8.10, *150, 151, 152–153,* 154, and 8.11}

Yuan dynasty (1271–1368 CE)—porcelain production—ruling class attitudes, 207; loosening of control to increase revenue (around 1320–1370 CE), 222, 235; political legitimacy of Mongol elites established through control of (around 1270–1320 CE), 222, 235

Yuan dynasty (1271–1368 CE)—porcelain production supervision. *See also Fuliang ciju* (浮梁磁局, Fuliang Porcelain Bureau [FLPB]): acculturation used as a lens by earlier scholars, 222; establishment of the FLPB in the Raozhou Circuit (1278 CE), 207, 212, 215; supervisory officials of porcelain production *(dutao guan),* 212–214, 215

Yuan dynasty (1271–1368 CE)—porcelain techniques—blue-and-white porcelain: analysis of porcelain glazes, 230, *231–232,* 232; Bayankhongor blue-and-white porcelain, 224, 227, *228–229,* 230, *231–233*; invention of, 220; Khanbogd

blue-and white porcelain, 224, 227, *228–229,* 230, *231–233*; sociopolitical role of, 4, 220, 222, 235; Sumali blue, 230, 234; symbolic significance of colors for, 222

Yuan dynasty (1271–1368 CE)—porcelain techniques—clay: imitations of elite styles using local clay, 223, 225; "porcelain stone," 224

Yuan dynasty (1271–1368 CE)—porcelain techniques—egg-white glazed porcelain: among porcelain sherds analyzed by Zeng, 221, 224; as an innovation derived from bluish-white glazed porcelains, 220; sociopolitical role of, 220, 222, 235; vessels dating to the Mongol period found in Inner Mongolia, 223

Yuan shi (元史, *Yuan History*): compilation of, 211–212; on the Directorate-General for Precious Metal and Jewel Artisan in Various Circuits, 212; the existence of the Jiangzuoyuan documented by, 210, 211; on the *Fuliang ciju* (浮梁磁局, Fuliang Porcelain Bureau), 210, 211; Fuliang's (浮梁, in modern northeastern Jiangxi) administrative status in, 207–208; on Jiangzuoyuan (將作院, Imperial Manufactories Commission), 210–211; Khalzan Shireg mentioned as Zhenghai (or Chinhai) in, 143; "Treatise on Officialdom," 208, 209–210

Yue-type (越) wares: animal forms of, 125, *126*; complexity, innovation, and diversity of, 122, *124,* 125, 138; influence on later ceramic production in China, 117, 136–137; tomb sites China yielding early Yue wares, 122, *123, 124*; tombs yielding pottery vessels and celadon compared, 125–126, *127*

Yue-type (越) wares—as celadon: early Yue wares as one kind of, 137–138; early Yue wares distinguished from proto-porcelain, 118, 119, 122, 125,

137, 138; the granary jar as a common type of, 123, 125, *126*; the name celadon associated with its green color, 136–137; Shangyu (上虞) as the production center of early Yue wares, 128, *129,* 138; Yue wares in forms and with ornaments influenced by Buddhism, 125, *126*

Yutang jiahua (YTJH) by Wang Yun: errors noted, 201n7, 201n8, 202n31; longer conclusion, 204n53; on Ouyang Xiu, 194, 202n19; poem attributed to Fang Xinru, 203n42; on Song emperor Gaozong, 199, 204n47; on the writing of the *Liao Official History,* 200, 204n52; Xiu Duan's "Debating the Legitimate Succession of the Liao, Song, and Jin" included in, 178, 188n3, 201n1

Z

Zeng, Lingyi: academic background of, 1

Zeng, Lingyi—study of porcelain: holistic consideration of archaeological and historical data, 2, 177–178, xv; macroscale trade networks across Eurasia revealed by, 1–2; political economy during the Yuan explored by, 4; on porcelain technologies, 7, 220, 222–223, 235; unique conditions of local contexts revealed by, 2, 223

Zhang, Senshui, 19

Zhang, Shangxin, 37–38

Zhang, Shuangquan, 13

Zhang, Xianrui, 37

Zhang, Xiaoling, 12

Zhang, Yan, 19

Zhang, Youyin, 37

Zhejiang Province: Dayuanping kiln site producing Yue ware, 118, 119, *134*

Zhejiang Province—Cixi (慈溪): kiln sites producing Yue ware (second- to sixth-century CE), *129, 130*; Yue ware from tomb site at, *123*

Zhejiang Province—Fenghuangshan: kiln site producing Yue ware at, 118; *Zun* vessel with beast head and Buddhist stylistic elements unearthed from, *126*

Zhejiang Province—Hangzhou (杭州): kiln site producing Yue ware at, *129, 130*; Yue ware from tomb site at, *123*

Zhejiang Province—Ningbo (宁波): kiln site producing Yue ware at, *129, 130*; Yue ware from tomb site at, *123*

Zhejiang Province—Shangyu (上虞): as the production center of early Yue wares, 128, *129, 130,* 138; Xiaoxiantan kiln site producing Yue ware at, 117, 118–119, *120*; Zhangzishan kiln site producing Yue ware, 117, 118–119, *120, 134*

Zhejiang Province—Shaoxing (绍兴): kiln site producing Yue ware at, *129, 130*; Yue ware from tomb site at, *120, 123*

Zhejiang Province—Yuyao (余姚): kiln site producing Yue ware at, *129, 130*; Yue ware from tomb site at, *123*

Zhong, Maohua, 19

Zhou, Chunlin, 15

Zhou, Ren, Fukang Zhang, and Yongpu Zheng, 31

Zhou dynasty (1046–256 BCE): carnelian beads incorporated into funerary attire, 148; dragon kilns during, 129

Zhoukoudian Locality 1: crania of *Sinanthropus pekinensis* found at, *10,* 11; dating confusion associated with, 14–15; as a natural trap, 13; as the Peking Man site, 9–11; processes of site formation as a recurring topic, 11; reconstruction of life in, 16, *17*; tale of six Locality 1 homin crania found at, 10–11

Zhoukoudian Locality 1—fire produced at: ashy deposits studied as evidence or not of, 16–19; in the cultural transmission hypothesis of Katharine MacDonald et al., 9, 13–14, 20, 22; evidence for the innovation of fire use, 20, *21,* 22; evidence from the stratigraphic sequence of layers, 18–20; in situ fire production, 19

Zhoukoudian Locality 1—stratigraphic sequence of layers: Brunhes/Matuyama (B/M) paleomagnetic boundary, 15; dating of the lower stratigraphic layers, 15–16; geological description of, 11–12, *12*; global climatic variations correlated with the site's stratigraphy, 15–16; "hearths" in layer 10 examined, 18–19

Zhu, Boqian, 117

Zhu, Fenghan, 73

Zhu, Jian, 37

Zhu, Xianmo, 14, 15

Zhukaigou (朱开沟) cultural period (around 2100–1300/1200 BCE), 71

Zizhi tongjian of Sima Guang, 196, 203n34